Urban Economics
and Public Policy

Urban Economics and Public Policy

JAMES HEILBRUN
FORDHAM UNIVERSITY

ST. MARTIN'S PRESS NEW YORK

ACKNOWLEDGMENTS

p. 50, Table 3.5: Data from Tables II-A and III-B, from Donald J. Bogue, *Components of Population Change 1940–50* (Oxford, Ohio: Scripps Foundation, 1957). Used with permission of the author.

p. 63, Figure 4.1: Adapted from Figure 6, p. 86, in *Regional Development and Planning* by John Friedmann and William Alonso by permission of The M.I.T. Press, Cambridge, Massachusetts. © 1964 by The Massachusetts Institute of Technology.

p. 85, Table 5.1, and *p. 86, Table 5.2:* Data from Brian J. L. Berry and William L. Garrison, "The Functional Bases of the Central-Place Hierarchy," *Economic Geography* (April 1958), pp. 145–54. Used with permission.

p. 90, Table 5.3: Derived from Howard L. Green, "Hinterland Boundaries of New York City and Boston in Southern New England," in Harold M. Mayer and Clyde F. Kohn, eds., *Readings in Urban Geography* (Chicago: The University of Chicago Press, 1959), pp. 185–201. © 1959 by The University of Chicago. Used with permission.

p. 102, Table 5.5: Data from Gerald Hodge, "The Prediction of Trade Center Viability in the Great Plains," *Papers* of the Regional Science Association, Vol. XV, 1965, Table 2, p. 95. Used with permission.

p. 124, Figure 6.5: Adapted from William Alonso, *Location and Land Use* (Cambridge, Mass.: Harvard University Press, 1964), Figure 32, p. 112. Used with permission.

p. 153, Table 7.3: Data from Britton Harris, "Comment on Pfouts' Test of the Base Theory," *Journal of the American Institute of Planners*, Vol. XXIV, No. 4 (1958), p. 236. Reprinted by permission of the *Journal of the American Institute of Planners* and Britton Harris.

p. 328, Table 12.3: Data from *Tax Burdens and Benefits of Government Expenditures by Income Class, 1961 and 1965* (New York: Tax Foundation, Inc., 1967), Table 3, p. 14. Used with permission.

For Carol

Preface

This book introduces the reader to the subject of urban economics. In the first chapter I define this relatively new field of study as one in which "we use the analytical tools of economics to explain the spatial and economic organization of cities and metropolitan areas and to deal with their special economic problems." These problems, including urban poverty, housing, and public finance, have been matters of intense social concern in the 1960's and '70's, and, with the nation becoming ever more highly urbanized, there is good reason to believe they will remain so in the foreseeable future.

In this volume I have tried to bring together three elements essential to an understanding of the present economic situation of cities. The first of these is a sense of where we are now and how we got there. Thus, following the Introduction, Chapters 2 and 3 of this book provide an economic explanation of the growth of cities and metropolitan areas. They emphasize the forces of technological change that first built up great cities during the Industrial Revolution and later brought about the massive dispersion of jobs and population into the metropolitan suburbs that is still going on.

The second essential element is an understanding of the forces that determine the location, form, and economic structure of cities. Chapters 4 through 7, which cover the fundamentals of urban economic theory, deal with these topics. The theoretical analysis in these chapters is buttressed with factual evidence at many points.

As the Introduction to this book points out, the analysis of urban size, growth, form, and structure is vital to an understanding of urban economic problems precisely because these problems are significantly affected by the spatial organization of the city. Consequently, Chapters 2 through 7 are not only interesting in their own right, but also provide the foundation for an understanding of the third part of the book, which examines three major contemporary urban problems: poverty, housing and urban renewal, and the organization and financing of the metropolitan public sector. In Chapters 8 through 12 these problems are analyzed in depth, and the various public policies that have been either tried or proposed to meet them are discussed in considerable detail.

The chapters on public policy are thoroughly up-to-date in covering recent legislative changes and significant judicial decisions. In addition, I have made every effort to use current statistics to illustrate the argument in all parts of the book. Much of this statistical information has been specially tabulated from the 1970 Census of Population and Housing, a source that has only recently become available.

The book as a whole will be easily intelligible to anyone who has had an introductory semester of economic principles. Except for a bit of high-school algebra employed in Chapter 7, the approach is entirely non-mathematical. Nevertheless, the economic arguments are, I believe, rigorously developed and carefully qualified. While the book is intended primarily as a text for an introductory course in urban economics or urban economic policy, the chapters on poverty, housing, and public finance will also prove useful as supplementary reading for courses in urban sociology and politics.

The reader will find, both in the body of the text and in the footnotes, numerous references to the names and the works of other urban economists. These have been deliberately inserted, in part to indicate my intellectual debts, but, more importantly, to provide students with a bibliography of the major writers on urban economics keyed to the topics on which I have found their works most relevant and useful. From these clues the inquisitive reader will easily find his way to the major works in any part of the discipline. The footnotes thus comprise my list of "suggested further readings." I hope it may be said that they are as valuable as any part of this book.

I am indebted to many people for indispensable assistance in bringing this volume to completion. Professors Benjamin Chinitz of Brown University and John F. Kain of Harvard reviewed the entire manuscript and made innumerable helpful comments and suggestions. Professors George F. Break of the University of California at Berkeley and William G. Grigsby of the University of Pennsylvania provided most helpful reviews of the chapters on public finance and housing, respectively. Of course, none of these gentlemen should be held·responsible for the views I have expressed or for any errors of fact or logic remaining in the text.

The Fordham University Faculty Research Grant Program generously helped to defray research expenses. Edward Sawicz, Beverly Brignoli, and John Mooney deserve thanks for able research assistance. Appreciation is also expressed to Joseph E. Earley for permission to use data from his as yet unpublished study of land values in New York City.

Above all, I am grateful to my wife, not only for her patience and encouragement, but also for taking countless hours from her own professional life to help with arduous and time-consuming tasks.

August 1973   James Heilbrun

Contents

143-45   152

144 -
152

SEVEN
The Urban Economic Base and Economic Policy   137

TEN
The Problem of Urban Housing   239

ELEVEN
Urban Housing Policy   267

THIRTEEN
Postscript: Problems of Decline and Growth   363

Urban Economics
and Public Policy

Introduction

ONE

[handwritten margin note: Industrial Revolution altered ways of life]

Since the Industrial Revolution began about two hundred years ago, man's way of life has been profoundly altered by the rapid growth of cities and metropolitan areas. The extraordinary pace of urbanization is one of the most striking facts of modern history. Archeologists assure us that cities have existed for at least five thousand years, yet we know that society down to the end of the eighteenth century remained everywhere predominantly rural. Then, within less than two hundred years, the Industrial Revolution radically transformed the pattern of human settlement: in the industrialized nations of the world the majority of men today live in cities.

Looking back, the statistics seem hardly credible. In 1790 the population of the United States was 5 percent urban and 95 percent rural; by 1970 it was 73 percent urban and only 27 percent rural. The population of Great Britain, both then and now the most urbanized of nations, was probably 80 percent rural at the eve of the Industrial Revolution in the mid-eighteenth century. By 1951 the pattern had reversed; the population of Britain was more than 80 percent urban. For the underdeveloped nations, too, rapid urban growth is one of the major facts of modern life.[1] In whatever country one lives today, it is inevitable that many of the most pressing social and economic problems will be associated with urban and metropolitan development.

---

1. Numerous concise studies of the history of urbanization are available. See, for example, Emrys Jones, *Towns and Cities* (London: Oxford University Press, 1966), Ch. 2; and Kingsley Davis, "The Urbanization of the Human Population," in *Cities* (New York: Alfred A. Knopf, 1965), a Scientific American Book, pp. 3–24.

1

THE SCOPE OF URBAN ECONOMICS

It is hardly surprising that in such a world students should be increasingly concerned about matters of urban public policy or that economists should have developed the special branch of their discipline that we now call urban economics. More remarkable, perhaps, is the fact that urban economics became a distinct and recognized specialty only in the last twenty-five years. It can be defined as a field of study in which we use the analytical tools of economics to explain the spatial and economic organization of cities and metropolitan areas and to deal with their special economic problems.

This definition has the advantage of putting first things first. Students are often impatient to go directly to the "issues." They want to investigate the problems of urban poverty, slum housing, land-use decisions, transportation, the delivery of urban public services, and they are eager to debate the merits of the various public policies that might be used to meet them. But neither the problems nor the policies can be discussed intelligently until one understands the highly complex urban-metropolitan environment in which they occur. Hence we must deal with the spatial and economic organization of the city first, and only then with its problems.

In the definition of urban economics, the word "spatial" deserves particular emphasis. Traditional economic theory omits any reference to the dimensions of space by treating all economic activity as if it took place at a single point. It refers to consumers and producers, firms and industries, but not to distance or contiguity, separation or neighborhood. The fact that population and economic activity are arranged in a spatial as well as a functional order is simply ignored. In recent years the discipline known as regional economics has sought to restore the balance. "Regional economics," in Hugh Nourse's apt phrase, "is the study of the neglected spatial order of the economy." [2]

Regions may be areas of any size from neighborhoods to cities, river basins, farm belts, nations, or continents. Urban economics is that subcategory of regional economics that deals with the regions we call cities and metropolitan areas. It concentrates on those economic relationships and processes that contribute to the important spatial characteristics of such places, especially to their size, density of settlement, and structure or pattern of land use. And, since cities and metropolitan areas undergo continuous change in all these spatial characteristics, urban economics is also vitally concerned with the forces that attract or repel economic activity and population and thus cause growth or decline, concentration or

2. Hugh O. Nourse, *Regional Economics* (New York: McGraw-Hill, 1968), p. 1.

dispersion, preservation or replacement. It seeks to understand, not only the present spatial order, but the direction of change and development.

Here are a few examples of the sort of question about urban spatial economic organization that this book attempts to answer:

What accounts for the enormous concentration of population and economic activity in cities and metropolitan areas?

Is migration from the countryside into metropolitan areas now falling off?

Within metropolitan areas, why has there been such a marked dispersion of jobs and population from the large cities to their suburban rings in recent decades?

Why is it principally the middle and upper classes that have been attracted to the suburbs, while low-income families continue to live in the central cities?

Can racial segregation within cities be explained by spatial-economic factors such as the location of low-skill jobs and low-income housing, without reference to race prejudice?

SPATIAL ASPECTS OF URBAN PROBLEMS

The analysis of urban size, growth, form, and structure is vital to an understanding of the problems of urban poverty, housing, and public finance precisely because each of these problems has significant spatial aspects. For example, the poverty population remains heavily concentrated in the core cities, while job growth is most rapid in the suburban ring. When antipoverty policies are framed, this spatial characteristic of the poverty problem must be taken into account. It is important to know, for example, whether the separation of the poor from the areas of most rapid job growth is significantly slowing their rise out of poverty.

Or consider the connection between the housing problem and the pattern of land use. In the United States, decisions as to what will be built, and where, are taken largely in the private market for land and structures. Does this market work efficiently to give us the optimum development of each parcel and neighborhood? Or are there significant defects in the market process that justify public intervention to stimulate the redevelopment of old neighborhoods? These questions can be answered only by a careful study of the way in which the urban land market influences the spatial organization of the city.

The problems of metropolitan public finance, too, have many strongly spatial characteristics. To cite only one: consider the question of jurisdictional boundaries. The typical metropolitan area of the 1970's contains a large core city surrounded by the numerous smaller political units of the suburbs. Jurisdictional boundaries generally were drawn a century or more before the metropolitan area became a highly integrated economic unit. In today's circumstances can this minutely parceled set of local governments be expected to provide the level and assortment of public services that best satisfy the desires of the metropolitan population as a whole, or do local political boundaries now interfere with the efficient and equitable operation of the public sector? If so, what changes are desirable? Urban economic analysis, as we will see, can help to answer such vital policy questions.

THE CRITERIA OF EFFICIENCY AND EQUITY

Efficiency and equity are two of the general criteria to be applied in comparing alternative economic policies. To the economist, efficiency means the most productive use of resources to satisfy competing material wants. The productive resources available in even the most affluent economy are limited. Every use that we decide to make of them has as its real cost the next best opportunity for their use that we had to forego in choosing the one we did. ("Opportunity cost," thus defined, is the fundamental basis of real cost in economics.) If we are to achieve maximum satisfaction of material wants by the application of limited resources, it behooves us not to waste resources by using them in less than the most productive way. In the context of urban economics this often means finding the most efficient spatial arrangements or configurations, as in the examples from land use and public finance policy cited above.

The term "equity" in economics usually refers to fairness in the distribution of income or wealth or, more broadly, "welfare." When we evaluate a particular public policy (such as urban renewal or subsidies for low-income housing) or a private policy (such as discrimination in housing or employment), we usually try to apply some standard of equity to the policy's outcome: Which groups does it help? On whom does it impose burdens? Are these results desirable?

The ultimate question—desirability—cannot be answered on strictly economic grounds. It requires an explicit ethical judgment, and economists, in their professional capacity, have no special claim to ethical authority. Nevertheless, their work is indispensable as a pre-condition for informed judgment of economic policies. Since we judge policies by their consequences, accurate judgment requires a clear understanding of what those consequences are. Unfortunately, causes and consequences in economics are not very easily identified. The economy is a complex network of markets that connects all persons, institutions, functions, and regions and that transmits impulses among them in ways that are not always obvious. Careful analysis, however, can help us to understand how the system works so that the results of past or present policies can be deciphered, even if imperfectly, and the likely consequences of proposed future programs foreseen. By contributing to such an understanding the economist lays a foundation upon which others can then base their own judgment about the desirability of the various alternatives.

THE THEME AND OUTLINE OF THE BOOK

Broadly speaking, this book moves from a historical description and economic explanation of the growth of cities in Chapters 2 and 3, through a theoretical analysis of their location, form, and economic structure in Chapters 4 through 7, to the investigation of current urban economic problems in Chapters 8 through 13. Running through the entire book is a connecting theme: the influence of technological innovation, rising living standards, and changing population size on the spatial organization of cities and metropolitan areas and on the major economic problems they face. To speak of innovation and growth is obviously to suggest that cities change through time. Yet there is a sense in which they are also imprisoned in their own past. For they cannot be built anew to adopt the technology and suit the needs of each new era. Although the grand designs, the structures, and the boundaries laid down at an earlier date are often inappropriate to the present, they can be changed only at great expense of money, or of effort, or of disruption—and therefore only very slowly. It is precisely this tension between the needs of the present and the legacy of the past that makes the subject matter of urban economics so unusually challenging and endlessly absorbing.

The Economics of Urbanization

TWO

Economics has always been a major force determining the pattern of human settlement. Man cannot live by bread alone, but neither can he live without bread. From the earliest age, when our ancestors at the margin of historical time settled in the fertile river valleys to live by farming, to our own century, in which the rural poor migrate to the city in search of higher wages, man has moved over the surface of the earth in search, perhaps not of El Dorado, but, at any rate, of a place where the living was easier.

Cities are themselves evidence that an economy has reached a certain stage of development. Since city dwellers do not grow food, they can survive only if some one else in the economic system produces a food surplus. As long as agriculture is relatively unproductive, most men necessarily are tied to the soil. In a society in which 90 farmers can produce enough food and fiber for only 90 families, all men must remain farmers. If agriculture improves to the point where 90 farmers can feed and clothe 100 families, then one-tenth of the population can move off the land.

This obvious proposition enables us to characterize three major phases in the history of human settlement. The first is a society in which either agriculture is unknown and men live by hunting and fishing or agriculture is so primitive that it yields almost no surplus for the support of nonagricultural workers. In such a society farming and fishing villages, of course, exist, but they remain very small and contain at most only a few people, such as a priestly class, who are not food producers.

The second phase is a society not yet industrialized, in which agriculture becomes productive enough to yield persistently a small

7

surplus beyond bare subsistence. This surplus enters into trade and can support a limited urban population. True towns and cities now arise in which men specialize in nonagricultural activity. The limit to such urbanization in most areas before the Industrial Revolution appears to have been around 10 percent of total population, though we lack anything like adequate statistics on the question. Something like that ratio probably prevailed in the Mediterranean civilization of the Roman Empire. Despite the existence of a few great cities—Rome itself may, at its zenith, have reached a population of a million or more—society remained predominantly rural.

The third phase, and the only one in which we find substantially urbanized societies, occurs with and after what we may loosely call the Industrial Revolution—loosely, because a necessary condition for industrialization is a rise in output per farm worker, either in the industrializing country itself or in an area with which it trades, to support the growing industrial population. Such a rise in farm productivity in turn requires the application of scientific and mechanical techniques to farming and so may itself be treated as an aspect of industrial revolution. In the third phase we do not know what the limit to urbanization may be. Suffice it to say that the United States is today 73 percent urbanized, that most of the rural population is no longer engaged in farming, and that the nation nevertheless continues to be a net food exporter. (See Chapter 3 for details.)

SPECIALIZATION, TRADE, AND URBAN GROWTH BEFORE THE INDUSTRIAL REVOLUTION

Wherever cities have existed, the city dweller lives by exporting something in exchange for the produce of the countryside. Clearly, trade and its necessary correlate, the geographic division of labor, are intimately bound up with man's pattern of settlement. The great metropolis of ancient times, however, was, as Scott Greer has pointed out, principally engaged not in the export of goods but in the export of "order." [1] Cities dominated society not because they were centers of economic activity but because they were centers of government. The "order" they "exported" to the rural territory of their state consisted of defense, of law, and of a system of communication. In exchange for these services the city collected taxes from the countryside, and the tax revenues in turn became the means of paying for the agricultural imports upon which the city depended for survival. Trade, except for the import of food, was limited in volume by

1. Scott Greer, *Governing the Metropolis* (New York: John Wiley & Sons, 1962), pp. 4–6.

trade was limited for ;—
① transportation costs .
② not enough production .

two factors: first, the high cost of transport and, second, the fact that there was little the city could produce that could not equally well be produced in the peasant village.

However limited the volume of trade may have been in late antiquity, it was sufficient to feed and clothe a considerable population in the urban centers of the Roman Empire. The later decline of the cities of Western Europe—say, from about the seventh to the tenth centuries—has been attributed not only to the breakup of the Empire but also, in Henri Pirenne's famous thesis, to the closing of the Mediterranean to European trade by the "abrupt entry of Islam" and its "conquest of the eastern, southern and western shores of the great European lake."[2] Western Europeans were thrown back upon the self-sufficient manor, or estate, as the fundamental economic unit. The territorial division of labor, trade, and consequently urban population all declined in a self-reinforcing spiral.

Just as the decline of the cities followed the decline of trade, their revival accompanied, and in turn reinforced, the restoration of commerce that took place at about the beginning of the eleventh century, when Western Europeans, led by the energetic and thoroughly commercial Venetians, once more extended their influence across the Mediterranean. Indeed, from the eleventh century onward, the rise of the towns is one of the major themes in medieval history, with implications going far beyond the mere economics to which we are here confined.

What had been a declining spiral of city life now became a rising one. The growth of urban population led to increased demand for the commodities needed to support it. Hence trade increased further, and more and more workmen were drawn into the specialized occupations of craft and commerce, further increasing the demand for trade. Centuries later Adam Smith observed that the division of labor depends upon the extent of the market: the growing urban-rural interdependence of the late Middle Ages was, in fact, a form of territorial division of labor, within which major division the ever finer specialization by trade and craft proceeded in its turn.

Then, as now, the process was a complex one: the goods and services a town exported in order to pay for its necessary imports accounted for only a fraction of its total employment. Much urban labor has always consisted of what we now call "service employment." Every medieval clerk, every apprentice working for a tradesman, required the goods of other trades and the services of other clerks, and so the population of the towns must always have far exceeded the number of those engaged directly in trade or service to other regions.

The expansion of European influence and settlement, the growth of

2. Henri Pirenne, *Economic and Social History of Medieval Europe* (New York: Harcourt Brace Jovanovich, 1961), a Harvest Book, pp. 1–7, 39–40.

trade, and the rise of urban population continued down to the end of the thirteenth century. With the opening of the fourteenth century, Europe's forward motion apparently ceased. A time of troubles set in. Trade and population seem to have leveled off even before the Black Death of 1347–50 reduced Europe's population by perhaps one-third. The end of the thirteenth and the beginning of the fourteenth century is thus, in a sense, the high-water mark of medieval European civilization. By that date the towns had been growing for some three hundred years. How large had they grown? Not very big by today's standard. Pirenne estimates that at the beginning of the fourteenth century only a few of the largest cities had attained a population of 50,000 to 100,000. Florence in 1339 numbered perhaps 90,000 inhabitants. Venice at that period probably exceeded 100,000, while Paris may have had as many as 200,000.[3]

Europe's trade and population surged ahead once more from the mid-fifteenth century onward. The age of exploration opened up new trade routes by sea. Banking, insurance, and trading enterprises were now undertaken on a truly grand scale. The cities of Europe began to expand once again. By 1800 London, by far Europe's largest city, contained more than 950,000 people. Yet because the techniques of agricultural production had improved but little, the bulk of European population remained tied to the soil. Kingsley Davis has pointed out that "urbanization" properly means, not simply the growth of urban population, but its growth relative to rural and hence to total numbers. In the three centuries before the Industrial Revolution Europe's cities grew considerably, but their margin of growth over that of the rural sector was slight, indeed. Hence, as Davis points out, "On the eve of the industrial revolution Europe was still an overwhelmingly agrarian region." [4]

THE IMPACT OF THE INDUSTRIAL REVOLUTION

Why did the Industrial Revolution suddenly cause mankind to congregate in cities and towns? Why couldn't it have taken a different course, leaving the laboring man in his rural surroundings and spreading industrial facilities thinly over the countryside? The answer emerges if we consider its effects in greater detail. Let us first note that the Industrial Revolution comprised (at least) three radical developments: a manufacturing revolution, a transportation revolution, and an agricultural revolution.

The last has already been described as the application of scientific

3. *Ibid.*, pp. 170–71.
4. Kingsley Davis, "The Urbanization of the Human Population," in *Cities* (New York: Alfred A. Knopf, 1965), a Scientific American Book, p. 8.

and mechanical techniques to farming to bring about a sharp increase in farm output per worker. Its effect was to make possible a shift of population from agricultural to nonagricultural pursuits, but in no respect did it *require* the urbanization of those released from farming.

The transportation revolution, on the other hand, certainly encouraged urban agglomeration. Cities have, throughout history, tended to locate at economical transport points: at seaports, on navigable lakes and rivers, or at junctures of important overland trade routes. The transportation revolution of the nineteenth century consisted chiefly in the improvement in water-borne transport following the development of canals and the invention of the steamship and the even more radical change in overland transport made possible by steam railroads. These developments combined to increase enormously the transportation advantages of those points they served as compared with all other points. Both modes of transport operated, not ubiquitously, but along lines of movement that formed rather coarse-meshed networks. The point of service for the steamship network was the port—and the number of good ports is limited by topography. The canal and later the railroad system, on the other hand, could serve many points. Despite the topographical constraints, many possible routes existed, and the choice among them was sometimes determined by noneconomic factors. Once the system was built, however, those points it served obtained decisive cost advantages over all other places, for overland travel apart from the railroad remained in the horse-and-buggy stage throughout the nineteenth century. Thus ports and points along the railroads and canals powerfully attracted industry and often became manufacturing towns or cities.

Indeed, so effectively did the railroad encourage villages to grow into towns and towns into cities that it proved to be the most powerful agglomerative invention of all time. To enjoy its benefits, one had to build directly along the right-of-way or on a short siding. Hence nineteenth-century factories huddled next to one another in the familiar railside industrial districts still visible in every manufacturing town. Moreover, the railroad was relatively more efficient for long than for short hauls. It was miraculously economical for intercity movement of both goods and people, but until the invention of the electric railway it did little to improve intra-urban transport. Thus the workers in their turn lived as close as possible to the factories, and the nineteenth-century city grew up at an extraordinarily high level of density.

That it could also grow to encompass an immense population was another effect of the transportation revolution. Since long-distance haulage had become relatively cheap, it was now possible to feed huge populations concentrated at any point on the transport network by bringing food from distant agricultural zones, which, incidentally, the railroad had often helped open up. Without such a network, even if cities could have obtained sufficient food from nearby farm areas, they would have run a grave risk of famine whenever the local crop was deficient. Indeed, the wide chronological fluctuations in local death rates that occurred in, say, medieval Europe were due partly to local famines, which a better transport network could have mitigated.[5]

The manufacturing revolution consisted essentially of the development of factory methods of production incorporating power-driven machinery in place of the hand-tool system of production that had prevailed for thousands of years. This encouraged urbanization for several reasons. First, the optimum scale for a single plant, even in the early days of the Industrial Revolution, was likely to be large enough to form the economic nucleus for a small town. Second, and perhaps more important, commercial activities show a marked tendency to locate where other commercial activities already exist, and it is this process of agglomeration we now wish to examine in detail.

THE AGGLOMERATION OF ECONOMIC ACTIVITY

It is important to note that economic activity displayed agglomerative tendencies long before the Industrial Revolution. We have already mentioned the obvious point that banking and financial services concentrated in the great ports and trading centers of Renaissance Europe. At the same period handicraft trades, such as the Flemish cloth-weaving complex, were geographically concentrated even though still organized as cottage industries. The economic basis of agglomeration, which we will analyze below, was not much different then than now. But one of the profound effects of the Industrial Revolution was vastly to increase specialization through increased division of labor. Before the Industrial Revolution most production was carried on within the home—do-it-yourself was the rule in those days—and homes were mostly rural, located wherever farming was possible. The Industrial Revolution split off more and more of these domestic activities, converted them into full-time occupations within factories, and freed them to find their optimum location, no longer bound to home and farm. Thus it vastly increased the possibilities of agglomeration.

In a capitalist economy entrepreneurs will build their plants at the location where they think they can maximize profits. Precisely where on the map that will turn out to be depends on a number of discoverable

5. Carlo Cipolla, *The Economic History of World Population* (Baltimore: Penguin Books, 1962), a Pelican Book, pp. 77–80.

factors, including the location of sources of supply and geographic differentials in transport costs, in wage rates, and in market potential. These factors are handled systematically in what is usually called "the theory of the location of industry," which will be taken up in Chapter 4. At this point, however, we will examine the matter from a different perspective, focusing on why economic activities in an industrial society generally tend to agglomerate rather than on the somewhat different question of why they tend to locate at particular points on the map, such as Buffalo, New York, or Peoria, Illinois.

The locational pattern of economic activity reveals a complex system of interrelationships among firms. One soon realizes that the location of any particular economic unit depends upon the location of all the others. No matter where we begin the analysis we are quite likely to find the argument running in circles. But we must cut into it somewhere. Let us start, therefore, by adopting Raymond Vernon's distinction between "local-market activities . . . which generate goods and services of the sort which are typically consumed in the area where they are produced," and "national-market activities . . . devoted to the generation of goods and services which characteristically are 'exported' over broad market areas." [6] Local market activities, as Vernon explains, "respond largely to changes which go on inside the region." Therefore, if we can explain the tendency for national market activities to concentrate at a certain place, we will also have explained the tendency of local market activities to do so: the latter expand wherever the local market expands, and the local market expands wherever the growth of national market activities stimulates local employment and income.

Within the category of national-market activities, agglomeration is the result partly of a kind of inverted pyramiding. One industry—say, shipping—locates at a place because it has a good natural harbor. That activity then attracts others linked to it—say, banking, insurance, inland transport. The concentration of those industries in turn attracts others linked to them—say, a stock market, a commodity exchange, a printing and publishing industry, a university. And, of course, all these build up a large demand for "local-market" products—that is, for the services of retail traders, bakers, dentists, plumbers, policemen, bus drivers, school teachers, and all the other members of the "local-market" sector, who provide services both to those in the national sector and to other local-market producers.

The linkages of which we speak consist of a need for either communication or the movement of goods between firms and individuals doing business with one another. Linkage, however, need not itself imply

6. Raymond Vernon, *Metropolis 1985* (New York: Doubleday, 1963), an Anchor Book, p. 25.

proximity: firms have links both to their suppliers and to their customers, and proximity to both is not always possible. The locational pull exerted by such connections depends on numerous factors including the technology of communication and transport, the functions performed by the firm, and the locations of its suppliers and customers. The pull varies directly both with the need for communication and with the unit cost of accomplishing it. Since improvements in technology have reduced the relative cost of communication and transport in recent years, "distance" has become relatively less expensive, and some of the linkages that formerly pulled economic activity into the urban core have grown weaker. Before one can gauge correctly the effects of such changes, however, it is necessary to understand the relationship between linkages and the functions and organization of the firm.

In a classic article R. M. Haig pointed out that what we call the "firm" actually comprises a "packet of functions," which may not all have the same communication and transportation needs.[7] If these functions are spatially separable, then the ideal solution for the firm might be to place each at a different location. The separability of functions is in fact dependent on the state of technology. One important result of the reduced cost of communication and transportation has been to make possible increased spatial separation of functions within firms. In principle this might either increase or decrease the tendency of economic activity to agglomerate. A corporation that formerly located both its manufacturing plant and head office in a low-wage small town might now move its head office to a large city. A firm that formerly operated a department store and warehouse in the central business district might now move the warehouse out to a lower rent area, still within the city. A book publisher who formerly maintained his head office downtown and his storage and shipping departments in a nearby warehouse might now locate the last two in a distant suburb.

In fact, if we mean by agglomeration not just the tendency of activities to concentrate in central cities but their tendency to concentrate in metropolitan areas, then the displacement of a warehousing operation from downtown to the suburbs is not deglomerating. It represents a loosening up, a spreading out of the structure of the metropolis rather than a dispersion of activity into nonmetropolitan areas. A genuine dispersion, ending at the point where urban and rural densities of activity converge and become indistinguishable, is a conceivable but still distant possibility. But this anticipates later discussion. Suffice it to say at this point that despite the telephone, the airplane, and the automobile, certain activities

7. R. M. Haig, "The Assignment of Activities to Areas in Urban Regions," *Quarterly Journal of Economics*, May 1926, pp. 402–34.

find their links to the center still strong enough to hold them. Many of these are industries that Vernon has characterized as requiring face-to-face contact with either customers or suppliers in the daily conduct of business. Such industries, he points out, generally combine two characteristics: their activities are nonroutine, and speed is crucial to their success. He calls these industries "communication-oriented" in their choice of location.[8] A list of them would certainly include at least some parts of banking and finance, law, government, advertising, publishing, and broadcasting. For these activities the letter and the telephone are not adequate substitutes for face-to-face contact; their personnel, or at the very least their management personnel, must remain close to the center.

Some kinds of manufacturing certainly fall within this category, too. In a telling illustration, Vernon contrasts two cases: first, the producer of standardized goods, whose communications needs do not dictate an urban location because he can probably use the telephone to order raw materials or parts by giving the catalogue number or standard specification to his supplier; second, the manufacturer of the unique or the highly styled product, such as ladies' dresses, who has to locate close to his suppliers because day in, day out, he must see and compare various combinations of color, quality, and design before he can decide what materials to buy.

ECONOMIES OF AGGLOMERATION

For a fuller understanding of the causes of the geographic concentration of industry we must go beyond the concept of linkages, even the face-to-face variety, to a discussion of what have sometimes been called "economies of agglomeration." When they operate on the input side such economies have generally been known as "external economies of scale," where the word "external" stands for "external to the firm." These are the economies (i.e., the unit cost savings) that depend not upon the size of the firm but upon the size of the industry. Stigler explains the matter succinctly: "When one component is made on a small scale it may be unprofitable to employ specialized machines and labor; when the industry grows, the individual firms will cease making this component on a small scale and a new firm will specialize in its production on a large scale. . . . The progressive specialism of firms is the major source of external economies."[9] What has this to do with urban agglomeration? Stigler goes on to explain: "Many of the functions which an industry can delegate to auxiliary and complementary industries must be performed in fairly close

8. Vernon, pp. 105–06, 139–43.
9. George Stigler, *The Theory of Price*, Rev. Ed. (New York: Macmillan, 1952), p. 146.

proximity, and this is a powerful factor making for the geographic concentration of industries."

When external economies of agglomeration are possible, individual firms will enjoy lower costs when the industry is geographically concentrated than they would if it were geographically dispersed. A classic case is, once again, the concentration of the ladies' garment industry in New York City, more specifically in midtown Manhattan. The industry in New York is large enough to provide a profitable local market for a host of specialized suppliers. Thus, without incurring the risks and costs of carrying large inventories, the garment manufacturer who locates in New York gains ready access to a full line of the inputs he needs in a trade where style requirements change rapidly and speed and flexibility are crucial. This advantage is not confined to material inputs but applies equally to his labor supply: he obtains access to a common pool of trained labor, so he can vary his work force without having to bear the expense of training or, alternatively, of carrying idle workers.

One must not suppose that the cost savings resulting from external economies are merely savings to one firm or industry at the expense of others; on the contrary, they are true social economies, reductions in the real cost of output to society. Thus urban agglomeration is economically beneficial.

The garment industry also provides an example of the advantages of agglomeration on the output, or sales, side: by locating in New York the manufacturer places his showroom in the major national market to which buyers regularly come from stores all over the country. He could not reach nearly as many potential customers if his showroom were in, say, Chicago. (Of course, this suggests only that the showroom, not the whole operation, need be in New York. Moreover, it may well pay to have a showroom in Chicago as well.)

Does this instance also yield social benefits, or is it merely a case of one manufacturer gaining sales at the expense of another? Again, society is clearly the gainer: the expenses incurred by the buyer in canvassing the market—expenses involving real costs of time and travel, which he must recoup from his customers—are minimized when markets are geographically concentrated. Moreover, similar gains accrue through geographic concentration of like stores at the micro-scale of the neighborhood: the consumer bent on comparative shopping saves time and money when stores are close together.

E. M. Hoover has pointed out that the external economies of scale that influence geographic concentration of production can be divided into two classes: *localization economies*, which result when firms of the same industry congregate at a given place, and *urbanization economies*, which result when firms of different industries locate in the same place.[10] This distinction would be more useful if "industry" were a less ambiguous term. One may observe, nevertheless, that the concentration of the garment industry in New York unambiguously produces localization economies. On the other hand, New York City also unquestionably offers urbanization economies. For example, the local labor market is so large that it can offer not merely a large number of employment agencies but a large number that specialize in finding particular kinds of personnel. It has not only many banks but banks large enough to maintain highly specialized departments for a wide variety of functions. Thus the concentration of industries, even though they be unlike industries, makes possible an efficient specialization of service firms, and these latter are the source of external economies for the congregating firms that made them profitable.

The concentration of corporate head offices in New York City testifies to the importance of urbanization economies. Union Carbide, Exxon, and General Motors have their head offices in New York not so much because they do business with one another as because they all want to do business with New York banks and investment houses, with Wall Street law firms, and with Madison Avenue advertising agencies. Just as in the case of localization economies, the advantage to be gained is essentially that of easy access to highly specialized services.

We spoke earlier of the fact that the location of any one economic unit depends upon the location of all the others. The complex interrelatedness of the forces that have produced agglomeration should by now be clear: within the national-market sector one industry attracted other, related activities to its locality; this increased agglomeration produced external economies that attracted still more firms and produced still more external economies. As employment and income rose, local-market industries also expanded, and this expansion too was potent for the creation of further economies of agglomeration and further urban growth.

OTHER ADVANTAGES OF COMMUNITY SIZE

In order to explain the growth of cities we have thus far emphasized the advantages of large communities as places of production. The primary importance of production advantages, however, should not lead us to overlook other factors associated with community size. As Chinitz points out, large communities also afford superior opportunities for consump-

---

10. Edgar M. Hoover, *Location Theory and the Shoe and Leather Industries* (Cambridge, Mass.: Harvard University Press, 1937), pp. 90–91.

tion.[11] The basic necessities of food, clothing, and shelter can be purchased anywhere, but the more specialized forms of consumption goods—the "luxuries" that people turn to increasingly as their income rises—are more readily available in the larger centers. In general, the range of types of goods and services offered to the consumer increases as community size increases. Some items, such as opera performances or major league baseball games, are found only in the largest cities.

The large community also offers important advantages to the worker. Obviously, the range of job choice increases with community size. Wage levels, too, are higher in the larger centers. Within specific occupational categories there is a fairly regular pattern of rising wages as one moves from smaller to larger metropolitan areas.[12] As we will show in Chapter 3, median family income is far higher in metropolitan areas than in the rest of the country, and the persistent flow of internal migration toward those areas suggests that workers do move to take advantage of the differential.

ARE CITIES "UNNATURAL"?

Implicit in most analyses of urban growth, including perhaps the argument of this chapter, is the assumption that one must, so to speak, "account" for the fact that men move from a "natural" rural life to a somehow "unnatural" urban one. The argument need not proceed that way, however. R. M. Haig, in a notable *tour de force*, shrewdly reversed matters and suggested that "the question is changed from 'Why live in the City?' to 'Why not live in the City?' "[13] He took as his starting point the observation that the economically most efficient pattern for the production and distribution of goods would assign to metropolitan areas all men except those needed to farm the land or extract minerals plus those needed to transport such raw materials. According to this logic what requires "explanation" is not the tendency of the population to concentrate in cities but the fact that it is not *all* concentrated there.

One might also draw upon the authority of the philosophers for this point of view: man, the social animal described by Aristotle, only fulfills his nature in association with his fellows. Or, in the current phrase, men want to go where the action is. Thus, one might argue, social as well as economic drives make the city the natural destination of man. Urbanism as a way of life then requires no special justification, and no apologies.

11. Benjamin Chinitz, ed., *City and Suburb* (Englewood Cliffs, N.J.: Prentice-Hall, 1964), editor's introduction, pp. 10–12.
12. See data in Edgar M. Hoover, *An Introduction to Regional Economics* (New York: Alfred A. Knopf, 1971), pp. 162–63.
13. R. M. Haig, "Some Speculations Regarding the Economic Basis of Urban Concentration," *Quarterly Journal of Economics*, February 1926, pp. 179–208; the quotation is from p. 188.

The Growth of Cities and Metropolitan Areas

THREE

When Mark Twain informs the reader of *Huckleberry Finn* that he has painstakingly incorporated seven different dialects into the book he excuses his explanation by saying that "without it many readers would suppose that all these characters were trying to talk alike and not succeeding." Unless a similar warning is issued here, the unwary reader may assume that "urban," "metropolitan," and "central city" are terms that sound different but have the same meaning, or that "rural," "suburban," and "nonmetropolitan" are nothing more than synonyms used to ward off fatigue. In short, the time has come for some definitions. And since to define is also to understand, the labor of definition will provide the reader with a kind of spatial paradigm, a map of the essential elements of urban and metropolitan structure.

In what follows we will also refer occasionally to the technical problems that arise when areal definitions are used as the basis for gathering statistics. Our purpose in so doing is, not only to warn the reader against the ambiguities in the data, but to forewarn those who wish to do their own empirical research concerning some of the problems they will face.

SOME DEFINITIONS

"City"

Let us begin with "city," the easiest of the essential terms to define. "City" is often used loosely as a generic term for all kinds of large or dense settlements. When used with precision, however, as in classifying population data, it simply denotes the area contained within the political boundaries of a large incorporated municipality. We will make frequent use of the term "central city" in this book. A central city is the principal city (defined as above) around which some larger unit— say, a standard metropolitan statistical area—is formed.

The definition of "city" and "central city" by political boundaries has two important consequences. First, the area of a city, and hence its population, is partly the result of historical accident. If a city is originally incorporated with a large geographic area or is able to grow by annexing neighboring towns as its population expands, then it will become larger than another city, equally prosperous and attractive, which either starts with a relatively small area or is unable, for political reasons, to gain much territory or population through annexation. Consider the contrast between Boston and Baltimore. In 1970 the population of the "Boston urbanized area" exceeded that of the "Baltimore urbanized area" by almost 1.1 million, yet the city of Baltimore contained 265,000 more people than did the city of Boston. Baltimore city accounted for 57 percent of the population and covered 34 percent of the land in the Baltimore urbanized area. The figures for Boston were, respectively, only 24 percent and 13 percent.

Since cities can expand by annexation, the second consequence of the use of political boundaries to define cities is that historical comparisons of population size (or other measures) can be misleading if care is not taken to adjust for boundary changes. The place on the map defined as Indianapolis, Indiana, increased in area from 71.2 square miles in 1960 to 379.4 square miles ten years later. During the same period its population rose from 476,258 to 744,624. Without all that annexation, Indianapolis would actually have lost population over the decade: the 1970 population within the 1960 boundaries was only 437,892, 8 percent less than in 1960. Which figure is the relevant one depends, of course, on the problem at hand.

"Metropolitan Area"

Consider next a definition for "metropolitan area." "It has long been recognized," the Census Bureau tells us, "that for many types of social and economic analysis, it is necessary to consider as a unit the entire population in and around the city whose activities form an integrated social and economic system. Prior to the 1950 census, areas of this type had been defined in somewhat different ways for different purposes and by various agencies." [1] Seeking uniformity, the government developed the concept of

1. This and the additional quoted passages defining SMSA's are from U.S. Bureau of the Census, *Census of Population, 1960, Supplementary Reports*, PC(S1)-1,

the "Standard Metropolitan Area" and introduced it into the 1950 census as a new geostatistical unit for which data were collected. For the 1960 census the definition, subsequently unchanged, was slightly modified and the name altered to "Standard Metropolitan Statistical Area," or, for convenience, "SMSA."

In 1970 the Bureau of the Census recognized 243 SMSA's in the United States and 4 in Puerto Rico. Except in New England, they are built up of units not smaller than whole counties. This has the practical advantage of making data collected for SMSA's readily comparable with local business or government information assembled on a county basis.

The SMSA is basically an economic unit. It defines the metropolis largely, though not entirely, by its character of being an integrated, non-agricultural labor market. An integrated labor market might, for our purposes, be described as the smallest area that is large enough to contain the workplaces of most of the people who reside in it and the residences of most of the people who work in it. In a major metropolitan region, such as the one centered on Philadelphia, for example, the smallest area that will answer such a definition is large indeed. The Philadelphia SMSA includes the city of Philadelphia plus four other counties in Pennsylvania and three in New Jersey. As we shall see, the Census Bureau definition treats the web of journeys from home to workplace as primary evidence that the regional population forms "an integrated social and economic system"—a metropolitan system, in truth, about which it is exceedingly useful to collect statistics.

Except in New England, where towns and cities replace counties, an SMSA is defined as

> a county or group of contiguous counties which contains at least one city of 50,000 inhabitants or more or "twin cities" with a combined population of at least 50,000. In addition to the county or counties, containing such a city or cities, contiguous counties are included in an SMSA if, according to certain criteria, they are essentially metropolitan in character and are socially and economically integrated with the central city.

The labor market emphasis of this definition emerges clearly if we examine the specific criteria employed with it. The Census Bureau explains that "the criteria of metropolitan character relate primarily to the attributes of the outlying county as a place of work or as a home for a concentration of nonagricultural workers." One of these criteria, for example, is that "at least 75 percent of the labor force of the county must

April 10, 1961, pp. 4–5. The "official" list of SMSA's, together with the precise areal definition of each, is periodically revised and published by the Office of Statistical Standards of the U.S. Bureau of the Budget.

be in the nonagricultural labor force." In addition, the outlying county must meet at least one of three other conditions relating to density of population, number of nonagricultural jobs, and number of nonagricultural workers living in the county.

The Bureau continues,

> The criteria of integration relate primarily to the extent of social and economic communication between the outlying counties and the central county . . . . A county is regarded as integrated with the county or counties containing the central cities of the area if either . . . 15 percent of the workers living in the given outlying county work in the county or counties containing the central city or cities of the area, or . . . if 25 percent of those working in the given outlying county live in the county or counties containing the central city or cities.

When the Census Bureau publishes SMSA data it generally subdivides them into "central city" and "outside central city." The latter category, which is simply the SMSA total minus the central city total, is often referred to as "the ring," since it comprises the ring of counties that commonly surround the central city and lie within the SMSA. Thus the Philadelphia SMSA consists of the central city of Philadelphia and a "ring" of seven contiguous counties.

Since counties are often large and contain diverse kinds of settlement, parts of the counties included in an SMSA frequently are thinly settled and essentially rural rather than urban. The people living in these rural areas within SMSA's may or may not be part of the region's integrated nonagricultural labor market. In either case, the fact we are confronted with is that if "metropolitan" can include "rural" then "metropolitan" does not equal "urban." What, then, do we mean by "urban" and what by "rural"?

"Urban" and "Rural"

"Urban" and "rural" have, indeed, proven difficult for social scientists to define. Economists offer no help here: apparently economic science has been able to get along without empirically meaningful definitions of these categories. Sociologists, however, to whom the concept of community is central, have given the matter a good deal of attention. The urban community, they find, displays social characteristics different from those of rural society, but they are not always in agreement as to the extent of the differences or the inferences to be drawn from them. Consequently there is no definition of "urban" and "rural" universally accepted among sociologists. Moreover, it is highly improbable, as Duncan has argued, that any single, scalable characteristic can provide an adequate system of classification for all purposes.[2] Hatt and Reiss, however, point out that

> A growing number of sociologists appear to share the point of view that the formal criteria of a scientific definition of urban phenomena is satisfactorily met by defining communities solely in terms of their demographic uniqueness—the variables of population and area. "Urban" usually is defined, then, as a function of absolute population size and density of settlement. Most so-called urban variables then are considered causal consequences of variation in size and density of settlement.[3]

A definition of "urban" in terms of population size and density is, in fact, what the U.S. Bureau of the Census has adopted for compiling statistics on urbanization. The economist will have no trouble accepting this. He is likely to be much more directly interested in the population characteristics of communities than in sociological variables such as degree of kinship solidarity or incidence of deviant behavior, the correlation of which with the population variables used to define "urban" may be doubtful. Hence he will not be disturbed at the choice of demographic features themselves as the sole criteria.

By common consent, however, any dichotomous definition—i.e., any definition that divides all places into two mutually exclusive groups labeled "urban" and "rural"—is bound to be arbitrary. Between the polar cases of rural and urban, along whatever scale we choose, there lie many intermediate situations. There is no obvious point at which to draw the line and say "all places larger and more densely settled than this one are urban, and the rest are rural." Yet a simple, two-way classification is so convenient that it continues to predominate in statistical studies.

The Bureau of the Census adopted its present definition of "urban" for the 1950 census. Included as urban are three kinds of places:

1. all incorporated municipalities having a population of 2,500 or more
2. the densely settled "urban fringe," whether or not incorporated as municipalities, around cities of 50,000 or more
3. unincorporated places of 2,500 or more population outside any urban fringe area.

The Census Bureau also publishes data for an important subcategory of urban places to which it gives the name "urbanized areas." An urban-

2. Otis Dudley Duncan, "Community Size and the Rural-Urban Continuum," in Paul K. Hatt and Albert J. Reiss, Jr., eds., *Cities and Society, The Revised Reader in Urban Sociology* (Glencoe, Ill.: The Free Press, 1957), pp. 35–45.
3. Hatt and Reiss, p. 20.

ized area is a ctiy of 50,000 or more plus its densely settled contiguous urban fringe. With a few exceptions, there is one urbanized area within each SMSA. Data are collected on this basis in order to sort out the population living at urban densities (i.e., those living in the central city and its urban fringe) from the population of the usually larger SMSA, which may, as a result of its definition in terms of whole counties, contain extensive, low density, rural areas.

All places not defined as urban in the census are counted as rural and further subdivided into rural-farm and rural-nonfarm. The neophyte should be warned not to confuse farm–nonfarm with rural–urban.

The definition of "urban" adopted for the 1950 census differed radically from that employed earlier, and the reasons for the change are highly instructive. Until 1950, the Census Bureau defined as urban any incorporated municipality with a population of 2,500 or more. With a few exceptions, other places, no matter how densely settled or populous, were not considered urban because they were not incorporated municipalities. As Bogue has pointed out, this definition had one important advantage and two serious disadvantages.[4] It was advantageous because, being simple, it could be applied readily to historical census figures to yield urban-rural data running all the way back to 1790. It was disadvantageous because it assumed, first, that every settlement would incorporate before reaching the minimum size of 2,500 and, second, that each city, as its population grew, would periodically expand its corporate limits to bring within the defined "urban" boundary the contiguous densely settled urban fringe. On both counts the old definition led to understatement of the urban population. Small places did not always incorporate before they reached the 2,500 line. More important, widespread use of the automobile and truck after 1920 led to a change in the pattern of metropolitan settlement (to be discussed at greater length below). Rubber-tired transport made it possible to live in areas well away from either the central city or the suburban railroad towns and still commute to jobs in the center or in satellite cities. These new suburban settlements were rarely annexed by the central cities and often remained unincorporated even though they attained a considerable population and density of settlement. The result was a growing discrepancy between the census category of urban, which excluded such unincorporated areas, and the common-sense observation that these communities were economically and socially integrated with large urban centers and themselves displayed most of the characteristics of incorporated towns.

The new criteria adopted in 1950 met the requirements of an up-to-date definition of urbanism about as well as possible. One must note,

4. Donald J. Bogue, "Urbanism in the United States, 1950," in *ibid.*, pp. 83–102.

however, that changes in the technology of communication and transportation during the twentieth century have made the distinction between urban and rural less clear and perhaps less meaningful than it had been. Down to the end of the nineteenth century urban settlement was typically quite dense, while rural areas were settled at the low density appropriate to farming. Rural life, built around horse-and-buggy transport for short journeys, was still relatively isolated from the influence of cities. Today the urban-rural distinction is less clear: urban settlement has spread out at a much lower density than before; rural life is increasingly tied to the country towns and the larger cities by rapid communication and transport, and it has lost many of the characteristics attributable to its isolation and relative self-sufficiency.

"Central Business District"

A few terms that do not have formal Census Bureau definitions remain to be mentioned. "Central business district," commonly abbreviated as "CBD," refers to the commercial center of a large city. There are no precise rules for defining a CBD according to which we could delineate comparable areas in various large cities. Thus, when the term is encountered in the literature it may quite properly mean simply what the analyst wants it to mean, or it may be defined according to local usage for a particular city. In New York, for example, CBD conventionally refers to Manhattan south of 60th Street. The steady migration of workplaces up the island now threatens this traditional dividing line with extinction. CBD's are anything but static.

"Suburb" and "Satellite City"

"Suburb" and "satellite city" are likewise terms usually defined *ad hoc*. In general, these two kinds of settlement make up the ring area of an SMSA. Suburbs are primarily "bedroom communities" containing relatively few places of employment; they may be either urban or rural. Satellite cities are urban localities within the SMSA that are places of employment and centers of commerce in their own right. As Margolis has shown in a study of the San Francisco Bay area, a set of formal definitions can be based on the ratio of local jobs to resident labor force. When the ratio was below .75, he defined the place as a "dormitory city" (i.e., suburb). When it fell between .75 and 1.25, he classified the municipality as a "balanced city" (i.e., satellite city). If the ratio exceeded 1.25 he considered the place an "industrial enclave." [5] Of course, the precise dividing

5. Julius Margolis, "Municipal Fiscal Structure in a Metropolitan Region," *The Journal of Political Economy*, June 1957, pp. 225–36.

lines between these categories, or others one might wish to interpose, are likely to be arbitrary. Especially since the rise of auto and truck transport, residential suburbs have increasingly sought or permitted the construction of light industry, research and office enterprises, while satellite cities may have growing residential districts the inhabitants of which commute to jobs elsewhere in the region.

So much for terminology. A useful device for making all these spatial distinctions concrete and fixing them in the reader's mind is the schematic map of Figure 3.1. It shows how SMSA, central city, urbanized area, urban fringe, urban place, and rural area might be related spatially within a typical metropolitan region.

FIGURE 3.1

Schematic Map of an Urban-Metropolitan Area

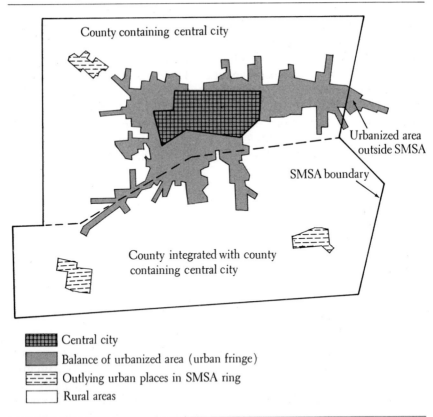

Central city
Balance of urbanized area (urban fringe)
Outlying urban places in SMSA ring
Rural areas

Source: Adapted from Bogue, *Population Growth in Standard Metropolitan Areas,* Housing and Home Finance Agency, December 1953, Figure 1, p.8.

THE URBANIZATION OF THE
UNITED STATES

Table 3.1 summarizes the history of urban and metropolitan development in the United States. At the earliest census, in 1790, only 5 percent of the whole population lived in cities of 2,500 or more—the definition of urban used until the 1950 census. If we take "urbanization" to mean a rise in the proportion of population living in urban areas, and "urban growth" to mean an absolute increase in urban population, then the United States has been experiencing both processes almost continuously since 1790. Urbanization obviously occurs whenever urban growth exceeds rural growth, and that condition has been fulfilled in every decade of our history except 1810–20. In the decades between 1790 and 1840, with that one exception, the urban population grew at an average rate almost twice that of the rural population. But because cities were so small at the beginning of the period—there were only 24 in all, of which only 5 exceeded the 10,000 mark—it took a long time for these high growth rates

TABLE 3.1
Growth of Urban and Metropolitan Population in the United States

| | PERCENTAGE OF TOTAL POPULATION | | PERCENTAGE OF TOTAL POPULATION | |
Date	Urban [a]	Rural [a]	Metro-politan [b]	Nonmetro-politan [b]
1790	5.1%	94.9%	—	—
1840	10.8	89.2	—	—
1900	39.6	60.4	31.7%	68.3%
1910	45.6	54.4	37.5	62.5
1920	51.2	48.8	43.7	56.3
1930	56.1	43.9	49.8	50.2
1940	56.5	43.5	51.1	48.9
1950	64.0	36.0	56.8	43.2
1960	69.9	30.1	63.0	37.0
1970	73.5	26.5	68.6	31.4

[a] Revised definition for 1950 and later. Using the older definition, proportions for 1950 would have been: urban, 59.6%, rural, 40.4%.
[b] Data for 1900 through 1950 refer to the areas that would have qualified as SMSA's at the given dates according to the 1950 definition, as estimated by Bogue. Data for 1960 and 1970 refer to SMSA's as defined at those census dates. "Nonmetropolitan" comprises all areas outside SMSA's.
Sources: Donald J. Bogue, *Population Growth in Standard Metropolitan Areas 1900–1950*, Housing and Home Finance Agency, December 1953; and U.S. Bureau of the Census, *Census of Population*, 1960 and 1970.

to urbanize very many people. As late as 1840 the country was still 89 percent rural, and only 11 percent urban.

By the 1840's, according to most students of the subject, the Industrial Revolution was well under way in the United States, and all the economic forces making for agglomeration were unleashed. Thereafter the ratio of urban to rural growth increased markedly, and the pace of urbanization quickened. Immigration from abroad contributed to the trend, since a disproportionate number of immigrants to the United States have always stopped in the cities. The urban portion of the population reached 20 percent in 1860 and 40 percent in 1900. Sometime between 1910 and 1920 the nation passed the historic milestone of a population half urban and half rural: by 1920, 51 percent of the population was urban. Indeed, the decade of 1910–20 was marked by an unusually high ratio of urban to rural growth. Economic mobilization for war attracted labor from the farms to the cities. The urban population grew 29 percent, while rural numbers rose only 3 percent.

Down to the present moment urbanization has continued without interruption. According to the old, pre-1950 definition of "urban," the Great Depression had appeared to halt the trend, for urban places contained 56.2 percent of the national population in 1930 and only 56.5 percent in 1940. But it now seems likely that the old definition was already becoming seriously inadequate in the 1930's through its failure to count as urban the increased settlement in unincorporated urban fringe areas. Had the new definition been used in 1930 and 1940, census data would probably have shown some further urbanization during that decade, even though the trend was undoubtedly slowed by the absence of job opportunities in the cities.

Urbanization proceeded rapidly again during and after World War II. In 1950 the nation was 59 percent urban by the old definition, 64 percent by the new. By 1970 the new definition placed 73.5 percent of the population in the urban category.

DECLINE OF THE RURAL POPULATION

During the 1950's another milestone of sorts was passed: for the first time the rural population of the United States declined not only relatively but in absolute numbers. The absolute decline was small, but it continued in the next decade as well. It was the net result of three different sources of change, all of which had been operating for many years. The 1950's were simply the first period in which the three added up to a negative sum.

The first source of change in rural population is the urban-rural classification system itself. Some areas, rural as of 1950, enjoyed sufficient population increases to be reclassified as urban in the 1960 census, thus diminishing the rural sector. This sort of change is a built-in consequence of any urban-rural classification system and has affected intercensal comparisons from the beginning.

The second source of change has been the continuously advancing mechanization of agriculture. As labor was displaced by machinery, young workers left the farms to seek urban employment. Actual depopulation therefore has long occurred in many rural areas, particularly in regions that are remote from large urban centers, such as the Great Plains farm belt and some parts of the agricultural South. The rural population of the West North Central states reached its peak in 1920. Between 1920 and 1970, it declined by 24 percent. So pronounced was this trend that between 1960 and 1970, 415 of the region's counties experienced a decline in total population (urban and rural), while only 204 enjoyed any population growth.

The third source of change has been the revolutionary impact of the automobile on patterns of settlement, and this has worked in the opposite direction: some rural areas, especially those close to industrial towns and cities, have actually gained inhabitants. The automobile has made it possible to drive from a rural home to an urban job. Thus the rural areas of the industrial states have, in recent years, been gaining rather than losing population, but these gains are attributable directly to the attractive power of the local urban sector with its variety of industry and jobs. The rural population of New England, for example, declined steadily from 1860 to 1910, as the West was opened up to agriculture and New England's farm acreage fell off. After 1910, however, the trend reversed, and New England's rural population again began to increase. Indeed, since 1950 it has been growing relatively as fast as the urban population.

Thus, for the nation as a whole the slight decline in total rural population since 1950 is the result of two rather pronounced but offsetting trends: the rapid depopulation of rural agricultural areas, largely offset by a somewhat less dramatic increase in the rural population in the nation's major industrial regions. Putting these two tendencies together with the population gains that occurred in the urban sector itself, we obtain the rather startling result that between 1960 and 1970, 1,369 of the nation's 3,141 counties experienced a loss of population. On a county map of the United States this appears as a flight of population from the remote agricultural regions of the Great Plains and of the inland South to the urban and metropolitan counties of the Great Lakes region and the Atlantic, Pacific, and Gulf coasts.

THE GROWTH AND DECENTRALIZATION
OF METROPOLITAN AREAS

We turn next to the metropolitan areas themselves, to look at the growth of the metropolitan population as a whole and at the profoundly important changes that have been taking place within metropolitan areas during the twentieth century. Systematic collection of metropolitan area statistics on the present basis began only with the census of 1950. However, since the SMSA (or, as it was then called, the SMA) is defined on a county basis, Bogue has been able to apply the definition retrospectively to census data running back to 1900. His figures refer to those areas that would have qualified as SMSA's if the definition used in 1950 had been in effect at the earlier dates. The number of areas included diminishes as one moves back in time because the number of central cities of 50,000 or more population diminishes. Bogue's work provides us with the basic statistics needed to study the rise of metropolitanism in the twentieth century.[6] In these data one can literally read the history of agglomeration in our times.

As Table 3.1 indicates, throughout the twentieth century, metropolitan areas have gained population far faster than nonmetropolitan areas. In 1900 areas outside SMA's contained 68 percent of our total population, while SMA's contained only 32 percent. By 1970 these figures had been almost exactly reversed: SMSA's accounted for 69 percent of the national population, nonmetropolitan areas for only 31 percent. Nonmetropolitan population increased only 7 percent between 1960 and 1970, while the population within SMSA's was rising 17 percent.

At the opening of the century the central cities of the SMA's were growing at a remarkable pace. Table 3.2 shows that from 1900 to 1910, their population rose 35 percent, while that of the ring areas of SMA's grew 28 percent and the population outside SMA's increased only 15 percent. In the next decade a pattern relatively the same persisted. After 1920, however, a dramatic reversal occurred: in every decade since that date the population of ring areas has grown faster than that of the central cities, and the margin between the rates of growth has greatly increased. Between 1960 and 1970 ring area population rose 27 percent, while central cities as a whole gained only 6 percent. So far has the reversal of trend now gone that in the 1950's and 1960's many of the older central cities for the first time actually lost population. Had the central city boundaries of 1960 been in effect in 1970, thus eliminating any gains through annexation, the 243 central cities of 1970 would have gained only

6. Donald J. Bogue, *Population Growth in Standard Metropolitan Areas 1900–1950*, Housing and Home Finance Agency, December 1953.

TABLE 3.2
Rate of Population Growth in Central Cities, Metropolitan Rings, and Nonmetropolitan Areas of the United States

Date	Number of SMSA's [a]	RATE OF GROWTH DURING PRECEDING DECADE (PERCENT) Standard Metropolitan Statistical Areas [a]		Nonmetropolitan Areas [a]
		Central Cities	Rings	
1910	71	35.3%	27.6%	15.0%
1920	94	26.7	22.4	8.1
1930	115	23.3	34.2	7.1
1940	125	5.1	13.8	6.2
1950	162	13.9	34.7	6.0
1960	212	10.7	48.6	7.1
1970	243	6.4	26.8	6.8

[a] Data for 1910 through 1950 refer to the areas that would have qualified as SMA's at the given dates according to the 1950 definition, as estimated by Bogue. Data for 1960 and 1970 refer to SMSA's, central cities, and rings as defined at those census dates. "Nonmetropolitan" comprises all areas outside SMSA's.
Sources: Donald J. Bogue, *Population Growth in Standard Metropolitan Areas 1900–1950,* Housing and Home Finance Agency, December 1953; and U.S. Bureau of the Census, *Census of Population, 1960* and *1970.*

.1 percent instead of 6 percent in population over the ten-year period. In 1960 there were 21 U.S. cities with a population above 500,000. Fifteen of them lost population during the next decade, and the losses ranged as high as 14 percent for Cleveland and 17 percent for St. Louis. Yet while these two central cities were losing population, their suburban rings were gaining 27 percent and 29 percent, respectively.

THE IMPACT OF SUCCESSIVE REVOLUTIONS IN TRANSPORTATION TECHNOLOGY

Railroads

Behind the changing patterns of settlement revealed in Tables 3.1 and 3.2 lie the successive revolutions in transportation during the nineteenth and twentieth centuries. The Industrial Revolution began with water but soon switched to steam, and the cities of the nineteenth century grew up on a pattern influenced largely by the strengths and limitations of steam transport. As we pointed out in Chapter 2, the steam railroad revolutionized long distance, intercity haulage, thus making possible great concentrations of urban population at favorable points on the rail network. Steam railroads, however, did little to improve transportation within cities, since they were not efficient for short hauls that involved frequent starting and stopping of their ponderous equipment. Indeed, mass transit in the age of steam was accomplished mostly on foot, while harnessed animal power helped to move local freight. Limited to such ancient modes of intraurban transport, the "hoof-and-foot city," as Blumenfeld has called it, could not extend over great distances. Factories crowded in close to the waterfront and the railroad lines, and workers' homes huddled as close as possible to the factories. Since distance within the city was costly to overcome, proximity was at a premium. And, since proximity was at a premium, close-in land was in great demand, brought high prices, and had to be used intensively. The nineteenth-century city therefore grew up at an extraordinarily high level of density.

Skyscrapers

In the second half of the century the introduction of the "skyscraper" made possible still greater intensity of land use. The skyscraper, in turn, was the product of two interdependent innovations, the passenger elevator and the iron and steel frame method of building construction. The passenger elevator, a revolutionary means of urban transportation in the previously unexploited vertical dimension, was first perfected by Elisha Graves Otis, who personally demonstrated it at the Crystal Palace Exposition in New York in 1853. First use of the fully developed iron and steel frame in a tall building is credited to the architect William LeBaron Jenney in the famous ten story "skyscraper" he completed for the Home Insurance Company of Chicago in 1885. Within a few years the steel frame largely replaced masonry construction; the race toward the modern skyscraper was under way.

Meanwhile, escape outward from the crowded center was reserved for those who could afford, if they wished, to commute to the city on steam railroads. Toward the end of the century commuter's suburbs grew up around the stations along the railroad lines leaving the principal cities. These suburbs were compact in form. Since local transportation was still by horse and buggy, commuters could not live far from the railroad station. Hence commuting towns were strung out like beads along the railroad lines that radiated from the city. By 1898 *Harper's Weekly* reported that more than 118,000 people arrived daily at New York City's Grand Central Terminal from Westchester and Connecticut alone.[7]

7. Reported by John A. Kouwenhoven in *Columbia Historical Portrait of New York* (New York: Doubleday, 1953), p. 422.

Streetcars and Subways

Between 1870 and 1900 the "hoof-and-foot city" was rapidly trans- formed into the "city of the streetcar." In various ways rail transportation was adapted to serve urban needs. Horsedrawn streetcars had been in use since the middle of the nineteenth century. They were not fast enough or large enough, however, to influence urban size and form. Although the cable car was introduced in 1872, its construction was expensive, and it remained for the electric streetcar, first operated on a large scale in the late 1880's, to alter matters by radically extending the distances city dwellers could conveniently travel to their workplaces. By the first decade of the twentieth century a web of streetcar lines crisscrossed every major city and made it possible for residential neighborhoods to spread far out from the old centers. Sometimes the new neighborhoods were more spa- cious than the old; sometimes they repeated the old high densities. In either case, vast new areas became accessible for housing, and cities were able to grow to unprecedented size.

In the largest cities the age of the streetcar also became the age of the elevated train and the subway. New York City began to build elevated intra-urban railroads in the 1870's and possessed an extensive network by 1890. Steam engines were used at first, but the lines were soon electrified. In 1900 the city began construction of its first subway, and service started in 1904. Boston had begun service on a small section of subway in the late 1890's.

THE MONONUCLEAR CITY

Rapid transit by subway or elevated train extended the feasible journey to work or to shop and thus reinforced the effect of the streetcar in stimulating the growth of great cities. Even more than the streetcar lines, however, the rapid transit systems were laid out like the spokes of a wheel. They were intended to move people from outlying residential areas to a central business and shopping district and back again to their homes. Such a system did little to improve communication between points in out- lying areas. It was intended to serve a mononuclear city, and once in place it provided formidable economic support for the mononuclear structure. Only in the central business district could the large insurance companies, banks, and other office enterprises daily assemble the thou- sands of clerks and bookkeepers they required. Light industry, too, was encouraged to remain near the center to take advantage of the availability of labor as well as easy access to other services. Centrality was even more crucial to the large department stores. Located at the hub of the transport network, they could serve not only the downtown work force but the crowds of shoppers the system funneled toward them from all parts of the city.

Thus supported by the great transportation innovations of railroad, streetcar, subway, and elevator, central cities reached what might be called their demographic zenith in the early years of the twentieth century. Between 1900 and 1920 the population of central cities grew considerably faster than that of their ring areas and incomparably faster than the nation's nonmetropolitan population.

We have already indicated the reversal of this pattern when, after 1920, ring areas of SMSA's began to gain population faster than central cities. For this reversal we can supply two principal explanations; the first might be termed the overflow effect and the second the automobile effect.

DECENTRALIZATION: THE OVERFLOW EFFECT

The overflow effect is easily described: if a central city with fixed boundaries enjoys continuous growth of numbers, vacant land will eventually be used up, and, even though growth continues in the form of higher density, additional metropolitan population will tend increasingly to spill over into the suburbs. Before the outward-moving margin of continuous development reaches the central city boundaries, suburban ring development will be relatively slight, based upon the growth of scattered suburbs and satellite cities. After the margin of development passes those boundaries, however, suburban population will rise at an incomparably faster pace than before and will certainly outstrip the growth rate of the central city.

Statistical evidence of the overflow effect can be obtained if we restate the relationship as follows: the greater the density of population per square mile in the central city, the greater the proportion of SMSA population growth that will be accounted for by the ring. Figure 3.2 demonstrates the existence of such a relationship. Its horizontal scale measures central city population per square mile in 1960. Its vertical scale measures percentage of total SMSA population growth between 1960 and 1970 accounted for by the ring area of the SMSA. Plotted on the diagram are points showing the central city density and ring proportion of SMSA growth for 12 SMSA's: the six largest (in 1970) in the North and East (marked by crosses) and the six largest in the South and West (shown by circles). The SMSA's were selected on a regional basis in order to bring out the contrast—which we will have occasion to illustrate along many socioeconomic scales—between the older, more densely settled SMSA's

FIGURE 3.2

Relationship Between Central City Density and Suburban Population Growth

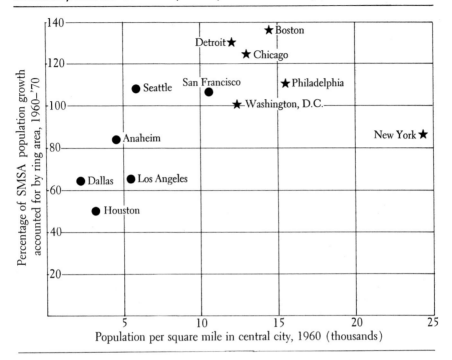

Notes: Data refer to 1960 areas of SMSA's, central cities and ring areas. The two groups of SMSA's are:

NORTH AND EAST (SHOWN BY ★)

New York, N.Y.
Chicago, Ill.
Philadelphia, Pa.–N.J.
Detroit, Mich.
Washington, D.C., Md.–Va.
Boston, Mass.

SOUTH AND WEST (SHOWN BY ●)

Los Angeles-Long Beach, Calif.
San Francisco-Oakland, Calif.
Houston, Texas
Dallas, Texas
Seattle–Everett, Wash.
Anaheim-Santa Ana-Garden Grove, Calif.

Orange County was deducted from the Los Angeles-Long Beach SMSA data for 1960, since that county was subsequently recognized as the independent Anaheim-Santa Ana-Garden Grove SMSA

Source: U.S. Bureau of the Census, *Census of Population, 1960* and *1970*.

of the former group and the newer, more "spread out" metropolitan areas of the latter.

The diagram shows clearly that the proportion of growth accounted for by the ring increases as central city density rises. With one exception, all the cities having a density above 6,000 persons per square mile in 1960 lost population in the next decade. In the SMSA's centered on those cities, the ring therefore necessarily accounted for more than 100 percent of SMSA population growth. The one exception was New York City. Although its population density is approximately double that of the other large central cities of the North and East, it nevertheless registered a small population gain during the 1960's. This suggests not that density and overflow are unconnected, but rather that New York City is literally a unique case—unique as the nation's "highest order city" and therefore able to exert an attraction for population and economic activity of a different order of magnitude than other large centers. (We will explore the notion of a "hierarchy" of urban centers in Chapter 5.)

Influence of City "Age"

Figure 3.2 shows a dramatic contrast between the large central cities of the North and East and those of the South and West. With the single exception of San Francisco-Oakland, the central cities of the South and West are grouped at the low end of the density scale; without exception those of the North and East fall at the high end. This striking difference is a function primarily of central city "age." As we have already pointed out, cities that achieved their major growth before the automobile era typically developed to very high densities; these are the "old" central cities of the North and East. On the other hand, as we will explain below, cities that grew rapidly after 1920 were laid out to be served by the automobile and truck and typically show a dispersed, low density pattern; such are the "new" cities of the South and West.

The "age" of an SMSA has often been measured by the census date at which it first would have qualified as a metropolitan area according to our present definition. Such a procedure, however, fails to draw the distinction intended here. The definition of an SMSA requires a central city of at least 50,000 population, but almost all the very large SMSA's of 1970 had central cities of 50,000 or more well before the automobile era. An "age" measure capable of distinguishing development before from development after the automobile era would have to be based on a different criterion than simply a 50,000 population size. One might, for example, assign as the "age" of a central city the census date at which it reached half its maximum size. Such a measure enables one to distinguish those cities that enjoyed half or more of their growth before the automobile age from those that did not. Applying that criterion, we find that all six of the northern and eastern cities in Figure 3.2 had achieved at least half their maximum size by 1920, and four had done so by 1910 or earlier. According to this measure, the western and southern cities are much newer: four achieved half their maximum size only by 1930 or later, and two achieved it in 1920. These two are Seattle and San Francisco-Oakland. The latter pair in particular display density and growth characteristics similar to the cities of the North and East, as one would expect from their similarity in "age."

As the older central cities in Figure 3.2 lose population, their population per square mile will diminish, and they will move leftward on the density diagram. As the newer central cities gain population, they will move to the right. Thus the two groups, now so widely separated, are gradually converging along the density scale. It seems unlikely, however, that they will meet in the foreseeable future. The newer cities, built on the principle of automobile transportation, cannot develop to anything like the densities achieved in the older cities, with their mass transit framework. Indeed, some of the denser new cities of the South and West appear already to have reached, or may be close to reaching, their maximum population size.

Data on the present size and recent growth of population in the 12 metropolitan areas discussed above are given in Table 3.3. From 1960 to 1970 the aggregate population of the "new" SMSA's of the South and West grew at more than twice the rate shown by the "old" areas of the North and East. The central cities in the former group gained 14 percent in aggregate population, while those in the latter lost 2 percent. Ring areas grew rapidly in both regions, but more rapidly in the new SMSA's than in the old.

DECENTRALIZATION: THE AUTOMOBILE EFFECT

The high ratio of ring to central city population growth in metropolitan areas with central city densities as low as those of Dallas, Houston, and Anaheim-Santa Ana-Garden Grove is strong evidence that the automobile effect as well as the overflow effect has been an important cause of the rapid development of suburbs since 1920. In addition, the overflow effect, acting alone, could never account for the decline in population experienced by so many central cities in recent years. With the automobile effect we come to the last revolutionary change in transportation technology that has shaped the geographic pattern of metropolitan settlement in our times.

TABLE 3.3
*Population Inside and Outside Central Cities of Selected
Metropolitan Areas, 1970, and Percentage Change in
Population, 1950–60 and 1960–70*

		PERCENTAGE CHANGE [a]	
Six Largest SMSA's in North and East [b]	*Population, 1970* [a]	*1960–70*	*1950–60*
New York, N.Y.	11,571,899	8.2	11.9
New York City	7,894,862	1.5	−1.4
Outside central city	3,677,037	26.2	75.0
Chicago, Ill.	6,978,947	12.2	20.1
Chicago city	3,366,957	−5.2	−2.0
Outside central city	3,611,990	35.3	71.5
Philadelphia, Pa.-N.J.	4,817,914	10.9	18.3
Philadelphia city	1,948,609	−2.7	−3.3
Outside central city	2,869,305	22.6	46.3
Detroit, Mich.	4,199,931	11.6	24.7
Detroit city	1,511,482	−9.5	−9.7
Outside central city	2,688,449	28.5	79.3
Washington, D.C.-Md.-Va.	2,861,123	37.8	37.7
Washington city	756,510	−1.0	−4.8
Outside central city	2,104,613	60.3	86.0
Boston, Mass.	2,753,700	6.1	7.5
Boston city	641,071	−8.1	−13.0
Outside central city	2,112,629	11.3	17.7
Aggregate of six SMSA's in North and East	33,183,514	11.8	17.2
Inside central cities	16,119,491	−2.1	−3.4
Outside central cities	17,064,023	29.0	59.3

Until the automobile and the truck came into widespread use, rail transport (including street railways) was the only rapid and efficient system of overland movement both for men and for goods. Rail transport, however, has important limitations. Obviously service is restricted to points along the right of way. Yet the number of rights of way that can be operated economically is limited because high fixed costs impose a need for heavy traffic. Within cities, population density was sufficient to support a rather fine-grained network of streetcar lines, but a highly articulated network of commuter railroads, even around the largest cities, was never feasible. Instead the commuter was restricted to a few lines radiating from the central city. Suburban streetcar service, if it existed at all, was subject to the same sort of constraint at its own scale of operation. One could not profitably operate streetcar lines through thinly settled residential districts. Before the advent of the automobile commuters therefore had to live near the railroad stations. Vast areas between the radiating spokes of

Six Largest SMSA's in South and West [c]	Population, 1970 [a]	PERCENTAGE CHANGE [a]	
		1960–70	1950–60
Los Angeles-Long Beach, Calif.	7,032,075	16.4	45.5
Inside central cities	3,174,694	12.5	27.1
Outside central cities	3,857,381	20.0	66.6
San Francisco-Oakland, Calif.	3,109,519	17.4	24.0
Inside central cities	1,077,235	−2.8	−4.5
Outside central cities	2,032,284	31.9	57.9
Houston, Texas	1,985,031	40.0	51.6
Houston city (urban part)	1,231,394	31.2	57.4
Outside central city	753,637	57.0	41.5
Dallas, Texas	1,555,950	39.0	43.4
Dallas city	844,401	24.2	56.4
Outside central city	711,549	61.8	27.0
Seattle-Everett, Wash.	1,421,869	28.4	31.1
Inside central cities	584,453	−2.2	19.1
Outside central cities	837,416	64.3	48.6
Anaheim-Santa Ana-Garden Grove, Calif.	1,420,386	101.8	225.6
Inside central cities	445,826	54.4	380.6
Outside central cities	974,560	34.7	165.9
Aggregate of six SMSA's in South and West	16,524,830	26.8	43.8
Inside central cities	7,358,003	14.3	29.4
Outside central cities	9,166,827	38.9	61.3

[a] For each SMSA as a whole, population in 1970 and percentage changes from earlier years are based on constant SMSA boundaries, as defined for the 1970 census. Central city boundaries, however, are not held constant. In some cases annexation by central cities took substantial population away from ring areas.

[b] Corresponds to Northeast and North Central Census Regions plus Maryland and Washington, D.C.

[c] Corresponds to South and West Census Regions less Maryland and Washington, D.C.

Source: U.S. Bureau of the Census, Census of Population, 1970, U.S. Summary, PC(1)A-1, Table 34.

the railroad system, if they were outside the range of the central city street-car or subway lines, were too inaccessible for suburban settlement.

Industrial and commercial activities were similarly restricted in their choice of location. Manufacturing plants could and did locate outside the central cities along existing railroad lines. Indeed, many satellite cities thrived and grew on such an economic base during the nineteenth century. But even the lightest of industries could not move away from the railroad lines on which they depended for the movement of goods. Nor could they have assembled a daily work force at any suburban point outside the satellite towns.

Large clerical enterprises were even more restricted. Nowhere but at the hub of the central city could they find a labor supply large enough for their needs. Retailing, too, was centralized. Highly specialized stores of all sorts could find enough customers only in the central city, and often only in its central business district. Department stores grew up in satellite towns as well as in central cities, but the suburban "shopping center" in open country was not yet even an inspired land developer's dream.

Thus, because rail transport could best serve a centralized metropolis, metropolitan areas grew up centralized. Indeed, centralization was a self-reinforcing process: the greater the concentration of employment in the central business district, the more it thrived as a center for specialized retail and business services; and the more it developed such services, the greater its attraction as a place of business and employment. Congestion could act as an automatic brake on centralization, but, contrary to our fantasies about the ultimate traffic jam, congestion limits but does not reverse concentration at the center.

Only a radical improvement in man's ability to overcome what Haig called the "friction of space" could break up this historic drive toward centralization. The automobile and the truck provided that improvement by freeing man from the need to live and work close to the fixed lines of the railroad, the subway, and the streetcar. Beginning about 1920 a vast loosening-up took place within the metropolis, and, as it proceeded, the self-reinforcing tide of centralization halted and was succeeded by what may prove to be an equally powerful process of decentralization.

What followed has sometimes been called the "suburbanization" of metropolitan America. That term may be misleading, however, if it connotes simply the rise of commuting suburbs, for the process of decentralization has involved jobs almost as much as residences.

DECENTRALIZATION OF JOBS

Job decentralization within metropolitan areas need not mean that firms close up shop within the central city, pack their movables into vans, and unload at new sites in the suburbs. Such moves can and do take place. But decentralization occurs also as a result of differential rates of expansion of existing firms and differential rates of formation of new establishments as between areas. In fact, these sources of decentralization cannot be disentangled except through painstaking case by case study of individual firms in each area.

We know, however, that the development of trucking made it possible for many firms to cut their ties to railroads and ports. Simultaneously, the widespread ownership of automobiles enabled them to break away from mass-transit-oriented urban labor markets. The need for more ground space often provided the impetus either to move old plants or, when expansion was desirable, to establish new ones at suburban locations. In order to take advantage of assembly line techniques and modern methods of materials handling, manufacturers and distributors needed extended single-story plants rather than the traditional multi-story mills of the nineteenth century. Space to build such plants was far too expensive in the old urban locations but was readily available in the ring areas of the metropolis. Hence many firms, whose face-to-face contact requirements with other industries in the central city were not overriding, either moved to the suburbs or opened new plants there. They acquired space without sacrificing effective proximity to either their suppliers or their customers in the metropolitan market.

The extent to which new manufacturing plants were truck rather than rail oriented has been documented by Hoover and Vernon in their study of the New York metropolitan region. One of their surveys revealed that the proportion of plants served by railroad sidings fell from 63 percent for sites acquired before 1920 to 40 percent for sites acquired between 1946 and 1956. Hoover and Vernon also show the extent to which modern production and materials-handling techniques have steadily increased the land requirements of factories and thus encouraged suburban rather than central city location. They found that plants built outside the central and old satellite cities of the region before 1922 occupied an average of 1,040 square feet of land per worker, while those built between 1922 and 1945 occupied 2,000 square feet per worker, and those built after 1945 took up an average of 4,550 square feet per worker, or almost as much as a very small suburban housing lot.[8]

In an economy built on specialization and interdependence, one new job at a particular place gives rise to others. As the manufacturers, the distributors, and the research laboratories moved out into the suburban rings, suburban employment in complementary service trades increased, too. The rise in job opportunities, of course, attracted population, and the increased population in turn enlarged the market for consumer services, creating still further job opportunities. In short, suburban areas were launched on a continuous round of self-reinforcing economic and demographic growth.

The decentralization of manufacturing within metropolitan areas in the period before World War II has been documented by Kitigawa and Bogue. They found that the proportion of metropolitan area production workers within central cities declined from 67 percent in 1929 to 63 percent

8. Edgar M. Hoover and Raymond Vernon, *Anatomy of a Metropolis* (Cambridge, Mass.: Harvard University Press, 1959), pp. 31, 37.

TABLE 3.4
*Decentralization of Employment and Population Within Selected
Metropolitan Areas*

Six Largest SMSA's in North and East [a]	EMPLOYMENT [b] (THOUSANDS) 1948	1967	PERCENTAGE CHANGE 1948–67	PERCENTAGE DISTRIBUTION BETWEEN CENTRAL CITIES AND RING AREAS 1948	1967
Manufacturing					
Central cities	2,386	2,019	−15.4	73.1	55.1
Outside central cities	879	1,642	86.8	26.9	44.9
Retail					
Central cities	1,066	908	−14.8	74.8	53.1
Outside central cities	358	801	112.4	25.2	46.9
Wholesale					
Central cities	640	599	−6.4	90.6	71.1
Outside central cities	66	243	247.6	9.4	28.9
Selected services					
Central cities	508	692	36.6	85.2	71.9
Outside central cities	88	271	207.6	14.8	28.1
Total, four industries					
Central cities	4,600	4,218	−8.3	76.8	58.8
Outside central cities	1,392	2,957	112.5	23.2	41.2
			(PERCENTAGE CHANGE		
Population [c]	(1950)	(1970)	1950–70)	(1950)	(1970)
Central cities	17,038	16,119	−5.4	67.2	48.6
Outside central cities	8,306	17,064	105.4	32.8	51.4

in 1939, while the proportion in ring areas rose from 33 percent to 37
percent. Despite the enormous increase in manufacturing production
that took place during the war, these aggregate ratios did not show further
change by 1947.[9] Since that date, however, decentralization has resumed,
and its pace has quickened. Table 3.4 shows the decentralization of manufacturing, retail, wholesale, and selected service employment that took
place within our 12 major SMSA's between 1948 and 1967.[10] In both the
older and the newer groups every category of activity shows marked decentralization, as indicated by the rise in the ring share and the fall in the
central city share of the industry total.

9. Evelyn M. Kitigawa and Donald J. Bogue, *Suburbanization of Manufacturing
Activity Within Standard Metropolitan Areas* (Oxford, Ohio: Scripps Foundation, 1955),
Table II–3, p. 22.
10. For a more detailed analysis covering 1948 to 1958, see J. R. Meyer, J. F.
Kain, and M. Wohl, *The Urban Transportation Problem* (Cambridge, Mass.: Harvard
University Press, 1965), Ch. 3.

Six Largest SMSA's in South and West [a]	EMPLOYMENT [b] (THOUSANDS)		PERCENTAGE CHANGE	PERCENTAGE DISTRIBUTION BETWEEN CENTRAL CITIES AND RING AREAS	
	1948	1967	1948–67	1948	1967
Manufacturing					
Central cities	400	765	91.6	57.6	45.3
Outside central cities	294	923	214.0	42.4	54.7
Retail					
Central cities	352	458	30.0	68.7	54.9
Outside central cities	160	376	134.6	31.3	45.1
Wholesale					
Central cities	198	253	28.0	84.0	66.3
Outside central cities	38	128	242.1	16.0	33.7
Selected services					
Central cities	130	314	141.9	78.2	67.1
Outside central cities	36	154	325.8	21.8	32.9
Total, four industries					
Central cities	1,079	1,790	65.9	67.1	53.1
Outside central cities	528	1,582	199.6	32.9	46.9
			(PERCENTAGE CHANGE		
Population [c]	(1950)	(1970)	1950–70)	(1950)	(1970)
Central cities	4,973	7,358	48.2	54.9	44.5
Outside central cities	4,092	9,167	124.0	45.1	55.5

[a] As defined in Table 3.3.

[b] With minor exceptions it was possible to gather 1948 employment data on the basis of 1967 SMSA boundaries. Thus SMSA boundaries are held virtually constant. No adjustment is made, however, for annexation of territory by central cities, which, in some cases, took a substantial number of jobs away from ring areas between 1948 and 1967. Manufacturing data are for 1947 rather than 1948.

[c] Population data are consistent with those in Table 3.3. See footnote (a) of that table.

Sources: U.S. Bureau of the Census, *Census of Manufactures, 1947* and *1967; Census of Business, 1948* and *1967;* and *Census of Population, 1970.*

It is interesting to note that in every industrial category the older metropolitan areas were more centralized in 1948 than were the newer areas. This is just what we would have expected, since the newer areas tended to develop during the age of the automobile, while the older areas were products of the railroad age. The table also seems to suggest that decentralization is proceeding faster in the older than in the newer areas. Here, however, the figures are probably misleading. With a few minor exceptions, SMSA boundaries have been held constant in Table 3.4 at the definitions that obtained in 1967. It was not feasible, however, to correct the data for annexations of suburban territory by central cities between the two dates. Such annexations were negligible in the older areas but quite substantial in the newer ones, where they added automatically to the central city share of total activity at the expense of the share reported for the ring. In the absence of such annexation, the SMSA's of the South and West would probably have displayed decentralization at least as rapid as that shown for the metropolitan areas of the North and East.

It is important not to lose sight of the fact that the decentralization of jobs has accompanied the decentralization of population. The last lines of Table 3.4 show the decentralization of population for our two groups of metropolitan areas between 1950 and 1970, a span of years that almost coincides with the period covered by the employment data. In the table, it appears that jobs have been decentralizing at about the same rate as population within the older SMSA's of the North and East and even faster than population in the South and West. However, the job data were not available for such categories as government and nonprofit institutions. Decentralization has probably been slower for these than for the categories shown. The table may therefore somewhat overstate the pace of overall job decentralization. In any event, the juxtaposition of the job and the population figures should serve to remind the reader that as the suburbs have grown, the proportion of suburbanites who work in the central city has steadily diminished. "Suburbanite" and "commuter" are not interchangeable terms.

DECENTRALIZATION OF POPULATION

We have yet to examine in detail the forces that led to the decentralization of metropolitan population in the twentieth century. Obviously this movement has depended on some of the same technological forces—especially the automobile effect—that led to the decentralization of jobs. Nevertheless, the change in residential patterns also depended on other factors and is important enough to warrant separate analysis.

For the resident of the metropolis, the automobile made possible a home in the previously inaccessible areas between the spokes of the railroad lines radiating from the central city. The commuting towns, which had once appeared as compact beads strung out along the railroad lines, began to spread out. Wholly new residential settlements were built in what had been rural areas, miles from the nearest railroad station. By the 1970's, after more than fifty years of "automobilization," the suburban rings around major cities were not yet "filled up," but open space was fast disappearing.

Evidence of the Automobile Effect

Population statistics dramatically illustrate the abrupt change in pattern that occurred in the age of the automobile. In every decade up to 1930, urban places in the ring—the satellite cities and the compact, rail-oriented commuter towns—had gained population far faster than had the rural ring areas. Even during the 1920's, when automobiles were coming into widespread use, the rates of growth were 48 percent for urban ring places and only 19 percent for rural ring areas. But with the decade of the 1930's the relationship suddenly reversed. Thereafter, rural parts of the ring gained residents far faster than urban ring places. In the 1940's the rates of growth were 41 percent and 29 percent, respectively.[11]

It is important to note that the change in pattern from faster ring-urban to faster ring-rural growth took place at the same date in all size classes of metropolitan area (except the very smallest).[12] This coincidence in time reinforces the belief that the change relates to the nationwide impact of the automobile on patterns of settlement rather than to factors associated with the size or stage of development of individual metropolitan areas.

The Influence of Rising Living Standards and Changes in Consumer Preferences

The advent of the automobile and the truck was a necessary condition for the rise of suburbia in its present low-density pattern. Even in conjunction with the overflow effect, however, it was not a sufficient force to produce the degree of suburbanization we find in metropolitan America today. Rising living standards is another factor that deserves mention. In the technical language of economics, living space is a "superior good" —that is to say, a good which people want more of as their incomes rise. To be sure, they can obtain more space by moving into larger quarters in the city. But there is reason to believe that many who lived in the city while they were poor will choose more space in the suburbs rather than more space in the city as they grow wealthier. That reason lies in the peculiarly fixed nature of commuting costs. A poor man might just possibly find inexpensive housing in the suburbs. But for any given location, his commuting costs are fixed: it will cost him as much to ride a train from Tarrytown to New York City as it costs any of the Rockefellers. A low income family will find that cost simply prohibitive. As income rises, however, the barrier of fixed commuting costs looms less and less large, and eventually the family surmounts it. Thus many who chose the city

11. Bogue, *Population Growth*, Table 1, p. 13.
12. *Ibid.*, Table 16, p. 31.

when they were poor will be found to choose the suburbs as their income rises, just as many who drove used cars when they were poor will buy new cars when their fortunes improve. It is their income, not their taste, that changes. The steady rise of living standards generates a flow of migration from city to suburb quite independently of any change in consumer tastes or in the cost of satisfying them.

Yet consumer preferences, or tastes, may have changed as well. Images of the good life are difficult (before the age of the sociological questionnaire one might have said impossible) to measure and quantify. It does seem likely, however, that the suburban life style—informal, fecund, child-centered—has exercised a more powerful appeal since the end of World War II than it did thirty-five or forty years ago, even for those who could then have afforded it. If this change in the underlying preferences of the population did, indeed, occur, it simply worked to reinforce a process of suburbanization that would have occurred, in any case, without it.

There are signs that the pendulum is now swinging in the other direction. The recent sharp drop in the birth rate, the rise of the new feminism, the increasing questioning of the desirability of the traditional nuclear family, all suggest that at least some Americans are now moving away from the values that have hitherto been the foundation of suburban life. But it is too early to speculate on the eventual magnitude of this change or on its implications for the pattern of settlement.

The Influence of Public Policy

The growth of the suburbs has, in the main, been a natural consequence of changes in technology and rising living standards. However, we should not overlook the fact that public policy has been an indirect influence. It has stimulated suburban as opposed to central city development by favoring home ownership, typical of suburban living, over home rental, which is largely a city phenomenon. This bias is manifold and coincides in time with the impact of the automobile.

First of all, the federal income tax, which was introduced in 1913 and reached the mass of Americans beginning with World War II, treats homeowners more favorably than home renters. Suppose that a man, now living in a rented house, inherits some capital. On the one hand, he can invest his inheritance in stocks and continue to live in a rented house. In that case his investment earns dividends on which he must pay income tax. On the other hand, if he invests the inheritance in a house he occupies himself, he pays no rent, and his investment yields no taxable income under U.S. law. An economically neutral tax system would add to the income of the owner-occupant an estimate of the gross rental value of the house and allow him to deduct interest, property taxes, maintenance, and depreciation as expenses of earning that income. The difference between these amounts is the imputed net income the owner could have earned had he leased the house to someone else at the going market price instead of occupying it himself. U.S. tax law favors homeowners twice-over. It does *not* tax them on the imputed net rental value of their homes, yet it *does* allow them to deduct the interest and property tax costs of producing that income. Because the homeowner's taxable income is being understated, his tax saving is greater the higher the marginal tax bracket in which his income falls.[13] Consequently, U.S. tax law not only favors home-ownership, it stimulates home-ownership by the rich more than by the poor and therefore encourages the segregation of the rich in the suburbs and the poor in the central cities.

The notion that the imputed rental value of housing ought to be counted as income is not, incidentally, as far-fetched as it may appear to the reader whose concept of income is based on conventional rather than logically consistent reasoning: the Department of Commerce, in measuring national income and gross national product, has always included an estimate of imputed annual home rental in the grand aggregate.

A second source of bias in public policy is the long-standing federal policy of intervening in the mortgage market to encourage home-ownership. Since the Great Depression this intervention has taken many forms, of which the most important was and is the Federal Housing Administration's program of home mortgage insurance. The FHA has been startlingly successful in achieving its purpose of reducing both the down payments and the monthly carrying costs on new owner-occupied housing, and that is all to the good. But its program has been administered so as to favor ownership in new suburban areas, and it has failed to develop equally powerful institutional supports for the construction of new urban rental housing. By and large the FHA, from the inception of its mortgage insurance program, underwrote the advertising man's version of the good American life as requiring a Cape Cod cottage, surrounded by a hedge and a well-cropped lawn, and filled with new home appliances. Since World War II policies to aid urban as well as suburban housing have gradually gained momentum. But for about twenty-five years—say, from the early 1930's until the late 1950's—the net effect of federal intervention was surely to hasten the flight to the suburbs.

To summarize briefly, we have now cited five forces that contributed to the rapid growth of suburban relative to central city population during

13. For detailed estimates, see Henry J. Aaron, *Shelter and Subsidies* (Washington, D.C., The Brookings Institution, 1972), Ch. 4. Aaron also examines depreciation provisions under the income tax that favor rental rather than owner-occupied housing. He suggests that under the most probable assumptions the value of these depreciation benefits to rental housing is much smaller than the value of the special treatment accorded to owner occupants (p. 68).

the twentieth century: the overflow effect, the effects of technological innovations, the rise in living standards, a probable change in consumer preferences among life styles, and, finally, the effects of biases in public policy. Each of these can be thought of as a separate force that would have acted even in the absence of the others. Acting together, they provided a remarkably powerful stimulus for change. (In Chapter 6 we will reexamine the first three in the tighter theoretical framework of an urban land-use model.)

MIGRATION AND METROPOLITAN GROWTH

Where did the people come from who filled the cities and suburbs of twentieth-century America? There are only two possible sources of local population growth: natural increase, which occurs when local births exceed local deaths, and migration from other places. The rate of natural increase of population has always been higher in rural than in urban areas, because rural birth rates are higher than urban while rural death rates are slightly lower. Hence, in the absence of migration, rural population would grow much faster than urban. Since, on the contrary, urban population has regularly grown faster than rural, we know that migration from rural to urban areas and/or from overseas into urban areas has long been taking place. (This abstracts from the relatively minor complication that rural places, after sufficient growth, are automatically reclassified as urban for statistical purposes.)

As we pointed out earlier, foreign immigrants into the United States have always moved disproportionately to urban destinations. Immigration from abroad was therefore a major source of urban growth down to the mid-1920's. Then restrictive quotas, and later the Great Depression, sharply reduced the inflow. Since 1950 it has gained in significance once again. More important, however, in explaining urban development is the internal migration from rural to urban areas that has probably been going on at least since the early nineteenth century. According to Shannon, farmers' sons who moved to the city outnumbered those who became owners of new farms by ten to one.[14] While aggregate earlier data are unavailable, figures for 1920 through 1954 show that during those 35 years the *net* migration from farms to urban areas totaled 24 million. For the

---

14. Fred A. Shannon, "A Post-Mortem on the Labor-Safety-Valve Theory," *Agricultural History* (1945), Vol. 19, pp. 31–7, cited in Conrad Taeuber and Irene B. Taeuber, *The Changing Population of the United States* (New York: John Wiley & Sons, for the Social Science Research Council and the U.S. Bureau of the Census, 1958), p. 106.

sake of comparison, the *net* migration of aliens into the United States during the 24 years 1907 through 1930, while immigration was still at a relatively high level, amounted to only 8.4 million.[15] The farm sector in the United States is now so small, however, that it cannot continue to be a major source of population for the rest of the country. Rather it is the nonmetropolitan areas of the nation, including small towns as well as farm areas, that are now supplying internal migrants to urban and metropolitan America.

Estimates of the flows of net migration from nonmetropolitan to metropolitan areas during the last three decades are shown in Table 3.5. (It should be noted that the number of SMSA's and their boundaries are *not* held constant over the three decade span, but this probably does not introduce major distortions into the data.) Interregional flows of migration within a country are rarely observed directly, since such movement is legally unobstructed. Instead, net migration into a given area is estimated as a residual by applying the formula: net change in population — change through natural increase = net migration. The first term is easily calculated from successive decennial census reports. Natural increase is estimated as the difference between local births and deaths. Net migration necessarily accounts for any remaining population change. It must be emphasized that figures derived in this way represent only the *net* flows— i.e., the difference between the number of people who moved into an area and the number who moved out during a given period. A small net flow may be the result of much larger but mutually offsetting movements in both directions. Rates of net migration are usually calculated as the flow during a period divided by the population at the period's starting date.

Comparing the last three decades, Table 3.5 shows that both the amount and the rate of net migration out of nonmetropolitan areas were highest during the 1940's, helped along, no doubt, by the attraction of wartime jobs in the cities. The *rate* of net migration into metropolitan areas was also at its highest level in the 1940's. However, the absolute level of net in-migration rose rather than fell during the 1950's. This asymmetry is made possible by net immigration from abroad, which accounts for the difference between the net outflow from nonmetropolitan areas and the net inflow to SMSA's. Obviously, net immigration from abroad rose sharply after World War II.

During the 1960's net migration out of nonmetropolitan areas fell to less than half the level of the 1950's, and there was a corresponding absolute drop in the net flow into metropolitan areas. Indeed, this drop in the net movement between the two areas is one of the major revelations of the 1970 census. Undoubtedly, it is a result of the previously mentioned

15. Taeuber and Taeuber, pp. 54, 107.

TABLE 3.5
Estimates of Net Migration: Metropolitan and Nonmetropolitan Areas of the United States, by Race

	NET MIGRATION [a]			
	METROPOLITAN AREAS		NONMETROPOLITAN AREAS	
	Number	Rate	Number	Rate
1940–50 (147 SMA's)				
Total civilian [b]	6,397,125	9.2%	−5,808,275	−9.3%
White	4,423,523	−	−	−
Nonwhite	1,605,631	−	−	−
1950–60 (212 SMSA's)				
Total [c]	8,125,354	9.1	−5,460,266	−8.8
White	6,489,380	8.1	−3,813,274	−7.0
Nonwhite	1,636,046	18.2	−1,646,992	−22.9
1960–70 (243 SMSA's)				
Total [d]	5,307,000	4.4	−2,306,000	−3.9
White	3,169,000	3.0	−885,000	−1.7
Nonwhite	2,138,000	15.5	−1,421,000	−21.2

[a] Minus sign indicates net out-migration. Rates calculated as net migration divided by population in base year. Migration of aliens accounts for difference between nonmetropolitan out-migration and metropolitan in-migration.
[b] Civilian population only. Because of differences in estimating procedures, white and nonwhite do not add to total. *Source:* Donald J. Bogue, *Components of Population Change 1940–50* (Oxford, Ohio, Scripps Foundation, 1957), Tables II–A, III–B.
[c] Includes military as well as civilian population. *Source:* Gladys K. Bowles and James D. Tarver, *Net Migration of the Population by Age, Sex and Color, 1950–60,* U.S. Department of Agriculture, Economic Research Service, November 1965, Table 4. Rates have been recalculated on 1950 population base to conform with footnote (a) above.
[d] Includes military as well as civilian population. State Economic Areas are substituted for the SMSA's of New England. *Source:* U.S. Bureau of the Census. *Census of Population and Housing, 1970,* U.S. Summary, PHC(2)-1, Table 7.

long decline in the nation's farm population, which is now so small that it can no longer provide much net migration to other sectors.

Since metropolitan areas gained 5.3 million through migration in the 1960's, while nonmetropolitan areas lost only 2.3 million, it is apparent that the net inflow of foreign immigrants amounted to 3.0 million. The census reports that "an overwhelming proportion" of foreign immigrants "gave urban areas as their place of intended permanent residence . . . ." [16]

16. U.S. Bureau of the Census, *Census of Population and Housing, 1970,* Final Report, U.S. Summary, PHC(2)-1, p. 4.

It is safe to say, therefore, that during the 1960's immigration from abroad actually outweighed internal migration as a source of metropolitan population growth.

Of course, this emphasis on migration should not lead us to overlook the importance of natural increase. During the 1960's metropolitan areas gained 20.2 million in population. Natural increase accounted for 14.9 million, or almost three-fourths of that total.

Patterns of Migration by Race

Table 3.5 shows a significant breakdown of net migration by race. Although the data for the 1940's are incomplete, they do indicate that nonwhites made up about a quarter of the net migration to metropolitan areas during that decade. The absolute level of this flow remained nearly the same in the 1950's and then rose moderately during the most recent decade. It is interesting to note that the white out-migration from non-metropolitan areas fell from 3.8 million in the 1950's to less than 1 million in the 1960's. Since total immigration from abroad and nonwhite migration from nonmetropolitan areas remained almost unchanged, it is this decline in white internal migration that explains the sharp reduction of the net inflow of population to metropolitan areas estimated for the 1960's.

The data in Table 3.5 are at a level of aggregation that conceals a good deal of regional difference in migration patterns as well as migration between SMSA's. They also conceal major differences in migration patterns between central cities and the ring areas of SMSA's. For example, the study by Bogue from which we have taken data for the 1940's showed that the 6.4 million net migration into metropolitan areas actually consisted of a 7.1 million flow into ring areas, offset by a .7 million net outflow from central cities. We know from other sources that there was a good deal of rural migration into central cities during the 1940's. Hence we can be sure that the relatively small net outflow from central cities was actually the result of considerable movement in both directions—a substantial inflow, primarily from nonmetropolitan regions, and an even larger outflow, primarily to metropolitan rings. The same general pattern continued in the 1950's and 1960's. It accounts, of course, for the recent rapid change in central city racial composition, since the in-migrants have increasingly been black, while the outflow to metropolitan rings consists largely of whites. (Race, migration, and urban poverty will be discussed in greater detail in Chapter 8.)

Table 3.6 permits us to compare central-city with ring-area migration by race for our 12 selected major SMSA's during the 1960's; it also shows total net migration for the same areas in the 1950's. SMSA boundaries have been held constant at the limits defined in 1970. For the six

TABLE 3.6

Estimates of Net Migration: Selected Metropolitan Areas, Central Cities, and Metropolitan Rings, by Race

Six Largest SMSA's in North and East [b]	NET MIGRATION [a]					
	TOTAL SMSA [c]		CENTRAL CITIES [c]		RING AREAS [c]	
	Number	Rate	Number	Rate	Number	Rate
1950–60, total	873,216	3.4	—	—	—	—
1960–70, total	314,241	1.0	−1,768,454	−10.3	2,082,695	16.0
White [d]	−635,225	−2.4	−2,519,510	−18.4	1,884,285	15.0
Nonwhite	949,466	23.8	751,056	21.5	198,410	39.2
Six Largest SMSA's in South and West [b]						
1950–60, total	2,287,051	25.2	—	—	—	—
1960–70, total	1,724,562	13.2	187,811	2.9	1,536,751	23.3
White [d]	1,213,316	10.4	−119,194	−2.2	1,332,510	21.3
Nonwhite	511,246	36.3	307,005	29.0	204,241	59.0

[a] Minus sign indicates net out-migration. Rates calculated as net migration divided by population in base year.

[b] Groups as defined in Table 3.3, except that Boston State Economic Area is substituted for Boston SMSA.

[c] Although SMSA boundaries are held constant in this table, central city boundaries are not. Since net migration is calculated as the residual in the formula: net population change − natural increase = net migration, population annexed by a central city appears as a component of net migration. In the South and West, where there was substantial annexation in the 1960's, net in-migration is therefore overestimated for central cities and underestimated for ring areas.

[d] Counties for which migration figures by race were not derivable were assigned in toto to the white sector, following the methodology used in the 1970 census.

Sources: Data for 1950–60, adjusted to conform with 1970 SMSA boundaries, from U.S. Bureau of the Census, *Current Population Reports*, Series P-23, No. 7, November 1962, Tables 1, 2, 3. Data for 1960–70 compiled from U.S. Bureau of the Census, *Census of Population and Housing, 1970*, PHC(2) series for states, 1970, Table 3.

older areas of the North and East the net inflow of migrants to the SMSA's in toto (the left-hand column) was very small in the 1960's, since the net outflow of whites was almost as large as the net inflow of nonwhites. Central cities as a whole showed a high rate of outmigration, while ring areas as a whole attracted substantial inward movement.

The pattern is quite different for the six newer areas of the South and West, where total in-migration was almost as great in the 1960's as in the preceding decade. Unfortunately, in this group the breakdown of migration between central cities and rings is inaccurate because of the effects of the considerable territorial annexation by these central cities during the decade. (In the six northern and eastern SMSA's, such annexation was negligible.) Population change resulting from annexation by central cities between 1960 and 1970 appears as a component of net migration. Net in-migration is therefore overestimated for central cities and underestimated for ring areas. The white out-migration shown for central cities of the South and West would have been much more substantial but for these annexation effects.

Geographic Income Differentials As Causes of Migration

What accounts for the persistent power of metropolitan areas to attract migrant population? The automobile and the truck may have made the modern metropolis *possible*, but they did not *compel* migration out of the countryside. On the contrary they did much to improve the rural way of life. Nor can the bias of public policy in favor of home ownership account for migration from nonmetropolitan to suburban areas, since both are characterized by a high degree of owner-occupancy in housing. Surely, economic opportunity has been the principal attractive force. Living standards are demonstrably higher in urban and metropolitan than in rural or nonmetropolitan areas.

Table 3.7 shows median family income (in constant dollars) by place of residence for two recent dates. In 1969 the median for nonmetropolitan families was only 78 percent as high as for residents of metropolitan areas. For nonmetropolitan farm families the comparable figure was only 60 percent. The table also allows us to compare white and black income by place of residence. It shows not only that white incomes are far higher than black at all locations but also that the ratio of nonmetropolitan to metropolitan income is considerably lower for blacks than for whites. No wonder, then, that blacks make up such a substantial portion of the net migration to metropolitan areas. Finally, Table 3.7 affords a comparison between median incomes in central cities and in suburban rings. Income levels are clearly higher in the ring areas than in central cities, and the margin has been widening over time. (We will take up this comparison in greater detail in later chapters.)

A few cautions must be issued with these data. First of all, there are differences in the cost of living that ought to be taken into account when incomes in different places are compared. Unfortunately, as Wilbur Thompson has pointed out, it is not clear how one can make meaningful comparisons of living costs between places that offer fundamentally different ways of life.[17] Second, differences in income levels *between* regions of the United States are of the same order of magnitude as differences

17. Wilbur Thompson, *A Preface to Urban Economics* (Baltimore: Johns Hopkins Press, 1965), pp. 90–98.

TABLE 3.7
Median Family Income by Place of Residence and Race
(in 1969 dollars; place of residence as of March 1970 and April 1960)

	U.S. TOTAL	METROPOLITAN AREAS				NONMETROPOLITAN AREAS			RATIO: Nonmetro/Metro	RATIO: Farm/Metro
		Total	Central City	Ring Area	Ratio CC/Ring	Total	Nonfarm	Farm		
All races										
1959	7,058	7,880	7,417	8,351	.89	5,647			.72	
1969	9,433	10,261	9,157	11,003	.83	7,982	8,215	6,140	.78	.60
White										
1959	7,360	8,198	7,881	8,486	.93	5,976			.73	
1969	9,793	10,646	9,797	11,155	.89	8,312	8,548	6,403	.78	.60
Negro										
1959	3,721	4,768	4,840	4,383	1.10	2,152			.45	
1969	5,998	6,836	6,794	6,986	.97	3,969	4,151	3,063	.58	.45

Sources: U.S. Bureau of the Census, *Current Population Reports*, Series P-23, No. 37, June 24, 1971, Table 7, and Series P-60, No. 75, December 14, 1970, Table 16.

between metropolitan and nonmetropolitan incomes *within* regions. It is unnecessary, however, for us to examine these complexities here. Suffice it to say that net migration within the United States has long been attracted toward areas of higher income (higher living standards), and the long-run, continued relative growth of urban and metropolitan areas is based squarely on this attraction. If the emphasis on money income differences as determinants of the flow of migration seems unduly materialistic, one can readily broaden the concept of income to take account of the value of the greater degree of choice offered by the metropolis—greater choice among jobs, among social groups, among the specialized forms of material goods themselves.

Just as one would expect migration to flow in the direction of higher income, so one would also expect the result of migration to be a gradual decline in the geographic income differentials that initially gave rise to it. This follows from the influence of migration on the local labor supply. In areas experiencing out-migration the labor supply is reduced, which tends to raise wages. On the other hand, areas to which migrants move enjoy an increase in the labor supply, which tends to hold wages down. The combined effect should be to reduce interarea differentials.

The available data do suggest that although geographic income differentials are far from being eliminated in the United States, they have been much reduced over time, in part, no doubt, as a result of migration. For example, a Department of Commerce study has shown that the ratio between per capita income in non-SMSA and SMSA counties across the nation rose from .43 in 1929 to .62 in 1950 and .67 in 1966.[18] Similarly, Table 3.7 shows a considerable reduction of relative income differentials between metropolitan and nonmetropolitan areas from 1959 to 1969. (The fact that income differentials between central cities and rings are widening rather than narrowing does not establish an exception to the principles outlined above, for central cities and suburbs are really part of a single labor market. The income differential between them is based on the spatial segregation of income classes *within* that market.)

INCREASING CONCENTRATION AND INCREASING DECENTRALIZATION

The long-run changes we have described in this chapter can be summarized very simply: a growing proportion of our population lives in metropolitan areas; within those areas, a growing proportion lives outside

18. Robert E. Graham, Jr., and Edwin J. Coleman, "Metropolitan Area Incomes, 1929–66," *Survey of Current Business*, August 1968, Table 1, p. 33.

the central cities. To put it still more succinctly, the pattern of settlement in the United States has become increasingly concentrated and increasingly decentralized. One must add that the recent decline in migration from nonmetropolitan to metropolitan areas has considerably reduced the rate at which concentration is taking place, but it would be rash to predict that the process will soon come to an end.

The Location of Economic Activity and the Location of Cities

FOUR

The rise of cities at particular places in an industrialized society depends largely on those forces that determine the location of economic activity. In Chapter 2 we explained that economic activity tends to concentrate geographically because external economies of agglomeration have the effect of reducing costs or increasing sales for many types of industry. A description of the external economies of agglomeration, however, is by no means a complete account of the forces affecting the location of firms or of people. In particular, it tells us nothing about *where* agglomeration is likely to occur. We must now look into the matter more systematically.

Traditional Anglo-American economic theory has been called "spaceless." As Isard puts it, "Transport costs and other costs involved in movement within a 'market' are assumed to be zero. In this sense the factor of space is repudiated, everything within the economy is in effect compressed to a point, and all spatial resistance disappears." [1] Even international trade theories have sometimes abstracted entirely from the elements of space and distance. Students of urban phenomena, however, generally have sought to incorporate in their theories as many regularities in spatial relationships as they could discover or accommodate. This and the following chapter deal with the interurban aspects of space. In this chapter we start with the individual location decisions of firms, explaining why firms locate in one place rather than another, and consequently account for the fact that cities of a particular kind and size are where they are instead of someplace else. Chapter 5, adopting a somewhat different

1. Walter Isard, *Location and Space-Economy* (New York: John Wiley & Sons and M.I.T. Press, 1956), p. 26.

but complementary point of view, looks at the spatial relationships between cities and explains why it makes sense to speak of a "system of cities" or of an "urban hierarchy." In Chapter 6 we will take up the problem of intra-urban location: why firms and people locate in one part of the city rather than another and why cities consequently display a certain regularity of form.

EFFECTS OF TRANSPORT COSTS ON CHOICE OF LOCATION

Isard has suggested that the forces affecting a given business firm's choice of location can be classified conveniently into three groups: (1) transport costs, the distinguishing feature of which is that they vary systematically with distance; (2) other input costs, which, if they vary at all from place to place, do so in what is, from the spatial point of view, a haphazard manner; (3) economies and diseconomies of agglomeration, which are a function not of geographic position but of the magnitude of activity gathered in one place, wherever it may be.[2]

It is convenient to begin by examining the influence on the location of a single firm of transport costs considered in isolation. To do so we must postulate a radically simplified world. It will suffice to assume the following:

1. The firm in question is so small in relation to the relevant markets that its activities have no perceptible effect on the prices of the goods it buys or sells and no effect on the location of other economic units.
2. The prices of land, labor, and capital are everywhere equal. Raw materials that are not ubiquitous are priced f.o.b. the source.
3. There are no economies or diseconomies of scale or of agglomeration.
4. The market for the product of the firm is concentrated at a point rather than geographically extensive. (This assumption is *not* necessary in order to isolate the effect of transport costs, but it helps to simplify the argument.)

The profit-maximizing firm will obviously seek out the profit-maximizing location. Under the conditions we have postulated, production costs are everywhere equal. The location at which profits are maximized

2. *Ibid.*, pp. 138–39.

will therefore be the one at which transport costs per unit of output are minimized.

The transport costs in question are the costs of transporting raw materials from their point of origin to the manufacturing plant and the costs of transporting finished goods from the plant to the customer. Using Alonso's terminology, we may call the former "assembly costs" and the latter "distribution costs." [3]

If the customer instead of the manufacturer were to bear the cost of transport from the plant it would make no difference; under our assumptions the price of the final good is already established at the market. If our producer were to require his customers to pay transportation they would not buy from him unless his price at the plant were below the established market price by the amount of the required transport costs. Hence, it is in the interest of the producer to minimize total transport costs per unit of output, including cost of delivery to the market, no matter who actually pays the carrier.

If the firm used only ubiquitous raw materials, like air, it is obvious that production at the market would minimize transport costs and maximize profits. It is only because indispensable raw materials are not ubiquitous that a manufacturing firm in our radically simplified world might find it desirable to locate close to his materials sources rather than to his market.

To begin with the simplest case, consider a firm that requires only a single raw material: a sawmill manufacturing finished lumber. Suppose that logs are available from a forest at point M and the firm wishes to manufacture lumber to be sold in a market at C. Points M and C are connected by a railroad. The railroad charges the same rate per ton-mile to haul logs or to haul finished lumber. Should the lumber mill locate at M, at C, or at some point between?

The answer can be seen at once. If the raw materials that have to be assembled at the plant weigh more than the finished product they yield, it pays to locate the plant at the source of the materials and pay transport charges only on the lighter product. On the other hand, if the finished product weighs more than the raw materials that must be assembled, it pays to locate the plant at the market and pay transport charges only on the lighter raw materials.

The former case is called a "weight-losing" process, the latter a "weight-gaining" one. Clearly lumber milling is a weight-losing process:

3. William Alonso, "Location Theory," in John Friedmann and William Alonso, eds., *Regional Development and Planning, A Reader* (Cambridge, Mass.: M.I.T. Press, 1964), p. 83.

the finished boards weigh less than the logs. Consequently the mill owner would build his plant at *M*, where the logs originate, rather than at *C*.

Materials Orientation Versus Market Orientation

Since, other things being equal, weight-losing processes tend to locate near their source of raw materials, they are often called "materials oriented." Prominent examples, in addition to sawmilling, are steel-making, smelting of other ores, and raw materials processing in general.

Weight-gaining processes, on the other hand, since they tend to locate near their markets, have been called "market oriented." One may well wonder, given the principle of the conservation of matter, how any process could be "weight gaining." The answer found in the traditional literature on location theory is that some processes use ubiquitous materials, such as air and water, whose weight has thus far been left out of account. Soda bottling, for example, involves a large weight gain if one does not count the water on the input side. The argument has traditionally been that since water is available everywhere it doesn't have to be transported and so may be left out of transport cost calculations. For the soda bottling industry this may be a supportable oversimplification. Water does, in fact, have to be transported, but the cost of moving it is so low in relation to the value of the soda produced that the bottler can afford to ignore geographic differentials in the cost of "assembling water." As a general rule, however, it is no longer safe to treat water as a ubiquity in the United States. Increasingly, it is becoming a scarce resource, exerting a locational pull of its own.

An effect similar to weight gain occurs when a finished good, though not heavier than the materials that go into it, nevertheless gains in bulk, fragility, or perishability and so takes a higher transport rate per ton-mile than do its constituent materials. Such a rise in transport rate has the same locational effect as a gain in weight, pulling the plant toward its market and away from its source of (nonubiquitous) materials. The automobile industry provides a good example of this sort of thing. The assembled car weighs no more than the parts that go into it. Nevertheless, the large multiplant firms build their assembly plants near important markets because it is cheaper to ship the constituent parts to an assembly plant than to ship the bulky, and in its own way fragile, finished vehicle to the market.

Broadly speaking, the early stages in a production process are likely to be materials oriented, since they frequently involve great weight loss in the refining of raw materials. The later stages, however, are often market oriented, since as a product approaches the final form in which it is to be consumed it is likely to gain in fragility or perishability.

The Mathematics of Rates, Weights, and Distances

It is worthwhile recasting what has been said so far in a simple mathematical statement.[4] We will employ the following symbols:

w_m = tons of material m needed to make one unit of final product

w_c = weight of one unit of final product in tons

r_m = rate per ton-mile to transport material m

r_c = rate per ton-mile to transport final product

t = rail distance in miles between M and C

K = transport cost per unit of output

Then transport cost per unit of output for location at M can be expressed as the cost of delivering the finished good to market, or

$$K_m = w_c \cdot r_c \cdot t$$

and for location at C as the cost of assembling the raw materials at the market, or

$$K_c = w_m \cdot r_m \cdot t$$

It follows that if

$$w_m \cdot r_m > w_c \cdot r_c$$

the firm will prefer location at M to location at C, and if

$$w_m \cdot r_m < w_c \cdot r_c$$

the firm will prefer location at C to location at M.

The product of rate times weight is what Alfred Weber, in his seminal book on location theory, called the "ideal weight" of the material or product in question.[5] In the one-material-one-market case we are dealing with, the firm will locate at the materials source if the ideal weight of the material is greater and at the market if the ideal weight of the product is greater. The reader can see by reference to these ideal weights the locational choice that is optimal in case of weight gain, weight loss, differences in transport rate on account of bulk, perishability, and the like, or some combination of these.

Thus far, however, we have dealt only with end-point locations. How do we know that transport costs will not be minimized at some intermediate point along the railroad line? The answer can be deduced as follows.

4. Adapted from *ibid.*, pp. 83–84, 99.
5. Written in German and published in 1909, the book was translated into English by Carl J. Friedrich under the title *Alfred Weber's Theory of the Location of Industries* (Chicago: University of Chicago Press, 1929).

For each mile that the firm shifts its location from M toward C, it adds $w_m r_m$ to its assembly costs and subtracts $w_c r_c$ from its distribution costs. The net change in total unit transport costs is therefore $w_m r_m - w_c r_c$ for each mile the firm moves from M toward C. If this difference is positive, transport costs rise continually as the firm moves from M toward C; hence no intermediate point can be as desirable as M. The firm is materials oriented. If the difference is negative, transport costs fall continuously as the firm moves from M to C, and no intermediate point can be as desirable as C. The firm is market oriented. Only if the ideal weights of material and product are equal could an intermediate location be as attractive as an end point.

Effect of Terminal Costs and Declining Rates

The likelihood of an end-point location is increased by two characteristic features of the structure of transport costs that we have thus far neglected. These are, first, the fact that the movement of goods involves terminal costs as well as ton-mile carrying charges and, second, the fact that ton-mile carrying charges themselves generally decline as the distance to be covered increases.

Terminal costs payable by the shipper arise because he has to bring his goods to the loading point of the carrier at one end of the journey and take them away from the unloading point at the other end. If he ships by rail or water he may have to haul the goods by truck to and from the freight terminal or pier. In addition, he will have administrative expenses in the form of supervision and paperwork.

We may speak of loading and unloading expenses as constituting one set of terminal costs. Terminal costs vary according to the mode of carriage. They are generally lower for truck than for rail and for rail than for water shipment. Since terminal costs do not vary with the length of the haul, they have the effect of making long hauls cheaper per ton-mile than short hauls, even if the carrier charges ton-mile rates that are constant for all distances.

In practice, however, carriers do *not* charge constant ton-mile rates. In general, the rate per ton-mile declines as distance increases because the carrier can spread his fixed expenses per shipment over a larger number of miles. Thus the charge for a single shipment of 1,000 miles will generally be far less than for five similar shipments of 200 miles.[6]

How do terminal costs and rates that decline with distance reinforce

6. For further discussion of "the structure of transfer costs," together with factual illustrations, see Edgar M. Hoover, *The Location of Economic Activity*, paperback edition (New York: McGraw-Hill, 1963), Ch. 2.

the likelihood of an end-point location? Consider the consequences if the mill owner should choose to build at some point, call it L, along the railroad line between M and C. He would now have to pay two sets of terminal costs: one set for loading at M and unloading at L; a second set for loading at L and unloading at C. If he located at M or at C he would have to pay only one set, clearly an advantage. Furthermore, the rate structure would generally penalize him for locating at L: the two short hauls, M to L and L to C, would cost more per ton-mile than a single long haul from M to C.

Figure 4.1, adapted from Alonso, summarizes the problem of choosing a minimum-transport-cost location exactly as we have discussed it so far. The diagram is drawn with one corner at M, another at C. The horizontal axis measures, in one direction, distance from M, and, in the other direction, distance from C. The vertical axis measures transport costs.

FIGURE 4.1

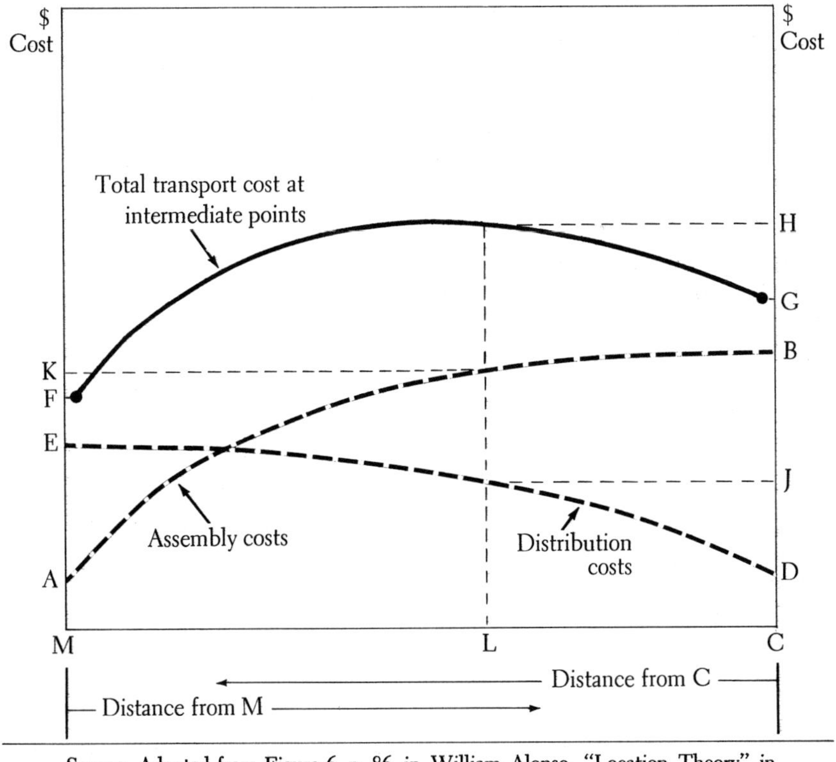

Source: Adapted from Figure 6, p. 86, in William Alonso, "Location Theory" in John Friedman and William Alonso, editors, *Regional Development and Planning*, Cambridge, Mass., The MIT Press, 1964.

The curve MAB shows how the cost of transporting a unit of raw material weighing w_m increases as plant location moves away from M toward C. Terminal costs of loading and unloading the material are indicated by the segment MA. If transport rates per ton-mile charged by the carrier were invariant with distance the segment AB would be an inclined straight line, its constant slope indicating the constant marginal rate. As drawn here the curve flattens out. Its diminishing slope indicates a diminishing marginal transport rate as distance increases. If the plant locates at C, assembly costs rise to CB per unit of material, while distribution costs are zero.

If the plant locates at M, assembly costs are zero, but now the firm must pay distribution costs of carrying the product all the way to C. These costs are indicated by the curve CDE, where CD is the terminal cost and the curve DE indicates the way cost of carriage to C rises as the plant moves away from C toward M. If the plant locates at M, distribution costs total ME per unit of product. Since $ME < CB$ it is clear that in this case location at M is preferable to location at C.

The curve FG shows transport costs for all intermediate points. FG is nothing but the vertical sum of the curves of assembly cost and distribution cost. At an intermediate point, such as L, the firm would pay assembly costs of MK for a unit of raw materials coming from M and distribution costs of CJ for a unit of product sent to C. The sum of these costs is CH, indicated by the height of the curve of total transport costs at L.

For any intermediate location the extra set of terminal costs incurred is shown by segment EF or BG. The disadvantage of making two short hauls instead of one long one is indicated by the fact that FG is higher in the middle than at either end. The diagram shows how these effects combine to reinforce the attractiveness of end-point locations.

Transport Advantages and Urban Growth

We can now begin to see how the transportation advantages of certain locations explain why they become great centers of economic activity. Let us start with a very simple case: raw materials deposits attract materials-oriented industry, industry creates markets for intermediate goods used in production and for consumer goods for its employees, and these markets in turn attract market-oriented industry. Thus great urban industrial complexes grow up in regions that are rich in raw materials: one thinks immediately of the Pittsburgh region in Pennsylvania or the Ruhr Valley in Germany, in both of which proximity to coal deposits (plus accessibility to other complementary materials) explains the subsequent growth of industry.

Yet we know that proximity to raw materials is only a small part of the story. New York, Chicago, Buffalo, and many other important manufacturing centers are not cheek-by-jowl with great raw materials deposits. These cities do, indeed, owe their unusual growth to transport factors, but of a different sort than those we have considered so far. Let us extend the analysis.

Returning to our original scheme of materials at M, market at C, and an intermediate point at L, we can imagine that M and L are on opposite shores of a body of water. (Figure 4.1 no longer applies.) Transportation is therefore by ship from M to L and by rail from L to C. Point L may now be a feasible location for industry. If a manufacturer or processor were to set up at L, he would no longer pay the penalty of extra terminal costs and higher transport rates. Terminal costs are incurred at L in any case, since the mode of transport changes there. For the same reason, two short hauls rather than a single long one are required whether one locates at L, M, or C. In this fashion, any point at which a break in the transport network requires transshipment of goods gains important advantages. Of course, an end-point location might still be preferable if there were a significant difference between the ideal weight of the materials $(w_m r_m)$ and the ideal weight of the finished product $(w_c r_c)$, but it would no longer be virtually dictated by the structure of transport charges.

Probably the most often cited case of a city that has attracted industry because it is a transshipment point is Buffalo. An enormous flour-milling industry developed there because grain could be carried inexpensively across the Great Lakes from the grain belt of the North Central states, unloaded at Buffalo, the easternmost port that could be reached before the St. Lawrence Seaway was built, there milled into flour, and then shipped by rail to the large East Coast markets. But there are many other examples. New York City receives crude oil by water, refines it, and then ships it out by other modes of transport to eastern markets. New York and Boston both refine sugar received by the shipload in crude form from overseas and then distribute it to regional markets by rail or truck.

In most cases port cities, in addition to being transshipment points, gain the further advantage of nodality. (New York City is an outstanding instance.) To return to our hypothetical example, the port L would be likely to develop shipping connections with other materials sources or markets in addition to M and would become a railhead for lines radiating to other points besides C. If a manufacturer required bulky materials from several sources or wished to be in close contact with several markets, a junction point such as a port, though not itself either a market or a materials source, might well be his best location. Of course, a junction has this advantage even when it does not connect unlike modes of transport but joins only different routes on a rail or road network.

Finally, as Hoover has pointed out, ports and other modal interchange points are apt to offer the advantage of economies of scale in terminal operations and will generally "be better provided than most other points with specialized facilities for goods handling and storage." [7] In short, economies of scale and of agglomeration in freight handling give major transportation centers an advantage that helps explain why they attract industrial activity.

Obviously the choice of a minimum-transport-cost location becomes more complicated when firms have multiple materials sources or markets. In some cases location at one market or at the source of one material will still be preferable—as, for example, when the ideal weight of one material or market is greater than the sum of all the others. When such a "dominant weight," to use Weber's term, is not present, the minimum-transport-cost location, taking account of terminal costs, may turn out to be at a materials source, at a market, or at an intermediate route junction.

Our primary interest is the city rather than the firm, however, and it would not be fruitful to that purpose to investigate the complexities arising from the existence of multiple materials sources and markets. The analysis so far suffices to show that transport considerations alone account for a good deal of the concentration of economic activity and population into large centers and also for the particular location of such centers.

LOCATIONAL EFFECTS OF PRODUCTION-COST DIFFERENTIALS

Up to this point we have restricted the analysis to cases of pure transport orientation by assuming (1) that the prices of land, labor, and capital are everywhere equal and (2) that there are no economies or diseconomies of scale or agglomeration. These two assumptions ensure that production costs will be everywhere equal and consequently that the firm will choose its location by reference to transport costs alone. Let us now relax these assumptions and see what effects geographic production-cost differentials might have.

Returning to our hypothetical example, suppose that we are dealing with a weight-losing process for which M is the minimum-transport-cost location. Suppose also that production costs are everywhere equal except that at L the prevailing wage rate for the same quality of labor is lower than elsewhere. A firm would locate at L instead of at M if the saving on production costs per unit of output at L exceeded the loss due to higher

7. Edgar M. Hoover, *An Introduction to Regional Economics* (New York: Alfred A. Knopf, 1971), p. 54.

transport costs per unit as compared with M. The same sort of calculus applies in the case of any geographic difference in input prices.

Note that L's advantage is measured in terms of reduced *production* costs per unit of output rather than reduced labor costs per unit of output. This is necessary because a firm producing at L would tend to use a more labor-intensive technique than a firm located elsewhere—it would substitute labor for other factors of production. Only by comparing all production costs per unit of output at L and M can we take account of the fact that as a result of substitution, the producer at L uses a different mixture of inputs than the producer at M.

Indeed, substitution is pervasive in economic processes. Isard has shown that location theory itself can be handled within the substitution framework of the traditional theory of production.[8] For example, we have assumed that transport costs per unit of output are higher at L than at M, while wages, and therefore production costs, are lower at L. Thus, in moving from M to L a firm would, in Isard's terminology, substitute dollar outlays on transport for dollar outlays on production, while at the same time substituting physical inputs of one factor of production, labor, for physical inputs of the others.

Production-Cost and Transport-Cost Orientations Compared

Industries for which geographic differentials in production cost are more important than geographic differentials in transport cost are said to be "production-cost oriented" rather than "transport-cost oriented." No precise classification is possible, however, since an industry may be significantly affected by both factors. In general—and again this is no more than a rough rule—an industry will be transport-cost oriented if the ratio of bulk to value in its manufacturing process is high and production-cost oriented if the ratio of bulk to value is low.

The iron and steel industry illustrates the first case. At the input end of the process, between 3 and $3\frac{1}{2}$ tons of raw material are required to produce one ton of crude steel, a ratio which insures that the transportation cost of obtaining materials will account for a significant fraction of total cost. At the output end, finished steel products sell for an average $165 a ton, or $8\frac{1}{4}\cancel{c}$ a pound. The low value of finished steel in relation to its bulk means that the cost of transporting it to market is bound to be high relative to its price. Thus transportation costs are important at both ends of the process, and the iron and steel industry is highly transport-cost oriented.[9]

8. Isard, *passim.*
9. Current figures are estimates by Professor William T. Hogan, S.J., Fordham University. On changes in the technology, materials sources, and locational pattern of

Steel mills tend to locate where the combined transportation cost of assembling the materials and delivering the product to market is minimized. Since the two principal materials—coal and iron ore—can be obtained from a number of sources, but not usually side-by-side, many locations for mills are feasible in the United States. For example, mills at Pittsburgh enjoy very low transportation costs on coal, which is mined nearby, but pay relatively high charges to obtain ore from Minnesota. Mills at the Great Lakes ports, on the other hand, can bring in ore relatively economically by water from Minnesota but pay higher transportation costs per ton of coal. Mills along the Atlantic coast in Maryland and Pennsylvania pay relatively low shipping costs to bring in ore by sea from Canada and Venezuela but bear higher costs than do Pittsburgh mills to obtain coal. All of these locations are relatively close to major market areas.[10]

Over the years the tonnage of material required to produce steel has been gradually reduced. Today's figure of 3 to $3\frac{1}{2}$ tons of material per ton of crude steel can be compared with a range of $4\frac{1}{2}$ to 5 tons in the late 1930's.[11] The reduction of input requirements has gradually made the industry less materials-oriented and more market-oriented. It bears repeating, however, that both of these are types of transport-cost orientation.

The cotton textile industry offers a good example of production-cost orientation. Originally concentrated in New England, the industry moved south beginning in the late nineteenth century, in order to take advantage of the lower wage level there. Cotton textiles illustrate the general rule that an industry will tend to be production-cost oriented if the ratio of bulk to value in its processes is low. At the input end, weight-loss in the production process is negligible. To choose one example, a 480-pound bale of cotton lint will yield enough yarn to weave about 450 pounds of cotton print cloth. This is not quite comparable to the weight-loss figure cited for steel since it ignores fuel consumption, but it suffices to show that textile production is not a heavily weight-losing process. Neither is it a fragility- or perishability-gaining process; hence it is not materials-oriented. At the output end, a cotton print cloth in its gray or unfinished state sells for about $26\frac{1}{2}\cent$ a yard, and runs about 4 yards to the pound, indicating a value of about $1.06 per pound.[12] This high value in relation to bulk means that the cost of transportation to market is a relatively small part of total cost, and the industry therefore feels little pressure to locate close to

the industry, see his *Economic History of the Iron and Steel Industry in the United States* (Lexington, Mass.: D. C. Heath, 1971).

10. See data in Walter Isard, *Methods of Regional Analysis* (New York: John Wiley & Sons and M.I.T. Press, 1960), Table 4, p. 351.

11. Hoover, *The Location of Economic Activity,* Table 3.1, p. 43.

12. All data on cotton supplied by courtesy of L. B. Gatewood, Economic and Market Research Service, the National Cotton Council of America, Memphis, Tenn.

its markets. We see at once why the steel industry is far more sensitive to intersite transport cost differentials than the textile industry: transport costs are an important part of the whole in the case of steel but only a very small part in the case of textiles.

Types of Production-Cost Orientation

Production-cost orientation is sometimes further subdivided according to the sort of input involved. One can distinguish "labor orientation" (e.g., textiles), "power orientation" (e.g., aluminum refining), or "amenity orientation" (e.g., research and development laboratories).

Amenity orientation is increasingly important in the United States. It means simply locating the plant in a place where the firm's most specialized, highly paid employees would particularly like to live. Research scientists and engineers, for example, seem to have a strong preference for areas with good schools for their children and interesting recreation for their leisure time. Consequently research laboratories are attracted to areas such as Southern California or the suburbs of New York or Boston, where, apparently, good schools and good living are found together.

Logically, amenity orientation is really a subclass of labor orientation: there must be some salary differential that would induce scientists to leave Santa Monica by the thousands and take up research employment on the plains of North Dakota. But as long as Santa Monica offers free sunshine and ocean sports there is no reason why the laboratory should not take advantage of them and acquire for itself a contented scientific staff at no premium in salary.

The concentration of research and development in certain areas cannot, of course, be accounted for solely by amenities of the physical and social environment. Economies of agglomeration probably play an important part, as well. Nevertheless, amenity orientation should not be dismissed as a mere curiosum. On the contrary, it probably foreshadows things to come. As the work week shrinks, leisure time grows; as living standards rise, people can afford increasingly complex and expensive forms of recreation and will increasingly wish to live where these are available. The income elasticity of demand for yachts is high. In the long run it is bound to influence the location of economic activity.

To complete the list of types of production-cost orientation, we must return briefly to the subject of agglomeration. When we analyzed the causes of industrial agglomeration in Chapter 2 we found two different forces at work. First, some industries are attracted to cities because of a special need for face-to-face contact with customers or suppliers. These are conveniently classified as "communication oriented." Second, we described the external economies of agglomeration and explained how these result in lower costs and so attract industries that can take advantage of them.

Both these forces can now be incorporated in a general analysis of the location of the firm. External economies of agglomeration usually result in lower costs.[13] Hence external-economy orientation can be treated as a subclass of production-cost orientation. Communication orientation can also be seen as a way of minimizing production cost. A firm that needs face-to-face contact with customers or suppliers at C could conceivably locate at M and maintain "contact" by having the appropriate personnel travel back and forth between M and C. But this would entail large travel outlays and would require a larger staff on account of the time lost traveling. If it is cheaper to operate at C than to locate elsewhere and pay the cost of maintaining "contact" with C, then we would say this is a "communication-oriented" firm. The choice we have suggested is not a fanciful one. Many firms do regularly maintain "contact" with other places by sending their personnel on expensive travels. (Of course, if one chooses to classify business travel expense as a subclass of transportation outlay, then communication orientation is a form of transportation-cost rather than production-cost orientation.)

Occasionally in the literature on the economics of location one encounters the term "foot-loose" or "foot-free." Sometimes this is used as a catchall for industries that locate without reference to any identifiable influence. As Alonso has pointed out, however, this usage might suggest erroneously "that one place is as good as any other," which is surely not the case.[14] It is better to describe as foot-loose those industries for which transport costs are relatively unimportant and which are therefore free to use some other criterion in choosing a location.

DECLINING IMPORTANCE OF TRANSPORT-COST ORIENTATION

Over the years technological progress has brought about a gradual decline of transport-cost orientation. This is probably one of the most important changes at work in our society, since it means that men and institutions are increasingly free to move away from the old transport-determined points of production and start over again in an environment of their own choosing.

Alonso has offered three cogent reasons for believing that transport

13. "Usually" because in some cases the advantage may be greater sales rather than lower costs. The same qualification applies in the case of communication-oriented firms. (See Ch. 2.)
14. Alonso, p. 101.

orientation is becoming less important.[15] Foremost is the long-run tendency for transportation to become cheaper, quicker, and more efficient. Second, one of the fruits of technical progress is a gradual reduction in the quantity of raw material used to produce a unit of a given product. Third, products have been gradually improved through ever more complex fabrication, so that value per unit of weight increases. Each of these tendencies reduces the ratio of transport costs to total costs and therefore also reduces the likelihood that geographic differences in transport costs will dominate location decisions.

SUMMARY OF LOCATIONAL ORIENTATION

Table 4.1 summarizes our analysis of the locational orientation of the firm. Necessarily, it omits much detail and many qualifications. The table, and indeed the analysis up to this point, may be misleading if it suggests that every firm can be classified according to a single factor that dominates its choice of location. Quite probably the optimum location will be determined by a combination of factors. For example, the decisive attraction may be a complex mixture of external economies and opportunities for face-to-face contact, two factors difficult to distinguish in practice. Or again, the optimum location may be one that offers neither the lowest transport costs *nor* the lowest production costs but the lowest combination of these. In short, the table simplifies a complex world.

LIMITATIONS OF THE ANALYSIS

Throughout this chapter we have used the method of partial equilibrium analysis, or, as it has sometimes been called, "one-thing-at-a-time" analysis. The method proceeds by saying, in effect, if all other things except the location of one firm are held constant, where will that one firm locate? We set the scene for this sort of analysis when we explicitly assumed that "the firm in question is so small in relation to the relevant markets that its activities have no perceptible effect on the prices of the goods it buys or sells and no effect on the location of other economic units." We thus assumed away the possibility that our one firm's decisions would in fact alter the prices, costs, and other magnitudes we had specified as "given." We could then find the equilibrium location for a single firm in a world of "given" markets, prices, and costs.

15. *Ibid.*

TABLE 4.1
Types of Locational Orientation of Industry

ORIENTATION	DECISIVE CHARACTERISTIC	OPTIMUM LOCATION	EXAMPLES
Transport-cost oriented	High bulk-to-value ratio, hence transport inputs relatively important		
Materials oriented	Weight- or perishability-losing process	Close to materials sources	Ore refining, steel, fruit and vegetable canning
Market oriented	Weight-, perishability-, or fragility-gaining process	Close to market	Brewing, baking, automobile assembly
Production-cost oriented	Low bulk-to-value ratio, hence transport inputs relatively unimportant		
Labor oriented	Labor-intensive process	Low wage area [a]	Textiles
Power oriented	Power-intensive process	Cheap power area	Aluminum refining
Amenity oriented	Employs high proportion of specialized, highly paid personnel	Attractive physical and social environment	Research and development
Communication oriented	Need for face-to-face contact with customers or suppliers	Close to customers or suppliers	Corporate head offices, advertising, law, investment banking
External-economy oriented	Need for specialized ancillary services	A city of appropriate size or specialized character	Apparel manufacturing, broadcasting

[a] For labor of the required skill level.

Suppose, however, that we are dealing with a firm so large in relation to its economic environment that it must in fact have an impact on local markets, prices, and costs. In that case the method of partial equilibrium analysis breaks down. For example, our analysis of transport orientation takes as "given" a market of a certain size and production costs of a certain level at C. But if a large firm decides to locate at C instead of M, won't that perhaps increase employment, wage rates, production costs, incomes, and market size at C, thus altering all the determinants of location not only for this firm but for others both at C and elsewhere? Clearly, there are limits to the valid use of the partial equilibrium method.

In contrast with this approach, the method of general equilibrium attempts to reveal simultaneously the equilibrium locations for all firms. To do this, it must, of course, also simultaneously yield equilibrium prices and quantities for goods and services in all markets. Needless to say, such an analysis is complex and difficult to carry through, but for certain problems such as planning a new city that will maximize some specified value, or calculating the impact of a proposed new urban transit facility on citywide real estate values, it would appear to be indispensable.

WHAT LOCATION THEORY
CONTRIBUTES TO AN UNDERSTANDING
OF URBAN GROWTH

In this chapter, we have attempted to explain why economic activities locate in particular places—for example, why a large flour-milling industry developed at Buffalo rather than Albany, or why textile mills are concentrated in North Carolina rather than northern New Jersey. The explanation has turned out to depend almost entirely on the existence of irregularities in space, including variations in the physical configuration of the land, discontinuities in the means of transportation, the fact that resources are localized rather than ubiquitous, or that climate is not spatially uniform. Because of these irregularities and discontinuities, the business firm's costs of production or transportation are potentially lower at some places than at others. Places offering lower costs attract economic activity, become centers of production, and therefore increase in market size and attract market-oriented activity, which contributes to further growth. As they grow they offer increasingly important economies of agglomeration, which then reinforce their initial locational advantage. By these processes the railroad junction or the little river port of 1850 becomes the large city of 1900 and the great metropolitan area of 1950. An entire urban-metropolitan economy grows from the small seed of initial locational advantage.

The next chapter continues the discussion of location theory. However, the focus shifts: instead of examining the question of why cities grow up at particular places, we will be investigating the spatial relationships *between* cities. The theories offered in the two chapters are entirely complementary. A full account of urban reality must recognize that there are not just individual urban places whose character, development, and location can be studied. Rather, there is a "system of cities," and this system is marked by important spatial-economic regularities.

The System of Cities
and the Urban Hierarchy

FIVE

It is meaningful to speak of there being a "system of cities" because the size and character of any one urban place, or in dynamic terms its power of attracting activity, is conditioned by the size, character, and location of other, related places. The nature of this system is dealt with in a branch of urban study known as "central place theory," which began with work done by Walter Christaller in the 1930's and was subsequently extended and systematized by August Lösch.[1] Central place theory is, in fact, an integral part of the theory of the location of economic activity. The link between the two is provided by market area analysis, as will emerge shortly.

CENTRAL PLACE THEORY

The analysis in the preceding chapter realistically assumed a world of differentiated topography, discontinuous transportation facilities, and nonubiquitous resources. Central place theory, on the other hand, is best expounded by assuming just the opposite sort of world. Instead of explaining the location of activity in terms of the unique features of particular places, it begins by assuming away all unique features. It postulates a perfectly uniform physical world,

1. Christaller's work was published in German. For an early description of it see Edward Ullman's well-known article "A Theory of Location for Cities," in Paul K. Hatt and Albert J. Reiss, Jr., eds., *Cities and Society, The Revised Reader in Urban Sociology* (Glencoe, Ill.: The Free Press, 1957), pp. 227–36.

Lösch's major work, published in German in 1941, appeared in an English translation by W. H. Woglom and W. F. Stolper as *The Economics of Location* (New Haven: Yale University Press, 1954).

consisting of a featureless plane on which transportation is equally efficient in any direction and resources are evenly distributed.

J. H. von Thunen had first postulated a uniform land surface as early
as 1826, in his explanation of the formation of concentric agricultural belts
around a market city. (See Chapter 6, footnote 1.) Central place theory
shows us how, in a similar environment, a regular network of urban places
would be expected to form to provide various services to an evenly distributed homogeneous rural population.

The Economic Basis for a Central Place

In explaining the development of central places, Lösch begins by
assuming that self-sufficient farms are the only producing units on the
uniform transport surface. He then asks, if one of the farmers decides to
produce a surplus of some commodity and offer it for sale, will he be able
to do so? The answer, fundamental to all analysis of market areas, is that
"he will be helped by the economies of large scale production, and handicapped by costs of transportation." [2]

In a much simplified version of Lösch's argument, let us assume that
farmer F has decided to produce a surplus of bread to sell to his neighbors.
They will be willing to buy it from him if he can deliver it to their farms
at a price below what it would cost them to make it themselves. Farmer F
will be able to deliver at such a price only if the cost he saves by baking in
larger quantities outweighs the expense of delivery. Otherwise the potential customers would be better off continuing to bake at home.

The situation is illustrated in Figure 5.1. Farmer F is located at
point O. Distances from O are measured along the horizontal scale and
unit costs along the vertical. The average unit cost of producing bread at
home is OA. Farmer F, however, produces on a larger scale and therefore
at lower cost. Suppose that he finds he can maximize profits by setting an
f.o.b. price of OB. His customers must also bear the cost of transportation,
which rises with distance from O as indicated by the line BC. The
delivered price at any given distance is shown by the height of BC above
the horizontal at that distance from O. Thus a customer at point D would
pay a delivered price of OG per unit, of which BG is the cost of transportation and OB the price at the source. Under the monopolistic conditions
assumed, farmer F would serve a circular market with a radius of OE
miles. Beyond that distance his delivered price would exceed the cost to

2. August Lösch, "The Nature of Economic Regions," in John Friedmann and
William Alonso, eds., *Regional Development and Planning, A Reader* (Cambridge,
Mass.: M.I.T. Press, 1964), pp. 107–15.

FIGURE 5.1

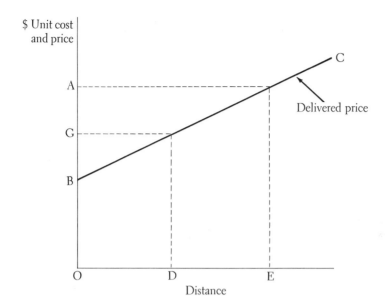

potential customers of producing at home; sales would be zero. (Through-out the following analysis matters are greatly simplified if we continue to assume that the producer sells to all customers at a uniform f.o.b. mill price. Buyers pay all delivery costs. The seller engages in neither price discrimination nor freight absorption.)

A more extended analysis of farmer F's situation would show explic-itly the relationship between price, market area, quantity sold, cost of production, and total profit.[3] Such a detailed picture, however, is not necessary for our purposes. It suffices, as in the general case for monop-olists, to say that the price, OB, at which he maximizes profits must be that price at which the marginal revenue from sales just equals the mar-ginal cost of production. The spatial-monopoly situation analyzed here differs from the standard, textbook monopoly case only in this respect: in the spatial setting it can be shown explicitly that a reduction in price results in a greater quantity being sold both because existing customers buy more *and* because a lower price extends the boundary of the market outward to take in additional customers.

3. This was one of Lösch's major contributions. It is lucidly developed in Hugh O. Nourse, *Regional Economics* (New York: McGraw-Hill, 1968), pp. 18–29, 33–39.

A Network of Central Places for a Single Service

Let us now assume that other farmers can set up bakeries under the same cost conditions enjoyed by farmer *F*. To maximize profits each would locate away from other producers so that he could sell as a monopolist to a circular market of optimum size (i.e., the same size as farmer *F*'s). If the whole region were to be filled up by such sellers, a map of their markets would show a series of tangent circular areas, each having a radius

FIGURE 5.2(a)

Network of Circular Markets Leaves Some Areas Unserved

Market radius = OE miles   Shading indicates unserved areas

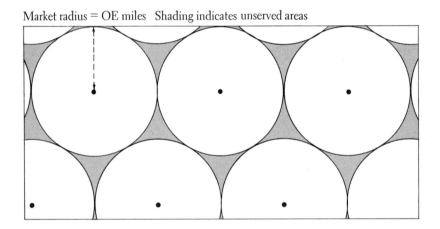

FIGURE 5.2(b)

Network of Hexagonal Markets Serves All Areas

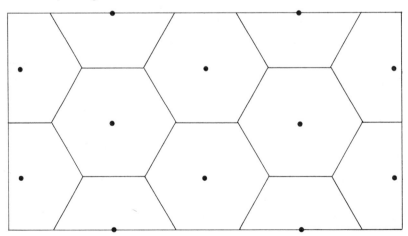

of OE miles as in Figure 5.2(a). Since each bakery would be earning monopoly profits, however, there is no reason to assume that this situation would persist. On the contrary, one would expect additional firms to be attracted by the high profits. The newcomers would locate between the existing producers, and by their competition reduce the market areas of the former monopolists.

The situation would now take on the characteristics of monopolistic competition as defined by E. H. Chamberlin.[4] We assume that bread is an undifferentiated product, so each customer buys from the nearest supplier. Producers are differentiated in the eyes of their customers not by differences in their product but by differences in their location. The effect is the same, however: instead of facing the horizontal demand curve of perfect competition, each producer faces a negatively sloped demand curve because as he lowers his f.o.b. price he sells more to his existing customers and also extends the radius of his market to take in new customers at the geographic margin. The competition of new firms pressing in to fill the terrain, however, ensures that no producer can take advantage of his spatial monopoly (with its negatively sloped demand curve) to earn monopoly profits. When competition is fully effective each producer will find that his market area has been so compressed by the entry of other firms that the most profitable nondiscriminatory price level he can establish will yield only the normal rate of return (i.e., his demand curve will be tangent to his average cost curve at that price level; it is assumed that average cost includes an allowance for "normal profit").

Since we assume that all firms produce under similar cost conditions and that population and effective demand are spread uniformly over the region, it follows that f.o.b. prices will be the same in all markets and that all markets will be the same size. As Lösch points out, this size will also be the minimum threshold size for a firm producing the given service.

The geometrical shape to be expected theoretically for such markets in a system that has reached equilibrium has been a matter of debate. The early central place theorists realized that if markets were circular, as in Figure 5.2(a), unserved areas would remain between the points of tangency of the circles. They argued that this could not be an equilibrium scheme and concluded that the most efficient arrangement that would leave no place unserved would be a network of regular hexagons, with a central place at the center of each, as shown in Figure 5.2(b). A more recent analysis, however, has shown that other outcomes are possible.[5]

4. E. H. Chamberlin, *The Theory of Monopolistic Competition*, 5th Ed. (Cambridge, Mass.: Harvard University Press, 1946), Ch. 5.

5. Edwin S. Mills and Michael R. Lav, "A Model of Market Areas with Free Entry," *Journal of Political Economy*, June 1964, pp. 278–88.

The hypothetical scheme of monopolistic competition in space that we have outlined above for a single good can readily be extended to take in any number of products or services. Let us call the goods so distributed "central services." Each such service would develop market areas of a characteristic size. The economy would thus contain not a single net of markets but a system of nets overlaid upon each other, each net delineating markets for a different good or service.

Determinants of Characteristic Market Size

The forces that determine the characteristic market size for each central service are a matter of great interest, since, as we will see below, they also determine the dimensions of the entire central place system. For each service, then, market size depends on three factors:

1. The extent of economies of scale in production of the service. Market areas will tend to be larger when economies of scale are attainable, since large-scale firms will then be able to produce at lower unit cost than smaller firms and will be able to drive the latter out of business. The survivors will necessarily have markets large enough to support large-scale output.

2. The "density" of demand for the service. The greater the demand for a service per unit of land area, the smaller the area needed to support a producing firm of optimum size. Demand per unit of land area is a function not only of price but of population density and income level per head of population. Therefore the greater the population density and/or the average income level in a region, the smaller the characteristic market areas for given services in that region will be.

3. The cost of transporting the good or service. At first glance it would appear that the lower the cost of transportation, the larger the typical market area would be. In Figure 5.1 the cost of transport per unit of output per mile is shown by the slope of the gradient BC. If transport were cheaper and this slope consequently were flatter, it would appear that farmer F's market could extend farther before his delivered price rose to the level of the home-production cost, OA. As we will see below, however, the case is more complicated than that. While transportation costs certainly affect market size, one cannot assume a priori that lower rates will always make for larger markets.

A HIERARCHY OF CENTRAL PLACES

The fact of wide variation in the characteristic market size for different central services implies the existence of a hierarchy of central places or, as it is sometimes called, an "urban hierarchy." In an economy of fixed extent, the number of individual markets necessary to handle the distribution of a given good, such as haircuts, over the entire economy would be inversely proportional to the characteristic area of a haircut market. Some goods, including haircuts, would in fact be distributed through many small markets; others, say finished lumber or television broadcasts, through a smaller number of larger markets. In order to take advantage of economies of agglomeration in both production and marketing, firms selling these various services will tend to cluster in villages, towns, and cities instead of seeking isolated locations. But if there are fewer television stations than lumberyards and fewer lumberyards than barber shops it is apparent that many towns will have only barber shops, while a smaller number will have barber shops and lumberyards, and still fewer will offer all three central services. Thus we could describe a central place hierarchy by classifying places according to the number and types of central services they offer. We would find that size of city increased and number of cities decreased as we moved up the scale from first order places (those offering the fewest services) to the highest order place (which offers the most services).

It is worth noting that higher order places offer not only more services but services of an entirely different sort than lower order places. A major center, for example, not only contains more kinds of retail stores than does a small town, but provides services like wholesaling and transshipment that are entirely absent in the smaller place.

Indeed, as Philbrick has shown, one can define a hierarchy of places in terms of the level or nature of the functions performed, rather than their sheer number. Using economic functions only, he suggests a sevenfold hierarchy in which the seven levels of function from lowest to highest order are: consumption (i.e., the household function), retail, wholesale, transshipment, exchange, control, leadership.[6]

Philbrick's scheme emphasizes the fact that a developed economy is highly specialized by function, that specialization requires exchange of goods and of information by means of flows along well-defined paths, that cities are focal places in the organization of such flows, and that their rank in the hierarchy is defined by the stage in the process of production and distribution for which they serve as a focal place.

Thus a town with a retail store is a focal place for the activities of a group of household consumption units, a city containing a wholesale establishment is a focal place for the activities of a group of towns containing retail stores, and so forth up the table of organization to the highest order place, which provides leadership to the economy as a whole.

6. Allen K. Philbrick, "Areal Functional Organization in Regional Geography," *Papers* of the Regional Science Association, 1957, Vol. III, pp. 87–98.

FIGURE 5.3

Schematic Diagram of an Urban Hierarchy

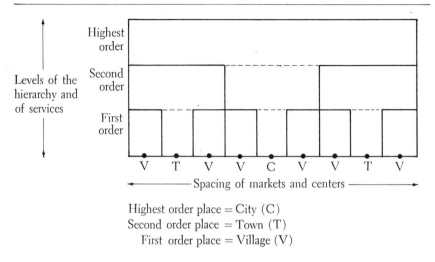

Highest order place = City (C)
Second order place = Town (T)
First order place = Village (V)

Such an organization is not unlike the plan of a telephone network. Each subscriber cannot have a direct line to every other; instead, each is connected to a local exchange, which in turn is connected to other focal points through a long-distance network. As Philbrick has pointed out, this sort of scheme can be used to describe the hierarchy of political and social as well as economic functions.

As the discussion to this point indicates, theoretical models of central place systems display a high degree of internal regularity. For example, at each level of the hierarchy all the towns serve market areas of the same size and shape. Each town is at the center of its market area, and the markets do not overlap. Consequently towns of each hierarchical order are uniformly spaced. The number of towns decreases as we move up the hierarchy, and, necessarily, the average distance between them increases at successively higher levels. At each level we could map out a perfectly regular set of mutually exclusive market areas that would exhaust the space of the economy. Each would contain a town of appropriate size at its center. Each city of a higher order would provide services to the same number of towns of the next lower order. In addition, each would provide for itself all the services performed for themselves by all places lower in the hierarchy. Figure 5.3 is a diagram of such a system containing three levels. The number of market areas decreases by a factor of three as we move up from level to level of this hypothetical system.

Systematic Exceptions to the Hierarchical Order

No central place theorist would expect to find in the real world a hierarchy of places as perfectly ordered as the one depicted in Figure 5.3. First of all, resources and population are not spread evenly over the earth as central place models usually assume. Extractive industries necessarily concentrate where the resources are and attract population to such regions. Topographical irregularities, too, obviously interfere with the uniform spacing of economic activity, both directly and through their influence on the transport network. Thus ports and navigable rivers attract concentrations of activity and population. Climate and other natural amenities also strongly influence the location of people and of industry. And if population and industry are unevenly distributed over the map, then obviously central places will also be unevenly distributed: their size and spacing will not display the regularity to be found in theoretical models of central place systems.

So far as manufacturing is concerned, the scheme applies, even roughly, only to those industries such as baking that are locationally consumer-market oriented. Manufacturing industries that are materials oriented locate near materials sources, and if the sources are not evenly distributed, they, like the extractive industries, will concentrate in a few favored areas from which they serve the entire economy. The geographic concentration of the coal, iron, and steel industries is a good example. In similar fashion, manufacturing firms that are production-cost oriented frequently breach the scheme by competing for the entire national market from a single plant, perhaps in some relatively small town that otherwise performs only the lowest order functions.

Large cities, too, may develop disproportionately in the sense that they perform one higher order function without performing others to the expected degree. Thus Pittsburgh, clearly not a highest order metropolis, nevertheless ranked fourth in the United States in nonlocal banking activity in 1950, ahead of Philadelphia, Boston, Los Angeles, and Cleveland, all larger cities and in many respects more "metropolitan." [7]

Central place theory best applies in two cases: consumer-market-oriented manufacturing and the general run of service industries. Even for these, however, there is an important qualification to the deductive model: the market areas of individual suppliers are rarely mutually exclusive. Since most products and services are differentiated either by brand names, like loaves of bread, or by the personal qualities of the supplier, like automo-

7. Otis Dudley Duncan *et al.*, *Metropolis and Region* (Baltimore: Johns Hopkins Press, 1960), pp. 116–17.

tive repair services, consumers do *not* always purchase from the nearest source. This alone would make for interpenetration of markets. In addition, however, many producers employ pricing practices, such as freight absorption, in a deliberate effort to foster sales to distant customers. Though usually mentioned in connection with industries serving national markets, freight absorption is equally important locally. Retail distributors of home heating oil or bottled gas, for example, do not charge for delivery. In such cases nearby customers are, in effect, subsidizing distant ones. The customer has no incentive to seek out the closest supplier. We must allow for a great deal of cross-hauling, both of goods going to customers and of customers shopping for goods.

THE PROBLEM OF EMPIRICAL VERIFICATION

A large number of empirical studies have sought evidence in the real world of economic geography for the regularities that central place theory predicts will exist. Most of these have examined relatively thinly settled agricultural regions, such as the farm belt of the American Middle West and Canada, where central place theory's assumption of an even distribution of population and resources is approximately realized. In such areas (and in many parts of the world) the central place system has, indeed, been found to display a high degree of regularity.[8]

At this point the alert reader may detect a problem in scientific methodology: is there really an urban hierarchy containing classes of cities with demonstrably different characteristics, or is there merely a continuum of cities from small to large on which we have arbitrarily imposed the character of hierarchy? For if we take the cities and towns of a given region and array them by size we will, of course, find that there are more small than large towns and more large towns than cities. Average market area size and average distance between places will therefore necessarily increase as we go up the scale from small to large places. We will also certainly find that the number of establishments performing central services and the number of different services performed typically increases as population size of centers increases. A town of 200 might have only 4 establishments providing 2 or 3 different services, while a town of 1,000 in the same region has 30 establishments covering 24 functions, and a town of 3,000 has 100 establishments in 40 service categories. Yet the plain fact

8. Much of the empirical work is reviewed in Brian J. L. Berry, *Geography of Market Centers and Retail Distribution* (Englewood Cliffs, N.J.: Prentice-Hall, 1967). Also see the many studies of central place systems published in the annual volumes of *Papers* of the Regional Science Association.

TABLE 5.1

Characteristics of the Central Place Hierarchy in Snohomish County, Washington

	CLASSES OF CENTRAL PLACES		
	Hamlets	*Villages*	*Towns*
Number of places in class	20	9	4
Average population per place	417	948	2,433
Total number of establishments in class of places	138	490	596
Average number of establishments per place	6.9	54.4	149
Total number of functions in class of places	118	289	239
Average number of functions per place	5.9	32.1	59.8
Average number of establishments per function	1.2	1.7	2.5

Source: Brian J. L. Berry and William Garrison, "The Functional Bases of the Central-Place Hierarchy," *Economic Geography*, April 1958, pp. 145–54.

is that we could use an arbitrary rule to partition an array of towns into a number of size classes, and no matter where we drew the lines we would certainly find those kinds of regularity. Consequently, such a finding would not demonstrate the existence of a hierarchy. In Berry and Garrison's phrase, the analyst would merely have "used an arbitrary division and then proved what he had in fact assumed . . . ."

Two Case Studies: Washington and Saskatchewan

Berry and Garrison set out to test the hypothesis that the central places in Snohomish County, Washington, form an observable hierarchy rather than merely a continuum from small to large.[9] They concluded that a hierarchy was indeed observable. Their procedure need not be described here in detail. In summary, they found that the towns in their study area could be "arranged into three types . . . defined on the basis of the presence of urban functions . . . in varying degrees." They then demonstrated that "these center types differ more one from another than they differ within types."[10] By using appropriate statistical tests they were

9. Brian J. L. Berry and William L. Garrison, "The Functional Bases of the Central-Place Hierarchy," *Economic Geography*, April 1958, pp. 145–54, reprinted in Harold M. Mayer and Clyde F. Kohn, eds., *Readings in Urban Geography* (Chicago: University of Chicago Press, 1959), pp. 218–27.

10. *Ibid.*, p. 220.

TABLE 5.2
Prevalence of Selected Functions in Central Places of Snohomish County, Washington

Type of Function [a]	NUMBER OF PLACES IN CLASS HAVING AT LEAST ONE ESTABLISHMENT		
	Hamlets, 20	Villages, 9	Towns, 4
Filling stations	17	9	4
Food stores	7	9	4
Churches	8	9	4
Restaurants	6	9	4
Elementary schools	13	9	4
Physicians	0	6	4
Appliance stores	0	8	4
Barber shops	5	9	4
Insurance agencies	0	5	3
Drug stores	2	9	4
Lawyers	0	5	4
Apparel stores	0	6	4
Banks	2	7	4
Dry cleaners	1	4	4
Jewelry stores	0	4	4
Department stores	1	3	4
Hospitals and clinics	0	1	3
Public accountants	0	1	3

[a] Functions are ranked from smallest to largest by estimated minimum threshold population size.
Source: Brian J. L. Berry and William L. Garrison, "The Functional Bases of the Central-Place Hierarchy," *Economic Geography*, April 1958, pp. 145–54.

able to show that their classification of types was not arbitrary but, instead, led to statistically significant groupings. Moreover, the three groups, or types, of central places differed significantly from one another not only in number of functions performed but in types of functions.

Table 5.1 summarizes the dimensions of the hierarchy revealed in Berry and Garrison's study. Obviously, the mean population size of central places increases as we move up the scale from hamlets to villages to towns. So also does the average number of establishments per place and the average number of different functions performed. Since the former increases faster than the latter, the number of establishments per function also increases as we move up the hierarchy. The individual hamlets rarely have more than one or two establishments of a single type. A town, on the other hand, might easily have six or more establishments in categories such as food stores, restaurants, churches, or filling stations.

A different perspective on the system is presented in Table 5.2, which measures the prevalence of selected functions in the three classes of central place. The functions are ranked down the table from most common (filling stations) to least common (public accountants) on the basis of Berry and Garrison's estimates of minimum threshold population size for each. Almost without exception, all four towns in the study area had at least one establishment in every functional class. The nine villages without exception offered all of the more common functions, but halfway down the table they show a pronounced falling off. Fewer than half of the villages are represented in the selected functions with the largest threshold sizes. As for the hamlets, they drop out almost completely when we reach central services with a population threshold larger than an elementary school. It is interesting to note this inference from Table 5.2: with very few exceptions, the central place hierarchy of Snohomish County possesses the characteristic (predicted by the theory) that places of a higher order provide for themselves all services that are found in places lower in the hierarchy.

A hierarchy is by definition a systematic arrangement of the classes of an object. Central place theory emphasizes especially the systematic nature of the spatial arrangement of centers. The best analogy is to a planetary system in which the units are held in place by the gravitational forces between them. Thus central place theory purports to show that each particular urban settlement is, so to speak, held in place within a system of cities; it suggests that the development of each is affected in a predictable way by its position within the system.

Gerald Hodge's study of central places in Saskatchewan verifies this characteristic of the system.[11] Hodge distinguished seven classes of trade centers in Saskatchewan and studied changes in the relative importance of each of these classes in the system as a whole between 1941 and 1961. A given trade center was said to "decline" between 1941 and 1961 if it either shifted downward one or more classes in the hierarchy or else disappeared altogether as a center. Central place theory would predict that, other things being equal, at any given level in the hierarchy, towns that are nearer than the average to centers of like character will be more likely to decline than the average in their class, for they will be too near their competitors. Hodge's study showed just such a result. He found: "Of hamlets thus situated [i.e., closer than average to other hamlets], 66 percent declined from 1941–61 compared to 46 percent for all hamlets in the same period. Similar differentials of decline were found for the other types of centers studied." [12] Here is direct evidence that central places be-

11. Gerald Hodge, "The Prediction of Trade Center Viability in the Great Plains," *Papers* of the Regional Science Association, 1965, Vol. XV, pp. 87–115.
   12. *Ibid.*, p. 101.

have not as independent entities but as parts of a coherent "system of cities."

DEFINING A CITY'S "HINTERLAND"

Sociologists have long spoken of cities as having "hinterlands" over which, in the language of that discipline, they extend their "dominance." By dominance is meant the power of exerting "an organizing influence upon the economic and social structure of the communities in their hinterlands." [13] In analyzing the central place system we have concentrated attention on the market areas served from central places. These market areas for outputs provide one means of defining hinterlands—but not a simple means, since all but the smallest central places produce a multiplicity of services, and the market areas for these services will typically differ widely in size. Moreover, outputs require inputs, and therefore each central place also has a set of supply areas from which it draws the resources that feed its production process. These supply areas provide another and equally important contribution to the definition of a city's hinterland. For example, the SMSA around each major central city, as delineated by the Census Bureau, is in effect defined by its character of being a labor market area. Roughly speaking, it is the area from which the metropolis daily draws its supply of workers—the labor-supply hinterland of the metropolis. It is almost always far smaller in extent than the hinterland of that same metropolis as defined by the market area of its highest order services. In the discussion that follows, we propose to simplify matters by focusing on the market area definition of hinterland. Even so, we will find more than enough ambiguities and complications.

In an urban hierarchy the highest, or "nth order," city has the entire nation as its hinterland, since the entire nation depends upon it for nth order services. Each city below that level has as its hinterland all the cities to which *it* supplies central services plus all *their* hinterlands. In a description of U.S. cities New York is likely to rank as the nth order place (although it lacks federal government functions found in Washington). Boston would probably rank as a city of $n - 1$ order. Thus Boston is within New York's hinterland for nth order services. But for services of the $n - 1$ order, each has its own hinterland.

In the perfectly ordered hierarchy of central place theory as we have defined it, these hinterlands at the $n - 1$ level would not overlap: one would be able to draw a line somewhere between New York and Boston

13. Rupert B. Vance and Sara Smith, "Metropolitan Dominance and Integration," in Hatt and Reiss, p. 103.

that would unambiguously divide them. We have argued, however, that hierarchies in the real world are not perfectly ordered. Hinterlands, for example, are not mutually exclusive. Here is some interesting evidence of how they overlap. Park and Newcomb in 1933 delineated regions around major cities by mapping the circulation of the leading morning newspaper of each. They defined the region of each city as consisting of those places in which its newspaper was the dominant one. By that definition Hartford, Connecticut, fell within the Boston region, while New London, Connecticut, and Newport, Rhode Island, came within New York's. Whatever else may be said about this classification, it should not be permitted to obscure the fact that many people in Hartford read the *New York Times*, and some in Newport and New London read the *Boston Globe*. Clearly the influence of one central place does not stop where the influence of another starts.

Since market areas inevitably overlap, hinterland boundaries can be drawn only by devising some rational rule of the sort used by Park and Newcomb. However, the boundary will vary greatly depending both on the rule and on the kind of central service it refers to. In 1955 Howard L. Green compared Park and Newcomb's findings with other attempts to locate the hinterland boundary between New York and Boston.[14] He showed that Dickinson's 1934 study using different service components had exactly reversed Park and Newcomb's findings by placing Hartford in New York's region and New London and Newport in Boston's. Green then made his own delineation of the hinterland boundary by taking the median of seven different functional indicators. The extent to which these seven give contradictory delineations of the regional boundary is indicated in Table 5.3, which shows how five cities close to the median borderline are classified according to the separate criteria. Green's composite, or median, line places Springfield, Providence, and Newport in New York's region, Holyoke and Pittsfield in Boston's. The table, however, shows that none of these cities fell unambiguously to one side or the other. In every case the indicators were split 5 to 2 or 4 to 3. Green recognized the existence of a broad band of hinterland overlap and placed all five of the above cities within it.

The overlapping of regions, the interpenetration of central place influences, obviously makes it impossible to map out a single exhaustive and unambiguous set of central place hinterlands for the United States. More important, it should remind us that the appropriate definition of a city's hinterland will depend upon the subject and purpose of the analysis.

14. Howard L. Green, "Hinterland Boundaries of New York City and Boston in Southern New England," in Mayer and Kohn, pp. 185–201.

TABLE 5.3

How Regional Classification of Cities Varies with Choice of Indicator

	REGIONAL CLASSIFICATION OF CITY				
Indicator of Region	*Springfield*	*Providence*	*Newport*	*Pittsfield*	*Holyoke*
Railroad coach ticket purchases	New York	Boston	New York	Boston	On the borderline
Estimated truck freight movement	New York	New York	New York	New York	New York
Metropolitan newspaper circulation	Boston	Boston	Boston	Boston	Boston
Long-distance telephone calls	Boston	Boston	Boston	Boston	Boston
Metropolitan origin of vacationers	Boston	New York	New York	New York	Boston
Business addresses of directors for major industrial firms	New York	New York	New York	New York	New York
Metropolitan correspondents for hinterland banks	On the borderline	New York	New York	Boston	Boston
Composite of indicators	New York	New York	New York	Boston	Boston

Source: Based on Howard L. Green, "Hinterland Boundaries of New York City and Boston in Southern New England," in Harold M. Mayer and Clyde F. Kohn, eds., *Readings in Urban Geography* (Chicago: University of Chicago Press, 1959), pp. 185–201.

HOW THE SYSTEM OF CITIES DEVELOPS AND CHANGES THROUGH TIME

Probably the most interesting contribution of central place theory is the help it provides in understanding the historical trend of changes within the system of cities. Under the impact of technological innovation and economic growth profound alterations occur in the pattern of urban settlement, the size distribution of cities, and the division of functions among cities at various levels of the hierarchy. Central place theory helps to illuminate these complex changes.

We have already shown that the various dimensions of the central place system (number, size, and spacing of cities; number and location of functions and of establishments; etc.) depend largely on the size of the characteristic market areas for central services. Therefore, the obvious point of entry for an analysis of changes in those dimensions is to consider what might cause the typical market area to alter in size.[15] It was pointed out earlier that market area size for any central service depends on three factors: the extent of economies of scale in its production; the level of demand for the service per unit of area; and the cost of transporting it. We must now examine the effects of technological change and economic growth on these three factors. Four aspects of change and growth will be analyzed:

1. Growth of population.
2. Rise in living standards (i.e., increased per capita income).
3. Innovation leading to the development of greater economies of scale in production.
4. Innovation leading to a reduction in transport costs.

To keep the discussion within bounds we will use retail trade as the illustrative case and derive conclusions from it that are applicable to central services in general. Figure 5.4 depicts three spatially separated competing retail outlets, A, B and C. As before, we measure distance along the horizontal scale, average unit cost of production and unit delivery cost along the vertical.

Delivery costs for retail activities require careful analysis. First of all, they consist of two distinct parts: (1) the cost to the consumer of making a round trip from home to store to buy the merchandise or service; (2) the cost of delivering the merchandise, if any, to the consumer's home. Part (2) is zero if we are dealing with services like haircuts or movies, which must be consumed at the point of sale. It is also zero when the consumer carries the merchandise home by public transportation or in his own vehicle—provided he had to make the trip in any event to select the merchandise. This is typically the case with purchases of food, clothing, drugs, and novelties. When the retailer delivers "free of charge" over a wide area, part (2) costs are *not* zero; they are simply concealed in higher prices at the source. Since, however, these higher prices are invariant with distance of the consumer from the source, we will not attempt to deal with the case here.

Assume that Figure 5.4 represents one of the cases in which part (2) costs are zero. Delivery costs are then to be interpreted as consisting of the cost of the consumer's round trip from home to market. Can we then speak of "unit delivery costs"? Not without a certain ambiguity, since the consumer can buy drugs, groceries, clothing—and more—all on the

15. For a more complex analysis that relates arithmetically the number and population size of centers at each level of the hierarchy to the population of the market areas they serve, see Nourse, pp. 40–44, 209–18.

FIGURE 5.4

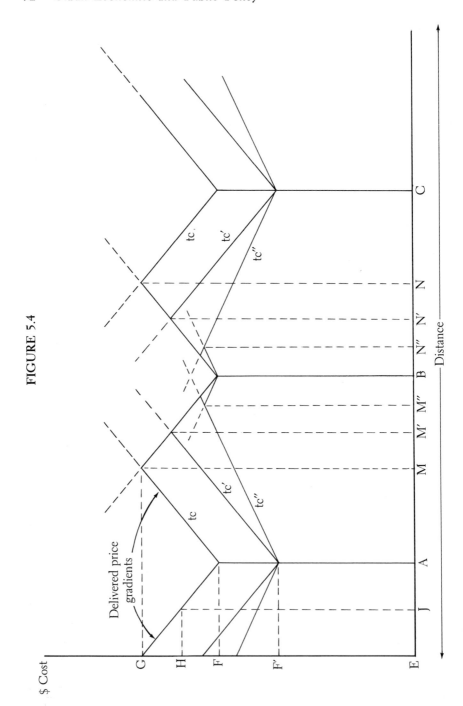

same trip. Let us, therefore, define the unit as a composite of those items having no part (2) costs which the consumer might buy on a single shopping trip. For simplicity we might imagine that a single "general store" can provide this composite unit. For our purposes it does not matter how large the composite unit of goods is, as long as we hold its size constant.

When the consumer goes shopping and carries the goods home himself, he reckons the "delivery cost" to be the sum of two elements: first, the money cost of the trip and, second, a nonmonetary cost, consisting of the disutility of the trip in terms of time lost and discomfort undergone. The disutility of the trip can, in principle, be given a money equivalent: the amount the shopper would pay not to have to undergo it. Thus the two costs can be combined into a single money equivalent. For a given route and mode of transport this can be expressed as a cost of so many cents per mile. Now in the ordinary case in which the nonmonetary disutility of a journey is positive, the faster the mode of transport, the less the disutility of covering a given distance, hence the lower the nonmonetary cost per mile.

In Figure 5.4 then, we start with three general stores located at villages A, B, and C along a line that represents geographic space. The villages are of equal size. Rural population and resources are spread uniformly in the space between them. We assume that more such stores are located at regular intervals to the left and right of the segment we are looking at. Initially these spatial competitors are in equilibrium. Each has a store of optimum size and can just manage to earn a normal return by supplying a unit of goods at an f.o.b. price of OF. The absence of monopolistic profits indicates that stores have been "packed in" as closely as is consistent with long-run equilibrium.

Shoppers who do not live in a village travel to market by automobile. Their round-trip travel costs, a combination of monetary and nonmonetary elements, are a linear function of their distance from the store. Each buys in that store for which the sum of f.o.b. price plus travel costs is least. Thus sum, which we may call the delivered price, is shown for any point of residence by the height above the horizontal at that point of the delivered price gradient from the supplier. The slope of the gradient equals round-trip travel cost per unit of distance. Initially, the relevant gradients are those labeled *tc*. Thus a customer living at *J* would pay *OF* for a unit of merchandise and incur travel costs of *FH* in going from his home at *J* to the store at *A* and return. His total cost per unit is therefore *OH*. The market boundary between stores *A* and *B* is at point *M*, where the delivered price gradients of these two suppliers intersect. A customer at *M* would incur a cost of *OG* per unit whether he bought from *A* or *B*. Similarly, *N* marks the boundary between the markets of *B* and *C*.

Effect of a Rise in Population or Income

We examine first the effect of a geographically uniform increase in the region's population. A rise in population, with income per capita remaining constant, would clearly increase the level of demand for general store services per unit of area. Store owners at A, B, and C would find demand for their output rising and would begin to earn above-normal profits. These profits would attract new firms to the industry. New points of service would spring up between previously existing centers, and the markets of store owners at A, B, and C would be compressed by this competition. At the higher level of demand density a store of optimum size could earn normal returns with a smaller market area. The end result would be an increase in the number of firms and in the number of central places and a decrease in the characteristic size of market areas for general stores. The distance between centers would decrease.

Let us assume that these general stores and the villages at which they are located make up the lowest order of the central place hierarchy. We can see that the changes taking place at this level would have their counterparts at higher levels, too. The number of higher order firms and centers would also increase (for example, more wholesalers would be needed to service the larger number of general stores), their market areas would grow smaller, and the distance between higher order centers would also diminish.

Berry has amply documented these and other effects of varying population density by comparing the central place systems in Iowa and in much more thinly populated South Dakota.[16] To be sure, this approach is cross-sectional rather than longitudinal: it examines areas having unequal densities at a single point in time instead of observing a single area as its population density changes through the years. Such a cross-sectional method, however, has the great advantage that it holds constant other crucial variables, such as the technology of transportation, which could not be held constant in a study running through time. With "other things remaining the same" one can isolate more successfully the effect of the single factor of population density.

The general effect of a rise in per capita income with population held constant would be much the same as the effect of a rise in population with per capita income held constant, since in both cases the areal density of demand increases. Consequently, we need not repeat the argument for the case in which income rises.

16. Berry, *Geography of Market Centers*, Ch. 2.

The Effect of Increased Economies of Scale

In order to examine the effect of a technological innovation leading to increased economies of scale in production, let us assume that the owner of store A "invents" the principle of the self-service supermarket. This innovation allows average unit cost to be reduced, provided that the scale of operation can be sufficiently enlarged. The owner of store A calculates that by creating a supermarket he can achieve economies of scale such that he will maximize profits by reducing his f.o.b. price from OF to OF'. With this lower price he can expect to increase sales for two reasons: first, if the demand of individual consumers is elastic, he will sell more to his present customers; second, if his competitors do not also build supermarkets he will capture their outlying customers. For example, when A lowers his price to OF', his delivered price gradient shifts to tc' (parallel to tc, since transportation cost is unchanged). If B does not respond in kind, A's market boundary now moves out to point M'.

If owner C also builds a supermarket, B's market area will be squeezed from both sides, contracting from MN to $M'N'$. Initially, B was earning a normal return. Now his return will fall, and he may decide to close up, leaving his customers to be divided between supermarkets A and C. This, of course, is precisely what has happened since the advent of the supermarket: many small stores have disappeared. But suppose B had also attempted to open a supermarket? In that case no one could have expanded his market area. Unless demand were so elastic that lower prices permitted considerably enlarged sales within fixed market boundaries, not all the supermarkets could survive. Some suppliers would be forced out until those remaining could earn normal returns by enlarging their market areas. This seems the most likely outcome provided that population, income, and transportation costs remain constant.

Granted that increased economies of scale will probably lead to a reduction in the number of establishments providing the given service, what effect will that have on the number and spacing of central places? The answer depends on the situation from which one starts. In Figure 5.4 we assume that general store retailing is the only service provided by villages, which are the lowest order places in the hierarchy, and that there is only one store per village. In that case, a reduction in the number of firms necessarily means a reduction in the number of villages and an increase in their spacing.

Of course, other possibilities abound. Initially, for example, villages A, B, and C might have provided several central services in addition to general store goods. In that case, B could continue supplying other central services even though supermarkets at A and C had eliminated its general store. Economies of scale would then have reduced the number of central service establishments in the system as a whole, but not the number of centers, although some centers would have been weakened relative to others.

If we assume, however, that economies of scale increase substantially in the production of many types of central services rather than in only one, then it seems highly probable that some of the smallest centers will be eliminated entirely as services are gradually concentrated into larger towns. Within the category of retail services, such consolidation is also affected by the importance of economies of agglomeration in shopping. Other things being equal, the retail customer will prefer to shop at the center where he can satisfy more of his needs on a single trip. If villages A and B provided the same services, the customer midway between them would be indifferent as to where he shopped. But if A provided more services than B, he would probably prefer shopping at A even for those goods also available at B. Thus the existence of agglomeration economies in shopping accelerates a process of consolidation that may begin with the development of scale economies in a particular service: each function lost at a small center weakens those that remain.

Effect of a Reduction in Transportation Costs

We come last to the question of transportation costs. How would a technological innovation that reduced transport costs per mile affect the central place system? This is both the most interesting and the most complex question we can ask about the response of the system to the forces of economic change.

Let us first examine a situation such as was described initially in Figure 5.4. Producers at competing centers operate under identical cost conditions. Their market areas are identical in extent and just large enough to afford each a normal rate of return from a plant of optimum size. In a recent analysis of this case Hoover has argued that a reduction in transport costs has two analytically distinguishable effects: an output effect (or, as he calls it, an "income effect") and a substitution effect.[17] Since the output effect of reduced transportation costs makes market areas smaller, while the substitution effect makes them larger, one cannot say, without knowing the details of each case, what will be the net effect.

This situation is a familiar one in the economic theory of production. For example, if a firm uses two production inputs, labor and machinery, and the relative price of machinery falls, the firm will tend to substitute machinery for labor in its production process. The "substitution effect"

17. Edgar M. Hoover, "Transport Costs and the Spacing of Central Places," *Papers* of the Regional Science Association, 1970, Vol. XXV, pp. 255–74.

will clearly be to use more machinery and less labor to produce a given quantity of goods. But there will also be an "output effect": since the cost of one of the firm's inputs has fallen, it will be able to sell at lower prices and therefore in larger quantities. Output will rise above its previous level, and the "output effect" will cause the firm to purchase more of both labor and machinery. Purchases of machinery will certainly rise, since both effects make for that result. But purchases of labor may either rise or fall, since the substitution effect reduces labor inputs, while the output effect increases them.

Using Isard's method of treating transport as an input to the production process that is substitutable for other inputs, Hoover shows how the output and substitution effects operate in the case of declining transportation costs. The output effect works as follows. When transport costs per mile are reduced, the delivered price of each supplier of a central service falls for all customers not located at the very center of the market. Consequently, at whatever f.o.b. price he chooses, each supplier can now sell more than he previously did to customers within his existing market area. His profits therefore rise above the normal rate of return he had previously been earning. This is the output effect of the fall in transport rates. It makes for smaller market areas because new firms are attracted to the production of the central service by the existence of extra-normal profits. They press in upon the previously existing firms. Market areas are compressed, the number of centers increases, and the distance between them falls.

The substitution effect, Hoover argues, works in the opposite direction. As transport becomes relatively cheaper, profit-maximizing producers increase the use of transport inputs relative to other inputs by delivering the service to greater distances. Market areas become larger, centers fewer and farther apart. Since the substitution and output effects work in opposite directions, the net effect of reduced transport costs is theoretically uncertain.

It is most important, however, to note the stringent initial assumption of this analysis that all firms operate with identical production costs. The outcome is quite different where production costs are *not* assumed to be equal for all suppliers. Moreover, the latter case is probably much the more significant in explaining the impact of economic change on the central place system. To illustrate it, let us return to the situation depicted in Figure 5.4.

Suppose that owners A and C have installed supermarkets but owner B has decided to continue running his general store, even though his market has been cut down to size M'N'. (This can be made more plausible if we recognize that in reality points A, B, and C may initially have had not one but two or three stores each and that the construction of supermarkets at A and C would then result in a reduction in the number of stores at all points. In that case a lone survivor at *B* could well continue to earn normal returns.) Now suppose that with the passage of time a technological improvement, in the form of better roads, speeds up travel, thus reducing transport costs. On the diagram this appears as a flattening of the delivered price gradients from *tc'* to *tc''*. Even though *B*'s gradients flatten out as much as the others, his market boundaries move inward from *M'* and *N'* to *M''* and *N''*. Thus *A* and *C* once again expand their territory at his expense. Indeed, *B* may well be forced out of business.

Why does *B* lose market ground to *A* and *C* when transportation costs drop uniformly in all three markets and the f.o.b. price differential between them does not change? The answer is that the lower transport costs per mile drop, the more miles a consumer will travel to save a price differential of given magnitude. An analogous principle was shown to be at work in connection with problems of industrial location: if, as a result of technological improvements, transport costs drop relative to other costs, industries tend to become less transport oriented and more production-cost oriented.

We have already argued that an increase in economies of scale in production interacts with economies of agglomeration in shopping to strengthen larger retail centers at the expense of smaller ones. Precisely the same interaction occurs when a reduction in transport costs eliminates high-cost suppliers while extending the markets of low-cost firms. To the extent that economies of agglomeration exist, either in shopping or in production, the centers at which low-cost suppliers are concentrated will find themselves gaining cumulative advantages over the smaller centers at which functions are being eliminated. The smaller centers will suffer progressive loss through what might be called "the diseconomies of deglomeration."

Transportation Costs and the Scale of Social Organization

The general principle that for any given industry a reduction in transport costs benefits low-cost and large-scale producers at the expense of high-cost and small-scale producers is of the greatest importance in spatial economics. It helps to explain why the scale of organization throughout society is steadily increasing. It lies at the root of Hoover's observation: "Other things being equal, high transport costs mean scattered local production, and cheap transport means localized (i.e., concentrated) production." [18]

18. Edgar M. Hoover, *Location Theory and the Shoe and Leather Industries* (Cambridge, Mass.: Harvard University Press, 1937), p. 20. Hoover has recently added a caveat, however. He notes that some interlocal variation in production costs may itself be related to transport costs insofar as the latter affect the cost of transported in-

With a little imagination the reader can change the terms employed in our example and see for himself that it is a paradigm for a large number of cases. For instance, it can be used to show the impact on the central place hierarchy of the substitution of the automobile for the horse and buggy as a vehicle for local shopping trips. Or, in the public rather than the private sector, it explains why the "scale" of local schools and their districts increased and the number of schools diminished when a faster form of transportation—the school bus, replaced a slower one— shank's mare. The change in organizational scale of the school system is easily verified from national data. Between 1930 and 1970, the number of elementary and secondary schools in the United States diminished from 275,000 to 112,000, while enrollments increased from 28.6 million to 51.6 million.[19] Average enrollment per school—a good measure of scale —consequently soared from 104 to 462. Finally, if we substitute cost and ease of communication for cost and ease of transportation, we can understand how technological improvements have enabled all kinds of economic and social institutions to expand from a local to a regional scale of operation or from a regional to a national or international scale.

Summary: The Effects of Growth and Development on the Central Place System

We have now analyzed the impact on the central place system of four factors associated with economic growth and development. It was shown that either rising population or increased income per capita would lead to smaller market areas and a larger number and closer spacing of centers. On the other hand, increased economies of scale in the output of central services would, under the most probable circumstances, reduce the number of very small centers and strengthen the larger ones. The impact of reduced transport costs is uncertain when all suppliers have identical costs of production but favors large, low-cost suppliers when there are interfirm cost differentials. This almost certainly leads to a cumulative strengthening of large at the expense of small centers—and probably to the elimination of some of the latter. The four factors associated with economic growth thus have offsetting effects on the development of the central place system.

A final complicating factor, largely ignored in the literature of cen-

puts or cause factor immobilities. "Consequently," he concludes, "cheaper transport might well be expected to narrow such cost differentials . . . and thus run against the tendency for the cheaper locations to eliminate the more expensive ones" ("Transport Costs and the Spacing of Central Places," p. 271). However, this reservation does not apply to cost differentials based on economies of scale.

19. *Statistical Abstract of the United States, 1972,* Table 152 and Table 154.

tral place theory, remains to be mentioned. The analysis to this point assumed implicitly that despite the impact of economic change and growth, the number of central services to be performed in the region remained constant. But this helpful simplification is wholly unrealistic. There are at all times and in any region "latent" central services that might be brought to the threshold of feasibility by either an increase in demand density or a decrease in transportation cost. For example, a given population with a given average level of income might have a desire to see motion pictures, but because local transportation is so costly it is impossible to collect enough customers at any one point to make even the smallest sort of establishment pay. Suppose that the nearest motion picture theater is 50 miles away. When transportation becomes cheaper the probable result is not that local residents now make a 100-mile round trip to the movies, thus extending the market area of the distant producer. Rather, a local theater now becomes feasible because the cost of reaching it has fallen. A central service new to the region comes into existence. A like effect, of course, occurs when rising population or per capita income lifts demand for some latent central service to the threshold at which it becomes commercially feasible to produce it.

It is clear, then, that economic growth and declining transportation costs increase the number of central functions actually provided. The impact of such an increase on the central place system, however, cannot be determined a priori. It might seem probable, for example, that an increase in the number of functions would reinforce the tendency of rising population and income to increase the number of centers and reduce their spacing. Such an outcome, however, cannot be taken for granted. If the new services are subject to significant economies of scale in production (as bowling alleys or movie theaters are, for example) they will tend to locate in the larger centers and, by adding to agglomeration economies at those points, further erode the position of smaller centers. Each new service, however, will have its own characteristics. There appears to be no general principle upon which to predict the impact of new services on the system as a whole.

EVIDENCE FOR THE EFFECTS OF
GROWTH AND DEVELOPMENT

In the actual course of economic history all the forces we have analyzed one by one have in fact been operating on the central place system simultaneously. Although this simultaneity makes it difficult to verify the impact of individual factors, we can at least observe the net effect

TABLE 5.4

Changes in the Number of Places by Size in the United States, 1900–70

| Size and Type of Place | NUMBER OF PLACES | | | PERCENTAGE INCREASE |
	1970	1930	1900	1900–70
Total, all places, urban and rural	20,768	16,643	10,673	95%
Urban, total	7,062	3,179	1,740	306
25,000–50,000	520	185	83	527
10,000–25,000	1,385	607	281	393
5,000–10,000	1,839	853	465	296
2,500–5,000	2,295	1,342	833	176
Less than 2,500 [a]	627	—	—	—
Rural, total	13,706	13,464	8,933	53
1,000–2,500	4,191	3,107	2,130	97
Less than 1,000	9,515	10,357	6,803	40
Urban and rural, less than 2,500	14,333	13,464	8,933	60

[a] Definition of "urban" changed in 1950. Previous to that date, all places with population under 2,500 were classified as rural.

Source: U.S. Bureau of the Census, *Census of Population, 1970,* U.S. Summary, PC(1)A-1, Table 7.

on the central place system of all of them operating together. Among the lower order places in the United States and Canada during the twentieth century the pattern of change is quite clear: towns and small cities have been growing in number relative to villages and hamlets. In recent years the very smallest places have declined not only in relative importance but in absolute number.

Two sets of data indicate this tendency. Table 5.4 shows how the number of places in the United States, classified by population size, has changed during the twentieth century. The table reveals that the rate of growth in the number of places per size class increases steadily as size class increases, for all classes from the smallest up to 50,000 population. Thus the number of places with population under 1,000 increased only 40 percent between 1900 and 1970, while the number of places with a population of 10,000 to 25,000 increased 393 percent, and the number in the 25,000 to 50,000 class rose 527 percent. Places with a population of less than 2,500 made up 84 percent of all places in 1900 but only 69 percent in 1970.

Precisely because they cover the whole United States, however, it may be objected that the data in Table 5.4 are too highly aggregated to

TABLE 5.5
Changes in the Hierarchy of Trade Centers in Saskatchewan,
1941–61

Class of Trade Center	1941		1951		1961	
	Num-ber	Per-centage	Num-ber	Per-centage	Num-ber	Per-centage
Primary wholesale-retail	2	0.2	2	0.2	2	0.2
Secondary wholesale-retail	5	0.6	8	0.9	9	1.2
Complete shopping	26	2.9	23	2.6	29	3.7
Partial shopping	57	6.3	66	7.4	85	10.9
Full convenience	171	18.9	169	18.9	100	12.7
Minimum convenience	287	31.8	191	21.4	150	19.4
Hamlet	358	39.3	433	48.6	404	51.8
All trade centers	906	100.0	892	100.0	779	100.0
Four highest orders	90	9.9	99	11.1	125	16.1
Three lowest orders	816	90.1	793	88.9	654	83.9

Source: Gerald Hodge, "The Prediction of Trade Center Viability in the Great Plains," *Papers* of the Regional Science Association, Vol. XV, 1965, Table 2, p. 95.

be really satisfactory. In each size class places located in growing regions and declining regions, in metropolitan areas and nonmetropolitan areas, are lumped together. In addition, the census definition of "place" changes over the interval covered and, in any case, does not correspond with the definition of "central place" employed in central place theory.

These objections, however, cannot be raised against the data in Table 5.5, which are drawn from Hodge's study of the central place system in the southern part of Saskatchewan. Hodge identified seven orders of central place in the study areas, which is a relatively homogeneous farming region. The total number of such places declined from 906 in 1941 to 892 in 1951 and 779 in 1961. The number of places in the four highest orders increased from 90 in 1941 to 125 in 1961, while the number in the three lowest orders fell from 816 to 654. The three lowest orders made up 90 percent of all places in 1941, but only 84 percent in 1961.[20] Studies by Berry and others of central place systems in farming areas of the U.S. Midwest reveal similar tendencies there.[21] These patterns of development

20. Hodge, Table 2, p. 95.
21. See Berry, *Geography of Market Centers*, pp. 114–17, and references cited therein.

are quite similar to the one suggested by the aggregate data for the United States in Table 5.4: under the impact of economic change and growth, central service functions have been gradually concentrating into fewer and larger places.

INTRAMETROPOLITAN PATTERNS ARE NOT EXPLAINED BY CENTRAL PLACE THEORY

It is no accident that this discussion of central place theory has focused on villages, towns, and small cities rather than on the great urban centers or metropolitan areas of the nation. True, we can observe hierarchical differences among large cities as well as among smaller places. Major cities and metropolitan areas can be differentiated into hierarchical classes by the order of services they provide and the regions for which they are the dominant provider. Thus they, as well as the smallest towns, are a part of the "system of cities," and our insight into urban phenomena is greatly enhanced by understanding that. Yet within metropolitan areas themselves it is not easy to discern the hierarchical pattern of market areas (and of centers) for the distribution of goods and services that is described in classical central place theory. Population is so dense and travel relatively so easy that shoppers habitually visit many suppliers, and the market areas of suppliers cease to be even approximately exclusive. Under these conditions, as Berry has pointed out, the locational pattern of central service firms becomes a complex of "ribbons" and "specialized areas" as well as of "centers." [22]

In the face of this complexity economists have, after the manner of their kind, looked for some underlying, simplifying principle that would explain the essence of the whole intrametropolitan pattern of location. They have employed as their point of departure a model that does not break the metropolis up into a hierarchically related system of submarkets but assumes instead that it is a single market area, organized into specialized districts around a single, unchallenged center. It is to this model that we turn in the next chapter.

22. *Ibid.*, pp. 44–58, 117–24.

Land-Use Patterns, Transportation, and the Form of the City

SIX

Just as transport costs influence the location of producers and, therefore, of cities, so, too, they systematically affect locational patterns within the city itself. We are all conscious of the general form of the city: concentrated activity and development at the center; a gradual decline of intensity as one moves out toward the edge. This characteristic form is constantly impressed on us by the clusters of tall buildings and the dense crowds of people and vehicles we see at the center, so dramatically different from the lower skyline and the smaller crowds we find at the periphery.

It is not difficult to construct economic models that will generate this easily observed pattern as a function of transport cost and the need for accessibility. Although these relatively simple models do not account for the full complexity of land-use arrangements that we find in the city, they do explain successfully the general pattern of land use, land value, and density of development. In addition, they are vitally important because they illuminate the process by which the real estate market sorts out potential occupants of land, allowing those who can make the most productive use of central sites to obtain them and pushing those less dependent on centrality out toward the edge. From an understanding of this process much can be gained. The city planner learns the strengths and weaknesses of a free market in land as a rational allocator of scarce central sites. Students of housing and urban renewal gain insight into the economics of "land-use succession," the process by which "renewal" occurs (or fails to occur) in a freely functioning market. The transportation analyst learns the interdependence of land values, land use, and the transportation network.

In all such models of land use, the price of urban land at various sites plays a crucial role. This price can be expressed either as the capital value of a site or as its annual rental value. Although land is more commonly sold than rented in the United States, it is usually more convenient for purposes of analysis to use annual rent rather than capital value as the measure of price. The relationship between the two concepts is, in any case, simple enough: the capital or market value of a site is the present value of the stream of net returns it is expected to yield in the future. Since land in uses other than agriculture does not "wear out," its expected future life is infinitely long. If, then, its yield is expected to be constant per year, the expression for its present capital value reduces to the formula for evaluating the worth of a perpetual income: capital value equals the expected perpetual annual net return divided by the interest rate appropriate for capitalizing an income of that degree of risk.

A SIMPLE MODEL: RESIDENTIAL LAND USE

Let us start with a drastically simplified model based on the following assumptions: (1) a city has sprung up on a flat plain, or "transport surface," of the sort assumed in the explanation of central place theory in the preceding chapter; (2) all production and distribution activity in this city takes place at a single point at its center; (3) the populace consists of families of uniform size, taste, and income who must live in rented single-family homes of uniform house and lot dimensions ranged around the central production and distribution point; (4) the cost of building and maintaining houses (site rent excluded) is constant throughout the city.[1] Since housing costs other than site rent are spatially invariant, differences in total rent paid by tenants at two different sites clearly represent differences in the site-rent component of the total. Site rent itself we define as the rent paid for a site less the rent it could command in an agricultural use.

1. The land-use model that we here apply to the city had its origin in J. H. von Thünen's work *Der isolierte Staat*, published in 1826. Von Thünen made use of the featureless plain and the need for access to a market center to explain the pattern of agricultural land uses that typically formed around a market town. In the twentieth century, urban economists have relied almost exclusively on a similar model to explain the pattern of urban land use. For a summary of twentieth-century theories of the economics of urban land use down to 1960, see William Alonso, *Location and Land Use* (Cambridge, Mass.: Harvard University Press, 1964), Ch. 1. The heart of Alonso's book is a model, far more elaborate than the one attempted here, that comprehends residential, business, and agricultural land uses within the now familiar von Thünen framework.

Under these assumptions it can be shown that site rent for residential lots will be highest adjacent to the business center, will decline along any radial from that point, and will fall to zero at the periphery. Beyond the periphery land will command agricultural rent only.

In Figure 6.1(a) we place the center of the city at O and measure distance from the center along the horizontal axis to the right. The vertical

FIGURE 6.1 (a)

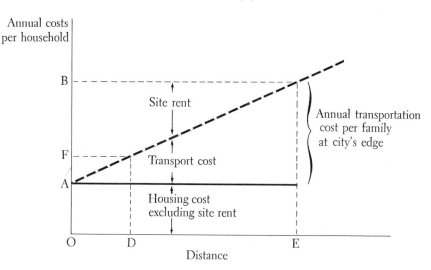

FIGURE 6.1 (b)

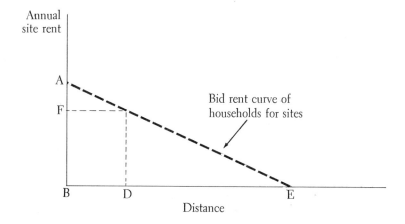

axis measures costs per family unit on an annual basis. Let us assume that for a given population and lot size and with no vacancies, the area needed to accommodate all families is provided when the city extends as far out as point E on the horizontal axis.

The vertical distance OA on the cost axis represents the annual cost of housing per unit, exclusive of site rent. This cost is equal for all locations, as indicated by the horizontal line at height OA. Since jobs and all consumer services are concentrated at the center, each household must bear an annual transportation bill for trips to the center and back. The annual cost of these trips increases with the household's distance from O and is shown by the rising transportation cost curve. Transport costs per family rise from zero at the city center to a maximum of AB for households located at the city's edge.

We can now show how site rent would arise as a payment for the saving in transport cost that could be obtained by living at any particular site. Consider, for example, a site adjacent to the city center. The owner of such a parcel could ask an occupant to pay as much as AB in site rent. If all houses are occupied, a householder would be willing to pay that much site rent to locate at the center, since his alternative would be to move just beyond the present edge of the city, where he would pay zero site rent but bear transportation costs equal to AB.

Under the usual assumptions about competition of occupants for houses and of landowners for maximum rent, the same argument can be extended to all sites: at any point within the city occupants would be willing to pay as site rent the difference between transportation costs at that site and the higher transportation costs that would be incurred if they moved to the city's edge. Under these conditions the combined cost of housing plus transportation plus site rent is the same at all sites and equals OB in Figure 6.1(a).

In Figure 6.1(b) we plot site rent itself against distance from the center. (We have simply inverted the site-rent triangle of Figure 6.1(a), while retaining its dimensions and labels.) Rent declines from BA at the center to zero at the edge. Thus our simple model approximates observed reality, in which land values are highest downtown and fall off with some consistency as one moves out to the metropolitan periphery.

The declining line in Figure 6.1(b) is usually described as a "bid-rent curve," since it shows the maximum site rent that households would willingly bid at each location. Since by assumption in this model no other land users compete with households for urban sites, the bid-rent curve of households becomes in fact the "rent gradient" for the city. Later, when introducing other land uses, we will show that the actual rent gradient in a city is produced from competition among uses and can be depicted by graphically combining their several bid-rent curves.

The Economic Character of Site Rent

The very simplicity of the model employed so far is a virtue, since it enables us to see clearly many of the important characteristics of rent in general and of site rent in particular. "Economic rent" is defined by economists as a payment to a factor of production in excess of its opportunity cost (for which reason it is also called an "economic surplus"). The opportunity cost of a factor in a given use is the payment it could command in its next best employment. The next best employment for urban sites is as agricultural land. Since site rent is a payment in excess of this opportunity cost for urban sites, it clearly conforms with the general definition of economic rent.

Factors of production command an economic rent only to the extent that they are "scarce," and they are scarce in the long run only to the extent that they are nonreproducible. Again urban sites illustrate the general case. While land on which to build is plentiful, land with accessibility to economic centers is scarce; it is the scarce attribute of accessibility that gives rise to site rent. In our simplified model sites can be added indefinitely by extending the edges of the city, but each incremental ring of sites has less accessibility than the adjacent ring closer to the center and commands correspondingly less rent. Accessibility to a given center cannot be reproduced, though it can be altered by changes in the technology of transportation.

Although rent is a payment in excess of opportunity cost and can therefore be described as an economic surplus, it is nevertheless a payment equal in value to the marginal product of the factor to which it accrues. Site-rent payments are therefore consistent in every respect with the marginal productivity theory of distribution and, as we will see, perform an essential function in bringing about an efficient allocation of land among competing uses. That site rent equals the marginal product of the site can easily be seen from Figure 6.1(a). Compare, for example, site D with site E. The rent at E is zero; at D rent equals FB. Suppose the site at D were vacant and a family moved there from E. At E the family would have borne transportation costs equal to AB, as compared with transportation costs of AF at D. The reduction in transportation costs through moving is given by $AB - AF = FB$. This reduction is a saving in real resource costs, and this saving is precisely the marginal product of the occupied site at D. It is also precisely the competitive site rent payable at D. Hence under competitive conditions rent equals marginal product.

Limitations of the Simple Model

The model developed above yields results that are unrealistic in several respects. First of all, numerous studies have been made in recent years of actual urban site-rent gradients. Most of these have concluded that the gradients are not linear—that is, they do not have a constant slope as in Figure 6.1(b). Instead they tend to be steepest at the center and to flatten out toward the edge, a shape that is often best approximated by a negative exponential curve.[2] Such a curve has the characteristic of declining at a constant *relative* rate, instead of at the constant *absolute* rate of a linear gradient. Along a negative exponential curve, site rent would decline by the same percentage for each mile of movement away from the center. It should be added that the rate of decline of the rent gradient appears to vary widely from city to city.

Our initial site-rent model is unrealistic in a second respect. We know from casual observation that density of urban settlement is not spatially uniform, as the model requires, but instead is much greater at the center. Again, statistical studies have verified the pattern. Like the gradient of site rent, the gradient of population density in modern cities has usually been best approximated by a negative exponential curve.[3]

Finally, greater population density at the center is associated with greater density of improvements—that is, with more cubic feet of building per acre. The visible evidence of this is, of course, the higher skyline we observe at the center, not just for office buildings, but for apartment structures as well.

Figure 6.2 shows the gradient of land value per square foot on the west side of Manhattan. The curve traces values along a ray extending from the edge of the central business district at Sixty-second Street to the northern tip of the island. It displays the diminishing slope with movement away from the center that is typical of large modern cities. In the next section we show how such a gradient can be generated by our residential model if we relax some of its initial simplifying assumptions.

2. See Edwin S. Mills, "The Value of Urban Land," in Harvey S. Perloff, ed., *The Quality of the Urban Environment* (Washington, D.C.: Resources for the Future, Inc., 1969). In addition to reporting his own findings (which are discussed at length later in this chapter), Mills summarizes the work of several other investigators.

3. See, for example, Colin Clark, *Population Growth and Land Use* (New York: St. Martin's Press, 1969), Ch. 9; Richard Muth, *Cities and Housing* (Chicago: University of Chicago Press, 1969), Ch. 7; Edwin S. Mills, "Urban Density Gradients," *Urban Studies*, February 1970, pp. 5–20; and Brian J. L. Berry and Frank E. Horton, *Geographic Perspectives on Urban Systems* (Englewood Cliffs, N.J.: Prentice-Hall, 1970), Ch. 9.

FIGURE 6.2

Gradient of Land Value on the West Side of Manhattan Island, 1970 [a]

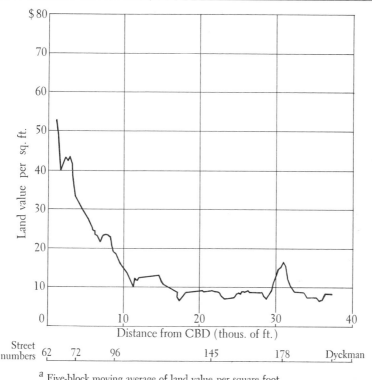

[a] Five-block moving average of land value per square foot

Source: Unpublished study of land value in New York City by Joseph E. Earley, Fordham University.

A MODEL THAT GENERATES SYSTEMATIC VARIATION IN DENSITY OF DEVELOPMENT

In constructing a more realistic model, we retain the assumption of a mononuclear city built on a "transport surface" with all commercial activity concentrated at a point in the center. Under these conditions, the transport-cost gradient remains as in Figure 6.1(a)—a linear function, rising as distance from the center increases. We continue to assume that families are uniform in size, taste, and income and that they occupy units of standard size. However, we abandon the requirement of uniform density of housing per acre. Instead, we allow developers to pile units up on a given lot by building vertically. We will assume that building developers do not own the sites on which they build but lease them from site owners. Tenants, in turn, rent space in buildings from the developers. Thus we have a three-tiered market: site owners, building owners, tenants. This institutional arrangement is used only occasionally in the United States, but it is quite common in England. We assume it only as a convenience. It does not affect the outcome of the analysis.

The new model is depicted in Figure 6.3. The right-hand panel shows transport costs and housing rent per family at various distances from the city center at O. The left-hand panel shows annualized costs to developers of building and operating standard size apartment units in multiple dwellings of varying heights.

Let us first examine the right-hand panel. Rent per apartment and transport cost per family are measured on the vertical scale between the two panels. To simplify the argument, we assume that all families arrange their budgets so as to pay a constant sum (equal for all families) for the combination of housing plus transportation. This outlay equals OP along the vertical scale, and the horizontal line through P indicates that the outlay is constant for all families regardless of location. At the center, transportation cost per family is zero, so OP is available as rent per apartment. Since transportation costs per family increase with mileage from the center, the sum available for rent decreases with distance and is shown by the housing-rent gradient, which declines from P at the center to E′ at the city's edge. Transportation costs at any site away from the center are shown by the vertical distance between the horizontal line through P and the declining housing rent gradient.

The left-hand panel is a mirror image of the conventional diagram of the long-run cost curves of a business firm, in which AC represents average cost and MC, marginal cost. In this instance the curves measure annual long-run average and marginal cost, per apartment, of building and operating apartment structures of varying heights on lots of standard size. Cost includes normal profit but, unlike the conventional case, excludes site rent. The horizontal scale shows number of apartments per structure, increasing in the leftward direction. Marginal and average costs per apartment rise, beyond a certain structure height, because the construction cost per apartment of adding additional stories begins to rise as the building grows taller. The rise in cost has two sources: first, the need for heavier foundations and structural elements and, second, the shrinkage of rentable interior space per story as height rises, on account of required building setbacks and the need for additional space-using elevator shafts.[4]

4. Concerning these increasing costs, see Ralph Turvey, *The Economics of Real Property* (London: Allen and Unwin, 1957), pp. 15–16. Edgar M. Hoover used a price line and a rising marginal-cost function to derive a site-rent gradient of increasing

FIGURE 6.3

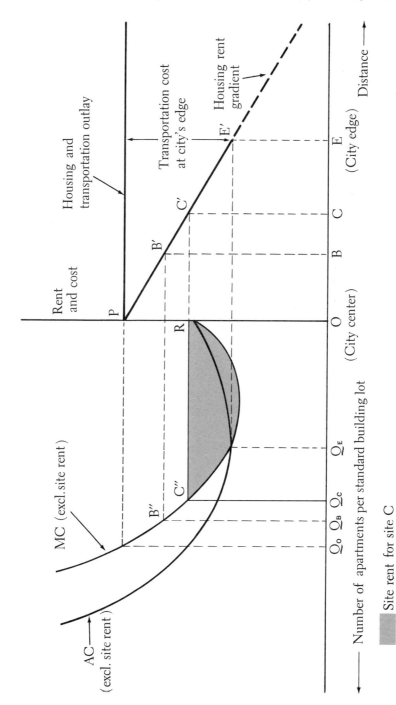

Taken together, the two panels of Figure 6.3 show the intensity of development that will occur and the site rent that will be generated at any distance out from the center. For example, at site C, tenants will be willing to pay CC′ in housing rent. We assume that builder-operators behave as perfect competitors, treating the going rent level at any distance from the center as if it were independent of their own decision to build. A builder at distance OC from the center will be guided by rent level CC′ in determining how intensively to develop his site. He will build his structure to the height at which the last story adds apartments whose marginal cost just equals the rent offer CC′. In other words, he follows the conventional rule for the perfect competitor, which is to extend output to the point at which marginal cost just equals price. Price at site C is shown by the horizontal line extending left from C′. This intersects the builder's marginal cost curve at C″. He therefore develops a building containing Q_C apartments.

What about site rent, which is not included in the cost curves depicted in Figure 6.3? The maximum annual site rent that a builder could pay at any site is the difference between total annual housing rent and total annual cost (excluding site rent) for an optimum size structure at that distance from the center. Total housing rent that could be realized in a building at site C containing Q_C apartments equals the product of the rent per unit times the number of units, which is shown by the area of the rectangle $OQ_CC″R$. Total cost (excluding site rent) equals the sum of all marginal costs and is shown, for site C, by the area under the marginal cost curve up to the quantity Q_C. Maximum site rent is the difference between these two areas, shown by the saucer-shaped shaded area on the left-hand panel. Since builders are competing to obtain scarce sites, actual site rent will in the long run tend to equal the indicated maximum.

Our example illustrates the fact that site rent arises as a residual in the pricing process. Out of the proceeds from the sale of output (in this instance, housing services) the producer must pay the going market price for whatever reproducible inputs he employs, including capital. The owners of nonreproducible scarce factors, such as urban sites, can then command as the price for the use of such factors whatever residual remains when all other inputs have been paid for by the producer. The size of this residual depends on the price the producer can obtain for his product and,

slope for agricultural land uses in *Location Theory and the Shoe and Leather Industries* (Cambridge, Mass.: Harvard University Press, 1937), pp. 24–26. The model in Fig. 6.3 applies his argument to the urban case. For a somewhat different derivation of an increasingly sloped urban site-rent gradient, see Harold Brodsky, "Residential Land and Improvement Values in a Central City," *Land Economics*, August 1970, pp. 229–47.

therefore, on the demand for it. It is for this reason that rent is usually said to be "price determined" rather than "price determining."

We can now use Figure 6.3 to demonstrate two points. First, as we move toward the city center, say from site C to site B, the intensity of development increases. Builders at B can obtain higher rents per unit than builders at C. They therefore carry development on the site further before reaching the point at which MC = rent: Q_B is to the left of Q_C, indicating that buildings at B are taller than those at C.

Second, it is easily seen that site rent is higher at B than at C, since the saucer-shaped site-rent area grows larger as rent per apartment rises to BB' and the number of apartments increases from Q_C to Q_B. But we can say more: the increase in site rent per mile of movement toward the center is greater for each successive mile. This means that the bid-rent curve for housing sites that could be derived from the left-hand panel of Figure 6.3 does not have the constant slope displayed by the simpler model in Figure 6.1. Rather, the increased intensity of development as we move toward the center generates increasingly large increments to site rent, so the bid-rent curve for sites grows steadily steeper as it nears the center. This result can easily be deduced from the shape of the site-rent area. Each mile of movement toward the center in the right-hand panel generates a constant increase in housing rent per apartment equal to the transportation cost saved by locating one mile nearer the center; apartment rent rises along a gradient of constant slope. But these successive, equal-per-mile increments to apartment rent, which could be measured along the vertical center scale, generate *increasing* increments to site rent, as demonstrated by the fact that the layers added to the saucer-shaped site-rent area are successively longer as they pile up in the vertical direction. These layers are longer only because intensity of development increases as we move toward the city center.

Intensity of development at the city's edge equals Q_E apartments per building lot. At that location, housing rent just equals the developer's average cost. Nothing is available for site rent, which is therefore zero. Tenants will not pay site rent to live in housing at the city's edge, since they have the alternative of building on adjacent vacant land for which site rent is zero. At the city's center, development reaches a density of Q_0 apartments per building lot and site rent (the saucer-shaped area above the marginal cost curve) is at a maximum.

We have shown that the model in Figure 6.3 generates a skyline that rises higher and a bid-rent curve for housing sites that grows steeper as we approach the center of the city. Since the model assumes housing to be the only land use, the bid-rent curve for housing sites is by assumption also the site-rent gradient for the city. It displays the characteristic shape found in empirical studies of land value in major cities.

THE EFFECT OF COMPETING LAND
USES ON URBAN FORM

The analysis developed above can now be modified to cope with something closer to the full complexity of land uses in a typical city. Although in principle the argument could be extended to any number of uses, let us for convenience combine city functions into three major groups and see how competition among them for sites will establish a land-use pattern and site-rent gradient for the city. The first group, which we will call central office functions, includes such activities as corporate headquarters offices, banks and other financial institutions, and law and accounting firms, all of which are complementary in providing high level business services that require frequent daily contact between firms. The second group, which we will call ancillary services, includes such categories as office equipment, parts and supply houses, printing shops, maintenance and repair firms, and telephone exchanges, whose function is to provide routine rather than high level services to the central office sector. The third category is housing.

We assume that each of the business sectors operates under conditions of perfect competition. We continue to posit a city on a flat transport surface so that movement is equally costly per mile in any direction. Within this city, central office functions and ancillary services, since they require frequent contact between firms, will exert a mutual attraction and will therefore locate close together rather than occupying scattered sites. Thus we can assume that the city will have a well-defined business district and that the center of this district will be the point offering greatest accessibility to other firms. The question to be answered is: how will the three kinds of land use locate in relation to this central point? The answer turns out to be that when various uses are competing for sites, the one that can pay the highest site rent at each particular location will come into possession there. Consequently the first point to investigate is: what determines the spatial pattern of demand for sites by each use?

To simplify the argument we make these additional assumptions: first, as in the housing case analyzed above, buildings are constructed and operated by developers who rent sites from landowners and in turn lease shelter space to tenants. Second, all structural types have similar cost characteristics. More specifically, all display identically increasing marginal and average cost per unit of floor space per year for building and operating structures of increasing height on lots of standard size. Thus the left-hand panel of Figure 6.4 shows cost curves resembling those of Figure 6.3. However, the horizontal scale to the left now measures quantity in square feet of floor space per structure rather than in number of apartments. As be-

FIGURE 6.4

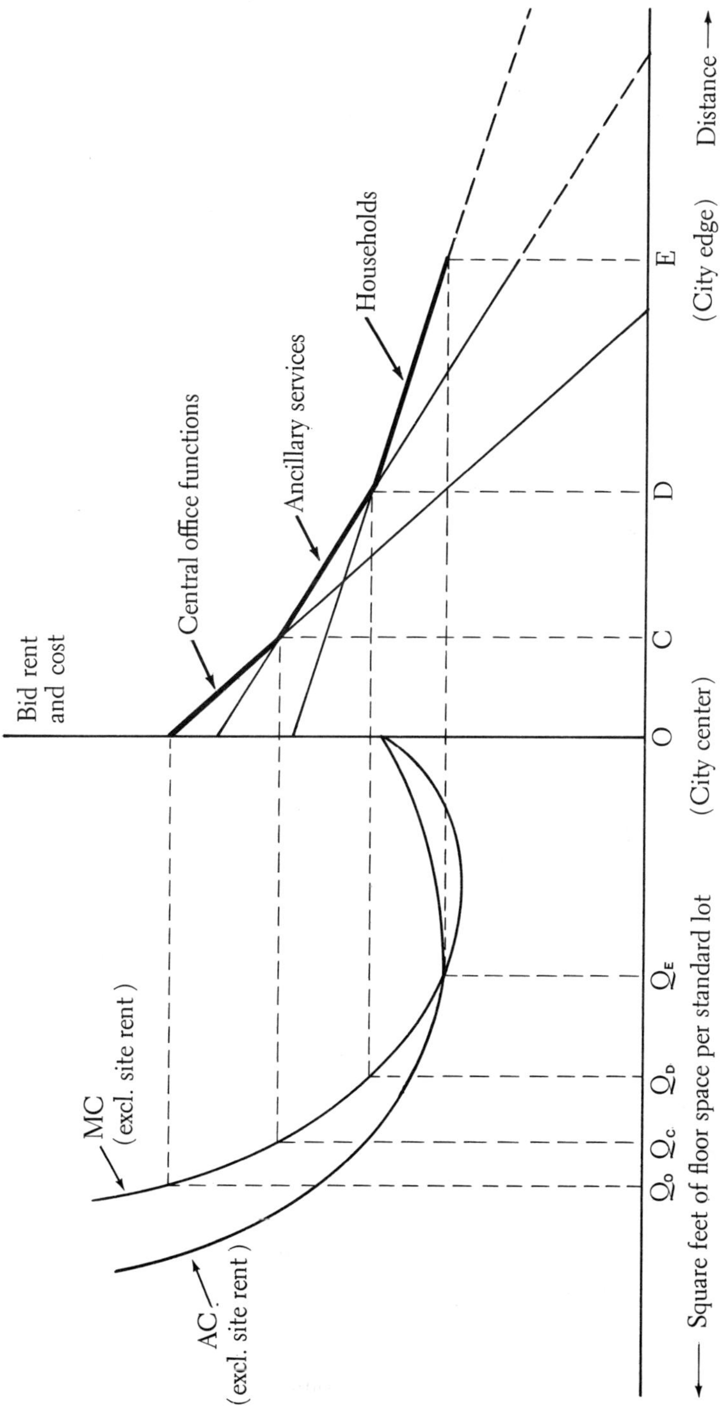

Bid rent
and cost

Central office functions

Ancillary services

Households

O (City center) C D E (City edge) Distance →

MC
(excl. site rent)

AC
(excl. site rent)

Q_O Q_C Q_D Q_E — Square feet of floor space per standard lot fore, increased quantity (i.e., increased output per site) is obtained by building higher.

In the right-hand panel of Figure 6.3 we drew a bid-rent curve of households for apartments, showing the maximum price that would be paid at each location as a decreasing function of distance from the center. The curve represented utility-indifferent positions for individual households. In the same fashion, bid-rent curves can be drawn for floor space to be occupied by each of the other types of activity, and each of these will show the maximum rent that can be paid consistent with earning a normal competitive return. As we will explain, this rent will decrease with distance from the city center.

First consider central office functions. Each firm in this group is heavily dependent on daily face-to-face contact between its own executives and their counterparts in firms with which it deals. The closer each firm can come to location at the center of the business district, the less costly to it in time and transportation outlay will be the task of maintaining contact with other firms. Thus a central location will reduce the firm's own costs (other than rent). For the same reason it will reduce the cost to others of maintaining contact with that firm. Hence a central location will also increase the firm's sales volume. Thus the rent per unit of floor space that a central office firm can pay while still earning a normal return will increase with proximity to the center both because transportation and communication costs will be decreasing and because sales will be increasing as distance from the center diminishes.

Much the same argument applies to the group of ancillary services. Firms in this group are in business to supply services to the central office firms (and to one another). They, too, will find costs (except rent) decreasing and sales increasing as distance from the center diminishes. Thus the rent they can pay per unit of floor space while still earning normal returns will also rise with proximity to the center.

Would the bid-rent curve for floor space be steeper for central office functions or for ancillary services? What determines its steepness in either case? Three factors can be distinguished. First, its steepness is greater, the greater the cost per unit of output of maintaining contact with the center. Second, its steepness is greater, the larger the number of units of output the firm produces per square foot of floor space occupied. Third, it is steeper, the less readily other inputs can be substituted for floor space in the production process as the price of floor space rises.[5]

It seems probable that central office functions would have a steeper bid-rent curve than ancillary services. First, since they are less routine and standardized than ancillary services, they are likely to require more fre-

5. For a more extended discussion of these factors see Hugh O. Nourse, *Regional Economics* (New York: McGraw-Hill, 1968), pp. 96–110.

quent personal contact between firms. In addition, since contact by central office firms frequently involves highest echelon executives, while contact for ancillary services is more apt to be carried out by lower-salaried personnel such as salesmen, truck drivers, or repairmen, it is probable that travel time would be valued far more highly for the former group than for the latter. Second, the quantity of output per unit of floor space is likely to be larger for a central office function than for an ancillary service. Comparable units of "output" are difficult to conceive of in this instance, but the point is that central office functions are, in some sense, able to make more intensive use of space than are ancillary services.

We show the bid-rent curve for households as the least steep of the three. The household typically has less need for central location than do business firms. Most commonly there is only one working member, hence only one required daily journey to the center. (We have not introduced shopping activity into the model.) To shorten this single daily trip households are willing to pay higher rent, which we show by drawing the household bid-rent curve with a slope that rises toward the center, but they are not willing to pay as much for centrality as do business firms, as we indicate by drawing the household curve below the inner (more central) portions of the other two.

The spatial distribution of the three land uses within the city is determined by the relationships among their bid-rent curves. At each location building owners, in order to maximize net income, rent space to the highest bidder. Hence the use with the highest bid-rent curve takes over occupancy at each point. In Figure 6.4, central office functions occupy the segment from O to C, ancillary services locate between C and D, and households occupy the segment from D to the edge of the city at E. Thus the highest portions of the three bid-rent curves (as indicated by the heavier line) become the rent gradient for the city. In this instance the gradient refers to rent per square foot of shelter space, but, as we have argued above, a unique land-rent gradient is, under the assumed conditions, associated with it. Both gradients become steeper as they approach the center. If we rotate either one about the city center we generate a corresponding rent surface. Looking down at such a surface from above we would see that the city is circular, that central office functions occupy the center and that the other land uses are ranged thereabout in concentric rings.

Interdependence Through Competition for Sites

The arrangement of land uses produced by the model depicted in Figure 6.4 forms an interdependent system. Not only are the several activities related to one another through the usual linkages of complementarity and substitution; they are also related by their competition for sites. In a more elaborate model that comes closer to articulating the general equilibrium nature of the problem, one would link the demand for sites by each activity to the quantity of output of each that could be sold in the markets served. In such a model the values of all supply and demand variables would have to be solved for simultaneously, since the site area occupied by each activity influences its output from the supply side, while at the same time the area that can be occupied by a given activity in competition with other uses depends on the demand for its output, the supply of complementary factors, and so on. The partial equilibrium model employed here can suggest the nature of these interdependencies, although it does not incorporate them explicitly.

For example, the outcome shown in Figure 6.4 was assumed to be an equilibrium division of land uses. In arriving at that division it was assumed implicitly that the quantity of central office functons that could be produced in the circular area of radius OC was just that quantity which could fetch a price sufficient to enable central office firms to exert the demand for space represented by their depicted bid-rent curve. Analogous assumptions held for the other land uses. Now suppose that an exogenous increase in the demand for central office services occurs. The price of such services would rise, and producers would seek to increase output. Their demand for sites—which is a "derived demand" based on the demand for their output—would increase. We could represent that increase by shifting their bid-rent curve up and to the right, which would cause the point of intersection of their bid-rent curve and that of ancillary services to move rightward. The immediate result would be an increase in the area occupied by central office functions at the expense of the ancillary service area.

But the chain of effects does not end there. If the area occupied by ancillary services shrank, output would fall and prices would rise. At higher prices for output, this industry, too, could bid more for sites. Hence the bid-rent curve of the ancillary service group would also move up and to the right (and thus would have an analogous effect on household demand for sites). The final equilibrium of the system would show that the margin of the central office area had moved out, but by less than would have occurred if the bid-rent curve of ancillary services had not thereby been forced up. Likewise the margin of the latter ring would have moved out, but by less than would have occurred had the household curve remained fixed. Finally, the upward shift of the household curve would have pushed the edge of the city farther from the center. All these effects are the result of direct competition between uses in the land market. We need not here trace out the effects of additional interdependencies, such as the increased demand for ancillary services when central office functions expand or the increased population that would be attracted into the household sector by these expanding industries.

We see, then, that a change in one part of the system causes a spreading wave of effects that in some degree alters the entire land-use pattern. Just as central place theory explains how cities are held in place, so to speak, by the location of all other cities, so, too, a fully developed model of intra-urban land use would have to explain how the whole array of urban activities is mutually held in place by intra-urban forces of attraction and repulsion operating through competitive land markets.

One might well ask whether our manner of combining the bid-rent curves in the model depicted in Figure 6.4 is not simply arbitrary. Why, for example, do the flatter bid-rent curves necessarily lie below the steeper ones at the center? The answer is that no other arrangement provides a stable equilibrium. If we were dealing with linear bid-rent curves for shelter space (i.e., each with constant slope throughout) and the curve that was highest at the center were also flattest, then it would be higher than all other curves throughout its length, and the city would be entirely devoted to that single land use. This is true a fortiori if the bid-rent curves are concave upward. But suppose one of them were concave downward? Then it might be higher but also flatter than the others at the center. This case can be ruled out, however, since it implies that the cost per mile of transportation to the center increases with the length of the journey, whereas the general tendency in transportation is for cost per mile to remain constant or else decrease with distance covered.

If these arguments seem to lean too heavily on mere geometry, consider the economic logic that lies behind them. The slope of a bid-rent curve measures the benefit that accessibility confers on a given activity: the greater their need for accessibility in terms of reduced cost or increased sales, the more firms of a particular type are willing to pay in higher rent to move one mile closer to the center. The more they are willing to pay per mile, the steeper their bid-rent curves. The slope of the bid-rent curve of a particular activity, therefore, measures the benefit accessibility confers on it. Industries that can benefit the most from accessibility have the steepest curves and occupy the center. Hence the model behaves efficiently in the economic sense: it allocates the scarce resource of accessibility to those who can make the most productive use of it.

The Doctrine of "Highest and Best Use"

Consistent with the foregoing argument, it is often said that a competitive real estate market allocates urban sites to their "highest and best use." Competition puts sites in the hands of the highest bidder. The highest bidder is the one who can make the most economically productive use of the site. The market operates so as to maximize rent from each site. We have already shown that site rent equals the marginal product of land. Hence the market also maximizes the contribution (i.e., marginal product) that each site adds to total output. It is in that sense that "highest" is also "best" from the viewpoint of society as a whole.

As we will see in Chapter 11, however, the process by which one use *succeeds* another on a given site is far more complicated than the above passage suggests. If a cleared site is thrown on the market it will obviously be sold to the highest bidder, who will then construct a building on it that represents the highest and best use of the site. If, however, a site has an old building on it that is still capable of rendering service, that old use may be sufficiently profitable to persist on the site even though it is not the kind of building that anyone would now construct if the site were already cleared. Frequently observed examples of this sort are the old four-story commercial buildings that stand cheek-by-jowl with skyscrapers in the CBD or the small, walk-up apartment houses scattered among tall, modern elevator structures in a residential district. These cases are not exceptions to the doctrine of highest and best use. Properly interpreted, the doctrine comprehends them. However, the matter will not be taken up in detail until we analyze the economics of land-use succession in Chapter 11.

EXTERNALITIES AND LAND-USE ZONING

A major qualification to the argument that a competitive land market allocates sites to their highest and best use must now be introduced. We have treated land uses as though they were independent of one another except for those connections made through market transactions. Thus we have ignored external, or neighborhood, effects. These arise when activity at one site confers benefits or imposes costs on the occupant of another site for which no fee can be charged or no recompense collected. For example, a beautiful garden in front of one house produces a free aesthetic benefit for neighbors and passers-by, while the noise and fumes from a boiler factory impose unrequited damages on the occupants of nearby sites. Such effects are especially likely to occur in densely built-up urban areas.

When they occur, externalities interfere systematically with the efficiency of the market in producing an economically optimal pattern of land use. For example, when bidding for a site, the owner of the boiler factory does not take into account the external cost of noise and fumes that his factory will impose on his neighbors. He locates without regard to the damage he imposes on others. Consequently, the resulting pattern of land use is likely to be suboptimal. If the owner could somehow be made to bear his factory's external costs, his choice of location would be affected. He would find it profitable to hold down external costs by seeking a neighborhood (perhaps an industrial district) where noise and fumes are not considered highly objectionable. A more desirable pattern of land use would result.

Land-use zoning arose as an attempt to meet the problem of externalities. Since it is generally difficult to force the occupants of sites to internalize all the external costs they might impose upon others, a second-best solution is to employ zoning to keep potentially incompatible uses apart. Thus boiler factories are forbidden to locate in residential districts. We will have more to say about the subject of zoning in Chapter 11.

INTRODUCING THE EFFECTS OF CHANGE AND GROWTH

The land-use model depicted in Figure 6.4 is wholly static. Ignoring time and change, it shows us what the equilibrium pattern would be if a city were suddenly to be built *de novo* under given conditions. It does not tell us how land-use patterns evolve as cities age or as the things assumed constant in the model—especially population, income level, and technology—change through time. It leaves out of account all the dynamic forces of urban evolution that for better or worse prevent the achievement of any final equilibrium. Because structures and—even more so—the underlying framework of streets and utilities are long-lived, the pattern of land uses that exists at any actual time is never the same as the optimal pattern that could be produced by a wholly fresh start at that moment. The aging of structures and the process of land-use succession on given sites will be examined in detail in Chapter 11. At this point we wish to analyze the general, or macrolocational, effects on land use of changes in technology, population, and income.

The consequences of such changes have been worked out very clearly by Alonso, and the following discussion is based largely on his work.[6] Although Alonso's study covers business and agricultural patterns as well as residential, he simplifies the formal analysis of the effect of changes in technology and the like by restricting it to the latter sector. (The results are fundamentally the same for urban business uses as well.) Alonso's model, like the highly simplified one used above, assumes a transport surface and a mononuclear city. It is far more complex than ours, however. Among other things, it explicitly rejects the assumption of constant resi-

6. Alonso, pp. 105–13.

dential lot size. Rather, lot size is one of the variables to be solved for. What follows below is not the Alonso model itself but one of its applications.

The Effect of an Improvement in Transportation Technology

Figure 6.5 shows the bid-rent curve of households for land (or, as Alonso calls it, the price structure for residential land) in a metropolis with its business and employment center at O. The land units in terms of which price is expressed may be square feet, acres, or what have you. Initially, the price structure is given by line AB. OA equals rent at the center and point B marks the edge of urban settlement. Now suppose that an improvement in technology takes place that reduces the time and/or money cost of transportation from the outlying areas to the center. Rent at the center is based on the saving in transportation cost obtained by locating there instead of at the city's edge. Accordingly, rent at the center will be reduced

FIGURE 6.5

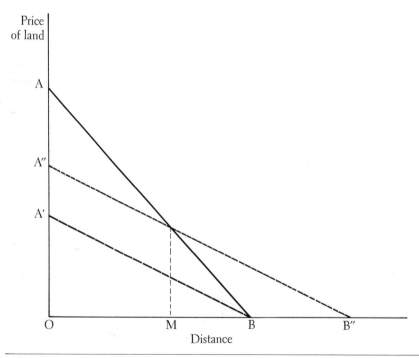

Source: Adapted from William Alonso, *Location and Land Use*, Figure 32, p. 112.

by the technological improvement, other things remaining the same. More specifically, if lot size were held constant the outer edge of settlement would remain at B and the bid-rent curve would fall to A'B. But with the price of land reduced, lot size will *not* remain constant. Alonso's model incorporates the important fact that to the householder space is a consumer good as well as an impediment to access. Other things being equal, if the price of land drops, householders will increase their consumption of it: lot size will increase. That, in turn, means that the area needed to house a given population will also increase. The margin of settlement will move out—say, to B″. Instead of falling to A'B, the bid-rent curve will shift to a position such as A″B″.

We know that A″ must be above A'—in other words, that rent at the center falls less than it would have if lot size had remained constant—because when the city's edge moves from B out to B″, the transportation cost saved at a central location increases, and therefore so does rent at the center. It is interesting to note that although the new bid-rent curve A″B″ shows rents lower than before at the center, it also shows them to have increased beyond some point, M. Why should households beyond M be paying higher rents after the improvement in transportation than they paid before? The answer is that people living farther out than M could pay more rent than before and still be better off than they were because the technological change has allowed them to gain utility through reduction in the time and/or money cost of transportation.

The Effect of an Increase in Population

The effects of population change also are easily deduced from Alonso's model. An increase in population will increase the demand for residential sites. In order to accommodate the new households, the margin of the city will move outward. As it does so, the cost of transportation from the edge to the center will increase, and the bid-rent curve will shift upward and to the right. That means higher land costs for all households and a tendency to reduce lot size. Hence the city's area will increase less than in proportion to the increase in population. Thus, as Alonso points out, a rise in population, other things being equal, will cause an increase in both land prices and density of settlement as well as in the physical extent of the urban area.

The Effect of an Increase in Income

We next examine the impact of changes in average household income. Alonso deals with the effect of differences in income among households rather than with the effect of a change in its average level. He notes that there is a well-documented tendency in large American cities for wealthier families to settle near the edge, while poorer households remain close to the center. As he points out, the explanation of this phenomenon has profound implications for housing and renewal policy. Let us examine the alternatives.

Some theories of urban form suggest that the outward movement of the middle and upper income classes is the result primarily of the growth of the city and the pattern of housing obsolescence associated with that growth. According to these theories the wealthier classes move away from the center for two reasons. First, the expansion of the CBD as the city grows encroaches on their close-in residential zone, destroying its amenities. Second, since the close-in housing is the oldest, it is also the first to become obsolete. Because it is easier to build new on vacant land than in built-up districts, the wealthy tend to move to the periphery to construct another round of up-to-date housing. Older housing is abandoned to poorer classes, and the oldest of all (adjacent to the CBD) to the immigrants whose arrival feeds the city's growth. Based on observations in Chicago, this theory of urban form was first put forward by the sociologist Ernest W. Burgess in 1925 and has been highly influential.[7] It is known as the "concentric zone theory" because Burgess described four distinct types of housing, which he believed were grouped in concentric rings around the CBD. He identified the zones and their residents as follows (moving from the center outward):

1. The Central Business District (in Chicago, "The Loop").
2. The Zone in Transition: as the CBD grows, business and light manufacturing encroach on old slums and rooming houses, making this the least desirable residential area.
3. The Zone of Workingmen's Homes: inhabited by laborers who have escaped from the deterioration of Zone 2 but wish to live close to their central workplaces.
4. The Residential Zone: a restricted or exclusive district consisting of high-class apartments and single family homes for the middle and upper classes.
5. The Commuters' Zone: suburban areas and satellite cities, outside the city limits but within commuting distance of the CBD.

This theory, and its later variants, finds the basic explanation for the peripheral location of the wealthy to lie in the growth, development, and aging of the city over time. If it is correct, then public policies that stimu-

---

7. Ernest W. Burgess, "The Growth of the City," Ch. 2 in Robert E. Park, Ernest W. Burgess, and Roderick D. McKenzie, *The City* (Chicago: University of Chicago Press, 1925).

late inner city renewal, and especially the construction of new luxury housing at the center, might succeed in overcoming the apparent preference of the wealthy for the suburbs and thus attract a large return flow. The case is entirely different, however, if the preference of families for space-consuming suburban living increases directly with income. In that event, the outward movement of the wealthy is simply the result of their rising living standards, and urban renewal in the older central cities will be relatively ineffective in stemming their outward migration or attracting a return flow.

By close theoretical argument Alonso shows why wealthy families may tend to have bid-rent curves less steep than those of poor families and therefore settle on large lots of relatively cheap land toward the city's edge, while the poor tend to occupy very small portions of higher priced land near the center. Alonso's argument is complex. An important factor in it, however, is the cost of commuting. This cost depends upon distance rather than upon income or the quantity of land occupied. For the poor family, the increase in commuting costs as distance increases will diminish rapidly the small fund of income available for housing. Consequently the poor cannot bid much for locations where commuting is expensive. On the other hand, since commuting costs are invariant with income or quantity of land occupied, the rich, who are prepared to spend large sums on housing, find the barrier of commuting costs rather inconsequential and can bid higher prices than the poor for land at distant locations. Of course, Alonso recognizes that individual tastes are not uniform. Some wealthy families with a strong aversion to commuting and a weak preference for added space will always continue to live in luxury housing near the center.

This interpretation of Alonso's argument can readily be extended to cover the effect of an increase in the average level of income as well as the effect of income differences among households. As the average income of American families increases over time, commuting costs, which do not vary with income, become relatively less burdensome, and the proportion of the population that chooses to take up suburban living increases. This means that even if population, tastes, and the technology of transportation were constant, rising living standards alone would suffice to increase the suburban population and diminish that of the inner cities. This process would also produce the trend in geographic income differentials that we do in fact observe and will discuss at length in later chapters: average family income is rising far faster in the suburbs than in the central cities.

Recapitulation: The "Automobile Effect," the "Overflow Effect," and the "Income Effect"

It is worth noting that with regard to the causes of dispersion within metropolitan areas, the inferences drawn from Alonso's formal land-rent model coincide with those cited in the essentially descriptive-historical analysis of the same process we presented in Chapter 3. Formal theoretical analysis supports the following conclusions:

1. An improvement in transportation, other things remaining the same, allows the margin of urban settlement to move out. If total population remains constant this causes population to rise in the suburbs and fall in the central city. This is the "automobile effect" of Chapter 3.

2. An increase in total metropolitan population, other things remaining the same, also pushes the margin of settlement out. It leads, by way of reduced lot size, to greater density and therefore to a larger population in the central city as well as in the suburbs. However, since the suburbs start with a smaller population base, the percentage increase recorded there will be greater than in the central city. This is the essence of the "overflow effect" cited in Chapter 3.

3. An increase in the average standard of living, other things constant, reduces the demand for central sites and increases the demand for more distant ones. Average lot size increases, and again the margin of settlement moves out. With no change in total numbers, this means a smaller population in the central city and a larger one in the suburbs. This is the "income effect" of Chapter 3.

We see then that each of the three effects, taken separately, leads to increased suburban population, while two reduce and one—the population effect—increases central city numbers. Since early in the twentieth century all three have operated simultaneously. What were the consequences for the pattern of settlement? As we showed in Table 3.2, the growth rate of central city population was at its height in the first decade of the century. It slowed down more or less steadily thereafter and actually turned negative for a great many of the older central cities in the 1950's and 1960's. But for the gains from annexation, the population of central cities as a whole would have been virtually unchanged during the latter decade. It thus appears that for a long time the strength of the population effect was sufficient to maintain some central city growth despite the strong impetus to dispersal from improved transportation and rising living standards. Eventually, however, despite the continued rapid growth of total metropolitan population, the forces making for dispersion were sufficient to offset the opposite effect of sheer population growth and in many cases brought an actual decline in the number of central city residents.

TOWARD GREATER REALISM:
SUBCENTERS, INTERPENETRATION OF
USES, THE DECLINE OF
MONONUCLEARITY

The model we have relied on so far is unrealistic in a number of ways. We have employed it nevertheless because its basic implications are valid and important, but we must now recognize some real-world complications.

Let us admit, first of all, that contrary to our starting assumption, cities are not built on featureless transport surfaces. Topographical irregularities abound: differences in elevation, view, wind direction, or proximity to natural features such as lakes, beaches, or mountans have an effect on locational choice. Equally important, transportation itself is not ubiquitous but is always channeled into corridors. These corridors themselves are often distorted by topographical irregularities, and the modes of transport vary according to corridor and purpose. These factors in turn account in part for a second complication: cities are not strictly mononuclear. Subcenters often arise at intersections on the transport grid. Each of these exerts its own attraction for certain functions and emerges as a lesser peak in the urban rent surface. Major corridors too, since they offer superior accessibility along their own length, command higher rents than minor streets or roads. Corridors, in effect, become centers.

It is not enough, however, to say simply that cities are often multinuclear instead of mononuclear. We must admit more—namely, that land uses are not arranged by the market into mutually exclusive districts, whether of concentric rings or any other shape. Not only are types of business intermixed within the CBD, but business and residential uses interpenetrate in both the central city and the suburbs. Retailing, for example, is found in all parts of the metropolis. This, however, is only the most obvious exception; other types of business, too, survive and prosper at a wide variety of locations. As we stressed in Chapter 3, urban evolution, driven by the force of changes in the technology of transportation, has moved steadily away from the nineteenth-century pattern of business activity concentrated at the center toward a much more decentralized arrangement.

We have shown above how an improvement in transportation causes the city's residential zone to spread out, its population dispersing to a pattern of lower density settlement. The results are similar for business firms. Cheaper transport allows them to both obtain from suppliers and offer to customers as much accessibility as before in terms of time and money cost at a greater distance out from the center where they can afford larger sites. Some firms, at least, will be induced by this change to move outward. The greater the possibility of substituting space for other inputs in the production process, the more likely they are to move. Thus automotive assembly plants or wholesale food distributors are more likely to disperse than are corporation law offices or advertising firms.

It should be emphasized that the business dispersion described here is not the spreading out of a discrete central business district at the heart of the city. Rather it is the dispersion of activity from that center toward the periphery; in other words, the suburbanization of industry. In Table 3.4 we showed the extent of this decentralization in 12 major SMSA's during the two decades following World War II. The analysis in Chapter 3 and the population data in Table 3.4 also made it clear that the outward movement of jobs encourages, and in turn is encouraged by, the simultaneous outward movement of population. Since jobs are moving outward simultaneously with people, it follows that the suburbanization of population does not imply an increase in commuting. This means, of course, that the forces making for dispersion render a mononuclear model of urban location increasingly unrealistic.

EMPIRICAL EVIDENCE OF LAND-VALUE CHANGES OVER TIME

The few empirical studies we have of changes in urban land-value gradients over time show that they have changed in the way our model would suggest under the impact of urban growth and decentralization. Mills recently estimated land-value gradients for Chicago from data gathered by Homer Hoyt for 1836, 1857, 1873, 1910, and 1928.[8] Mills' technique was to regress land value on distance from the CBD. He tested three forms of relationship at each date: linear in both variables, which fitted poorly at all dates; log of land value against arithmetic distance—the equation for a gradient of the negative exponential type; and log of land value against log of distance. Since the negative exponential form fitted as well as any, we use it as the basis for this discussion.

Mills found that between 1836 and 1857 the slope of the land-value gradient increased moderately. The coefficient of determination, R^2, of the line of regression also increased, indicating that the negative exponential curve provided an increasingly good fit to the data. From 1857 to 1928, however, both the slope of the gradient and the value of R^2 gradually diminished. The flattening of the gradient is just what theory would have led us to expect as a result of successive improvements in the technology of intrametropolitan transportation. Moreover, Berry and Horton, build-

8. Mills, "The Value of Urban Land."

ing on Mills' analysis, have shown that the decline in the slope of Chicago's land-value gradient over that period is paralleled by a decline in the slope of the population-density gradient—again, just the combination that theory would predict.[9]

Mills' analysis also shows that while the slope of the land-value gradient was diminishing, its height at the center was steadily rising, so the whole gradient at each later date lay above its position at each earlier time. This rise in the level of the gradient is precisely what the mononuclear model would predict as a result of the vast increase in population during the period.

The decline in the value of the coefficient of determination, R^2, for the fitted gradients between 1857 and 1928 suggests, as Mills himself points out, that the mononuclear model has become less valid with the passage of time. As a result of the dispersion of business activity and the growth of other centers, distance from the CBD is gradually losing its once commanding power to explain intrametropolitan variation in site value. Economists are now developing more sophisticated approaches to the problem of intrametropolitan location, primarily through the use of urban simulation models that can be run on high speed computers. The need for these complex techniques, however, does not render the simpler mononuclear theories useless as explanatory devices. Even in more advanced models the fundamental logic of business location decisions depicted in this chapter remains essentially intact: firms locate where they expect to maximize profits and are strongly influenced in so doing by the trade-off between accessibility to customers and suppliers on the one hand and the site rent they must pay to obtain that accessibility on the other. Despite the complexities of real-world location patterns, each class of urban activity does display a characteristic, measurable locational tendency. The observed complexity, in fact, is simply evidence that for most functions there remains a sufficiently wide range of feasible locations at going rent levels to produce considerable overlapping in spatial distribution.

THE ROLE OF SITE RENT UNDER
DYNAMIC CONDITIONS

Whatever their differences in either structure or complexity, theories of intra-urban location do not disagree on the crucial role of site rent as the free market's allocator of land among alternative uses. We opened

.9. Berry and Horton, p. 302 and Fig. 9–18. Ch. 9 of their volume reviews the extensive empirical work that has been done on population density gradients and their change over time.

this chapter with the analysis of rent as an allocator under static conditions. It is appropriate now to examine the role of rent under the impact of change and development.

Consider the situation in a city with a rapidly growing population. Land value per acre in such a city will generally be rising, just as theory suggests. The rise in value and the growth of population stem from a single source: the economic advantages that the city offers in terms of individual income and business profit as compared with other places. To the extent that his site confers valuable access to these gains, each landowner can appropriate a share of the city's net advantages in the form of urban site rent. In a suitably defined long-run equilibrium, landowners as a group would, in theory, be able to appropriate the entire value of the city's locational advantages. This would equal the difference between the aggregate returns that the nonland factors of production earn when used in the city and the returns they could obtain if employed at a place where urban site rent was zero. The aggregate of site rent in a city is thus one measure of the economies of location and agglomeration that the city offers.

To the individual businessman who must rent space, high site costs per se are, of course, a *dis*advantage. As the city grows, some firms that found it profitable to locate there when rents were low may find it unprofitable to remain as they rise and will choose to move away. But the fact that site rents are rising (by which we mean rising relative to the general level of prices) in itself is sufficient evidence that the city's net advantages to land users as a whole have increased. Were it otherwise, bidders would not be pushing site rents up. Thus, from the point of view of society as a whole, high site rents should not be regarded as one of the "diseconomies of agglomeration." On the contrary, they measure the extent of the positive economies of agglomeration and location to be found there.

In practice the spatial redistribution of activity that occurs under the pressure of rising site rents may take other forms than the movement of whole firms. Haig long ago pointed out that business firms actually comprise many distinct functions that need not all be carried on at the same place.[10] As site rents in the CBD rise, firms often separate out those functions that do not require centrality—manufacturing, warehousing, and record-keeping, for example—and move them to less costly areas on the periphery or even to points outside the metropolis. In the end perhaps only the head office will remain in the CBD. A prominent recent example

10. R. M. Haig, "The Assignment of Activities to Areas in Urban Regions," *Quarterly Journal of Economics*, May 1926, pp. 402–34.

of this has been the tendency of book publishers, who are still heavily concentrated in New York, to move their distribution, storage, and billing operations to low rent areas in New Jersey, while retaining head office, editorial, and sales functions in New York City.

THE IMPACT OF PUBLIC POLICY:
TRANSPORTATION PLANNING

Up to this point the argument of the chapter has focused exclusively on the way the private land market determines patterns of urban land use. No mention has been made of public planning or intervention. This was deliberate but also unrealistic, for we have continually emphasized the crucial importance of accessibility, and accessibility obviously depends upon the layout of streets, roads, and the mass transit network (if any). These features, especially in recent decades, have been planned and financed almost entirely by the public rather than the private sector. Hence the influence of public decisions on land-use patterns cannot be ignored.

New transportation facilities are typically laid down in large sections rather than in small increments. Their relationship to the market sector is a reciprocal one. To some extent new transportation links, whether urban expressways or additional subway lines, are built in response to visible traffic demand generated by private market locational decisions. But casuality runs the other way, too. A major traffic facility, once in place, exerts a powerful influence on subsequent private market development. This is obvious at the microlocational scale. For example, commercial development inevitably springs up around subway stations, highway interchanges, and airports.

More important, however, are the macrolocational effects of transportation systems as a whole. The transportation framework a city installs profoundly influences its future development. Cities that rely heavily on mass transit, like New York or Chicago, tend to become highly centralized and densely developed. On the other hand, if a city relies mainly on highway transportation as it grows, it develops into a decentralized, low-density metropolis such as Los Angeles. (Figure 3.2 shows how greatly these cities differ in population per square mile.)

One must be careful not to overemphasize the role of choice, however; historical necessity plays a part, too. New York and Chicago developed before the age of the motor car and the truck. For them it was mass transit or nothing. Moreover, they were already highly centralized and densely settled when their present transportation systems were built. The installation of electric mass transit reinforced centrality and density; it did not create it.

The case for historical necessity is not quite so clear in newer cities such as Los Angeles. Highway and mass transit technologies were both available at the time of the city's major growth. Once the great freeway system had been built, however, a decentralized, low-density urban pattern developed that could not be served effectively by a rail mass transit system. The latter requires concentrated trip destinations to operate economically; the former operates economically only when destinations are *not* concentrated. Hoover has pointed out that since each system tends to promote the pattern of settlement that it can serve efficiently, the choice of a transportation system is to some extent self-justifying.[11]

Mass Transit Versus Highways

Since the early 1960's there has been a revival of interest in rail mass transit, in cities that previously lacked it, as an alternative to continued expansion of urban highway systems. Many influences have converged to bring this about, among them the rising concern with air pollution, to which automobiles are a major contributor; the "energy crisis," which suggests that we may come to regret an exclusive commitment to the fuel-hungry automobile; and, finally, the increasingly effective opposition to the destructive effects of major highways on the aesthetic character and daily life of urban neighborhoods. To avoid congestion in a large and growing metropolis that depends entirely on motor transportation, extensive areas must be made available for the expansion of highway and parking facilities. Eventually opposition to these land-use demands may become intense enough to slow down or halt highway expansion and turn public effort toward the construction of rail mass transit.

Such at least has been the case in the San Francisco Bay Area and Washington, D.C., two major metropolitan areas that had reached great size without rail mass transit. The Bay Area Rapid Transit System (BARTS), connecting downtown San Francisco with Oakland, Berkeley, and other communities across the bay, opened its first section for service in 1972. Construction began in December 1969 on a major subway-surface rail system to serve Washington, D.C., and the surrounding suburban counties in Maryland and Virginia.

Economists disagree about the wisdom of these huge new undertakings. Some, like John R. Meyer, doubt that any of the cities that still lacked rail mass transit in the 1960's had the population densities or concentrated trip destinations necessary to make such systems an economical

11. Edgar M. Hoover, *An Introduction to Regional Economics* (New York: Alfred A. Knopf, 1971), p. 383.

alternative to an improved highway system.[12] Meyer would stress instead the better utilization of urban highways through more sophisticated and rational traffic controls and by the introduction of express bus service where feasible. Other economists, like William S. Vickrey, are convinced that the real economic costs of urban highway construction and operation are understated in the conventional analysis and that if costs were correctly calculated the case for mass transit would improve considerably in large cities.[13]

Disagreement in this area is difficult to resolve for several reasons. It is not an easy matter to say what a transportation system ought to optimize. Minimizing cost per trip, for example, does not appear to be a valid objective, since the comfort and convenience of the trip vary with the mode of travel. Including benefits as well as costs, however, does not make matters easier. The benefit-cost approach to evaluating investment alternatives cannot readily be applied to whole transportation systems. That method of analysis assumes a given economic context, or state-of-the-world, in which the benefits and costs of alternatives can be measured. It is therefore useful in dealing with increments to existing networks. Entire alternative systems, however, are likely to produce environments so different as to render quantitative comparison between them virtually impossible.[14]

The long-time horizon appropriate for evaluating transportation investments also creates difficulties. For example, in analyzing prospects for a new subway system, the planner or economist is called upon to predict land-use and traffic patterns forty or fifty years into the future. Since he cannot do that "scientifically," his judgment in the case is apt to rest ultimately on his general views concerning the long-run trend toward dispersion. If he believes, as Meyer does, that this trend is ineluctable and will continue almost unabated even in the face of improved mass transit, then he will advise against spending large sums on new rail systems de-

12. See J. R. Meyer, J. F. Kain, and M. Wohl's theoretical and empirical study, *The Urban Transportation Problem* (Cambridge, Mass.: Harvard University Press, 1965). Meyer's views on public policy are summarized in his paper on "Urban Transportation" in James Q. Wilson, ed., *The Metropolitan Enigma* (Washington, D.C.: Chamber of Commerce of the United States, 1967), pp. 34–55.

13. William S. Vickrey, "Pricing in Urban and Suburban Transport," *American Economic Review*, May 1963, pp. 452–65; and Lyle Fitch and Associates, *Urban Transportation and Public Policy* (San Francisco: Chandler Publishing Co., 1964), Ch. 4. Vickrey participated in the latter study.

14. Fitch and Associates, pp. 110–11. For an introduction to the theory and practice of cost-benefit analysis that includes numerous citations to its application in the area of transportation investment, see A. R. Prest and R. Turvey, "Cost-Benefit Analysis: A Survey," in International Economic Association, *Surveys of Economic Theory*, Vol. III (New York: St. Martin's Press, 1966), pp. 155–207.

signed inflexibly to serve today's traffic needs.[15] He will admit that centralized traffic patterns are well served by subway systems and ill-suited to highway transport. But he will insist that centralization is passing away and that scarce public funds should not be sunk irretrievably in a fruitless effort to preserve it. On the other hand, if he is convinced that central cities will retain at least their present economic importance, especially if well served by mass transit, he may reach the conclusion that, should major additional facilities be needed, mass transit would be preferable to further highway expansion.

These observations are intended only to indicate, not to resolve, the complexities of urban transportation economics, a subject we will not deal with in detail. We have tried to emphasize, however, that whatever sort of transportation network a city provides for itself, the response of the private sector to public transportation decisions takes place through the process of competition for access that we have described in this chapter. In any setting, therefore, an understanding of that process is essential to an understanding of the metropolis.

15. In an empirical test, Meyer, Kain, and Wohl found no evidence that the availability of mass transit service slows down decentralization within SMSA's (*The Urban Transportation Problem*, pp. 44–47). Hoover subsequently reanalyzed Meyer, Kain, and Wohl's data and reached the opposite conclusion—that they "support the idea that better transit service can be of assistance in fighting downtown and central city decline" (*An Introduction to Regional Economics*, pp. 371–72). However, the association between age of central city and degree of transit system development makes it difficult to interpret these results.

The Urban Economic Base
and Economic Policy

SEVEN

The economics of location have dominated the first six chapters of this book. We have examined, both historically and theoretically, the forces that draw industry and population together to form cities and metropolitan areas and, within those places, distribute them into orderly patterns of settlement. We have examined linkages among industries and between industries and population in a spatial context, emphasizing the way the technology of transportation and communications establishes physical connections between activities and determines the distance at which they can best locate with respect to one another. This chapter brings a change of perspective. We will look at the urban community as a functioning economic unit, examining the employment- and income-creating relationships between activities instead of their spatial relationships, which can now be taken for granted.

The employment- and income-generating activities of the city have often been called "the urban economic base." We now wish to examine the structure and behavior of that base and to see especially how its internal characteristics interact with external forces to determine the level, stability, and growth of local income and output. When those relationships have been made clear, we will move on to the problem of local economic policy, explaining the methods by which local authorities try to influence the level of income and output and examining the implications of these methods for both local and national welfare.

It is well to start with the distinction between internal structure and external relationships. At any moment in time the city possesses a stock of useful resources in the form of labor skills, land, capital, entrepreneurship. These are the available factors of production. When they are fully and efficiently employed, the city is producing as much as it can. These factors of production and the relationships among them make up the internal economic structure.

It is obvious, however, that a city is very much an "open economy." It does not produce everything it consumes; nor does it consume everything it produces. Even if a great city could turn out all the manufactured goods its residents wanted, it could never be the source of all the necessary food and raw materials. These goods, at least, must be imported, and to pay for them the city must send exports to the rest of the world. Trade is not merely incidental to the city's life; it is absolutely indispensable. Thus even if there were no migration of the factors of production between areas, trade would suffice to open up the city to the influence of exogenous forces —that is to say, forces arising outside its boundaries.

All the methods that have been devised to analyze the urban economic base recognize the fundamental openness of the urban economy and therefore stress the importance of its relationships with the outside world. They differ, however, in the extent to which they simplify the complex reality of the city's internal structure and therefore of its external relationships. The three principal methods that have been used, in ascending order of complexity, are the basic-nonbasic approach, the foreign-trade multiplier method, and input-output analysis. We will take them up in that order. Our purpose in so doing is not so much to elucidate the methods themselves—although that is important—as to provide an understanding of how the urban economy functions, and the simplifications these methods impose on reality, both when they are tenable and when they are not, are the best means we have to that understanding. Indeed, the weaknesses of these theories are often as instructive as their strengths, and we will show that despite some very important differences they share a common logical structure and therefore common weaknesses and limitations.

THE BASIC-NONBASIC THEORY

The basic-nonbasic theory derives its odd name from the causal significance it attaches to exports as compared with other local activity. (Strictly speaking, it is a "theory" rather than a "method" precisely because it does postulate a particular causal relationship between the variables it deals with.) According to this theory, a city's export industries are its economic foundation, its source of growth, and therefore rightly called "basic." Other industries are said to live by servicing these basic industries (and one another) and are therefore called "nonbasic." If there is a

TABLE 7.1
Employment Forecast for a Hypothetical City

	ACTUAL EMPLOY-MENT 1970	PREDICTED EMPLOYMENT 1980
Basic employment (exports)	20,000	30,000
Nonbasic employment (service)	40,000	60,000
Total employment	60,000	90,000
Ratio of nonbasic to basic	2	2
Ratio of total to basic ("the multiplier")	3	3

change in the level of employment, or of activity measured in some other way, in the basic (i.e., export) sector, it will lead automatically to a change in the same direction in the nonbasic (i.e., service) sector. The theory holds that the ratio of nonbasic to basic employment (or activity) can be measured and is sufficiently stable so that future changes in total employment can be derived from forecasts of basic employment. And from future total employment it is but one step further to a prediction of future population.

Although references to an export-versus-service dichotomy can be found in the literature a decade earlier, the basic-nonbasic theory was first worked out in full by Homer Hoyt in the 1930's.[1] As an economist with the Federal Housing Administration in Washington, he needed a simple model of urban economic performance in order to assess the economic prospects of a multitude of cities. Thus from the very beginning simplicity has been an intended feature of the basic-nonbasic theory. And despite subsequent refinements, when the theory is compared with other methods, simplicity remains its leading virtue today.

Table 7.1 illustrates an application of the theory using hypothetical data. Suppose that in 1970 total employment in a certain city was 60,000, of which 20,000 was basic employment and 40,000 was nonbasic. The ratio of total to basic employment was therefore 3:1 in 1970. The analyst is asked to predict total employment in 1980. The basic-nonbasic theory (at least in its simplest form) tells him that the total-to-basic ratio will remain constant over time. Therefore if he can predict employment in the basic sector his problem is solved. Total employment in 1980 will simply be 3

1. For an account of the origin of the basic-nonbasic theory, see Richard B. Andrews, "Mechanics of the Urban Economic Base: Historical Development of the Base Concept," in R. W. Pfouts, ed., *The Techniques of Urban Economic Analysis* (West Trenton, N.J.: Chandler-Davis Publishing, 1960), pp. 5–17.

times basic employment. In the hypothetical case the analyst predicts that basic employment will rise to 30,000. It follows that nonbasic will increase to 60,000 and total to 90,000. As this example makes clear, the total-to-basic ratio is, in effect, an employment "multiplier." The change in basic employment times the multiplier yields the change in total employment.

The multiplier in the table is stated in terms of an average relationship, and the example shows that this average relationship is expected to be maintained over time. As a city grows, however, the ratio of total to basic employment typically increases (for reasons we will explain below). If this is the case, then the ratio of total to basic employment for changes at the margin must be greater than the average ratio. When the analyst has reason to believe that the marginal ratio differs from the average, he will prefer to use the marginal multiplier, which equals the ratio of change in total employment to change in basic employment. Stated that way, the relationship takes on a strong resemblance to some forms of the Keynesian multiplier. Later, when describing the foreign-trade multiplier method, we will show that the Keynesian and the basic-nonbasic multipliers are, in fact, formally equivalent. It is interesting to note, however, that the latter was developed quite independently of the Keynesian analysis.

The operational simplicity of the basic-nonbasic method derives from several factors. First of all, instead of having to predict changes in each industry, the analyst need concern himself only with the export trades. In any city these are a minor fraction of the whole. In addition, they often have the added virtue of being characterized by large firms. The time and effort needed to make predictions are thus minimized. Second, the method makes use of the most easily available local data, those on employment. True, the basic-nonbasic theory could be stated instead in terms of total payrolls or value added. Indeed, value added might be theoretically the soundest unit of account. But employment is an acceptable proxy for value added, and the data are easier to come by.

Lack of data on economic activity in cities is an acute problem and frequently dictates the form that a study of the urban economic base must take. In particular, although measurement of the relationship between the local economy and the nation as a whole is important in any such study, no data are regularly collected by any statistical agency on the flow of goods or capital funds into or out of even the largest cities. Unless the analyst can pay the cost of a sample survey to measure the size of such flows, he must fall back on some form of approximation. Here again, the basic-nonbasic method has the advantage of simplicity. It requires information only about the volume of local and export activity. Imports and capital flows are ignored. In the absence of direct data, the technique of approximation most frequently used to estimate export activity is the location quotient method.

Location Quotients As Export Allocators

The "location quotient" is a statistical device that measures, usually in terms of employment, the degree to which a given industry is concentrated in a given place. Quite apart from its role in estimating the level of exports, it is an extremely useful descriptive measure in urban studies. It is defined as the percentage of local employment accounted for by a given industry divided by the percentage of national employment in that industry. Suppose that in our hypothetical city shoe production makes up 2.5 percent of all employment, while in the United States as a whole it accounts for 2.0 percent. Then the location quotient for shoe production in the hypothetical city is .025 ÷ .020 = 1.25. When the value of the quotient is exactly unity the industry in question is present at the given place just to the same extent as in the whole nation. When it is above unity the industry is relatively concentrated at that place; when below unity, relatively scarce.

Now let us see how this device can be used to estimate the level of export activity. It will be convenient to use the following terms:

$$e_i = \text{local employment in the } i\text{th industry}$$
$$e = \text{total local employment}$$
$$E_i = \text{national employment in the } i\text{th industry}$$
$$E = \text{total national employment}$$

Then the location quotient for the ith industry is

$$\frac{e_i/e}{E_i/E}$$

To use this coefficient as the basis for estimating export activity, we must make the three following assumptions: (1) patterns of consumption do not vary geographically; (2) labor productivity does not vary geographically; (3) each industry produces a single, perfectly homogeneous good. Suppose that we are dealing once again with the shoe industry in our hypothetical city. Given the assumed uniformity of consumption patterns, local residents will wish to buy the same quantity of shoes per capita as does the nation as a whole. Barring international trade, the nation as a whole obtains the desired quantity of shoes when E_i/E percent of the national labor force is devoted to shoe production. Given the assumption of uniform labor productivity, it follows that the local demand for shoes can be satisfied from local production when $e_i/e = E_i/E$, which occurs when the location quotient for shoe production equals one. In short, when the location quotient for a particular industry is unity, local consumption can just be satisfied by local production. There will be neither exports nor imports. It follows that when the quotient exceeds unity, the city will be exporting, and when it falls short of unity, importing. The amount of employment in each industry that can be assumed to serve the export sector is precisely the amount that, so to speak, pushes the location quotient above one. This may be written algebraically as follows: let

$$X_i = \text{export employment in the } i\text{th industry}$$

Using terms previously defined,

$\dfrac{E_i}{E} = $ the percentage of local employment that would have to be devoted to production of the ith good to supply local demand

$\dfrac{e_i}{e} = $ the actual percentage of local employment devoted to such production

Then

$$X_i = \left(\frac{e_i}{e} - \frac{E_i}{E}\right) \cdot e$$

If the two terms inside the brackets are equal, the location quotient equals one, and export employment in the ith industry is zero.

In the hypothetical city described earlier, total local employment in 1970 was 60,000. For shoe production we gave the following: $e_i/e = .025$, $E_i/E = .020$. In that case we can calculate export employment in the shoe industry as follows:

$$X_i = (.025 - .020) \cdot 60,000 = 300$$

If we make a similar calculation for every local industry for which the location quotient exceeds one and sum the results, we obtain an estimate of total basic employment in the city. All other employment can then be classified as nonbasic. Thus the location quotient method allows us to estimate the size of the basic (or export) sector even though we have no direct observations of goods flows.

Unfortunately, such an estimate is open to question because the three assumptions on which the analysis rests are in varying degrees doubtful. The assumption of geographically uniform consumption patterns is not strictly valid. Climate in particular causes variation in the consumption of such things as clothing and heating fuels and equipment. Nor is the assumption of uniform productivity entirely accurate. These are minor shortcomings, however. The real difficulty lies in the third assumption: that each industry, taken over the whole nation, produces a single homogeneous good. Unless this is true, there is simply no warrant for assuming that when the location quotient equals one, local production will be entirely absorbed by local consumption, leaving nothing for export.

Suppose, for example, that the location quotient for book publishing

TABLE 7.2

Estimates of Export Percentages Based on Surveys and on Location Quotients, 1955–56

Manufacturing Industries	DECATUR		INDIANAPOLIS	
	Survey	Location Quotient	Survey	Location Quotient
Food	87%	71%	63%	24%
Chemicals	98	44	100	50
Printing	—	—	51	24
Primary metals	97	20	99	0
Fabricated metals	—	—	98	11
Nonelectrical machinery	97	74	98	38
Electrical machinery	—	—	100	67
Transportation equipment	100	45	100	68

Source: Charles M. Tiebout, *The Community Economic Base Study* (New York: Committee for Economic Development, December 1962), Supplementary Paper No. 16, Table 10, p. 49.

in Boston were equal to unity. The analysis requires us then to believe that the literary public in Boston reads only books published there and that no books published there are read in other places. The assumption of homogeneous goods is, in most cases, obviously wrong. What we call an "industry," even at the finest level of classification in the Bureau of the Budget's Standard Industrial Classification system, contains a multitude of firms that more often than not make differentiated products. Consequently there is a great deal of geographic cross-hauling of goods within given "industries." Boston's books are read in San Francisco and San Francisco's in Boston. Since this effect is systematically present in our economy, estimates of the amount of basic (or export) employment arrived at by the location quotient method are systematically biased downward. That means, in turn, that the multiplier, which equals total employment divided by basic employment, is biased upward.

A questionnaire survey is probably the most accurate method of estimating exports. Charles M. Tiebout, who wrote extensively on economic base studies, compared export percentages estimated by survey techniques with those arrived at by the location quotient method.[2] His figures for Indianapolis and Decatur are reproduced in Table 7.2. Clearly, the downward bias imparted by the location quotient method is not trivial.

2. Charles M. Tiebout, *The Community Economic Base Study* (New York: Committee for Economic Development, December 1962), Supplementary Paper No. 16. Data originally supplied by the Federal Reserve Bank of Chicago.

Measuring Indirect Exports

Tiebout concluded that despite its shortcomings the location quotient method should not be rejected out of hand, since it does cope, even if imperfectly, with the tricky question of indirect exports. This problem deserves careful attention. Suppose that in order to measure the export sector of a city the analyst decided to send a questionnaire to all local firms asking them how many workers they employed and what percentage of their sales were made to purchasers outside the city. He could then divide each firm's labor force between export and local employment by using the export percentage revealed in the questionnaire. Summing for all industries, he would arrive at a figure for total export employment. But this would be a measure of "direct exports" only. In leaving out "indirect exports," it would understate the true size of the local export sector.

Indirect exports occur whenever one local firm sells to another that in turn ships its products outside the city. Any local supplier of a local exporter is thus producing indirect exports. His dependence on the export market is just as real as that of the direct exporter and must be appropriately taken into account. Does the location quotient method do so? To some extent, yes. For example, if the shoe manufacturing industry has a high location quotient in our hypothetical city, then activities that specialize in direct service to the shoe industry are likely to have high location quotients, too, and will therefore also appear as exporters. As we will see, however, this is not the best way of taking the indirect effects of exports into account. Only the input-output method comes close to representing the true interrelatedness of industries in the local economy. We will take up that method after examining the foreign-trade multiplier analysis.

THE FOREIGN-TRADE MULTIPLIER APPROACH

The fundamental relationship posited by the basic-nonbasic theory is the dependence of total local employment on the level of employment in the export sector. The foreign-trade multiplier method, which developed out of Keynesian income-determination theory during the 1930's and 1940's, allows us to examine the same relationship at a much higher level of sophistication. This method has not been used widely in empirical studies of urban areas because it requires data on local income and the flow of trade into and out of local areas that are not ordinarily available. It merits attention, nonetheless, for the insights it provides into the behavior of the urban economy. The following version is necessarily highly abbreviated.

In the Keynesian system the aggregate income generated in an economy during a given period is shown to be equal to the aggregate of spending on final goods during that period. In a "closed economy"—that is, an economy with no foreign trade—spending on final goods comprises private consumption, private investment, and government spending on goods and services. This closed economy model is the one ordinarily dealt with in detail in a first course in principles of economics. Foreign trade can be introduced into it quite easily, however, to cover the case of an "open economy." The model including foreign trade was, of course, originally developed to deal with national economies, but since urban areas are also engaged in trade with places outside their own boundaries it applies with equal logic to them.

Exports, since they represent foreign spending to buy domestic final goods, make up a part of the aggregate spending on those goods just as do domestic consumption, investment, and government spending. By the same token, however, imports, which represent domestic consumption or investment that pays for foreign goods, are a subtraction from the demand for domestic output. Introducing foreign trade into the model, therefore, requires adding exports to and subtracting imports from the aggregate of spending that creates domestic income.

To simplify matters, let us make the following assumptions:

1. We are dealing with an urban economy in which there is no public sector. Therefore, all spending is either for private consumption or private investment.
2. All business income is paid out to individuals (i.e., there are no retained corporate profits). Therefore net national product and personal income are identical.
3. Imports are entirely for consumption, never for investment.
4. The level of investment spending is determined autonomously (i.e., is not dependent on the level of local income). For the purposes of this analysis it will be assumed constant.

The usual symbols for the components of aggregate spending are the following:

Y = net national product generated in the local area (by assumption equal to personal income)

C = spending on local consumption goods (including imports)

I = net spending on local investment (above depreciation allowances)

E = exports

M = imports (assumed to be only for consumption)

The relationship between income and spending is then expressed by the following identity (it is written as an identity because it is necessarily true by definition of its components):

$$Y \equiv C + I + E - M$$

While consumption is one of the components of aggregate spending that generate income, its level is also determined by the level of income generated. The dependence of consumption on income can be expressed by the following equation (or "consumption function"):

$$C = a + mpcY$$

where a is a positive constant and mpc is the marginal propensity to consume. The marginal propensity to consume expresses the relationship between increments of income received by consumers in the aggregate and the amount by which they increase consumption out of that increment. Empirical studies demonstrate that its value is positive but less than one— i.e., some income is saved. The above equation is written on the assumption that its value is also constant as income changes.

Imports are entirely for consumption, of which they form a part. We will assume that, like consumption, they are dependent on the level of income, that the marginal propensity to import (mpm) is positive but less than one and constant as income changes.

Personal income is either spent on consumption or saved. Since consumption varies with the level of income, it follows that saving must do so as well. In fact, the marginal propensity to save (mps) equals one minus the marginal propensity to consume.

Since imports are entirely for consumption, we can obtain the level of spending for locally produced consumption goods by subtracting imports from total consumption. The same relationship holds for incremental changes: the marginal propensity to consume local goods ($mpcl$) equals the marginal propensity to consume minus the marginal propensity to import.

We can write the marginal relationships in the system as follows:

$$\text{marginal propensity to consume} = mpc = \frac{\Delta C}{\Delta Y}$$

$$\text{marginal propensity to import} = mpm = \frac{\Delta M}{\Delta Y}$$

$$\text{marginal propensity to save} = mps = 1 - mpc$$

$$\text{marginal propensity to consume local goods} = mpcl = mpc - mpm$$

Using the fundamental income identity and the terms defined above we can now derive an equation for the "foreign trade multiplier." This multiplier shows how much local income will change for a given change in the level of exports. If we use the symbol K for the multiplier, then we may define it as

$$K = \frac{\Delta Y}{\Delta E}$$

The fundamental income identity tells us that $Y \equiv C + I + E - M$. It follows that any change in Y must equal the sum of changes in the terms on the right side of the identity. Thus we can write

$$\Delta Y \equiv \Delta C + \Delta I + \Delta E - \Delta M$$

However,

$$\Delta C = mpc\ \Delta Y$$

and

$$\Delta M = mpm\ \Delta Y$$

Substituting these expressions into the preceding equation and rearranging the order of the terms, we obtain

$$\Delta Y = mpc\ \Delta Y - mpm\ \Delta Y + \Delta I + \Delta E$$

This can be rewritten as

$$\Delta Y = \Delta Y(mpc - mpm) + \Delta I + \Delta E$$

Transposing the first term on the right to the left side, we obtain

$$\Delta Y - \Delta Y(mpc - mpm) = \Delta I + \Delta E$$

After factoring, this becomes

$$\Delta Y[1 - (mpc - mpm)] = \Delta I + \Delta E$$

Whence

$$\Delta Y = \frac{1}{1 - (mpc - mpm)}(\Delta I + \Delta E)$$

Assuming $\Delta I = 0$ and recalling that $K = \dfrac{\Delta Y}{\Delta E}$ we find

$$K = \frac{1}{1 - (mpc - mpm)}$$

This can be stated in many equivalent forms. For example, since $mpc - mpm$ has been defined as the marginal propensity to consume local goods, or $mpcl$, we can also write

$$K = \frac{1}{1 - mpcl}$$

Thus any change in local exports, ΔE, will lead to a change in local income, ΔY, that is K times as great, where the value of K is given by either of the above expressions. Strictly speaking, this version of the multiplier is only a first approximation, a sort of partial equilibrium statement that ignores interregional feedback effects. A version that sought to capture all the effects of a change in one area's exports would take into account the following sequence for two regions trading with each other: a rise in region A's exports to region B leads to an increase in A's income and hence in its imports from B. These imports are region B's exports and induce a rise in region B's income, which leads to a further rise in B's imports, which are A's exports, and so on in diminishing series. If, however, we are analyzing an urban area that is relatively small in relation to the national economy with which it trades, these repercussions may safely be ignored.

As the derivation above illustrates, the same multiplier effect occurs if the level of investment spending rather than the level of exports changes, or if both change simultaneously. Indeed, for any autonomous change in spending, including government spending on goods and services (which would be included in a more complete model), or a shift in the consumption function, the same multiplier operates.

Some of the characteristics of the multiplier can be read directly from its formula. We know that its value must be positive and greater than one from the following argument: If there is any local service sector at all, the marginal propensity to consume local goods will almost certainly be greater than zero. If there is any foreign trade at all, it will almost certainly be less than one. Consequently the denominator of the multiplier must also be positive but less than one. The multiplier itself must therefore have a value that is positive and greater than one. Moreover, this value will be greater, the larger is the marginal propensity to consume and the smaller is the marginal propensity to import.

The Similarity of the Keynesian and Basic-Nonbasic Multipliers

The resemblance between the Keynesian multiplier and the basic-nonbasic multiplier, mentioned earlier, goes beyond the fact that both relate increases or decreases in total local employment to increases or decreases in export employment. In addition, there is a strong formal similarity between the two formulas. The marginal form of the basic-nonbasic multiplier has already been given (in units of employment) as:

$$K = \Delta \text{ total}/\Delta \text{ basic}$$

Since

$$\Delta \text{ basic} = \Delta \text{ total} - \Delta \text{ nonbasic}$$

we can also write the multiplier as

$$K = \Delta \text{ total}/(\Delta \text{ total} - \Delta \text{ nonbasic})$$

which can readily be transformed into

$$K = \frac{1}{1 - \dfrac{\Delta \text{ nonbasic}}{\Delta \text{ total}}}$$

The basic-nonbasic theory is usually stated in terms of employment units. However, as we noted, this is done largely for statistical convenience since employment data are the most readily available. The theory could equally well be posed in terms of factor income arising in each of the sectors, with sector employment regarded simply as an acceptable proxy for that measure in applying the theory. If the multiplier were stated in terms of income arising in each sector it would read:

$$K = \frac{1}{1 - \dfrac{\text{nonbasic sector income}}{\text{total income}}}$$

Now compare that formulation with the Keynesian multiplier, where

$$K = \frac{1}{1 - mpcl}$$

The term *mpcl* in the Keynesian version is the marginal propensity to consume locally produced goods. The term "Δ nonbasic sector income ÷ Δ total income" in the basic-nonbasic multiplier is analogous to that. Nonbasic sector income is income arising from sales within the local community. Although imports are sold locally, their consumption, as Nourse points out, does not give rise to local employment or income.[3] Any change in nonbasic sector income that occurs must therefore be the result of the consumption of locally produced goods. When such a change is divided by the change in total income that causes it we have a ratio that is equivalent to the marginal propensity to consume locally produced goods in the Keynesian multiplier. Hence the two multipliers are essentially the same.

The analogy should not be pressed too far, however. The basic-non-basic theory makes no distinction between employment to produce consumption goods and employment to produce investment goods. Ordinarily the nonbasic sector will include some investment activity—for example, via employment in the local construction industry, which builds investment goods such as houses and factories for local use. It may be convenient to assume that the investment component of nonbasic activity responds to

3. Hugh O. Nourse, *Regional Economics* (New York: McGraw-Hill, 1968), p. 161.

changes in the export sector via precisely the same multiplier that determines the level of other nonbasic activity. The assumption is tenuous, however, since local investment is often influenced not only by the level of local exports but by other forces, both internal and external, that are not specified in the model. It is precisely in this regard that the Keynesian multiplier analysis is conceptually superior to the basic-nonbasic: it introduces investment as an explicit category of spending and allows the relationship of investment to income and to other variables in the system to be handled in a variety of ways. We will not trace out these variations, however, because, despite its conceptual superiority, the Keynesian analysis has rarely been applied to urban areas. As we have already pointed out, the necessary data are simply too difficult to obtain at the local level.

A CRITIQUE OF THE BASIC-NONBASIC METHOD

Because its data requirements were so much easier to meet than those of the foreign-trade multiplier model, the basic-nonbasic method was frequently used for empirical studies in the 1940's and 1950's. Unfortunately, the method suffers from so many serious defects, both in theory and practice, that few economists today would endorse its use. It will suffice here to mention just a few of these difficulties.

Excessive Aggregation

First of all, the model loses a great deal in being so highly aggregated. The division of activity into only two classes is too gross to capture the complex interindustry relations of an urban economy. This is not merely a matter of theoretical nicety. It also reduces the accuracy with which the model does its job of prediction. The basic-nonbasic multiplier represents the average response of the whole nonbasic sector to a change in the level of all exports. If only one industry's exports were to increase there is no reason to assume that nonbasic activity would respond in this average way. For example, an export industry that relies heavily on imported components and materials will certainly transmit weaker impulses to the nonbasic sector than will an export industry that buys heavily from local suppliers. Hence predictions made by the model about the level of total activity are likely to be wrong unless all exports are expected to change simultaneously by the same percentage.

This problem can be looked at in another way. One of the purposes of economic base analysis is to predict the impact on the local economy of expected changes in the export sector. For example, a city with a large defense plant wants to know what will happen if a policy of disarmament closes that plant down. Not only will the basic-nonbasic model probably predict the wrong overall impact for the reasons just given, but also it will be unable to say which parts of the nonbasic sector will suffer more and which less. Such details would be far more useful than a simple statement about the average impact, even if it were correct. As we will see, the difficulties that result from excessive aggregation can be overcome by using the more complex input-output method.

The Instability of the Multiplier in the Short Run

A second series of difficulties centers around the time dimensions of the basic-nonbasic model. The analysis may be thought of as dealing either with the short run or the long run. A typical short-run problem would be a defense-industry impact study of the sort just described or a prediction of the consequences for the local community of an expected swing in the national business cycle. The method assumes that impulses from the export sector have a multiplied effect on the local economy as a whole, that the size of the multiplier can be calculated, and that its value will be sufficiently stable over the short run to warrant using it to predict the extent of the local economy's response to exogenous change. Unhappily the multiplier has not proven to be stable in the short run and is consequently unreliable as a tool for short-run prediction.[4]

The instability of the multiplier in the short run can probably be ascribed to lagged adjustment. Let us grant that for a city with a given population, economic structure, and location, at a given time in economic history, there is a "true" or equilibrium ratio of service to basic activity. If the level of basic activity changes, the response of service activity will not occur instantly and may well be drawn out over many years. Indeed, if its export sales are continually in flux, a city may be always moving toward its "true" ratio without ever reaching it. Under these circumstances the difficulty of determining the "true" ratio or of deciding what other ratio to use and how to allow for time lags in making short-run forecasts is obviously enormous. Given the other weakness of the basic-nonbasic method this sort of refinement has not seemed worth undertaking.

Changes in the Multiplier over the Long Run

Even if the basic-nonbasic analysis is ineffective for short-run prediction, might it still be reliable for long-run forecasts? Here the objective would be to predict the long-run growth of employment and population

4. See evidence cited in Walter Isard, *Methods of Regional Analysis* (New York: John Wiley & Sons and the Technology Press of Massachusetts Institute of Technology, 1960), p. 201. The book offers a detailed analysis of the basic-nonbasic method at pp. 189–205.

in a metropolitan area on the basis of the long-run prospects for its exports. Will the method perhaps work better in the long run when fluctuations in the multiplier can somehow be averaged out to determine its true value and the usual adjustment lags will no longer matter? The answer is clearly "no," for in the long run all the variables of taste, technology, population size, and economic structure that must be held constant in order even to conceive of a "true" or equilibrium ratio are free to vary. If there is a true ratio it will almost certainly change as time passes. Once again, the effort that would be required to overcome the difficulty—for example, by estimating long-run changes in the multiplier for a particular city—is simply not justified, given the other limitations of the basic-nonbasic method.

One source of long-run change in the ratio of basic to nonbasic activity is the growth of a city's population. Central place analysis, already presented in Chapter 5, tells us that the larger the market in a community the more services that community will provide for itself and the fewer it will have to import from other centers, for as a city grows in population it will pass successive "threshold" levels at which local provision of additional services becomes profitable. Translated into basic-nonbasic terminology, this means that the ratio of nonbasic to basic activity will rise as a city grows and that the multiplier, which equals the ratio of total to basic activity, will also rise. Not surprisingly, population growth has the same implications when the multiplier is expressed in Keynesian terms. As the city's economy grows, its average propensity to import will fall. A lower marginal propensity to import is likely to be associated with this lower average propensity. The Keynesian multiplier increases in size as the marginal propensity to import falls. Consequently the value of the Keynesian multiplier will also increase as a city's economy grows.

Empirical studies do confirm the tendency of the nonbasic sector to grow relative to the basic as a city's population rises through time. For example, Britton Harris calculated values of the basic-nonbasic multiplier for 67 Standard Metropolitan Areas in 1940 and 1950.[5] Population increased in each of these metropolitan areas over that interval. The nonbasic-to-basic ratio—which necessarily equals the multiplier minus one—rose in 57 of the 67 cases. Its failure to increase in the remaining 10 cases might well be evidence of the lagged adjustment process mentioned above.

The same tendency can be observed if we compare the nonbasic-to-basic ratios of large and small cities at a given moment in time. Table 7.3, derived form Harris' data, compares the ratios for 1950 in the six metropolitan areas with population above 2 million and the six metropolitan

5. Britton Harris, "Comment on Pfouts' Test of the Base Theory," *Journal of the American Institute of Planners,* November 1958, p. 236. Harris' calculations are based on data from the *Census of Population.*

areas in his sample having the smallest population. The nonbasic-to-basic ratio averaged 4.02 in the largest areas but only 2.77 in the smallest ones.

To be sure, empirical studies also show that the relationship between size and the nonbasic-to-basic ratio is a far from perfect one. Cities of the same size vary widely in economic structure. For example, Table 7.3 shows that Detroit has a much smaller nonbasic sector than the average metropolitan area of its size. Indeed, Detroit is known to be a not very metropolitan metropolis, and the economic data confirm this.

Undoubtedly, as central place analysis would suggest, the location

TABLE 7.3

Ratios of Nonbasic to Basic Activity in Large and Small Metropolitan Areas, 1950

STANDARD METROPOLITAN AREA	POPULATION [a]	NONBASIC EMPLOYMENT ÷ BASIC EMPLOYMENT
Six areas with largest population [b]		
New York-Northeast New Jersey	10,232,039	4.03
Chicago	4,285,902	3.65
Los Angeles	3,405,797	4.15
Philadelphia	2,848,698	5.99
Detroit	2,269,725	2.19
Boston-Lawrence-Lowell	2,049,947	4.13
Mean—largest areas		4.02
Six areas with smallest population [c]		
Erie	163,850	2.37
South Bend	155,535	1.84
Charlotte	144,579	3.33
Fort Wayne	138,110	2.88
El Paso	137,221	3.42
Evansville	120,695	2.75
Mean—smallest areas		2.77

[a] Population data based on 1950 definitions of Standard Metropolitan Areas.

[b] The six largest SMA's in Harris' sample were also the six largest in the nation.

[c] These were the six smallest SMA's in Harris' sample, though not the smallest in the nation.

Source: Britton Harris, "Comment on Pfouts' Test of the Base Theory," *Journal of the American Institute of Planners,* November 1958, p. 236.

of a given city in relation to competing centers affects the relative size of its nonbasic sector. We would expect a small city that is close to a large metropolis to have fewer local service activities than a city of equal size that is geographically isolated. Table 7.3 perhaps illustrates the point. South Bend, which is less than 100 miles from Chicago, has a nonbasic-to-basic ratio of only 1.84, while El Paso, a smaller metropolitan area that is many hundreds of miles from any large center, has a ratio of 3.42.

The inability of simple two-sector models adequately to depict urban economic structure has been amply demonstrated. In recent years most students of the urban economic base have therefore favored the multisector approach known as input-output analysis. This method, as we will see, enables one to lay bare both the internal and the external relationships of an urban economy in great detail. In this respect it overcomes many of the defects of the simpler methods, especially for purposes of short-run analysis. So far as long-run applications are concerned, however, input-output analysis does not in itself offer a solution to the problem of predicting growth and change. We will return to this problem below.

INPUT-OUTPUT ANALYSIS

Input-output analysis was developed by Wassily W. Leontief at Harvard, beginning in the 1930's. Inspired by Walras' theory of general equilibrium, which depicted the interrelationship of each economic sector with every other, Leontief sought a scheme in which those interrelationships could be quantified to yield an actual working model of the economy. The result was input-output analysis, a method specifically designed to portray in great detail the actual interindustry relationships of a real economy. The method was first applied to the national economy of the United States. In the 1950's economists began to adapt it for regional and urban use.[6]

Although input-output analysis can become highly complex, its analytical framework is based on a simple accounting identity that can be stated as follows: for each sector or industry the sum of all outputs (sold to other sectors or industries) must equal the sum of all inputs (purchased from other sectors or industries), provided we take care not to omit any transactions. This is equivalent to the accounting identity for an individual firm, which states that total receipts must equal total costs plus profit. If

6. For a more detailed account of input-output analysis in a regional setting (but one that is nevertheless comprehensible to the beginning student) see Isard, Ch. 8. William H. Miernyk's *The Elements of Input-Output Analysis* (New York: Random House, 1965) also provides an excellent introduction to the subject.

such an identity holds for each industry and sector separately it must also be true in the aggregate: total inputs to the economy equal its total output.

The full array of input-output relationships for an economy can be shown conveniently in a two-way table or matrix such as Table 7.4. Down the left-hand side are listed the sectors or industries producing outputs. Across the top the same sectors or industries are listed as purchasers of inputs from the sectors at the left.

A crucial assumption is introduced in order to simplify the relationships between the sectors: the assumption that all production processes have fixed technical coefficients. This means that no matter what the level of production in a given industry, it is assumed that inputs are required in fixed proportions to output. For example, the same number of tons of coal will be required to produce a ton of steel whether steel output is high or low, and the same number of yards of cloth and hours of labor will be needed to make a suit of clothes whether clothing production is up or down.

As a further simplification, the input-output method states the input coefficients not in physical units but in cents worth of input per dollar of output. Thus the input of electric power needed to produce aluminum would be stated, not as kilowatts per ton, but as cents worth of electricity per dollar's worth of aluminum output. An input-output model is generally employed to analyze change through time rather than simply to describe a perfectly static situation. In that case, the use of constant input coefficients expressed in monetary units implies an assumption that as

TABLE 7.4
Input-Output Table for a Hypothetical City
(Flows expressed in millions of dollars)

| Sector Producing \ Sector Purchasing | PROCESSING SECTOR | | | FINAL DEMAND SECTOR | ROW TOTALS |
	1 Manufac-turing	2 Services	3 House-holds	4 Exports	(Output)
1. Manufacturing (X_m)	—	10	40	50	100
2. Services (X_s)	30	—	60	10	100
3. Households (X_h)	30	70	—	—	100
4. Imports	40	20	—	—	60
Column Totals (Inputs)	100	100	100	60	360

the level or composition of output changes through time the relative prices of all goods will remain as they were in the base year.

Table 7.4 shows a highly compressed version of an input-output table for a hypothetical city. The unit of measurement is millions of dollars per year. To simplify matters we assume that labor and management are the only factors of production. Since capital is not employed, all transactions are on current account, and it is unnecessary to have a heading for capital transactions. The government, if there is one, exists without levying taxes or spending money, so no government sector appears in the table.

Of course, our example contains nothing like the detail that would be incorporated in an actual input-output study. In addition to including separate sectors for government and capital transactions, such studies attempt to divide industry into relatively fine classes. The degree of detail achieved depends upon the time and money available for the study. Generally it varies from 20 to 30 sectors to the nearly 600 used in the Philadelphia Region Input-Output Study directed by Walter Isard.[7]

In our highly compressed model, industry is divided into only two types—manufacturing and service. In addition, the table shows a household sector and a foreign trade sector. Moving across each row one reads the sales by the industry or sector named at the left to the industries and sectors named across the top. For simplicity it is assumed that there are no sales within sectors (an assumption that is not made in actual studies). Thus the first column in the first row is blank. Reading to the right across the first row we see that manufacturers sell $10 million of output per year to the service sector and $40 million to households and that they ship $50 million of exports to purchasers outside the area. The sum of these sales is total manufacturing output of $100 million shown in the right-hand column. Output and sales by the service industry are shown in row 2.

Household "output," recorded in row 3, consists of labor and management compensated by wages and salaries. The table indicates that each year households sell $30 million worth of labor and management to manufacturing and $70 million worth to service industries. The total value of this output—$100 million, as shown in the last column—is also total household income.

Just as each row shows sales by the sector listed at the left, so each column shows purchases by the sector named at the top. The entry at the bottom of each column is the sum of that sector's purchases. Because inputs equal outputs for each sector, the figure for total purchases at the bottom of each sector's column equals the figure for total sales at the end of that sector's row. Since the table shows the sales of each local sector to

7. Walter Isard, E. Romanoff, and T. W. Langford, Jr., *Working Papers, Philadelphia Region Input-Output Study* (Philadelphia: Regional Science Research Institute, 1967).

every other as well as the transactions of each with the outside world, it offers a complete and logically consistent picture of economic activity in the area under study.

Our highly simplified model, unrealistic though it may be, is convenient for showing how input-output analysis works. The logical starting point for such an explanation, however, is not Table 7.4 but Table 7.5. The latter shows the same industries and sectors as the former, but instead of presenting sales and purchases it records the values of the various input coefficients for industries in our hypothetical city. For example, reading down column 1 we see that the manufacturing industry requires 30 cents worth of service inputs, 30 cents worth of household inputs (i.e., labor and management), and 40 cents worth of imports for each dollar of output. A somewhat different set of coefficients appears in the service industry column: the service industry uses more labor and less imports per dollar of output than does manufacturing. The input coefficients for households, while analogous to those for industry, might better be thought of as representing the division of household purchases between locally produced manufactures (40 percent) and locally produced services (60 percent). Households import nothing directly. The input coefficients in every column add up to unity.

The Relationship Between the Structural Matrix and the Final Demand Sector

In any application of the input-output method the analyst must divide his industries or sectors into two groups, one called collectively the "final demand sector," the other collectively the "processing sector" or

TABLE 7.5
Input Coefficients of Industries in a Hypothetical City

	DOLLARS WORTH OF INPUTS PER DOLLAR OF OUTPUT IN:		
	1 *Manufacturing*	2 *Services*	3 *Households*
Inputs Purchased from Sources Below:			
1. Manufacturing	—	.10	.40
2. Services	.30	—	.60
3. Households	.30	.70	—
4. Imports	.40	.20	—
Sum of coefficients	1.00	1.00	1.00

"structural matrix." The division will vary according to the scope and purpose of the analysis. It is intended to reflect in each case a distinction between those "outside" (exogenous) sectors in which the level of activity is
autonomously determined and those "inside" (endogenous) sectors in which
the level of activity can be explained by the model. The former group make
up the final demand sector, the latter group the processing sector. The
entire analysis rests on the premise that the autonomous "outside" forces
to which the processing sector responds are those issuing from the final
demand sector. The level and composition of final demand thus determine the level and composition of activity inside the structural matrix.
The relationship can be expressed another way. The industries within the
structural matrix are regarded as a set of "processors" whose output goes
to satisfy the requirements of the final demand sector. Once the dollar
value of those final demand requirements is specified, the value of all the
inputs and outputs necessary to supply it is automatically determined.

The manner in which industries within the structural matrix respond
to demands put upon them from the outside is controlled entirely by the
input coefficients that establish relationships within the matrix. The logic
of input-output analysis therefore reduces to this: calculate input coefficients to delineate the processing sector, confront that sector with a set of
final demands, and it follows that the output of every industry, its transactions with every other industry, and the output of the system as a whole
will be fully determined.

In the hypothetical urban economy shown in Tables 7.4 and 7.5,
the final demand sector consists only of exports. Manufacturing, services,
and households are placed within the structural matrix. Thus the model
posits that the level of activity in the two local industries and the income
of households, which depends on that level, are determined entirely by
the demand of the outside world for the city's exports. In a more complex
and realistic analysis the final demand group would also include the government and capital-formation sectors omitted here. These sectors would
be placed in the category of final demand because the levels of activity
within them cannot reasonably be explained by means of fixed coefficients
relating their output to the level of activity in the industries within the
structural matrix. Instead, the dollar value of government activity and of
capital formation is assumed to be autonomously determined.

The Simple Mathematics of Input-Output Analysis

The relationship between the parts of an input-output table can
best be understood by means of some simple mathematics. Each row of
the table of input coefficients can be read as part of an equation for the

total output of the industry named at the left end of that row. Let us employ the following terms:

$$X_m = \text{total manufacturing output}$$
$$X_s = \text{total service output}$$
$$X_h = \text{total household output}$$

Using the input coefficients given in Table 7.5, we can show that the equations for these outputs are

$$X_m = .1X_s + .4X_h + \text{exports}$$
$$X_s = .3X_m + .6X_h + \text{exports}$$
$$X_h = .3X_m + .7X_s + \text{exports}$$

What the first equation states is that total manufacturing output must be sufficient to supply the required manufacturing exports (i.e., final demand) and in addition to supply the other two processing sectors with the manufacturing inputs that *they* need. What the other sectors require is given to us by the table of input coefficients. We know that the service industry needs 10 cents worth of manufacturing inputs for every dollar of its output. Its output will be X_s. Therefore the service industry will require $.1X_s$ of manufacturing inputs. This is the first term in the equation for required manufacturing output. Similarly the table of input coefficients tells us that households will require 40 cents worth of manufacturing inputs for every dollar of their output. Therefore the second term in the equation for manufacturing output is $.4X_h$. The equations for service output and household output are similarly constructed.

We have written three equations, which appear to contain six unknowns: X_m, X_s, X_h, and the level of exports for each of the three sectors. Exports, however, are not an unknown to be solved for in the analysis. Rather they are the "final demands" that the local economy responds to. Their value is determined outside the system. Let us assume that the manufacturing sector must produce $50 million of exports, the service sector $10 million, and the household sector none. Then our equations become

$$X_m = .1X_s + .4X_h + 50$$
$$X_s = .3X_m + .6X_h + 10$$
$$X_h = .3X_m + .7X_s + 0$$

We now have three equations containing only three unknowns. A solution must exist, and anyone who recalls his high school algebra can find it by the usual method for solving "simultaneous equations." (In actual practice, input-output tables contain far too many sectors and therefore too many simultaneous equations to permit solution by simple hand methods. The job can be done, however, by using matrix algebra and a high-speed computer.) In this instance the solution has already been given in Table 7.4. Total output of each of the processing sectors will be $100 million, which, as the input-output table shows, will enable each sector to supply the required exports plus the inputs simultaneously needed by each of the other sectors. Since total inputs equal total output for each sector, we can calculate imports for each by subtracting all other inputs from total output. The total income generated by the local economy is the sum of all returns to local factors of production. Since the factors of production—in this case labor and management—are provided by households, locally generated income equals household receipts of $100 million.

The Advantages of a Disaggregated Model

Input-output analysis is flexible enough to serve many purposes. The simplest of these is straightforward description. A detailed input-output table is a unique map of an economy as it functions in a particular year, showing the flows of goods and services among all the local sectors and between each of them and the outside world. More interesting, however, is the way in which the method can be used to answer questions about the effects of predicted changes. Because it is so much more highly disaggregated than the basic-nonbasic or foreign-trade multiplier models, it answers questions not only in greater detail but, in all likelihood, with far greater accuracy.

Suppose, for example, that we wish to know what the effect on the local economy will be of a predicted change in the level of exports. Both of the other methods use an aggregate multiplier that is averaged over all the export sectors. Therefore the predicted effect of, say, a $10 million increase in exports will be the same no matter which exporting industry enjoys the increase. Not so with input-output analysis, as the following example will demonstrate.

Let us assume that the situation in the base year is represented in Table 7.4. Exports total $60 million, of which $50 million is from the manufacturing and $10 million from the service sector. Local income equals $100 million per year. Now compare the effects of a $10 million increase in exports alternatively of the manufacturing sector and of the service sector. The results are shown in Table 7.6, which contains two entries in each cell of the input-output table. The upper entry in each cell shows the outcome when manufacturing exports rise from $50 to $60 million while service exports remain at $10 million. The lower entry shows the results when service exports rise from $10 to $20 million while manufacturing exports are held constant at $50 million.

TABLE 7.6

Results of Export Expansion in a Hypothetical City: Two Cases [a]
(Flows expressed in millions of dollars)

Sector Producing		1 Manufac-turing	2 Services	3 House-holds	4 Exports	(Output)
	Sector Purchasing	PROCESSING SECTOR			FINAL DEMAND SECTOR	ROW TOTALS
1. Manufacturing	1st case	—	11.5	46.2	60.0	117.7
	2nd case	—	12.7	48.9	50.0	111.6
2. Services	1st case	35.3	—	69.4	10.0	114.7
	2nd case	33.5	—	73.4	20.0	126.9
3. Households	1st case	35.3	80.3	—	—	115.6
	2nd case	33.5	88.8	—	—	122.3
4. Imports	1st case	47.1	22.9	—	—	70.0
	2nd case	44.6	25.4	—	—	70.0
Column Totals (Inputs)	1st case	117.7	114.7	115.6	70.0	418.0
	2nd case	111.6	126.9	122.3	70.0	430.9

[a] The two cases are: 1st case—manufacturing exports = $60 million, service exports = $10 million
2nd case—manufacturing exports = $50 million, service exports = $20 million

We can see at once that the outcome is entirely different in the two cases. Most notably, household income rises to $122.3 million when service exports increase by $10 million but reaches only $115.6 million when manufacturing exports rise by that amount. Why should service exports have so much stronger an effect, dollar for dollar, on local income? The answer can be deduced from an examination of the input coefficients in Table 7.5. The manufacturing sector uses 40 cents worth of imports per dollar of production, while the service sector uses only 20 cents worth. Consequently a dollar increase in service exports involves much less leakage of spending outside the economy in the form of increased imports than does a dollar increase in exports of the manufacturing sector. Less leakage means a larger increase in the demand for local output and hence a greater ultimate expansion of local output and income.

The expansion process can be viewed as a round by round series of increments. When manufacturing exports rise by $10 million, the input coefficients in column 1 of Table 7.5 show that the direct requirements to produce that output are $3 million of service inputs, $3 million of household inputs, and $4 million of imported goods. But that is only the first round of requirements, since those inputs themselves must be produced, giving rise to a second round of expansion. Specifically, in order to produce that $3 million of output sold to the manufacturing sector, the service sector requires $2.1 million of household inputs, $.3 million of manufacturing inputs, and $.6 million of imported goods. Likewise, the household sector receiving $3 million of additional income from sales to the manufacturing sector will buy (as, so to speak, its additional inputs) $1.2 million of manufactured goods and $1.8 million of services. These requirements comprise the second round of the expansion. Since they, too, must be produced there is a third round, and so on in diminishing series. The final expansion, as shown in Table 7.6, is the sum of this infinite series of rounds. We can now see that a $10 million increase in service exports leads to a greater expansion of local income than a similar increase in manufacturing exports primarily because on the first round of service industry expansion $8 million of spending remains within the community, while for an equal increase in manufacturing exports only $6 million of first-round spending would do so. And if the first round is smaller, subsequent rounds based on it will be reduced, too.

This illustration suggests another of the many uses for input-output analysis: it can show precisely what the total direct and indirect input requirements would be for an expected increase in output for final demand by a particular sector. Information of that kind might be crucial to city planners—for example, in anticipating the requirements for indirect services such as housing and transportation that would accompany a projected expansion of a major local industry. Or, if the trend is reversed and cutbacks are expected in a major local industry—say, a defense plant—the analysis will tell not just the aggregate output reduction to be expected as the sum of direct plus indirect effects, but also precisely which sectors will suffer how much of a decline in activity.

Input-Output Multipliers

The expansion or contraction of a local economy in response to a change in final demand as explained by input-output analysis is as much a multiplier process as were the expansions previously described by means of the other two models. This is one ground for stating, as we did earlier, that the three models are fundamentally similar in their logical structure. A second ground is the division of the economy in all three cases into an

TABLE 7.7

Variation in Multiplier Effect Depending on Which Sector Expands Exports

	CHANGE IN EXPORTS	CHANGE IN INCOME	MULTIPLIER
	($ MILLIONS)		
	(ΔE)	(ΔY)	$\Delta Y/\Delta E$
1st case: manufacturing exports rise by $10 million	10	15.6	1.56
2nd case: service exports rise by $10 million	10	22.3	2.23
3rd case: each export category rises by ⅙ (manufacturing rises $8.33 million; service rises $1.67 million)	10	16.7	1.67

NOTE: In each case the total increase in exports = $10 million. All changes are measured from initial equilibrium shown in Table 7.4. Full results for the first two cases, but not the third, are shown in Table 7.6.

outside, or exogenously oriented, sector in which the level of activity is autonomously determined and an inside, or endogenous, sector that responds passively to the stimulus transmitted from the other. A third is the mathematically similar character of the three multiplier relationships. In each case the multiplier is based on one or more system coefficients that are assumed to be fixed, at least in the short run: the basic-nonbasic ratio, the marginal propensity to import, and, finally, the set of technical input coefficients.

As we have shown, however, the value of the multiplier under input-output analysis varies according to which sector receives the initial impulse. Conceptually a variety of multipliers can be distinguished in an input-output model.[8] We have been discussing one that can be defined as the change in income divided by the change in exports. For our hypothetical city, the different values this multiplier takes—depending on the composition of the change in exports—are shown in Table 7.7. The first two rows we have already explained. The third represents the special case of a uniform expansion of exports: each sector's exports increase by the same ratio, in this case one-sixth. The resulting rise in income is $16.7 million. Initial income was $100 million, and 16.7 ÷ 100 = ⅙. Thus income has increased by the same proportion that exports increased. The case illustrates a basic property of the input-output model: if every element in the final demand sector increases by a given percentage, the entire trans-

8. See Miernyk, pp. 42–55.

actions matrix expands by the same percentage. In short, it "blows up" uniformly. This characteristic results from the assumption that input co-efficients remain constant as the economy expands, which means, in effect, that marginal relationships and average relationships are equal. If this equality were assumed in either of the other two models it would have precisely the same results: an increase of k percent in exports (or, in the Keynesian model, in exports plus other autonomous components of spend-ing) would lead to an increase of k percent in output and income.

The theoretical superiority of input-output analysis to other methods of analyzing the urban economic base is abundantly clear. Unfortunately, there are severe data problems. It is difficult enough to gather the numbers required for an input-output table for the United States as a whole. It is even more difficult for smaller regions, since in general the smaller the area, the less statistical detail is available in published sources. Basically the analyst has two alternatives: he can gather his own technical data by conducting an independent interview and questionnaire survey of the local area, or he can use the technical coefficients already calculated by the De-partment of Commerce for national input-output tables. The first is ex-pensive if carried out in any detail. The second, though widely adopted, runs the risk of throwing away just those special features of the local economy that may have suggested the need for a study in the first place and that, in any event, it is risky to suppress.

The Limitations of a Static Model

The input-output model discussed up to this point is essentially a static one. Fundamentally, it is a highly detailed map of the interindustry relationships in an economy *at a moment in time*. Such a model is highly effective for analyzing short-run problems such as the impact of an antici-pated change in final demand on the level and composition of local activity and income. A static model, however, cannot cope with the long-run prob-lems of urban change and growth. Economic development and urbaniza-tion are processes in which crucial relationships are continually changing. They cannot even be approximated by the linear expansion of a system whose internal relationships are fixed. The assumption of fixed input co-efficients is not tenable over the long run.

As numerous students of input-output analysis have pointed out, fixed coefficients of production and fixed relative prices are unlikely to prevail in the long run for a variety of reasons. Most basic of these is the pervasive influence of technological innovation, which consists precisely either of changes in the way inputs are combined to produce given outputs or in the development of entire ranges of new products that render old goods and the methods of producing them obsolete. The revolutionary effect of the automobile and truck suggests how profound these influences can be over a period of a few decades. They not only made other modes of transportation obsolete for certain purposes but rendered obsolete the physical layout of the older central cities themselves.

Technological change affects relative input prices directly. Quite apart from that, however, differential price changes between inputs or, for a given input, between regions may occur either because resource supplies are limited or because the demand for various resources changes differentially over time. And we know that as relative input prices change, producers will substitute those that are becoming relatively cheaper for those that are not. Input coefficients will not remain fixed.

In the long run, local growth itself is bound to affect local input coefficients. First of all, growth fosters economies of agglomeration. These, by their very definition, are increases in the technical efficiency of certain inputs as city size increases. Second, there are the central place effects of growth operating through market size. As an urban market grows, it becomes profitable to produce locally services that were formerly imported. Thus increasing urban size inevitably means change in urban economic structure.

Changes in local population characteristics, especially as a result of migration, are also likely to have important effects over the long run. Population change might affect both supply conditions, via changes in labor productivity, and demand conditions through shifts in the pattern of consumption.

There is no need to extend the list. Most of what we see currently as major urban problems have been caused by the long-run, dynamic forces of technological change, economic growth, and population movement. Can input-output analysis be made to handle these dynamic forces? The best answer, perhaps, is that its proponents believe it can, and they are trying. Fundamental technological innovations are unpredictable, but the rate at which existing technical improvements will be adopted by industry can be estimated. Long-run trends in relative prices can be measured. One can also estimate the effects of local market growth in bringing about the substitution of local production for imports. As Miernyk has shown, the probable results of these changes can be incorporated in a new set of local input coefficients to be used when making long-run projections based on input-output analysis.[9] The application of these dynamic adjustments, depending heavily as it does on the judgment of the analyst, is still far from an exact science. Nevertheless, it appears to offer the only real hope we have for obtaining useful long-run projections of local economic activity.

9. *Ibid.*, Ch. 6.

URBAN AND REGIONAL SIMULATION
MODELS

In recent years economists and city planners, spurred by the capacity of computers to operate with large systems of equations, have used computer simulation techniques in an attempt to create dynamic models of the urban economy that are even more comprehensive than an input-output analysis. What these models "simulate" is the movement of a city's or a region's economic system through time. Prescott and Mullendore, for example, constructed a simulation model for the eight-county region centered on Des Moines, Iowa.[10] The model contains five sub-sectors, labeled demographic, employment, output, final demand, and capital. The last three actually constitute an input-output model made dynamic by the inclusion of a sector linking net capital formation with the expansion of output. Thus the system as a whole is actually a dynamic input-output model with two additional sectors included to explain the growth of employment and population in a way that is consistent with the growth of output.

The following simplified explanation suggests how the parts of such a model are put together. The rate of growth of local output depends on the growth of exogenous demand and also on population growth determined in the demographic sector of the model and investment demand determined in its capital sector. Employment growth depends on the growth of output, moderated by an assumed trend in labor productivity. Employment provides a link between the output sector of the model and the demographic sector. To convey the sense of how simulation models work, let us examine the latter in somewhat more detail. The size and age distribution of the population and the local birth, death, and labor-force participation rates are found or estimated for the base period. From this data the natural annual increase in the labor force is calculated. Migration is then made to depend on the difference between job growth and natural increase in the labor force. When the model runs through time, in-migration occurs if job growth exceeds natural labor force growth, out-migration if vice versa. Migration plus natural increase yields change in total population. The effects of population change are continuously fed back into the input-output sector of the model via changes in household demand and in outlays by the state, local, and federal governments, which are assumed to rest on a per capita basis.

The accuracy of such a model can be tested by seeing how closely it reproduces actual changes over some observed past period. If it fits the facts reasonably well it can be used to predict the future course of the

10. James R. Prescott and Walter Mullendore, "A Simulation Model for Multi-County Planning," *Proceedings of the American Real Estate and Urban Economics Association,* Vol. IV, 1969, pp. 183–207.

economy, given various assumptions about future changes in demand, productivity, fertility, and so on. That it fits the past data from which its parameters were estimated does not, of course, ensure that it will accurately predict future trends. Because simulation models are so recent a development, their predictive accuracy can scarcely be said to have been established. If they prove successful, however, they will become an indispensable tool for urban and regional planning.

The sort of simulation model we have just described is a nonspatial one. Although it generates a level of business activity, employment, and population for a region, it makes no attempt to specify the location of these activities within the study area. Spatial concerns are simply omitted. We have used that particular sort of model as an illustration both because it is relatively simple and because its aims are similar to those of the other methods of economic base analysis dealt with in this chapter. In principle, however, simulation models can be developed to reproduce the movement of any social or physical system through time. For example, much research effort is now going into the construction of models to simulate the spatial form and land-use pattern of an actual metropolis. These models attempt to reproduce spatial reality by assigning population and business activity to specific sites within the metropolitan area. Thus they deal, at a very high level of sophistication and complexity, with the whole range of topics in intra-urban location that we introduced in Chapter 6. Like other simulation models, they are intended to be used ultimately as tools for policy planning and evaluation.[11]

STUDYING THE "SUPPLY SIDE" OF THE LOCAL ECONOMY

Traditional methods of studying the urban economic base have long been criticized for overemphasizing the role of demand in determining the level and rate of growth of local economic activity. In a widely cited article Chinitz wrote that "our efforts so far have been almost exclusively devoted to the demand dimensions of interdependence. The supply side has been virtually ignored." [12]

11. See, for example, Gregory K. Ingram, John F. Kain, and J. Royce Ginn, *The Detroit Prototype of the NBER Urban Simulation Model* (New York: National Bureau of Economic Research, 1972); and Robert F. Engle III, Franklin M. Fisher, John R. Harris, and Jerome Rothenberg, "An Econometric Simulation Model of Intra-Metropolitan Housing Location: Housing, Business, Transportation and Local Government," *American Economic Review*, May 1972, pp. 87–97. An earlier influential intra-urban location model was developed by Ira S. Lowry. See his *A Model of Metropolis* (Santa Monica, California: RAND Corporation, 1964).

12. Benjamin Chinitz, "Contrasts in Agglomeration: New York and Pittsburgh," *American Economic Review*, May 1961, p. 279.

168 Urban Economics and Public Policy

This comment applies with as much force to input-output and simulation methods as it does to the simpler basic-nonbasic and foreign-trade multiplier models. The fact that the input-output and simulation methods depict the flows of goods and services between the sectors of local industry in great detail is all to the good but does not bear on this point. Chinitz argues that we must look not only at the flows between local industries but at the way in which the structure of local industry affects factor supply prices, production costs, and entrepreneurial behavior within the local economy. He suggests, for example, that the supply of entrepreneurship and risk capital for launching new ventures may be significantly greater in a city where the industrial structure is largely competitive than in one that is dominated by a few very large firms. Thus the organizational structure of local industry may in the long run affect the way the local economy responds to opportunities for growth and diversification.

As Tiebout puts it, a study of the supply side "deals with the nature of the local economy as an economic environment." [13] An examination of the supply side would attempt to uncover the strengths and weaknesses of the community as a place in which to live and to conduct business. Once these were known, local policy makers could set about using its strengths and ameliorating its weaknesses in order to increase the area's productivity and attractiveness and help to ensure the long-run growth of its output and living standards.

It is a limitation, if not a defect, of the methods of economic base analysis reviewed above that (with some modification in the case of simulation models) they ascribe changes in the level of local activity entirely to changes in the level of an exogenously determined final demand. As John F. Kain has pointed out in another context, this way of looking at the local economy inevitably focuses attention on matters over which local authorities have no control—the exogenously determined components of final demand—while distracting attention from the very thing they *can* influence—the nature and attractiveness of the local economic environment.[14] It is well to recognize that in the short run, local activity will fluctuate in response to shifts in outside demand, but that is no reason to neglect the importance of internal supply factors in determining the course of events over the long run.

Precisely what can be done to take the supply side into account? First of all, location or feasibility studies can be made to discover what industries can best make use of the area's physical location and economic advantages. Second, the city can examine its local supply of labor, land,

13. Tiebout, p. 18.
14. See his review of Wilbur R. Thompson's A *Preface to Urban Economics* in *Journal of the American Institute of Planners*, May 1966, pp. 186–88.

capital, and entrepreneurship to see whether these can be marshaled more effectively for economic growth. Third, the city can survey its entire "infrastructure" of housing, transportation facilities, schools, hospitals, public services, and recreation areas—indeed, its whole "physical and social plan" —to see whether they are ample, well balanced, and life-enhancing or inadequate, uncoordinated, and stultifying.

LOCAL ECONOMIC POLICY AND NATIONAL WELFARE

The argument up to this point suggests an implicit assumption that the aim of local economic policy is or should be to promote local economic growth. Here is a matter that has received far too little attention either by economists or by public policy makers. Growth undoubtedly serves the special interests of the individual class of local "boosters" who typically own real estate that will appreciate in value or commercial firms whose profits will rise if the local economy expands. The question to be answered, however, is whether growth will benefit the local population as a whole. Is it likely to produce a general increase in local living standards? The question is so complex that a categorical answer is probably not possible, but a qualified "yes" can be defended on the following grounds.

First, growth is likely to bring increased economies of agglomeration, which will benefit local workers, businessmen, and consumers, as well as local landowners. Second, wages will tend to be higher and job preferences easier to satisfy in the "tight" labor market of a growing area than in the "easy" labor market of a static or declining one. This, however, is a one-time rather than a cumulative effect. If we assume that the local wage level is connected to the national level by the force of migration, then wages in a growing area can be higher than wages in a declining area by whatever differential is required to induce migration from the latter to the former. A similar argument applies to the return on local capital.

More generally, we can argue that policies to improve the local environment as a place to live and conduct business, and which thereby attract business and population, are in their very nature policies that increase both material productivity and population well-being. However, one can readily think of qualifications to this statement. For example, if growth occurs principally in very low wage industries and attracts an inflow of low skilled population, the average level of local family income might fall rather than rise with growth. This illustration raises precisely the issue that is most frequently and wrongly overlooked in discussing the aims of local economic policy: any statement about welfare requires a definition of the relevant population. Consider the above case. The low skilled in-migrants are presumably better off in the town to which they moved than in the place from which they came; they would not otherwise have migrated (barring ignorance and uncertainty). On the other hand, the pre-existing local population may be worse off after the low income population increases, if the newcomers cost the locality more via increased public expenditure than they contribute in additional tax revenue.[15] If we somehow aggregate the well-being of both groups, welfare may be found to increase as a result of in-migration. If we count only the welfare of the pre-existing population, it may decrease. A full account of the welfare effects of a local policy would have to go even further and look not only at changes in the welfare of the pre-existing local population and of the potential in-migrants, but at effects on the rest of the nation. If we fail to examine this last element, we run the danger of advocating policies that benefit a local area while harming the nation as a whole. In short, the relevant welfare universe for discussing the effects of local economic policy is not the local population, either before or after the policy takes effect, but the entire nation. Where does this lead us?

To simplify matters, let us assume that localities will not knowingly pursue policies harmful to themselves and that all policies that are beneficial locally will either be neutral toward other areas in the nation or else impose some loss on them. In that case we can say that for any local policy, the net effect on national welfare must be equal to the local gain less the losses (if any) elsewhere. For the nation as a whole it would be desirable (if it were possible) to insist that localities act not to maximize local gain but to maximize national welfare. This is not quite the same thing as saying "maximize local gain subject to the condition that local gains exceed outside losses." For under the latter rule localities might adopt policies that would lead to large local gain at the expense of large outside loss when from the national point of view it would have been better for them to choose alternative policies that entail moderate local gain at the cost of much smaller losses elsewhere.

We see, then, that consideration of the nation's welfare requires, not that localities avoid policies that hurt other localities, but only that losses elsewhere be properly taken into account. Of course, this proposition is, in the present state of economic knowledge, quite impossible to put into effect. It requires some way of quantifying welfare for various populations so that gains and losses can be compared along a common scale. Economists are not hopeful of discovering the "social welfare function" (or formula) that would make such comparisons possible. Even if we were to

15. This should not be taken to imply that the tax-expenditure calculus gives an adequate account of changes in individual welfare. On this point see Julius Margolis, "On Municipal Land Policy for Fiscal Gains," *National Tax Journal*, September 1956, pp. 247–57.

retreat from welfare to income as the relevant unit of account, the rule is presently impracticable because the effects of alternative policies on local income and, even more so, on outside income are extraordinarily difficult to measure.

Repelling Low Income Migrants

Despite the absence of reliable measurements of welfare, the above argument does help us to judge some real policy questions. Consider, for example, the matter of low income population movement. No urban policy issue is more intensely current. High income suburbs all over the United States quite correctly see that their own self-interest is served by keeping low income populations out. Even our great central cities that have always contained large numbers of the poor are beginning to wonder if they should now be less open to new arrivals. It should be obvious, however, that local policies to exclude the poverty-stricken do not diminish the total number of the poor in the nation. Indeed, by denying full mobility and therefore maximum choice of occupation and environment to the poor, such policies probably interfere with progress toward reducing poverty. At the very least this is an area where policies that maximize local welfare are unlikely to be in the national interest. Yet we know that local voters and local politicians will always be tempted to serve local self-interest. If the national interest is to prevail it will have to be asserted via state and national policies that limit local discretion to control the variables of housing, zoning, and welfare benefits through which localities currently influence the movement of the poor.

These conclusions may seem painfully obvious. Unfortunately they are easily lost sight of when attention is focused on solving intense local problems. A stunning example of this occurs in Jay Forrester's influential study entitled *Urban Dynamics*.[16] Forrester wished to examine the effects of alternative public policies in combatting the stagnation and decay of the older central cities. To do this he devised a simulation model, calibrated it with hypothetical "data," and ran it through centuries of time. He deliberately set his hypothetical city in what he described as a "limitless environment." The connections between the city and the environment he put in the form of "attractiveness for migration multipliers," the size of which depended upon the values of key variables within the city. For example, the attractiveness for migration multiplier that affected the influx of low income workers was made to depend in part upon the vacancy rate in the city's low rent housing. The multiplier would rise as the vacancy rate increased. As the model ran through time it showed that a

16. Jay W. Forrester, *Urban Dynamics* (Cambridge, Mass.: M.I.T. Press, 1969).

rise in the city's low income population either caused or exacerbated a great many problems and was a principal factor in the city's stagnation and decay.

Forrester "tested" the effects of various public policies on the city's economic health by building them into the model and running it through time. One of these policies was a subsidy for low income housing. He found that even if the subsidy cost were paid entirely from sources outside the city, a policy of building low income subsidized housing would have deleterious effects on the city's economic health because it would attract a larger number of the poor. The reader was left to draw the conclusion that subsidies to low income housing must be avoided if we wish to rescue our older cities from decay.[17] Surely one must ask whether that is the right way to view the problem.

The issue is not whether low income populations create problems for cities—quite obviously they do. The point is, rather, that Forrester's framework is wholly inappropriate for judging the welfare consequences of alternative policies. In his model, everything outside the city is part of the "limitless environment." It could better be described as a limitless void, since we do not know what goes on out there. Given this void, the model can tell us nothing about the national welfare effects of either local or national urban policies. It is capable of registering nothing but the local gains or losses from local policies. Forrester concludes that a policy of low income housing subsidies is bad because it attracts low income families. This overlooks two crucial points: first, if low income housing were equally subsidized everywhere, the subsidy would have *no* effect on migration. Consequently, if the heavy concentration of low income populations in large cities is undesirable, the solution is not necessarily to do away with housing subsidies but rather to use state or national policy to achieve a more desirable spatial distribution of the poor. Second, the low income population may be better off in Forrester's central city than in the place from which it came. A model that considers only one city is simply incapable of addressing this important welfare question.[18]

17. *Ibid.*, pp. 65–70.
18. Forrester does attempt, in a two-paragraph afterthought, to meet the criticism that his model overlooks effects on the outside world. He writes (*ibid.*, p. 116):

> The policies for controlling population balance that the city must establish are not antisocial. No purpose is served by operating a city so that it is a drain on the economy of the country and a disappointment and frustration to its occupants. An urban area that maintains effective internal balance can absorb poor people from other areas at a faster rate than can one that is operating in deep stagnation.

Indeed, this may be so. But the Forrester model is certainly incapable of demonstrating it. The inadequacy of Forrester's single-city model as a basis for testing national policies is developed at greater length by Leo P. Kadanoff in "From Simulation Model to Public Policy," *American Scientist*, January–February 1972, pp. 74–79. Also see the

Local Export Promotion

Local export promotion is another issue on which our proposed welfare rule casts important light. The earlier formulations of the basic-nonbasic theory stressed the view that exports were the "city-building" activities (hence "basic") and therefore that if the city of West Greenbush, for example, were to grow, it would have to expand its exports. How these additional sales were to be achieved was not altogether clear. Somehow, so the advice went, one must attract export industries to West Greenbush from their locations in the outside world. Local politicians were likely to put this advice into practice by offering subsidies to attract industry from elsewhere.

Now if we look at such a policy carefully we see that it violates our welfare rules. Let us measure gains and losses simply in terms of net changes in local income. Suppose that West Greenbush, suffering from unemployment, attracts a textile mill from some other location by means of a subsidy sufficient to overcome the higher transportation costs from West Greenbush to the market. The mill's output and exports, we may assume, are the same in West Greenbush as they were at the previous location. The factor incomes added by the mill at its new location will therefore just equal the incomes lost by its leaving the other place. In effect, West Greenbush exports its unemployment. From a welfare point of view, however, the situation is not a stand-off, because the net income gain to West Greenbush equals the rise in factor incomes *less* the locally financed subsidy needed to attract the mill from its preferred location. Hence the net gains at West Greenbush must be less than the losses at the old location by the amount of the annual subsidy.

Since we do not assume *general* unemployment, the added transportation costs cannot be counted as net increases in factor incomes. They measure only the opportunity cost of factors transferred from some other employment into transportation. The added transportation cost—or its equivalent, the reduced output in other industries from which factors were shifted into transportation—equals the net annual loss to society as a whole from this method of attracting export industry. (To this must be added the once-over loss equal to the cost of moving the firm.)

Pollution Control

Pollution control is a third area in which self-interested local policy may conflict with national welfare objectives. Here again the motive may be a desire to offer location inducements to industry. An industrial town

penetrating critique by Gregory K. Ingram in his review of *Urban Dynamics* in *Journal of the American Institute of Planners*, May 1970, pp. 206–08.

may fear that if it raises its antipollution standards it will drive industry away. Taking account only of their own welfare, the local citizens may correctly prefer to suffer the consequences of pollution rather than lose their jobs. In so deciding, however, they overlook the pollution costs thrown off by local industry onto neighboring towns whose interests they have not consulted. This is the familiar problem of external costs. Local industry is, in effect, being subsidized to stay put, and the subsidy is paid partly by those living outside the benefiting jurisdiction, who bear some of the pollution costs. The solution here, as in the somewhat different case of low income housing policy, is to raise the decision-making power to a higher level of government: a pollution-control jurisdiction must be found or created that is large enough to capture most of the externalities. Efficient pollution control requires a combination of regional and national standards.

Policies to Improve the Local Economic Environment

There are, of course, many ways in which localities can attract or hold industry that do not violate a national welfare rule. We have already described them above in the discussion of taking the supply side into account. These, by and large, are policies that would improve the local economy as an economic environment. As the environment becomes more productive for industry and more desirable for residents it will attract additional industry on its own merits, and growth will be achieved without special subsidies. While competition among cities to attract industry by means of subsidy is, as we have shown, necessarily harmful from the point of view of the nation as a whole, competition that takes the form of creating more attractive environments can hardly fail to be generally beneficial. True, not all places would prosper under such a regime, but it would not be difficult to show that the national welfare would be enhanced. Of course, the question of subsidy is not so easily put aside as the above statement may seem to suggest. We have already pointed out that location subsidies may take an indirect form, as in the case of low pollution-control standards. "Fair competition" would likewise rule out attracting industry by reducing business taxes to the point where firms receive local services at less than cost.

In a classic article criticizing the basic-nonbasic theory for its irrational export bias, Hans Blumenfeld performed the *tour de force* of turning the theory upside down. He pointed out that the great cities of modern times are centers of production that have shown remarkable persistence in the face of economic change and concluded with this passage:

> The bases of this amazing stability are the business and consumer services and other industries supplying the local market. They are

the permanent and constant element, while the "export" industries are variable, subject to incessant change and replacement. While the existence of a sufficient number of such industries is indispensable for the continued existence of the metropolis, each individual "export" industry is expendable and replaceable.

In any commonsense use of the term, it is the "service" industries of the metropolis that are "basic" and "primary" while the "export" industries are "secondary" and "ancillary." The economic base of the metropolis consists in the activities by which its inhabitants supply each other.[19]

In this sense the service sector is essentially the "economic environment" of the city, and the appropriate aim of local economic policy is to render that environment efficient and attractive by means that are consistent with the objectives of national policy.

19. Hans Blumenfeld, "The Economic Base of the Metropolis," reprinted in Pfouts, pp. 229–77.

The Urbanization of Poverty

EIGHT

Ever since America rediscovered her poor in the early 1960's, the words "poverty" and "city" have been almost automatically linked in our public vocabulary. It was not always so. To an earlier generation, poverty had appeared to be mainly a rural phenomenon. As late as 1959 considerably more poor people were living outside metropolitan areas than in them. Since then the proportions have changed dramatically, and the end is not yet in sight. In this chapter we briefly examine definitions of poverty, then investigate recent changes in its geography and explain some of the causes and consequences of those changes. In the chapter that follows we will analyze the great variety of policies that have been either tried or proposed to combat poverty in our cities.

DEFINING POVERTY

Definitions of poverty may be either relative or absolute. An absolute definition specifies some level of purchasing power per person or per family that is deemed sufficient to buy a minimum of life's necessities. Households with incomes below that level are classified as living in poverty. A relative definition, on the other hand, classifies households as living in poverty if their income falls below some fraction of the national median or mean. For example, a family with an income of less than half the national median might be defined as living in poverty.

In compiling "official" poverty statistics for the United States, the federal government employs the absolute definition of a poverty-line income that varies according to family size, sex of family head, and farm versus nonfarm residence and is adjusted annually in step with changes in the cost of living. The poverty-line income in 1971 for a nonfarm family of four with male head was $4,139.[1] In principle most analysts would prefer a poverty band rather than a poverty line when framing an absolute definition, since the choice of a particular line will always convey a degree of precision in both concept and measurement that is entirely unwarranted. As Thurow argues, we should recognize "that there is a band over which definite poverty shades into economic sufficiency. . . ." [2] Responding to this view, the federal government has recently begun publishing a limited amount of data on persons with incomes between the poverty line and a line 25 percent higher. As yet, however, the full range of poverty statistics is not available on that basis.

When an absolute definition of poverty is retained for a number of years while the average living standard in the nation gradually increases, the incidence of poverty (as defined) is almost certain to diminish. Only if the distribution of income became more unequal as income per capita rose could a reduction in absolute poverty fail to occur. So it should occasion neither surprise nor self-congratulation that, as Table 8.2 shows, the incidence of poverty in the United States, according to the official, absolute definition, has fallen markedly since the late 1950's.

The situation is quite different when a relative definition is used. The extent of poverty then depends entirely on the distribution of income and not at all on its level. A reduction in poverty can occur only if the distribution of income among families is changed in an appropriate fashion; a uniform percentage increase in living standards for all income classes has no effect. According to relative definitions, poverty in the United States has diminished only slightly since the end of World War II. In 1947 the poorest 20 percent of families in the United States received just 5.0 percent of all family income. By 1971 their share had increased only to 5.5 percent.[3]

Indeed, it may well be argued that the progress registered under an absolute definition of poverty is in part illusory. Historical experience demonstrates that in a dynamic economy the absolute standard of income sufficiency accepted by the social consensus at one period will no longer seem appropriate at a later date. Thus absolute standards tend periodically

---

1. For a detailed explanation of the federal definitions, see U.S. Bureau of the Census, *Current Population Reports*, P-60, No. 86, December 1972, pp. 17–19. Poverty-line income levels for 1971 are given in Table M.

2. Lester C. Thurow, *Poverty and Discrimination* (Washington, D.C.: Brookings Institution, 1969), p. 21.

3. U.S. Bureau of the Census, *Current Population Reports*, P-60, No. 85, December 1972, Table 14.

to be revised upward by common consent, which washes out some, though not all, of the reduction in poverty that seems to accrue during the intervals in which the standards remain fixed. In effect, we do think of poverty as partly a relative matter.

Since it was first introduced in the mid-1960's, however, the federal government's definition of a poverty-line income has not been substantially revised, except to adjust it for changes in the price level. As the years pass this standard is bound to appear increasingly unrealistic, and sooner or later it will be revised upward. But one must add that no single definition should be expected to serve for all purposes. Whatever its limitations in other connections, the federal definition does provide an easily understood, unambiguous standard for measuring the geographic distribution of poverty in the United States. It is to this subject that we now turn.

THE CHANGING GEOGRAPHY OF POVERTY

Table 8.1 shows the level of poverty in absolute numbers and also the percentage distribution of the poverty population by place of residence and by race. It clearly documents the increasing concentration of U.S. poverty in metropolitan areas. In 1959 the poor of all races living outside metropolitan areas outnumbered those living inside them by almost 5 million persons. During the 1960's, however, poverty declined much more sharply outside SMSA's, so that by 1971 a considerable majority of the nation's poor were metropolitan residents.

If we turn from the absolute level to the rate or incidence of poverty, we see a somewhat different picture. For any population class the rate of poverty is simply the proportion of that class living below the poverty line. Table 8.2 shows such rates by race and area. Notice, first of all, that although the number of the poor living inside metropolitan areas is now larger than the number living outside, the *rate* of poverty remains far lower inside. For all races in 1971, the rate inside SMSA's stood at 10.4 percent, as against 17.2 percent in nonmetropolitan areas. On the other hand, the rate has been falling faster outside than within metropolitan areas. Between 1959 and 1971 it dropped by about one-third inside SMSA's, but fell by almost one-half in the nonmetropolitan United States.

If we look at the metropolis itself these facts stand out:

1. Within metropolitan areas as a whole the incidence of poverty is far higher in the central cities than in the suburban rings.
2. The incidence of poverty is declining faster in the rings than in the central cities.

TABLE 8.1
Number of Persons Living in Poverty, by Race and Area

	ALL RACES [a]		WHITE		NEGRO	
	1971	1959	1971	1959	1971	1959
Number of persons below poverty line (thousands)						
United States	25,559	38,766	17,780	28,336	7,396	9,927
Metropolitan areas	14,561	17,019	9,798	11,825	4,586	5,002
Central cities	8,912	10,437	5,178	6,513	3,612	3,816
Outside central cities	5,649	6,582	4,620	5,312	974	1,186
Nonmetropolitan areas	10,999	21,747	7,982	16,511	2,810	4,925
Distribution of persons by area (percent)						
United States	100.0%	100.0%	100.0%	100.0%	100.0%	100.0%
Metropolitan areas	57.0	43.9	55.1	41.7	62.0	50.4
Central cities	34.9	26.9	29.1	23.0	48.8	38.4
Outside central cities	22.1	17.0	26.0	18.7	13.2	12.0
Nonmetropolitan areas	43.0	56.1	44.9	58.3	38.0	49.6
Distribution of persons by race (percent)						
United States	100%	100%	69.6%	73.1%	28.9%	25.6%
Metropolitan areas	100	100	67.3	69.5	31.5	29.4
Central cities	100	100	58.1	62.4	40.5	36.6
Outside central cities	100	100	81.8	80.7	17.2	18.0
Nonmetropolitan areas	100	100	72.6	75.9	25.6	22.7

[a] Includes other nonwhite, in addition to Negro.

Sources: U.S. Bureau of the Census, *Current Population Reports*, P-23, No. 37, June 24, 1971, Table 19, and P-60, No. 86, December 1972, Table 3.

TABLE 8.2
Incidence of Poverty, by Race and Area

	PERCENTAGE LIVING BELOW POVERTY LINE					
	ALL RACES [a]		WHITE		NEGRO	
	1971	1959	1971	1959	1971	1959
Incidence of poverty among persons, by area and race (percentage)						
United States	12.5	22.0	9.9	18.1	32.5	55.1
Metropolitan areas	10.4	15.3	8.0	12.0	26.9	42.8
Central cities	14.2	18.3	10.6	13.8	27.9	40.8
Outside central cities	7.2	12.2	6.3	10.4	23.8	50.9
Nonmetropolitan areas	17.2	33.2	13.9	28.2	48.9	77.7
	ALL RACES		WHITE		NEGRO AND OTHER	
	1969	1959	1969	1959	1969	1959
Incidence of poverty among families, by size of SMSA and race (percentage)						
Central cities in SMSA's of 1,000,000 or more	10.1	13.8	7.0	10.2	19.5	30.7
Central cities in SMSA's of 250,000 to 1,000,000	10.1	17.0	7.7	13.0	21.3	41.0

[a] Includes other nonwhite, in addition to Negro.
Sources: U.S. Bureau of the Census, Current Population Reports, P-23, No. 37, June 24, 1971, Tables 19 and 30, and P-60, No. 86, December 1972, Table 8.

3. Central cities of small SMSA's show a much sharper decline in the rate of poverty than do central cities of large SMSA's.

The first two points are shown clearly in the upper panel of Table 8.2. For all races combined, the incidence of poverty in the central cities was 18.3 percent in 1959 and 14.2 percent in 1971. In the suburban rings the comparable rates were 12.2 percent and 7.2 percent. These figures demonstrate both that the incidence is far higher and that its rate of decline is far lower in the central cities than in the rings.

More surprising, perhaps, is the third point. The bottom panel of Table 8.2 shows that the rate of poverty is declining faster in the central cities of the smaller metropolitan areas. In 1959 the poverty rate was 17.2 percent in the central cities of metropolitan areas with a population of between 250,000 and 1 million, far above the 13.8 percent incidence in central cities of the largest metropolitan areas. By 1969 the two rates were equal at 10.1 percent. As we will see, this rather dramatic change is at least partly the result of differences in the pattern of in-migration.

RACE AND POVERTY

Thus far we have not considered racial differences in either the level or rate of poverty. So far as the level is concerned, Table 8.1 shows that whites continue to make up the majority of the nation's poor—over two-thirds in 1971. Yet the same table shows that the white share has been gradually declining. Poverty is becoming increasingly concentrated among blacks. In the nation as a whole they made up 28.9 percent of the poverty population in 1971 as against 25.6 percent in 1959. Their share of the total increased both in metropolitan and nonmetropolitan areas.

On the other hand, Table 8.2 shows that the rate, or incidence, of poverty among blacks is dropping rapidly. It fell from 55.1 percent in 1959 to 32.5 percent in 1971. The rate of decline was not quite as rapid for blacks as for whites, however: the white poverty rate fell from 18.1 percent to 9.9 percent over the same period. This is one reason why poverty is increasingly concentrated in the black population. In addition, the total black population is increasing faster than the white, so even if the incidence of poverty in the two groups fell at an equal rate, blacks would make up an increasing proportion of the poor.

The fact that the incidence of poverty is declining less rapidly among blacks than among whites does *not* mean that the average level of black income is rising less rapidly. The rate of escape from poverty for each group depends on where in its income distribution the poverty line happens to lie, as well as on the average rate of increase of income. In fact, as Table 8.3 indicates, median black family income as a percentage of white has risen considerably in recent years. A continuous statistical series for Negroes as a separate category extends back only to 1964. For earlier years we must rely on figures for all nonwhites combined. The latter series, which is closely correlated with the Negro figure, shows considerable fluctuation but no pronounced upward movement until after 1963.

It is important to note that because their families are larger, blacks individually are worse off in relation to whites than appears from the usual comparisons of family income that ignore family size. For example, in 1971 average black family income was $7,695, or 64 percent of the $11,997 white family average. But black families contained an average of 4.1 members, as compared with only 3.5 members for white families. Consequently,

TABLE 8.3
Ratio of Negro to White Income

	MEDIAN FAMILY INCOME	
	Ratio of Negro and Other Races to White	*Ratio of Negro to White*
1950	.54	—
1951	.53	—
1952	.57	—
1953	.56	—
1954	.56	—
1955	.55	—
1956	.53	—
1957	.54	—
1958	.51	—
1959	.52	.51
1960	.55	—
1961	.53	—
1962	.53	—
1963	.53	—
1964	.56	.54
1965	.55	.54
1966	.60	.58
1967	.62	.59
1968	.63	.60
1969	.63	.61
1970	.64	.61
1971	.63	.60

Source: U.S. Bureau of the Census, *Current Population Reports*, P-23, No. 42, July 1972, Table 16.

black income per family member was only 55 percent as high as the level for whites.[4]

WHY POVERTY IS CONCENTRATING IN THE CITIES

The recent urbanization of poverty in the United States is not difficult to account for. It is the logical outcome of the changing pattern of settlement that has already been described in earlier chapters. With the mechanization of agriculture in the twentieth century there has been a massive migration of displaced labor from rural areas and small towns to metropolitan areas. Superimposed on this, so to speak, has been a marked flow of migration from relatively poor regions, such as Appalachia, the South, and Puerto Rico, to relatively prosperous regions, such as the Middle Atlantic, Great Lakes, and Pacific states. Both the poor and the non-poor have migrated. The simple statistical consequence of this massive movement of population has been, first, to shift the principal locus of poverty from the countryside to the cities and, second, to slow the reduction in the incidence of poverty in the cities below the rate that otherwise would have obtained.

Within the metropolitan areas the concentration of poverty in the central cities and its relative absence in the suburban rings can be explained largely as the result of three sets of forces: the process of metropolitan growth and development, the impact of public policy, and the pressure of race prejudice. The process of metropolitan development tends to hold the poor close to the center both because the center is the place with the largest concentration of old, and therefore cheap, housing and because it is the area that provides easiest access to a large number of jobs —especially to the types of casual employment that the unskilled are often forced to rely on. Easier job access at the center, in turn, has two aspects. First, the center contains more jobs than does any single place in the ring. Second, it is usually served by a public transportation network that efficiently connects close-in residential neighborhoods with central city places of employment.

We have described previously the process by which the development of highway transportation, the rise in family incomes, and the force of public policy in home finance and income taxation induced the middle and upper classes to move to the suburbs. These inducements scarcely affected low income families who could not afford either new suburban housing or the relatively high cost of suburban self-transportation. How-

4. *Ibid.*, Table 19.

ever, the exodus of the middle class from the central city reinforced its attraction for the poor and the blacks by releasing large quantities of housing in the older neighborhoods that they could afford or that could readily be adapted to their low rent-paying capacity. Here was an example of the "filtering" process in the housing market operating on a huge scale. (Filtering will be examined in detail in Chapter 10.) The process of racial and income-class change became a circular, or self-reinforcing, one because racial tensions rose as the black population of central cities increased and provided the white middle and upper classes with an additional impetus to move to the largely white suburbs.

If the "natural" process of metropolitan spatial-economic development and the indirect effects of public policy were the only operative forces, we would expect to find poor whites almost as heavily concentrated in the central cities as poor blacks. Since we do not find an equal concentration of poor whites in the cities, it is difficult to avoid the conclusion that racial factors are also at work. Persuasive evidence on this point has been assembled by Kain and Persky, demonstrating that in large urban-metropolitan areas the residential location pattern of poor whites is strikingly different from that of poor blacks. For example, in the Detroit area in 1960, 45 percent of poor white families lived in the suburbs, compared with only 11 percent of poor black families. Differences of a similar order of magnitude were found in most of the nation's ten largest urban-metropolitan areas.[5] The point is reinforced by the data in the upper panel of Table 8.1, which cover U.S. metropolitan areas as a whole. In 1971, 47 percent of poor metropolitan whites lived in the suburban ring, while only 21 percent of poor metropolitan blacks did so. To a significant extent, then, the concentration of poverty in the central cities appears to be reinforced by the essentially noneconomic forces of prejudice that prevent the low income black population from dispersing into the suburbs. (We take up the question of race prejudice and housing segregation in Chapter 11.)

SHIFT IN RELATIVE INCOME LEVEL: CENTRAL CITIES VERSUS SUBURBS

As might be expected, the dispersion of the middle and upper classes to the suburbs and the influx of a substantial low income population to the central cities has brought about a historic shift in the relative income levels of the two areas. Scattered evidence from earlier periods indicates

5. John F. Kain and Joseph J. Persky, "Alternatives to the Gilded Ghetto," *The Public Interest*, Winter 1969, Table 1, p. 76.

that prior to 1950 the level of per capita income was higher in central cities than in the surrounding ring areas. More recently the advantage has lain with the ring areas and has been steadily widening.

For example, Hoover and Vernon estimated that per capita personal income in the "core" counties fell from 108 percent of the regional average in 1939 to 105 percent in 1947 and 98 percent in 1956, while per capita income in the "inner ring" of suburban counties rose from 88 percent of the regional average in 1939 to 97 percent in 1947 and 111 percent in 1956.[6] Thus the mean income in the suburbs rose from 19 percent below the core county average in 1939 to 13 percent above it in 1956.

Table 3.7 confirmed the existence of a similar pattern for metropolitan areas in general. It showed that the ratio of median central city family income to median ring income fell from .89 in 1959 to .83 ten years later. Table 8.4 shows a like pattern of differentials developing from 1949 through 1969 in the 12 large SMSA's that were examined in detail in Chapter 3.

It is interesting to note that the income differentials in favor of the suburbs are larger in the six metropolitan areas of the North and East than in the six of the South and West. The former are far the "older" metropolitan areas, and therein lies the explanation. In a careful statistical study, Schnore has shown that the "age" of an urbanized area is a significant predictor of city-suburban income differentials.[7] Based on the discussion of the historic pattern of metropolitan growth in Chapter 3, we can hypothesize that the influence of age has operated as follows. The older central cities were built up to high densities during the railroad age of the nineteenth century. When, after 1920, the automobile and the truck, coupled with rising living standards, made possible a more dispersed pattern of metropolitan residential and business settlement, it was uneconomical to redevelop the older cities on the new pattern. Instead, the middle and upper income classes, in their search for low density neighborhoods, tended to move out into new suburbs beyond the city limits. Their places in the central city were (and continue to be) taken by families of lower income, immigrating from less affluent rural areas. On the other hand, the newer central cities, products of the auto- and truck-oriented twentieth century, were either themselves laid out in the much sought-after low density pattern or else still contained extensive rural fringe areas within their city limits that could accommodate such development. In either case the middle and upper classes did not have to move out of

6. Edgar M. Hoover and Raymond Vernon, *Anatomy of a Metropolis* (Cambridge, Mass.: Harvard University Press, 1959), p. 226.

7. Leo F. Schnore, *The Urban Scene* (New York: The Free Press, 1965), pp. 206–09. Schnore measured "age" by the census year in which a central city first reached a population of 50,000. In Ch. 2 we applied a somewhat different age measure.

TABLE 8.4

Income Differentials Between Central Cities and Their Metropolitan Areas

	MEDIAN FAMILY INCOME		
	Ratio of Central City Median to SMSA Median		
Six largest SMSA's in North and East	1949	1959	1969
New York-N.E. New Jersey [a]	.95	.91	.87
Chicago, Ill.	.97	.92	.86
Philadelphia, Pa.-N.J.	.96	.90	.85
Detroit, Mich.	.99	.89	.83
Washington, D.C.-Md.-Va.	.89	.79	.74
Boston, Mass.	.92	.86	.80
Average of six SMSA's in North and East	.95	.88	.83
Six largest SMSA's in South and West			
Los Angeles-Long Beach, Calif. [b]	.98	.98	.96
San Francisco-Oakland, Calif. [c]	1.00	.95	.89
Houston, Texas	1.02	.98	.97
Dallas, Texas	1.03	1.01	.96
Seattle-Everett, Wash. [d]	1.03	1.01	.95
Anaheim-Santa Ana-Garden Grove, Calif. [e]	—	—	.96
Average of six SMSA's in South and West	1.01	.99	.95

[a] Data are for Standard Consolidated Area in 1959 and 1969 in order to achieve comparability with 1949.
[b] Ratio is for Los Angeles only.
[c] Ratio is for San Francisco only.
[d] Ratio is for Seattle only.
[e] Ratio is for Anaheim only.
Sources: U.S. Bureau of the Census, *Census of Population, 1950, 1960, 1970.*

the central city in search of space. And if the rich were less inclined to move, there was less likelihood of housing being left behind that could be easily adapted for use by lower income groups. Consequently, as Table 8.4 shows, income levels in some of the newer cities, such as Houston, Dallas, and Los Angeles, have not fallen much below the level in their suburbs.

GROWTH OF THE URBAN BLACK POPULATION

The same internal migration pattern that brought about the urbanization of poverty has, of course, also produced the urbanization of the American black. Philip Hauser points out that "In 1910, before large migratory streams of Negroes left the South, 73 per cent of the Negroes in the nation, as compared with 52 per cent of the Whites, lived in rural areas. . . . By 1960, the distribution of Negroes by urban-rural residence had become completely reversed, with 73 per cent of the Negro population residing in urban areas. . . . In fact, in 1960, Negroes were more highly urbanized than Whites. . . ." [8] By 1970, 81 percent of the black population was living in places classified by the Census Bureau as urban.

Within metropolitan areas the blacks, like the poor, are highly concentrated in the central cities. As Table 8.5 shows, blacks in 1970 made up almost 21 percent of total central city population as compared with less than 5 percent of population in the suburban ring. Moreover, the black proportion of population rose substantially in central cities during the 1960's, while in suburban ring areas it remained virtually unchanged.

It is interesting to note that in Table 8.5, when SMSA's are grouped by size, the black percentage of central city population increases markedly as size increases. Likewise, the rate of change of central city population for each of the races is related to SMSA size. The black central city population in the largest class of SMSA's increased 37 percent between 1960 and 1970. In the smallest class it rose only 21 percent. For whites the relationship runs just the other way. White central city population is actually decreasing in the largest class while still increasing substantially in the smallest. The net effect of these opposite trends is that the black proportion of population is increasing much more rapidly in the central cities of large than of small SMSA's.

Obviously, migration patterns account for this difference in the speed of racial change within central cities. Kain and Persky have pointed out that blacks moving out of the South display a marked tendency to settle in large rather than medium-sized or small metropolitan areas in other parts of the country.[9] In Chapter 3, Table 3.6, we have already shown the high rate of net nonwhite in-migration to central cities in 12 large metropolitan areas. In central cities of smaller SMSA's the rate of nonwhite in-migration is usually lower and frequently even negative, indicating net out-

8. Philip M. Hauser, "Demographic Factors in the Integration of the Negro," in Talcott Parsons and Kenneth B. Clark, eds., *The Negro American* (Boston: Beacon Press, 1967), p. 75.

9. John F. Kain and Joseph J. Persky, "The North's Stake in Southern Rural Poverty," Ch. 17 in *Rural Poverty in the United States: A Report by the President's National Advisory Commission on Rural Poverty*, 1968, pp. 291–92.

TABLE 8.5

Population Growth by Race in Central Cities and Suburbs, by Size of SMSA

	PERCENTAGE CHANGE IN POPULATION 1960 TO 1970			NEGRO AS PERCENTAGE OF TOTAL POPULATION	
	Total [a]	White	Negro	1970	1960
Inside central cities					
All SMSA's	5.3	−1.2	32.6	20.6	16.3
SMSA's 1,000,000 or more	1.8	−8.0	37.3	25.3	18.8
SMSA's 250,000 to 1,000,000	8.5	5.0	25.0	16.7	14.5
SMSA's under 250,000	12.5	11.0	21.0	11.3	10.5
Outside central cities					
All SMSA's	28.2	27.5	29.0	4.8	4.8
SMSA's 1,000,000 or more	31.4	29.8	51.7	4.7	4.0
SMSA's 250,000 to 1,000,000	26.1	26.4	10.8	4.8	5.4
SMSA's under 250,000	16.4	17.4	−2.4	6.0	7.2

[a] Includes other nonwhite, in addition to Negro.

Source: Census of Population and Housing, 1970, U.S. Summary, Final Report, PHC(2)-1, Table 9.

migration. The latter occurs if the growth in local nonwhite population is less than would result simply as the sum of local births minus deaths.

The preference of black migrants for the larger metropolitan areas undoubtedly helps to explain the striking fact, brought out in Table 8.2 above, that since 1959 the overall poverty rate has been falling far less rapidly in central cities of large than of small SMSA's. Southern poverty is being exported to the large northern and western cities. Yet this cannot be the whole explanation, for the lower panel of Table 8.2 shows that the incidence of white poverty has also fallen somewhat less rapidly in the central cities of the larger areas. Perhaps this tendency in the white sector can be explained as the effect of a higher rate of out-migration of well-to-do whites to the suburbs in the larger SMSA's.

A late 1960's projection based on a careful assessment of the data suggests that by 1985 nonwhites are likely to account for 31 percent of the population of central cities, although they will then make up only 14 percent of the whole U.S. population.[10] It is important to note that this ex-

10. Patricia L. Hodge and Philip M. Hauser, *The Challenge of America's Metropolitan Population Outlook—1960 to 1985,* Research Report No. 3, National Commission on Urban Problems, 1968.

pected increase in the nonwhite proportion in central cities results from two factors: continued net in-migration of nonwhites and net out-migration of whites, and also a considerable excess of nonwhite over white fertility. Black migration to the cities may now be slowing down as the rural black population of the South diminishes. But even if it were now to cease entirely, the black population of central cities would continue to grow rapidly over the next few decades simply as a result of natural increase. Only a massive outflow of blacks to the suburbs on a scale that will not occur without the active encouragement of public policy can prevent, at least in the near future, the continued development of macro-segregation in metropolitan areas: increasingly black central cities surrounded by a ring of largely white suburbs. This prospect has implications for antipoverty policy, to be discussed in the next chapter; for housing policy, taken up in Chapter 11; and for public finance, to be analyzed in Chapter 12.

THE SOCIAL IMPACT OF BLACK MIGRATION TO CITIES

Apart from altering the color composition of central cities and contributing to the urbanization of poverty, has the massive migration of blacks exacerbated other urban social problems? Certainly there is a widespread belief that the typical black migrant is a poorly educated, unskilled rural laborer, unable to withstand the shock of migration, who soon falls into antisocial behavior patterns that create problems in the city that receives him. Is there any truth in this view? Let us begin by examining the effect of black migration on the average socioeconomic status of the central city population.

It is difficult to make general statements about the impact of migration on the socioeconomic characteristics of the population in a receiving region. On the one hand, it is well established that migrants (with certain exceptions for those leaving farms) are generally younger, better educated, and more highly skilled than the average in their place of origin. On the other hand, it is also indisputable that migration tends to flow from places of meager opportunity and low income to regions of expanding opportunity and high income. Since the population of the former regions is likely to be less educated and lower skilled on the average than that of the latter, it is entirely possible for migrants to be above average in status in their region of origin and yet below average at their destination. Migratory flows must be examined individually.

In a well-known study, Karl and Alma Taeuber compared the characteristics of nonwhites who migrated to ten major metropolitan areas during 1955–60 with the characteristics of the resident white and nonwhite population in 1960.[11] They divided nonwhite in-migrants into two groups —those coming from other SMSA's and those coming from nonmetropolitan areas. This division is crucial if one wishes to isolate the impact of black migration on the characteristics of metropolitan or central city populations.

The Taeubers found that nonwhite migrants coming from other metropolitan areas were generally younger and higher in socioeconomic status than the resident nonwhites in the SMSA's to which they moved. This is consistent with the usual finding that the mobile portion of any nonfarm population is below average in age and well above average in status at the point of origin. In this instance if we specify that the originating population is "United States metropolitan nonwhite," the usual rule holds: nonwhites leaving Detroit, Buffalo, Atlanta, Chicago, etc., and moving to Atlanta, Chicago, Buffalo, Detroit, etc., turn out to be well above the nonwhite average in status at their destinations because in the aggregate their destinations are largely the same places as their origins.

It should be obvious, however, that blacks who migrate from one metropolitan area to another cannot affect the socioeconomic status of metropolitan populations as a whole. The only *net* effect can come from migrants originating in *non*metropolitan areas. The Taeubers' analysis shows that this group is younger than, but also lower in socioeconomic status than, the nonmigrant, nonwhite population in the receiving areas and is far below the socioeconomic level of the white population. Earlier investigations cited by the Taeubers suggest that this was also true of migration during the 1930's and 1940's.

Additional evidence comes from data on the population of the North Central region of the United States. Kain and Persky show that residents of central cities in that region, both white and nonwhite, who were born in the South, have far lower educational attainments than resident members of the same racial groups born elsewhere.[12] These findings are consistent with the Taeubers', since Kain and Persky's "nonwhite migrants born in the South" undoubtedly make up a large fraction of the group classified by the Taeubers as "nonwhite migrants originating in nonmetropolitan areas." The relatively low educational attainment recorded for this group in the Taeuber study is probably a result of their predominantly southern origin.

With this much evidence, it is difficult to avoid the conclusion that over the last several decades blacks migrating to the metropolis from small

11. Karl E. Taeuber and Alma F. Taeuber, *Negroes in Cities* (Chicago: Aldine Publishing, 1965), Ch. 6.
12. Kain and Persky, "The North's Stake in Southern Rural Poverty," Table 9, p. 295.

towns and rural areas have been less skilled and less well educated than the resident populations in the areas that received them. They have also been considerably younger, which in itself is economically advantageous to the city, since their expected productive life is therefore longer. But they do have relative disadvantages in the attainment of skill and education which it becomes the task of the central city either to accommodate or to overcome.

Whether the black immigrant from nonmetropolitan America contributes disproportionately to the incidence of broken families, crime, and civil disorder in the cities is quite another matter, however. Charles Tilly cites abundant evidence for an opposite conclusion: recent black in-migrants have far *lower* rates of juvenile delinquency than locally born black youths; blacks immigrating from the South have lower rates of imprisonment in the North than those native to the North; recent migrants are not heavily represented among those booked or prosecuted for rioting; the incidence of "broken families" is far lower among blacks moving into cities from nonmetropolitan places than among resident blacks or those coming from other metropolitan areas.[13] As Tilly argues, all this evidence points to a single conclusion: it is not the shock of moving but the situation that the black faces in the city over the long years after his arrival that breeds social disorganization. Seen in that light, the black migrant is the victim of a disorganizing urban society, not the cause of its disorganization. If that is the case, the expected gradual tapering off of black migration to the cities will not automatically solve the problem of urban social disorganization, and the task of making possible a good life for the black population of the metropolis becomes that much more challenging.

13. Charles E. Tilly, "Race and Migration to the American City," in James Q. Wilson, ed., *The Metropolitan Enigma* (Washington, D.C.: Chamber of Commerce of the United States, 1967), pp. 132–36.

Antipoverty Policies

NINE

Broadly speaking, there are three ways of relieving poverty. The first is to give money income to the poor; the second is to provide the poor with goods and services either free or below market price; the third is to help them acquire the skills and find the jobs with which they can earn adequate incomes by their own effort. The first method can be accurately described as "income-maintenance policy." It includes both the existing forms of public assistance (or "welfare"), which had their origin in the Social Security Act of 1935, and numerous recent proposals to supplement or replace those programs with a guaranteed minimum income or some other comprehensive system of direct income transfers. The second category, sometimes described as "benefits in kind," includes such programs as medical assistance (Medicaid), food stamps, and housing subsidies. The third category covers a variety of strategies that are difficult to describe with a single phrase; for want of a better term they are usually called "employment policies."

A fourth group, which does not fit easily into this system of classification, comprises policies directed toward specific, geographically identifiable areas. Because these policies (when applied in the urban context) are concerned explicitly with the question of where the poor live within metropolitan areas and what effect location has on their welfare, they are of particular interest to students of urban economics. Included in this category are programs to stimulate economic activity inside black urban ghettos as well as policies to encourage the dispersion of the poor—out of their central city neighborhoods and into the suburbs.

We will look first at employment policies, then at income-maintenance schemes, and finally at programs that are area oriented. Programs to provide benefits in kind will not be analyzed as a separate category. Since Medicaid was authorized under the Social Security Act, it will be discussed simultaneously with the other forms of public assistance to which it is closely linked. Housing subsidies will be examined at length in Chapter 11.

It must be emphasized at this point that employment policies and income-maintenance policies are complementary rather than alternative ways of dealing with the problem of poverty. Obviously, employment policies can help only the employable poor. Those who cannot work, including children, the disabled, and others who are for some reason unemployable; those whom society decides ought not to be forced to work, including the elderly and the head of household with young children and no spouse present; and those whose earning capacity even after reasonable training leaves them still impoverished will always require some form of income maintenance to raise them out of poverty. Nor can the time dimension be ignored: some, though not all, employment policies operate slowly, whereas income maintenance, once established, can be effective immediately.

If it is true that the two policies are complementary, it must also be recognized that a system of income maintenance liberal enough to raise people out of poverty may possibly weaken the incentive to work among some of its beneficiaries. Thus there may be a trade-off between the immediate benefits of income maintenance and the longer run gains to be expected from employment policies. It is important to know the precise terms of this trade-off in designing antipoverty policies. Consequently, the Office of Economic Opportunity and the Department of Health, Education, and Welfare have financed several experimental income-maintenance projects in order to observe the effects of income-maintenance programs on labor force participation.[1]

THREE TYPES OF EMPLOYMENT POLICY

Employment policies have been heavily emphasized in federal legislation since the early 1960's. The War on Poverty may be said to have begun with the passage of the Economic Opportunity Act in 1964. The very title of that act reveals its commitment to employment: the "opportunity" it sought to open up to the poor was the chance to rise out of poverty by improving their skills and finding decently paid jobs.

Using the categories of economic theory one can logically divide

1. Interim reports on three experimental programs can be found in *American Economic Review*, May 1971, pp. 15–42.

employment policies into three groups according to the point at which they have impact on the labor market. As Sar A. Levitan has pointed out,

> Some programs focus on the supply side of the labor market, preparing the poor for gainful employment . . . . Other programs are directed to the demand side, opening doors for the poor in the private labor market and providing public employment for those who are not absorbed in the private sector. A third group of programs seeks to improve the functioning of the labor market for the poor, matching up supply and demand more effectively . . . .[2]

We will first describe these three types of policy in some detail and then attempt to evaluate them.

Training, Education, and Human Capital

Policies "on the supply side" are those that try to improve the training and education of the poor. Their purpose is to raise individual productivity so that the poor become better qualified to fill existing vacancies or to advance out of low-end jobs that leave them still impoverished. These policies operate on the supply side of the labor market because their effect is to increase the supply of productive skill. By themselves, however, they do not increase the employer's demand for labor in the sense of shifting his demand curve upward.

The provision of training and education can be regarded as a form of investment—investment in human resources, or, as it is now called, "human capital." Human capital is the store of productive knowledge and skill that the individual possesses. Lester Thurow explains the link between human capital and income as follows:

> Human capital . . . is one of the key determinants of the distribution of income. Individuals with little education, training, and skills have low marginal productivities and earn low incomes. With very little human capital they earn poverty incomes . . . . What might be called the productivity approach to the elimination of poverty and low Negro income is thus aimed at improving the quantity and distribution of human capital.[3]

The formal economic analysis of human capital and the quantitative measurement of its importance began only in the early 1960's. Interest in the subject grew rapidly when the battle against poverty became a national

---

2. Sar A. Levitan, *Programs in Aid of the Poor for the 1970's*, Policy Studies in Employment and Welfare, No. 1 (Baltimore: Johns Hopkins Press, 1969), p. 49.
3. Lester C. Thurow, *Poverty and Discrimination* (Washington, D.C.: Brookings Institution, 1969), p. 66. See Thurow's "Appendix K" for an extensive annotated bibliography on the economics of poverty, discrimination, and investment in education and training (i.e., human capital).

concern, and human capital analysis, as we will see, now has much to contribute to our understanding of poverty. At a less formal level, of course, the connection between education, training, and economic welfare has long been understood.

Job Creation

At the other end of the spectrum of employment policies are those that operate on the demand side of the market. These strategies attempt to help the poor by stimulating the demand for labor. In effect, they operate by shifting the demand curve for labor upward and to the right, so that the total number of jobs available at existing wage rates increases. This group comprises such policies as subsidizing the private employment of the hard-core unemployed and the proposal that the government act as "employer of last resort" for those who cannot obtain jobs elsewhere. Under the latter plan, the government would, in effect, guarantee a job to every citizen by agreeing to hire him in a public agency if he could not find a job in the private sector. In this way, it is argued, all sorts of much-needed, labor-intensive public services could be expanded at very little real cost, since the added workers would otherwise be unemployed. The newly created jobs would be mostly in state and local agencies, although financed by federal funds. The policy was first suggested by the National Commission on Technology, Automation, and Economic Progress in 1966.

Job creation also includes the macroeconomic policy of operating the economy at high pressure in order to hold overall unemployment to a bare minimum. According to the "queuing" theory of the labor market, employers rank the corps of job seekers available to them at any particular moment along a continuum from most to least desirable. This continuum is the "queue" from which employers always hire as near to the front end as possible. The low-skilled, the disadvantaged, the minorities are concentrated at the rear end of the queue. The theory consequently predicts that they will be "last hired, first fired." If nation-wide unemployment rises, their rate of unemployment will rise faster than the average; if nation-wide unemployment falls, their rate will fall faster than the average. If these propositions are true, then the relative economic position of poor minority groups and the disadvantaged can be improved substantially by macro-economic policies that maintain tight labor markets.

Overcoming Discrimination

Between the policies that increase supply and those that stimulate demand lies a third group, which attempt to help the poor by overcoming "imperfections" in the labor market itself. Among those imperfections that have serious effects on the poor, the foremost is probably employment discrimination against blacks and other minorities. The problem of discrimination in employment has been attacked by all levels of government through various forms of fair employment practices legislation.

The effects of employment discrimination have been demonstrated repeatedly in studies comparing the returns to education earned by whites with those earned by blacks. Using the human capital approach and nation-wide data for 1960, Thurow studied the returns to education and to work experience. He estimated that with 20 years of experience and 8 years of education, white males earned $1,367 more per year than blacks similarly situated. Holding experience constant but increasing education to 12 years raised the white advantage to $1,750. With 16 years of education completed (a college degree), the gap widened to $3,556.[4] As Thurow stresses, not all of this difference can be attributed to employment discrimination against blacks. Many other factors are at work, including differences among regions where blacks and whites live and differences among the industries in which they are typically employed. But a part of the difference is undoubtedly caused by discrimination in the sense of lower pay for equal work, restricted access to better paying jobs, and less opportunity for promotion.

Bennett Harrison's study of residents of poverty areas in 12 large SMSA's in 1966 produced very similar results. He analyzed the effects of education on annual earnings of whites and blacks, while controlling for such factors as age, sex, and industry in which employed. He estimated that a white male resident of a poverty area with a high school diploma earned $394 more than a similarly situated black. A college degree increased the margin of white over black earnings to $1,714.[5] Bearing in mind that all the subjects of this study come from similar areas in large central cities, and that Harrison controlled statistically for the effects of most other factors that affect earnings, it is hard to escape the conclusion that much of the remaining earnings differential is the result of employment discrimination.

The existence of employment discrimination probably has serious effects on individual incentives to acquire education. The human capital approach suggests that individuals invest in their own education at least in part to obtain the higher future incomes that education makes possible. If blacks can look forward to lower levels of earnings than whites with similar educational attainment, then they have less incentive to invest in their own education and might, quite rationally, provide themselves with

---

4. *Ibid.*, Table 5–2, p. 79.
5. Bennett Harrison, "Education and Underemployment in the Urban Ghetto," *American Economic Review*, December 1972, Table 4, p. 805.

less of it than do similarly qualified whites. (This effect is not eliminated by the existence of "free" public education, since one of the principal elements of cost in obtaining education for a person old enough to join the labor force is the earnings he or she must forego during the years in school.) Thus, eliminating employment discrimination should have a double impact on the incomes of the disadvantaged. First, it will raise earnings at given levels of training and education. Second, by doing so, it will increase the rate of return to investment in education, and therefore it will encourage people to obtain more education and training, leading to an additional round of improvement in their earnings.

Lack of job and career information is another form of market imperfection that is thought seriously to restrict the earnings of the poor and especially of those living in poverty areas where they are out of the economic mainstream. As we will see, counseling and information services have therefore been made an important component of many antipoverty programs.

Finally, we might regard the spatial extent of the urban labor market as a form of market imperfection, since it keeps potential buyers and sellers apart. In that case, programs to help the poor by subsidizing transportation between low income neighborhoods and the less accessible centers of employment are also properly classified as policies to improve the functioning of the market.

THE SCOPE OF PRESENT EMPLOYMENT PROGRAMS

For the sake of brevity, the three types of employment policy outlined above might be called "skill creation," "job creation," and (less felicitously) "market improvement policies." To assign actual government programs to one and only one of these classes, however, is likely to be misleading. In practice, actual programs are usually multifaceted. Aware that the causes of poverty are complex, the architects of antipoverty policy have often sought comprehensive countermeasures that combine the features of two or more of the three basic policy types.

The diverse array of employment policies that have been actually tried or seriously proposed since the War on Poverty began is truly bewildering. Some notion of their variety and growth is provided by Table 9.1, which shows first-time enrollments in federally assisted manpower programs at selected dates. The growth of federal concern is illustrated by the fact that first-time enrollments increased from 278,000 in 1964 to an estimated 2.3 million in 1972. The number of major programs in operation multiplied several times over during the same period. The table is by no

TABLE 9.1

Growth of Federally Assisted Manpower Training Programs

	FIRST-TIME ENROLLMENTS (THOUSANDS) FISCAL YEARS			
	1964	1969	1971	1972 (est.)
Institutional training under the Manpower Development and Training Act	278	1,745	2,109	2,318
JOBS (federally financed) and other on-the-job training	9	136	184	136
Neighborhood Youth Corps:				
In-school and summer program	—	430	562	583
Out-of-school program	—	74	53	49
Operation Mainstream	—	11	22	22
Public Service Careers	—	4	45	32
Concentrated Employment Program	—	127	77	69
Job Corps	—	53	50	53
Work Incentive Program	—	81	96	112
Veterans programs	(a)	59	86	83
Vocational rehabilitation	179	368	468	517
Public Employment Program	—	—	—	160
Other programs	21	267	311	335

[a] Included with "other programs."
Sources: U.S. Department of Labor, *Manpower Report of the President, 1971*, Table 1; *1972*, Table 1.

means a complete list of "employment" programs, even at the federal level. Left out are such functions as the U.S. Training and Employment Service and the employment programs of the Office of Economic Opportunity (OEO) for which "enrollment" is not an appropriate measure.

Federal expenditures on manpower training, vocational education, employment services, and miscellaneous manpower aids increased from $389 million in 1964 to an estimated peak level of $4.4 billion in 1973. The President's 1974 budget called for a moderate reduction in federal outlays.[6] A detailed examination of individual manpower programs will not be attempted here. The following paragraphs, however, describe briefly the programs listed in Table 9.1 and indicate for each whether the major objective is skill creation, job creation, improving the functioning of the market, or some combination of those three.[7]

6. *The Budget of the United States Government*, Fiscal Year 1974, Table 17, p. 366.
7. For further detail see the annual *Manpower Report of the President*, prepared by the United States Department of Labor for transmission to the Congress each spring.

Institutional training under the Manpower Development and Train-ing Act (MDTA). The Manpower Development and Training Act of 1962 was the first major manpower legislation of the 1960's. It was originally conceived as a program to retrain the technologically unem-ployed. After the War on Poverty began in 1964, however, MDTA pro-grams were redesigned to give greater emphasis to helping the poor. Today they provide institutional courses and supporting services to a clientele the majority of whom reported their pre-enrollment earnings to be below the poverty level. As its name indicates, the program aims primarily at skill creation.

Job Opportunities in the Business Sector (JOBS). This program is run jointly by the Department of Labor and the National Alliance of Businessmen. Started in March 1968 in response to the previous summer's riots, it places seriously disadvantaged, unemployed workers in jobs in private industry where they receive on-the-job training. The program combines skill creation with a degree of job creation. Since federal sub-sidies are available to employers to help defray the extra cost for a portion of the program, a temporary expansion in the total number of jobs may result. However, the principal long-run effect is probably to divert jobs from the regular labor market toward the program's special clientele.

Neighborhood Youth Corps (NYC). Established under the Eco-nomic Opportunity Act and originally administered by the Office of Economic Opportunity (OEO), this program is now run by the Depart-ment of Labor. Its primary purpose is part-time job creation for youths aged 16 through 21. The jobs, in public service and nonprofit agencies, are viewed as a means of providing income, so that students will not drop out of school, and work experience, to prepare them eventually for the job market. In addition to the in-school program, there is a program for those who have dropped out of school and also a large-scale summer operation. NYC aims more at job creation than at specific skill acquisition, but there is an increasing emphasis on remedial training for out-of-school youths.

Operation Mainstream. This relatively small program combines training and job creation for chronically unemployed adults and the elderly in rural areas.

Public Service Careers (PSC). Essentially, this program is the counterpart in the public sector of the JOBS program in private industry. Disadvantaged workers are placed in temporarily subsidized entry-level jobs with the federal, state, and local governments or in private, nonprofit agencies. They receive on-the-job training and usually a permanent job with at least some prospect of future advancement. Like the JOBS program, PSC relies on job diversion rather than long-run job creation.

Concentrated Employment Program (CEP). Initiated in 1967, this program attempts to provide a full range of manpower services to disadvantaged residents in selected areas that suffer from high unemployment and poverty rates. Much of the effort under CEP involves provision of information and referral of clients to other agencies and through them to job openings.

Job Corps. The Job Corps, like the Neighborhood Youth Corps, was established in 1964. Initially administered by the OEO, it has since been transferred to the Department of Labor. Alone among federal programs it provides training and counseling in special residential centers. Youths aged 16 through 21 from low income areas are eligible to enroll and may remain in the program up to two years. Despite its name, the program aims at skill creation rather than job creation.

Work Incentive Program (WIN). Initiated in 1968, the Work Incentive Program is intended to help welfare clients to achieve economic self-sufficiency and thereby to reduce welfare costs. WIN is one of the fastest growing federal manpower programs. It concentrates on basic education and skill development rather than on job creation.

Veterans programs. Included under this head are a variety of manpower services to help men and women find civilian employment upon leaving the armed forces. These programs focus on training and information rather than on job creation.

Vocational rehabilitation. This large-scale joint federal-state program has been in operation since 1920. It is open only to persons who have physical or mental disabilities that are capable of responding to rehabilitation services. Recently, the program has increasingly sought to serve the disabled poor and to help reduce welfare rolls through rehabilitation of disabled clients.

Public Employment Program (PEP). Unlike most federal manpower programs, PEP concentrates on job creation rather than on training or on improving the efficiency of the labor market. The program was authorized in 1971, partly in response to persistent high rates of unemployment, partly to help communities to expand essential public services. The essence of PEP is a federal subsidy of up to 90 percent of the cost of approved new public employment programs in state and local governments. The authorizing legislation requires that funds be allotted only for jobs that would not otherwise exist, that 85 percent of all funds go toward employee compensation (thus limiting the amount available for training and supportive services), and that all jobs created be transitional to permanent employment (thus ruling out "leaf-raking" enterprises).

What can we say about the success of employment policies in reducing poverty? Which of the many kinds we've tried have worked? How much improvement have they produced? These questions will surely have occurred to anyone who delves into this new and very complex area of applied social and economic theory. Careful evaluation of the results of employment policies is recognized as important both inside and outside the government. Such evaluation not only is necessary in deciding which programs should be continued and which should be dropped, but also is essential in developing desirable modifications to ongoing programs.

Evaluation of Manpower Training Programs

Manpower training programs are relatively amenable to benefit-cost analysis. Consequently, policies aimed at skill creation have been subject to systematic evaluation far more frequently than have other antipoverty efforts. As we will see, however, there remains considerable disagreement as to just what these studies demonstrate.

In a benefit-cost analysis of a training scheme, benefits are usually defined as the gain in earnings when the earnings of trainees after they have completed the course are compared either with their pre-enrollment level or with the earnings of a control group of nontrainees. Since the studies are generally conducted within a year or two after the program ends, the analyst must supply an estimate of how far into the future the gain in earnings is expected to persist. Usually counted as costs are the costs of instruction and administration and the foregone earnings of trainees while enrolled in the program. The expected benefit stream and the computed costs are then both discounted to obtain present values, and the end result is a comparison between the present value of benefits and that of costs. As long as the former exceeds the latter, undertaking the program will produce a net gain for society. In principle, if budget funds are limited, public authorities should choose the combination of programs that will produce the largest total net gain within the budget constraint.[8]

---

8. A. R. Prest and R. Turvey, "Cost-Benefit Analysis: A Survey," *Economic Journal,* December 1965, pp. 683–735, provides an excellent introduction to the theory and practice of cost-benefit analysis. It discusses applications to general education but refers only briefly to manpower training.

The first benefit-cost studies of manpower training dealt with programs that were carried out in the early 1960's. For the most part these analyses found that from the point of view of society as a whole the economic benefits of training programs outweighed their economic costs, sometimes by a very wide margin. For example, Einar Hardin reviewed five early benefit-cost studies and recomputed the findings to put them as nearly as possible on a comparable basis. Using rather conservative assumptions, he found that the ratio of benefits to costs for programs as a whole varied from 1.5 upward to 5.9. Benefits were found to be less than costs only for one subgroup of trainees who received an unusually long, and therefore expensive, training course.[9]

It was objected that the studies reviewed by Hardin threw little light on antipoverty programs because they were based on experience in the early 1960's, when federal manpower operations were directed toward the technologically unemployed rather than toward the poor and the disadvantaged. The implication was that the impoverished, the disadvantaged, and the hard-core unemployed would be less easily retrained, leading to less favorable benefit-cost ratios. More recently, however, there have been benefit-cost studies of several poverty-oriented manpower programs. For example, David O. Sewell in 1971 published a study of a training effort in North Carolina that was designed to serve severely disadvantaged rural workers. He calculated that the average benefit-cost ratio for all clients was an impressive 3.1.[10] Borus, Brennan, and Rosen studied the Neighborhood Youth Corps out-of-school program in Indiana, using 1967 data, and found that benefit-cost ratios were far above one for boys, but less than one for girls.[11]

In 1972 the staff of the Joint Economic Committee of the Congress surveyed and summarized existing benefit-cost studies of federally sponsored training programs. They found far more studies of Manpower Development and Training Act programs than of any other group, no doubt because MDTA is the oldest of current efforts (apart from veteran's services and vocational rehabilitation). Almost without exception, these analyses estimated favorable benefit-cost ratios for MDTA programs. The staff report found that other federally sponsored efforts were more difficult to evaluate. Basic data on the JOBS and WIN programs are so inadequate

9. Einar Hardin, "Benefit-Cost Analyses of Occupational Training Programs: A Comparison of Recent Studies," in G. G. Somers and W. D. Wood, eds., *Cost-Benefit Analyses of Manpower Policies*, Proceedings of a North American Conference (Kingston, Ontario: Industrial Relations Centre, Queen's University, 1969), Table 1, p. 113.

10. D. O. Sewell, *Training the Poor* (Kingston, Ontario: Industrial Relations Centre, Queen's University, 1971), Table 13, p. 98.

11. Michael E. Borus, John P. Brennan, and Sidney Rosen, "A Benefit-Cost Analysis of the Neighborhood Youth Corps: The Out-of-School Program in Indiana," *Journal of Human Resources*, Spring 1970, pp. 139–59.

that no benefit-cost analyses have been carried out. In other cases—the Jobs Corps and the Neighborhood Youth Corps in-school program—benefit-cost studies have been performed, but the staff report found them unreliable, because of either poor data or questionable methodology.[12]

There are, in fact, a good many unresolved questions about the manner in which benefit-cost analysis should be applied to manpower training programs.[13] Analysts continue to disagree, therefore, about the validity of many of the existing studies. We will mention only a few of the critical questions here, but they are questions that do illuminate the central issue: what is the economic impact of training programs on society as a whole? First, there is the problem of separating out training effects from job-placement effects. How can we be sure that the higher earnings recorded by trainees are not attributable to the organized job-placement effort that accompanies each training program rather than to the value of the training itself? To take up an allied point, does the training program increase a worker's real productivity or does it just fill a "credentialing function," opening up a better job to a trainee than to a nonparticipant solely because employers use training credentials as a screening device in filling jobs? If training does increase worker productivity and we observe this in the first year after training, how far into the future can we expect the gain to persist, given the rapid obsolescence of specific skills? Unfortunately, follow-up studies rarely extend beyond the first year, so the probable duration of benefits remains an unresolved question. In the absence of specific information, a ten-year stream of benefits is often assumed by the analyst. A decision on this point obviously can be crucial. Some studies that yield benefits in excess of costs on the assumption of a ten-year benefit stream produce costs in excess of benefits when the latter are assumed to last only five years.[14]

A final source of uncertainty in the evaluation of manpower training programs is the possible existence of indirect benefits. Economists generally recognize that training programs may have socially beneficial indirect effects associated with the increased incomes they produce, such as a reduction in crime and civil disorder or an improvement in family stability or health. However, these indirect benefits are usually omitted from benefit-cost calculations because it is so difficult to estimate their

12. Joint Economic Committee, Congress of the United States, *The Effectiveness of Manpower Training Programs: A Review of Research on the Impact on the Poor,* Studies in Public Welfare, Paper No. 3, November 20, 1972.

13. In addition to the study cited in note 12, above, see: the papers in Somers and Wood; Thomas I. Ribich, *Education and Poverty* (Washington, D.C.: Brookings Institution, 1968), Ch. 3; and Anthony H. Pascal, "Manpower Training and Jobs," in A. H. Pascal, ed., *Cities in Trouble: An Agenda for Urban Research*, Memorandum RM-5603-RC (Santa Monica, Calif.: The Rand Corporation, August 1968), pp. 47–79.

14. *The Effectiveness of Manpower Training Programs*, p. 30.

monetary value. Leaving them out may impart a significant downward bias to measured benefit-cost ratios. On the other hand, it could also help to offset the opposite effect of overly enthusiastic estimates of the direct economic gains from training.

Evaluation of Job Creation, Job Placement, and Antidiscrimination Policies

Among policies for job creation we have listed the proposal that the government act as "employer of last resort" for those who wish to work but cannot find jobs in the private sector. This virtually open-ended commitment to a guaranteed job has not been put into effect. Numerous objections have been raised to it. Probably the most telling is that the jobs would tend to be of the low-skill, dead-end, leaf-raking variety, an outcome that would be unsatisfactory both to the worker and to the public employer. The worker (assuming he were willing to accept such a job) would find himself in a position that neither he nor the rest of society could look on with pride, hope, and respect. Perhaps even more serious would be the long-run effects on efficiency in the public agencies. Netzer points out that to encourage labor-intensive methods through the deliberate proliferation of low-skilled jobs is to push local governments—now badly in need of raising worker productivity—in precisely the wrong direction.[15] As a practical matter, how could any mayor successfully mount a campaign to raise output per worker through either improved methods or greater mechanization in the face of an open-ended commitment to produce not public services but public "jobs"?

The Public Employment Program (PEP), described earlier, is not a commitment by the government to act as employer of last resort, although it might be regarded as a very small step in that direction—"small" because it was expected to provide only 145,000 jobs in fiscal 1972, at a time when the unemployed numbered more than 4 million. Because it is so small, however, PEP may be able to avoid concentrating on dead-end, low-skill jobs. Such at least is the intent. The program is still too new to be evaluated.

Maintaining Tight Labor Markets

Job creation programs and skill creation programs are complementary. If the demand for labor is weak, graduates of training programs will have difficulty in obtaining jobs. Their training may go to waste.

15. Dick Netzer, *Economics and Urban Problems* (New York: Basic Books, 1970), p. 58.

Furthermore, the power of training programs to attract and hold trainees depends on their record of success in leading to employment.

On the other hand, if trainees *do* find jobs while unemployment is widespread, it may be reasonable to assume that they have taken positions that otherwise would have been filled by qualified nontrainees. If one-for-one job displacement occurs, there is no gain to society in the form of increased total output; there is only a transfer of employment achieved at considerable public cost. From such a transfer the disadvantaged may gain, but it will be at the expense of other members of the working class, a doubtful benefit from the point of view of society as a whole and one likely to strengthen political opposition to poverty programs. Thus tight labor markets are probably essential to the efficient operation of training programs.

Causality runs the other way as well. If labor markets are tight, an opportunity exists for employing the hard-core unemployed or for upgrading some of those presently in low-skilled jobs. Without adequate training programs, some of these opportunities may be wasted. The real output of society will remain below its attainable level even though labor markets are tight.

Tight labor markets are achieved by using the macroeconomic tools of monetary and fiscal policy to keep aggregate demand at an appropriately high level. Is there any evidence that such a policy has improved the relative economic standing of the disadvantaged, as the queuing theory of the labor market (described earlier) would suggest? Studying the period 1954 through mid-1966, Thurow found that "the large relative employment gains predicted for Negro workers by advocates of unbalanced [i.e., tight] labor markets certainly exist . . . ." [16] It is easy to verify that these relative employment gains were associated with relative income gains. As the data in Table 8.3 show, when labor markets were tight during the 1950's and 1960's, the ratio of median nonwhite family income to median white family income tended to rise. ("Nonwhite" income is used here instead of "Negro" because the data on that basis extend much farther back in time. There is no reason to think this affects the argument.) For example, the ratio increased from .53 in 1961, a year of high unemployment, to .60 in 1966, a year of low unemployment. When labor markets were slack, the reverse tended to occur. The nonwhite-to-white income ratio fell from .57 during the period of high employment generated by the Korean War in 1952 to .51 in 1958, during a sharp recession. After a brief recovery, it fell again during the economic downswing from 1960 to 1961.

On the basis of data down through 1967, Thurow concluded that "better utilization of economic resources improves job and income oppor-

16. Thurow, p. 57.

tunities of Negroes, but after adjustment for cyclical effects there have been no favorable (or unfavorable) trends in those opportunities in the postwar period." [17] If this statistical finding were correct, it would mean (as Thurow elsewhere pointed out) that we have no evidence that efforts to raise the relative income level of blacks through training programs, antidiscrimination laws, and job placement services (which he nevertheless strongly endorses) have thus far produced any significant aggregate effects. Macroeconomic cycles alone could account for the improvement in the relative income level of blacks since the inception of the Civil Rights Movement and, later, the War on Poverty.

Fortunately, events since 1967 suggest a less gloomy view. First of all, the ratio of median nonwhite-to-white family income rose from .60 in 1966 to .63 in 1969, even though overall unemployment rates changed very little during the period. That may be evidence that antipoverty policies other than macroeconomic stimulation were finally beginning to take effect. Second, if cyclical forces alone governed the ratio of nonwhite-to-white income, the recession of 1970–71 should have produced a downturn in the ratio. To the contrary, however, the ratio rose from .63 in 1969 to .64 in 1970, its highest recorded level. In 1971 it slipped back to .63 but was still ten points higher than it had been a decade earlier. One swallow does not make a summer, and one recession in which relative black gains were not washed out by rising unemployment does not finally disprove the experience of two earlier decades. Nevertheless, the evidence since 1966 does provide ground for a tentative conclusion that training programs, antidiscrimination laws, and job placement services are now beginning to pay off.

Unfortunately, there seems to be no way to evaluate the independent effects of either job placement programs or antidiscrimination laws. Whatever effects they have in producing a favorable long-term trend in the ratio of average nonwhite-to-white income are indistinguishably merged with the influence of training and education in raising the skill level of the nonwhite population. Consequently, it is difficult to identify the optimum "mix" of policies. In the present state of our knowledge, even the most sophisticated analyst can do no more than call for "coordinated programs to promote the employment of the poor."

Meanwhile, the policy of maintaining tight labor markets in order to fight poverty has clearly run into trouble. Advocates of that policy have always recognized that it would cause some price inflation, perhaps even a higher rate of inflation than most people had previously thought tolerable. They argued, however, that given the unavoidable trade-off between price stability and full employment, it was desirable to accept some price

17. *Ibid.*, p. 111.

inflation for the sake of greater success in the fight against poverty. Washington thought otherwise, and anti-inflationary monetary policies contributed to the recession of 1970–71. In the early 1970's, with sentiment against price inflation running strong and the United States balance of payments under continuing pressure, it remained uncertain when the government would again be willing to risk the inflationary effects of a return to tight labor markets.

THE NEED FOR INCOME MAINTENANCE

No matter how successful employment policies may prove to be, income maintenance in the form of transfer payments from the government is undoubtedly necessary if we are to eliminate poverty. In any society there is a large number of families whose adult members are outside the labor force either because they have retired or are disabled or because society believes they should not work. If these families have inadequate pensions or other sources of income, they can be raised out of poverty only by some form of income maintenance. Another large group consists of families with heads whose earning power is so low that even when they are employed full time, their families remain below the poverty line. Although some of these "working poor" may raise themselves out of poverty by acquiring higher skills or better paid jobs, others will remain impoverished unless they are relieved by direct cash payments.

Table 9.2 indicates the importance of these two groups. In 1971, 36 percent of all families living in poverty contained no wage earner. In the same year 20 percent of all families living in poverty were headed by a

TABLE 9.2
Characteristics of Families Below the Poverty Line

	1971		1960	
	Number (thousands)	*Percentage of Poverty Families*	*Number (thousands)*	*Percentage of Poverty Families*
Families below the poverty line	5,303	100.0%	8,243	100.0%
With no earners	1,907	36.0	1,841	22.3
With head who worked year round at full-time job	1,084	20.4	2,577	31.3

Sources: U.S. Bureau of the Census, *Current Population Reports*, Series P-60, No. 68, December 31, 1969, Table 7 and Table 8, and Series P-60, No. 86, December 1972, Table 24.

person who worked at a full-time job for the whole year. It is highly significant that the proportion of poor families with no wage earner has increased steadily over time, rising from 22 percent in 1960 to 36 percent eleven years later, while over the same period, the proportion with a family head who worked year round at a full-time job fell from 31 percent to 20 percent. Both of these trends result from the same cause: the general, year-after-year rise in labor productivity. As Thurow points out, "Those who are able to take advantage of better job opportunities or of government programs to increase individual productivity are gradually drawn out of the poverty pool. Those who cannot benefit are left at the bottom of the income distribution and consequently represent an increasing fraction of the poor . . . . The bottom of the income distribution will be increasingly made up of those not in the labor force." [18] Thus, as time passes and the number of families living in poverty declines, we must expect the proportion (though not necessarily the number) who need income maintenance to increase markedly.

In what follows we will use "income maintenance" as a general term to cover proposals known variously as the negative income tax, the credit income tax, the family assistance plan, or the guaranteed minimum income. These proposals embody a common social commitment and share a common technical structure that distinguish them clearly from existing cash transfer programs. The commitment is that the government guarantees a specified minimum annual income to every person or family as a matter of right. The individual or family qualifies for aid on the basis of need, taking into consideration only two factors: income in the absence of aid and family size. This commitment marks a radical break with the tradition under which government transfer payments have been made in the past. We do already have a large number of public assistance and other cash transfer programs in the United States, and they do provide a rapidly growing total of cash transfers to those who qualify under a bewildering variety of headings. But the existing set of programs was designed to alleviate certain carefully defined categories of hardship, not to attack poverty across the board. Thus many of the poor are not its beneficiaries, and many of its beneficiaries remain poor.

Public Assistance and Other Cash Transfer Programs

The dimensions of existing cash transfer programs are indicated in Table 9.3. Expenditures have increased sharply since the War on Poverty began in the early 1960's. They totaled $102 billion in fiscal 1971–72, more than two and one-half times the level recorded in 1964–65. Among the

18. *Ibid.*, pp. 140–41.

TABLE 9.3
Government Cash Transfer and Medical Assistance Programs

	EXPENDITURE BY ALL LEVELS OF GOVERNMENT (MILLIONS OF DOLLARS, FISCAL YEARS)		STATE AND LOCAL AS PERCENTAGE OF TOTAL EXPENDITURE	
	1964–65	*1971–72*	*1964–65*	*1971–72*
Total expenditure, including administrative costs	$39,688	$102,146	22.7%	22.9%
Public assistance, total	5,875	21,446	45.8	45.0
Payments	5,285	18,091	45.4	46.7
Old-age assistance	2,043	1,846	35.2	36.6
Aid to families with dependent children	1,725	6,476	44.5	44.8
Aid to the blind	99	98	52.5	40.8
Aid to the permanently and totally disabled	513	1,227	44.0	42.9
Medical assistance (Medicaid)	—	6,744	—	45.6
General assistance	382	851	100.0	100.0
Other payments	523	849	48.4	43.1
Administration	588	3,160	49.3	38.3
Miscellaneous programs	1	195	0	0
Social insurance, total	28,123	75,063	22.5	18.3
Old-age, survivors, disability and health insurance	16,998	48,259	0	0
Other social insurance	11,125	26,804	56.8	51.1
Veterans' pensions, medical care and insurance	5,690	8,992	0	0

Sources: Alfred M. Skolnik and Sophie R. Dales, "Social Welfare Expenditures, 1971–72," *Social Security Bulletin,* December 1972, Table 1, p. 5. Public Assistance subcategories are from unpublished worksheets of the Office of Research and Statistics, Social Security Administration.

programs shown in the table, only those under the heading of "public assistance" are really aimed at the relief of poverty. These programs accounted for only 21 percent of total expenditures in 1971–72. However, they are growing much faster than either social insurance or veteran's programs, the other major categories of transfer expenditure.

The administrative costs of each transfer program are included in the expenditure totals shown in Table 9.3, but these costs are given separately only for public assistance. Not included as transfer expenditures are "benefits in kind" provided through housing subsidies, food stamps, and nutrition programs, in part for the relief of poverty. Federal expenditures for these purposes came to about $1.5 billion in 1970 and are rising rapidly.

With the exception of general assistance, which is paid for by the states and localities, the public assistance programs were established under the original Social Security Act in 1935 or under later amendments to it. The federally authorized programs are paid for by a system of grants to the state governments. Matching formulas vary from program to program. Since the states are given considerable freedom of action within limits set by federal law, benefit levels and the details of eligibility rules vary widely among the states. So, too, does the financial contribution required by the state of its local governments. Table 9.3 shows that state and local governments financed 45 percent of public assistance expenditures in 1971–72. Localities provided about one-fourth and the states about three-fourths of that share.

The individual public assistance programs can be very briefly described as follows.[19] Old-age assistance (OAA) provides cash to old persons who receive either no retirement benefits or inadequate benefits under Social Security. Aid to the blind (AB) provides cash support to people with seriously impaired vision. Aid to the permanently and totally disabled (APTD) offers income supplements to those whose disability prevents them from earning a living.[20] General assistance is the name given to whatever aid the states and localities see fit to offer those of the poor who do not qualify for any federally authorized program.

By far the largest and fastest growing categories of public assistance are medical assistance (Medicaid) and aid to families with dependent children (AFDC). Medicaid was written into the Social Security law in 1965. It pays medical expenses for persons who are on the rolls of AFDC, AB, APTD, and OAA and for others who qualify by having sufficiently low incomes.

AFDC accounts for most of what is commonly referred to as "welfare." Until 1961 families were eligible only if one parent was absent or had died. This provision was widely believed to encourage desertion (either real or pretended), a remarkable instance of a social policy rule having perverse, antisocial consequences. The law was amended in 1961 to permit states also to assist families in which the father was present but

19. For further detail see Alan B. Batchelder, *The Economics of Poverty*, 2nd ed. (New York: John Wiley & Sons, 1971), Ch. 7; Levitan, Ch. 2; and Charles L. Schultze, *et al.*, *Setting National Priorities, the 1973 Budget* (Washington, D.C.: Brookings Institution, 1972), Ch. 6.

20. After January 1, 1974, these three will be consolidated into a single program entitled Supplemental Security Income. Known as SSI, the new program will be financed entirely by the federal government, rather than by matching grants, but states will be permitted to supplement the standard federal benefit.

unemployed, but only about half the states have adopted this policy. In any event, the new rule does not eliminate the incentive to desert on the part of the *employed* father: society will assist his family if he leaves but not if he stays.

AFDC provisions regarding earned income have also probably had perverse incentive effects. Down to 1967, beneficiaries who worked gave up a dollar of benefits for each dollar earned. In effect they were placed in a 100 percent income tax bracket for their initial earnings, thus facing the ultimate disincentive to work. A 1967 amendment permits beneficiaries to retain $30 a month plus one-third of earnings. But that is still nearly a 67 percent marginal tax rate on earnings, hardly a powerful incentive to work.

Benefits paid under AFDC vary greatly from state to state. At the end of 1972 the average monthly payment per recipient (i.e., per family member) ranged from a low of $14.41 in Mississippi to a high of $95.01 in Massachusetts. The nation-wide average was $53.95.[21]

As Table 9.3 shows, old-age, survivors, disability, and health insurance (what is usually called Social Security) is much larger than any of the public assistance programs. We have not included OASDHI among those programs aimed at the relief of poverty, first, because the benefits are paid for largely (though not entirely) out of a fund to which the beneficiaries have contributed and, second, because benefit levels are not dependent on the beneficiaries current income. It is true that two-thirds of those receiving Social Security would be classified as poor in the absence of such aid and that almost half of that two-thirds are raised out of poverty by their benefits. Nevertheless Social Security is properly thought of as a program for financing retirement rather than for relieving poverty. That most of its beneficiaries would be poor in its absence is not persuasive, since if Social Security did not exist many of them would have made other arrangements for retirement.

Criticism of Current Public Assistance Programs

No aspect of American social policy has been more widely criticized in recent years than its "welfare," or public assistance, programs. The multitude of objections refer essentially to three points. The first is that our public assistance programs are inadequate—they do not come close to eliminating poverty. This failure results partly from gaps in a hodge-podge of programs that were intended to relieve specific categories of hardship,

21. Social Security Administration, *Social Security Bulletin*, May 1973, Table M-27. Included in the national average are Puerto Rico, Guam, and the Virgin Islands, as well as the 50 states.

rather than poverty as such, and partly from the grossly inadequate level of benefits offered in many states.

The inadequacy of public assistance programs to relieve poverty has been measured statistically. Batchelder calculates that in 1965 public assistance went to 1.8 million households headed by persons less than 65 years old. He estimates that 77 percent of such households were poor according to federal government criteria before receiving aid, but that only 14 percent of that 77 percent were lifted out of poverty by the aid they received. The record was only a little better for households headed by persons 65 or over. Of the 1.1 million that received public assistance, 87 percent were poor without such aid, and 24 percent of that 87 percent were raised out of poverty.[22] The situation appears even grimmer than these figures suggest if one recalls that a considerable number of poor families do not even qualify for public assistance and are omitted entirely from these calculations.

The second major criticism of American welfare policy is that it lacks geographic uniformity. Although poverty in a society open to easy internal migration is essentially a national problem, our public assistance programs, as we have already indicated, allow enormous interstate variation in benefit levels. Instead of using the national tax base to relieve poverty uniformly throughout the land, we have allowed a system to develop under which the poor are treated very unequally, depending on where they live. For example, a recent analysis calls attention to the following dramatic evidence of disparities in benefits between two major cities: "In Detroit . . . a nonworking mother of three children on welfare can receive cash, food, and medical benefits worth $4,894 a year—benefits equivalent to $5,373 before taxes. If the same family moved to Atlanta it would be eligible for $2,710 in benefits . . . ." [23]

The real problem, of course, is that families will be tempted to move the other way. From the point of view of society as a whole, it is desirable for the poor to move to areas of better economic opportunity, where they can earn higher incomes on the basis of higher real productivity. On the other hand, it is certainly *not* desirable that their decision to move should be influenced by interarea differences in the level of transfer payments, since these are not connected with differences in productivity.

Some taxpayers in states with high benefit levels are convinced that their states' relative generosity has attracted an influx of poor people in search of aid. To refute the view that high benefit levels attract the poor,

22. Batchelder, Table 7–4, p. 163.
23. Schultze, *et al.*, p. 197, citing a study prepared for the Joint Economic Committee of the Congress.

others have cited the fact that very few of those "on welfare" in the high benefit states are recent arrivals. But this counter-argument is hardly sufficient: it may be that the availability of high benefit levels holds recent migrants in areas they would otherwise leave when their initial expectations about income and employment are disappointed. Thus without actually attracting the poor from elsewhere, high local benefit levels might nonetheless cause them, so to speak, to "pile up" locally.

Regardless of possible effects on migration, interstate variations in benefit levels raise grave questions of equity for taxpayers as well as for beneficiaries. States that seriously undertake to relieve poverty through public assistance must tax themselves heavily to do so. If localities within the state are required by state law to contribute to local public assistance programs (as is sometimes the case), then a heavy burden is placed on localities having a high proportion of citizens in need of aid.

The incidence of poverty is now much higher in the central cities than in the suburbs. Consequently arrangements under which localities must contribute toward the cost of public assistance programs penalize central cities but are advantageous to wealthy suburbs, since the latter would contribute more toward the support of welfare if financing depended on state-wide taxes. We will return to this problem in Chapter 12, which deals with metropolitan public finance.

The third major criticism of our current public assistance programs is that they are badly designed in detail. They are cumbersome and expensive to administer, sometimes degrading to beneficiaries, and often perverse in their social and economic consequences. Important examples of perverse effects were cited in the discussion of AFDC.

Income-maintenance policies, so their advocates argue, can overcome most of the defects of our current public assistance programs. Let us first see how income maintenance works and then discuss its possible advantages.

How Income Maintenance Works

All rational income-maintenance proposals call for 100 percent financing by the federal government. Whatever benefits they provide would be paid for entirely out of national tax revenues, with no contribution by state or local governments. The objective is to create a uniform national standard for the relief of poverty. It would be impossible to accomplish this without federal financing, since the poorer states could never afford to pay benefits at the level deemed appropriate by the nation as a whole.

The technical structure, shared by all income-maintenance proposals, consists of three elements. First, a guaranteed minimum income per person or per family, which the government will provide when the beneficiary has no other income. Second, a "take-back rate" at which the government reduces cash payments if the beneficiary does have any earned income. Third, a "break-even level" at which earned income is high enough so that benefit payments under the plan cease.

A simple illustration worked out in Table 9.4 shows how these elements fit together. Suppose that the income guarantee is set at $750 per person. A family of four would then receive $4 \times \$750 = \$3,000$ per year if it had no other income. Next, assume that benefits are reduced by $40 for every $100 of income the family earns. The "take-back rate," in other words, is 40 percent. For example, if the family earns $4,000 during the year, benefit payments will be reduced by $.40 \times \$4,000 = \$1,600$. The family will receive net benefits of $\$3,000 - \$1,600 = \$1,400$. Its total income will be $\$4,000 + \$1,400 = \$5,400$. (See the fifth line of Table 9.4.)

If the family's earned income rises year by year, its benefits under the plan will steadily decrease. When earned income reaches $7,500 a year, net benefits will fall to zero, since the take-back rate applied to earned income will yield a sum just equal to the initial income guarantee $(.40 \times \$7,500 = \$3,000)$. Thus $7,500 would be the break-even level of earned income at which net benefit payments under the plan cease for a four-person family.

How does such a plan affect the income tax liability of its beneficiaries? It is always necessary to provide for the meshing of an income-maintenance plan with provisions of the ordinary income tax. The simplest method is to make the take-back tax rate applicable as the marginal rate of income tax for incomes above the break-even level up to the point at which it would generate tax liability equal to that under the pre-existing income tax schedule. Beyond that point, the family "switches over" to the ordinary bracket rate tax schedule.

The result of meshing the two systems in this way is illustrated by the last three columns of Table 9.4. Income tax liability is calculated on the basis of 1971 rates and provisions. If there were no income-maintenance program, the family would pay $582 in ordinary income tax when earned income was $7,500. When income maintenance is in effect, the family pays no income tax at that point. Thus, although net benefit payments from the government are zero at the break-even income level of $7,500, there is nonetheless a $582 saving on income tax. As income rises above $7,500, taxes under the income-maintenance scheme begin to catch up with ordinary tax liability. The tax saving diminishes and reaches zero for a family of four when earned income is $10,000.

The three structural elements of an income-maintenance plan are

TABLE 9.4
A Hypothetical Income-Maintenance Plan, Illustrated for a Family of Four

INCOME GUARANTEE (Y_g) = $750 PER PERSON
TAKE-BACK TAX RATE (t_e) = .40

1	2	3	4	5	6	7	8
Earned Income (Y_e)	Guaranteed Minimum Income, or Benefit Level When $Y_e = 0$ (Y_g)	Reduction of Benefits on Account of Earned Income $(t_e \cdot Y_e)$	Net Benefit Paid by Government (Col. 2 − Col. 3)	Total Income Before Income Tax (Col. 1 + Col. 4)	Income Tax Liability on Earned Income in the Absence of Income-Maintenance Plan [a]	Income Tax Liability Under Income Maintenance, Above Benefit Break-even Level (Col. 3 − Col. 2)	Tax Saving Under Income-Maintenance Plan (Col. 6 − Col. 7)
0	3,000	0	3,000	3,000	0	0	0
1,000	3,000	400	2,600	3,600	0	0	0
2,000	3,000	800	2,200	4,200	0	0	0
3,000	3,000	1,200	1,800	4,800	0	0	0
4,000	3,000	1,600	1,400	5,400	39	0	39
5,000	3,000	2,000	1,000	6,000	181	0	181
6,000	3,000	2,400	600	6,600	334	0	334
7,500	3,000	3,000	0	7,500	582	0	582
9,000	3,000	3,600	0	9,000	839	600	239
10,000	3,000	4,000	0	10,000	1,000	1,000	0

[a] Calculated by applying 1971 federal income tax rates to incomes in Column 1.

related by a simple mathematical formula, as Christopher Green has shown.[24] Let

Y_g = income guarantee per person when earned income is zero
Y_e = earned income
t_e = take-back tax rate on earned income
R = break-even level of earned income

Then the relationship between the three structural elements is given mathematically by

$$R = \frac{Y_g}{t_e}$$

This equation can be explained as follows: by definition, R is that level of Y_e such that

$$Y_g - t_e Y_e = 0$$

which can be rewritten as

$$Y_e = \frac{Y_g}{t_e}$$

Substituting R for Y_e, we obtain

$$R = \frac{Y_g}{t_e}$$

Putting data from Table 9.4 into the equation we observe that

$$\$7,500 = \frac{\$3,000}{.40}$$

It is apparent that once the values of any two of the three structural elements are specified, the value of the third is mathematically determined. In other words, we can freely choose values for any two of them but not for all three. This is obviously an important constraint on the design of income-maintenance schemes.

Each of the three structural elements described above is related specifically to one of the major objectives of antipoverty policy. Consider first the objective of eliminating poverty by transferring income: the adequacy of an income-maintenance plan to relieve poverty depends directly upon the level chosen for Y_g. In measuring the adequacy of a transfer program to relieve poverty, the concept of a national aggregate "poverty gap" is helpful. This gap is defined as the aggregate sum of money that

24. Christopher Green, *Negative Taxes and the Poverty Problem* (Washington, D.C.: Brookings Institution, 1967), p. 63.

would have to be transferred to the poor population to raise each poor person just to the poverty line. In 1971 the poverty gap amounted to $12.0 billion.[25] In our hypothetical illustration Y_g is clearly too low to close the poverty gap completely. For example, poverty line income for a four-person family is calculated to be about $4,100, but the proposed income guarantee to that family is only $3,000. That still leaves a considerable "gap."

A second objective of antipoverty policy is to encourage (or at least not to discourage) work effort by the poor. In this connection, the level of the take-back tax rate, t_e, is important since it helps to determine the way in which the plan affects the work incentives of its beneficiaries. If a person who is not employed receives $3,000 a year for his family as a gift, how great is his incentive to go out and work to gain additional income? Clearly the incentive depends in part on the tax rate he will pay on the earned income. The higher the marginal tax rate, the less he will be able to keep of the additional income, and therefore the less incentive he has to work for it.

We pointed out earlier that one of the major objections to AFDC has been that benefits are reduced too sharply as the family begins to earn income. Until 1967 the effective marginal tax rate under AFDC was 100 percent, since benefits were reduced one dollar for each dollar of earnings. Subsequently the effective marginal rate was lowered to 67 percent, still a formidable disincentive to work effort. Income-maintenance plans would generally lower the rate to 50 percent or less in order to encourage beneficiaries to work.

The effect on work incentives of substituting income maintenance for AFDC would probably vary, depending on the initial situation of the beneficiary. The adult who was not working while on AFDC might well be encouraged to work by the lower marginal tax rate of an income-maintenance scheme. On the other hand, it is one of the advantages of income maintenance that it could systematically pay benefits to the working poor —those whose earning power is so low that even when fully employed they remain below the poverty line, and it is at least possible that the introduction of income maintenance would discourage some of this group from working. Imagine a man who has been employed full time but earns only $4,000 a year. Now suppose that income maintenance is introduced; he finds that his family will be given $4,000 a year if he does no work but that if he earns income it will be "taxed" at a 50 percent take-back rate. He might decide to remain unemployed, living on his accustomed $4,000 a year rather than work full time for the sake of $2,000 of additional income. In short, the strong "income effect" of a generous income-mainte-

25. U.S. Bureau of the Census, *Current Population Reports*, Series P-60, No. 86, December 1972, Table J.

nance plan might discourage some people with low earning power from working at all.

The final structural element to be examined is R, the break-even level of earned income. The level of R strongly influences the budgetary cost of an income-maintenance plan. Antipoverty policy is required by the realities of politics to achieve results at an acceptable cost to those who must pay taxes that support it. Consequently the level of R is a key factor in comparisons between alternative proposals.

Everyone with earned income less than R receives net cash benefits under income maintenance. Hence, the higher the level of R, the greater the number of persons receiving benefits and, for any given value of Y_g, the greater the total cost of benefits paid. In 1971 the median income of four-person families in the United States was $11,626. About 22 percent of them had incomes below $7,500.[26] Thus a scheme such as the one illustrated in Table 9.4 would have paid net benefits to more than one-fifth of all four-person families. In addition, the number of persons whose income tax liability is reduced will increase as R increases. Presumably the lost revenues have to be made up. The effect is a further increase in the tax cost of the plan that must be borne by nonbeneficiaries.

Balancing the Objectives of an Income-Maintenance Program

Let us now examine the trade-offs among major objectives that are implicit in the structural equation for an income-maintenance scheme. We have seen that the plan outlined above might be criticized as inadequate to relieve poverty. Then why not increase the minimum income guarantee for a family of four to $4,000 a year and close the poverty gap completely? The obvious answer is that doing so would raise the break-even level from $7,500 to $10,000 and add enormously to the cost of the program. We would be paying net benefits to about 38 percent of all four-person families, the wealthiest of them clearly living at close to a middle-class standard.

Closing the aggregate national poverty gap by means of income allowances requires large-scale transfers, not because the gap itself is so wide, but because there is no way of closing it, consistent with the other objectives of antipoverty policy, that does not involve a good deal of "excess redistribution." Part of this "excess" goes to raise people from below the poverty line to some point above it (example: the family in Table 9.4 with $3,000 of earned income). Another part goes to supplement the incomes of those who were above the poverty line even before receiving benefits (example: the family with $6,000 of earned income in Table 9.4).

26. U.S. Bureau of the Census, *Current Population Reports*, Series P-60, No. 80, October 4, 1971, Table 18.

The result is an aggregate redistribution that far exceeds the size of the poverty gap itself.

The only way to avoid all "excess redistribution" would be to guarantee everyone a poverty line income while at the same time reducing the benefit payment by one dollar for every dollar of earned income. Under that arrangement no one initially above the poverty line would receive anything and no one initially below the line would receive net benefits that would raise him so much as a dollar above it. But we would be imposing a 100 percent take-back tax rate on the first few thousand dollars of people's earnings. As we have already argued in connection with AFDC, such a policy seriously reduces work incentives for those whose earning power is low. To avoid this weakening of work incentives we must keep the take-back tax rate down, but in so doing we build a good deal of "excess redistribution" into the plan. And the lower the take-back tax rate, the greater the amount of the excess redistribution.

Some notion of the magnitudes involved is provided by Tobin's study using data for 1966.[27] The poverty gap in that year amounted to $11 billion. An income-maintenance plan with guarantees high enough to raise everyone out of poverty and with a 50 percent take-back tax rate on the earnings of beneficiaries would have transferred a total of $21.2 billion from the nonpoor to those who would have been poor but for the benefit payments. (Not included in the total is the redistribution that would occur among the nonpoor.) With a take-back tax rate of 33⅓ percent the total transfer would have increased to $23.2 billion. Public assistance grants to the poor amounted to $4.3 billion in 1966. Deducting that sum from the above total yields the net *additional* transfer that would have been required in 1966 to eliminate poverty under these plans.

The trade-off among the objectives attainable through income maintenance is frustrating to the policy designer but surely not fatal to the case for income maintenance. A compromise among contending values can yield a scheme, along the lines shown in Table 9.4, that substantially reduces poverty, maintains work incentives, and yet does not impose a prohibitive cost on taxpayers. Benefit levels under such a plan are higher than those currently provided by public assistance in many of the poorer states, especially in the South. By superseding public assistance in those states, the plan would make a start at reducing the geographic differentials in benefits that are such an objectionable feature of current public assistance programs. It would come nowhere near eliminating them, however, since in the wealthier states of the North and West benefits under categorical public assistance are already much higher than those implied in Table 9.4.

27. James Tobin, "Raising the Incomes of the Poor," in Kermit Gordon, ed., *Agenda for the Nation* (Washington, D.C.: Brookings Institution, 1968), pp. 104–05.

Very probably any plan that would raise benefits everywhere to the level now prevailing in the wealthiest states would be too costly to win political acceptance. Many advocates of income maintenance are willing to accept a less ambitious initial effort in the belief that benefit levels can later be increased gradually to bring about the desired national standard. Only at that point would we have finally eliminated the possibility that the poor are being attracted to the large northern and western cities by differentially high welfare benefit levels as well as (or perhaps instead of) by real economic opportunity. In the interim, wealthier states would continue to pay more than the national minimum, and we would require a transitional arrangement in which the federal government would pay part of the extra cost in the high benefit states.

To be realistic we must recognize that income maintenance would not at a single stroke overcome all the weaknesses of our present "welfare" system.[28] For example, families are not eligible for AFDC benefits if an employed father is in the household. This undoubtedly encourages desertion and broken families. But the situation is only slightly better under income maintenance. If an employed father is present, the family's earned income is higher and its benefits lower than they would be if he deserted. A strong incentive to desert remains, even though desertion is no longer a necessary precondition of eligibility. Thus income maintenance does not automatically overcome all problems of perverse incentives.

Or consider the high administrative costs of our present welfare system and the unpleasant prying and managing that are now required of the system's administrators. A major claim for income maintenance has been that it would make all this "bureaucratic overburden" unnecessary. This claim must be looked at skeptically. It is unlikely that income maintenance would replace all special forms of public assistance or that it would be operated without a small army of investigators to hold down cheating or without extensive supporting services to help beneficiaries find jobs or otherwise improve their lot. The arguments in favor of income maintenance are weighty enough, however, without relying on exaggerated notions of its administrative simplicity.

URBAN POVERTY AND RACIAL SEGREGATION

We come last to those antipoverty strategies that are oriented toward particular geographic areas. In the urban context these are policies that take specific account of the connections between race, segregation into

28. The excessive claims made for income maintenance are examined by Nathan Glazer in "Beyond Income Maintenance—a Note on Welfare in New York City," *The Public Interest*, Summer 1969, pp. 102–20.

ghettos, and preponderant poverty. The urban riots of the 1960's, coinciding with the rapid increase in the black population of central cities and with the early years of the War on Poverty, inevitably drew the nation's attention to the problems of the ghetto. What would be the most effective public policy to deal with them? Although discussion has tended to concentrate on black poverty, the analysis itself is usually applicable to the situation of other poor urban minorities as well—the Mexican-Americans of the South and West or the Puerto Ricans and other Spanish-speaking groups in the North and East.

Debate has focused on three kinds of policy that are distinguished by differences in the way they approach the fact of racial segregation.[29] In the heat of debate, advocates have often spoken as if these three policies were mutually exclusive. We will argue that they are not and that the wisest strategy would probably include elements of all three.

The first has sometimes been called "ghetto economic development." This policy would attempt to relieve poverty by taking advantage of possibilities for direct action within the racial ghetto itself. The second policy, a sort of polar opposite to the first, would attempt to relieve ghetto poverty by helping and encouraging the population of central city ghettos to disperse into the largely white metropolitan suburbs. The third policy, standing logically between the other two, would use the conventional tools of antipoverty policy to integrate urban racial minorities into the central city's economy. Supporters of this policy may not approve of segregation into ghettos, but they do not usually believe that the ghetto itself is a crucial factor that must be dealt with in antipoverty policy.

This third, or intermediate, policy relies on the conventional tools of manpower training, job information, and placement services focused intensively on residents of poverty areas. Since we have examined these programs above, nothing more need be said here. However, we will now examine the other two policies—ghetto development and ghetto dispersal —in greater detail.

Ghetto Economic Development

The branch plant strategy. Policies to stimulate the economic development of the ghetto may take numerous forms. One approach would attempt to bring jobs into racially segregated neighborhoods by inducing

29. See Anthony Downs, "Alternative Futures for the American Ghetto," *Daedalus,* Fall 1968, pp. 1331–78; John F. Kain and Joseph J. Persky, "Alternatives to the Gilded Ghetto," *The Public Interest,* Winter 1969, pp. 74–87; Matthew Edel, "Development vs. Dispersal: Approaches to Ghetto Poverty," in Matthew Edel and Jerome Rothenberg, eds., *Readings in Urban Economics* (New York: Macmillan, 1972), pp. 307–25; William K. Tabb, *The Political Economy of the Black Ghetto* (New York: W. W. Norton, 1970).

large employers (primarily major white-owned corporations) to open branches there. Some racial ghettos, such as the Watts district in Los Angeles, are relatively isolated from major centers of employment. Thus, the rationale of this first approach is to improve the ghetto resident's access to jobs, both physically and in terms of informal job information flows.

To date the federal government has not gone beyond experimental efforts at using subsidies to induce the relocation of plants in or near urban poverty areas. The late Senator Robert F. Kennedy introduced a bill offering substantial tax incentives for that purpose, but his proposal was not adopted. Meanwhile, some of the major firms that have moved branches into poverty areas have done so without government aid.

There have been both successes and failures in these attempts to move jobs to the ghetto. An extensive set of case studies by the Conference Board documents the frequent start-up difficulties of poverty-area plants. It concludes, however, that there is "reassuring evidence" on a number of points about which investors have expressed concern: "1. Outside investment has been well-received in ghetto communities . . . . 2. The disadvantaged have been quick to seek work . . . . 3. The disadvantaged have become reliable, productive workers . . . . 4. White managers have been accepted . . . . 5. The safety of property has not been a problem . . . ."[30]

Nevertheless, it is no simple matter to find large-scale business operations that can be carried on profitably from a ghetto location under a commitment to hire the hard-core unemployed and to pay them competitive wages. Start-up losses on poverty area plants may be tolerated by large corporations or could be systematically subsidized by the government. However, it would be difficult to justify substantial permanent government subsidies to maintain such plants, since that would imply very high costs per additional ghetto job created. Yet if high costs are to be avoided, great care must be taken in choosing projects, and the program will necessarily remain small in relation to the magnitude of the ghetto poverty problem.

The "black capitalist" approach. A second approach to ghetto economic development is to stimulate the growth of minority-owned private business enterprise. The failure of American blacks to develop the strong business tradition found among many other ethnic minority groups in America has long been recognized. The most recent figures show that in 1969, when blacks made up 11.2 percent of the population, they owned only 2.2 percent of all business firms, and those firms were so small that they accounted for only .3 percent of all business receipts.[31]

30. James K. Brown and Seymour Lusterman, *Business and the Development of Ghetto Enterprise* (New York: The Conference Board, Inc., 1971), pp. 59–60.

31. U.S. Bureau of the Census, *Minority-Owned Businesses: 1969*, August 1971, Table B.

The weakness of the black business tradition can readily be explained as the result of a long history of slavery, followed by oppressive economic discrimination. Unfortunately, it deprives the black community of effective economic power and a chance to enjoy what is now often referred to as "a piece of the action." The "action" includes not only current profits but an ownership stake in expected economic growth. The policy of fostering "black capitalism" is intended to make good these deficiencies. Federal action to support the growth of minority-group business ownership has come principally through such agencies as the Small Business Administration and the Office of Economic Opportunity. The SBA has developed special programs to assist minority-group businessmen with direct loans. It also offers guarantees (for a fee) that reduce the risk on loans to small businesses and thus make them more attractive to commercial banks. Minority-group businessmen are often short of experience and expertise as well as capital. The SBA therefore provides a modest amount of management counseling to minority-group loan recipients. Independent councils of businessmen in many cities have probably contributed an even greater counseling effort, some of it in cooperation with the SBA. The Office of Economic Opportunity has supported minority-group business ownership indirectly through its grants to community action agencies. Some of these have taken ghetto economic development as their task and have used OEO funds in a variety of ways to assist minority-owned enterprises.

A policy of fostering minority-owned business can contribute to ghetto economic development if it helps to bring new businesses into existence or to expand old ones within the poverty area.[32] The problem is to discover what kinds of business can thrive in the ghetto. Opportunities for expansion in the retail and service sector are severely constrained by the near-poverty level of average local income. Of course, it is possible for blacks to expand their share of local activity either by competitive success or by buying out white-owned retail firms. Either of these outcomes would increase the share of profits going to the black community, but neither would be likely to increase the total number of local jobs. Significant expansion of the ghetto economy can only come with the establishment of firms that sell to a wider market than the ghetto—for example, to an entire metropolitan area or to the nation as a whole.[33] Finding such business opportunities is a slow process, however, and usually requires the skills of an experienced entrepreneur.

32. See James Heilbrun and Stanislaw Wellisz, "An Economic Program for the Ghetto," *Urban Riots: Violence and Social Change,* Proceedings of the Academy of Political Science, July 1968, pp. 72–85.
33. For evidence of the constraining effect of low neighborhood income, see James Heilbrun, "Jobs in Harlem: A Statistical Analysis," *Papers* of the Regional Science Association, Vol. XXV, 1970, pp. 181–201.

Unfortunately, experienced black entrepreneurs are in short supply, and this shortage—which, of course, is an aspect of the initial problem—becomes an effective bottleneck in the expansion of the black business sector. What it limits is not the rate of expansion but its absolute amount. Even the most concerted efforts to expand the black entrepreneurial class cannot eliminate the bottleneck overnight. Moreover, experience has shown that a policy of forcing the pace of expansion in the minority-owned sector leads to a sharp increase in the new-business failure rate and therefore entails high financial cost.[34] Finally, it must be kept in mind that new minority-owned firms are likely to start small and initially create only a few new jobs. Thus, although the expansion of minority-owned enterprise is a highly desirable long-run goal, it cannot be expected to have much immediate impact on economic well-being in the ghetto.

Community development corporations. A third approach to ghetto economic development calls for the use of "community development corporations," a number of which were created during the 1960's. These corporations (known as CDC's) vary considerably in structure and intent.[35] Some, such as the Rochester Business Opportunities Corporation, are "strictly business" and operate for the most part through the conventional institutions of private enterprise. They devote themselves to assisting new minority-owned firms by providing management counseling and direct loans and by arranging access to banks and other sources of financial assistance and to markets for their products. They aim at nothing more complex than the creation of independent black-owned business firms—in other words, "black capitalism" in the most traditional sense.

Other CDC's, such as those established by the Reverend Leon Sullivan in Philadelphia, take a more active role in planning and financing development. They substitute a degree of community initiative for reliance on individual enterprise. Sullivan's organization raises the necessary initial equity capital by means of small contributions from thousands of parishioners. However, these subscribers do not have an exclusive claim to the profits of successful business ventures. Instead, a portion of net income is paid into a charitable trust that undertakes nonprofit community service activities.

Legislation has been proposed to give federal assistance to CDC's. In 1968 a group headed by Roy Innis, the national director of CORE,

34. Sar A. Levitan, Garth L. Mangum, and Robert Taggart III, *Economic Opportunity in the Ghetto: The Partnership of Government and Business* (Baltimore: Johns Hopkins Press, 1970), pp. 79–80.
35. See *ibid.*, pp. 75–79; Tabb, pp. 51–55; and Martin Skala, "Inner-City Enterprise: Current Experience," in William F. Haddad and G. Douglas Pugh, eds., The American Assembly, *Black Economic Development* (Englewood Cliffs, N.J.: Prentice-Hall, 1969), pp. 162–70.

drafted a Community Self-Determination Bill that was introduced into Congress with considerable support but has never been acted on. The bill would have encouraged broad-based community development corporations by granting them federal subsidies and preferential tax treatment. The corporations in turn would be expected to devote part of their net income to the performance of nonprofit community services.

Innis himself strongly advocates a "separatist" policy of black economic development and believes that the CDC's can become its vehicle.[36] However, CDC's need not pursue separatist aims. The Reverend Sullivan, for example, though he takes the idea of "community" seriously, does not on that account endorse separatist goals for black economic development.

Unfortunately, the proposition that CDC's can play an important role not only in economic development but in the provision of community services clearly rests on the counting of unhatched chickens. Creating new businesses in the highly competitive American economy is a risky and difficult undertaking—and probably riskier and more difficult in the ghetto than elsewhere. CDC's will do well enough if they earn modest profits while establishing new businesses; despite the Reverend Sullivan's success story, we ought not count on them to finance social services out of net business revenues.

Cumulative Effects of Development

Advocates of ghetto economic development policies—including the branch plant strategy, the black capitalist strategy, and the CDC approach —argue that these policies gain strength by mutual reinforcement, that their whole effect is, so to speak, more than the sum of their individual parts. There are several reasons for believing this to be true. First of all, we recognize the existence of external economies of agglomeration at the neighborhood level. Producers are attracted to neighborhoods that can provide supporting services; consumers are more likely to shop in retail centers that offer a wide variety of goods. Thus activity attracts activity and growth begets growth.

Second, there are local multiplier effects. If we define the neighborhood as the unit of analysis, then there exists a neighborhood income multiplier that is formally identical to the income multiplier for a nation, a region, or a city. In Chapter 7 we showed that this multiplier (k) can be written as

$$K = \frac{1}{1 - mpcl}$$

36. Roy Innis, "Separatist Economics: A New Social Contract," in The American Assembly, *Black Economic Development*, pp. 50–59.

where *mpcl* stands for the marginal propensity to consume locally produced goods.

Though there is no doubt that local multiplier effects exist, recent studies indicate that their magnitude is likely to be very small. The reason for this is not that poverty area residents fail to spend money in their own neighborhoods: estimates of the proportion of income spent locally vary from 38 percent in the Hough area of Cleveland to 55 percent in Brooklyn's Bedford-Stuyvesant. The reason for the small size of the multiplier is, rather, that a high proportion of the money spent in local stores and service establishments necessarily goes for the purchase of imported goods or factor services.[37] Since the marginal propensity to import is high, a very large proportion of local spending "leaks out" of the neighborhood instead of recirculating to generate more local income.

Finally, local economic development is likely to have favorable social and psychological effects. In communities where deprivation has produced apathy and hopelessness, demonstrations of success either in business or in job-holding will encourage others to emulate the pattern of success. Furthermore, local development opens up opportunities for talented and ambitious residents and encourages them to remain in the poverty area instead of taking their exceptional energies and abilities elsewhere. Thus it helps to prevent poverty areas from being deprived of some of their best human resources. Advocates of local development policy believe that success will attract the talent and create the self-confidence out of which greater success can flow.

Yet we must conclude by recognizing the limitations on ghetto development policy as a means of relieving urban poverty. Most residents of minority ghettos work in the larger, outside economy and must continue to do so, for ghetto neighborhoods are essentially residential in character. While they could usually accommodate more work places than they do now, it would be virtually impossible and very probably undesirable to make them over into major centers of employment.

Consider, for example, the case of Harlem, which is probably one of the more highly developed black ghettos. A recent study estimated that in 1966 there were approximately 19,500 jobs located in Harlem. The number of employed Harlem residents was about five times as large. Thus even if Harlem residents held every local job (which was certainly not the case), no more than one-fifth of them could have worked inside their own community.[38] Since available vacant industrial and commercial space in

37. See William H. Oakland, Frederick T. Sparrow, and H. Louis Stettler III, "Ghetto Multipliers: A Case Study of Hough," *Journal of Regional Science*, December 1971, pp. 337–45.
38. Heilbrun, "Jobs in Harlem," pp. 185–86.

or near Harlem can accommodate only a few thousand more jobs, extensive rebuilding would be needed to increase greatly the ratio of local jobs to resident workers. It is extremely doubtful whether the massive subsidies required to bring about such rebuilding would be an efficient use for public antipoverty funds.

All this means, not that development policies are useless, but only that they cannot make more than a modest contribution to the relief of deprivation in the ghetto. Integration into the larger metropolitan and national economies must remain the principal avenue of escape from poverty. It has been proposed that one way to speed this integration on terms favorable to urban minorities is to encourage and even subsidize their movement to the suburbs. We examine next the rationale for this policy of "ghetto dispersal."

Urban Poverty and Metropolitan Decentralization

It is one of the ironies of our times that the poor have been migrating to the cities at the very moment when job opportunities there are threatened by the forces of decentralization. The problem is usually described this way: in recent decades jobs have been dispersing within metropolitan areas. (On this point, see Table 3.4.) Many of the older central cities have actually suffered a loss in total jobs since the late 1940's. The suburbs, on the other hand, have enjoyed enormous job growth. Dispersion is most marked among blue collar jobs in manufacturing, wholesaling, and distribution, least pronounced in white collar jobs and in service industries. The poor are usually better qualified for blue collar than for white collar employment. Hence the inner portions of the central cities, where the poor typically live, are an increasingly disadvantageous base from which to look for work. Not only are blue collar jobs moving steadily away from inner-city poverty areas; they are moving to places that are scarcely accessible by public transportation. To the inner-city worker with no automobile, the cost in time and money of reaching a suburban job by commuter railroad and/or multiple bus connections is often prohibitive when compared with his low earning capacity. Moreover, the casual, informal sort of employment information on which many job seekers rely also thins out with distance. In short, the inner-city resident, especially if he is isolated in a racial ghetto, is increasingly out of touch with the market for his labor.

To be sure, this statement of the problem is somewhat oversimplified. First of all, it leans rather heavily on the assumption that white collar jobs are higher skilled than blue collar jobs, whereas, in fact, many white collar jobs in the central city do not call for particularly high levels of skill. Then, too, as Table 3.4 suggests, many of the central cities even today contain more jobs in manufacturing (i.e., blue collar jobs) than do their suburban rings. Finally, the dispersion of jobs has been accompanied by a dispersion of the resident population (again, see Table 3.4). Jobs as well as housing have been left behind for newcomers to the city. A sort of "job filtering" process is at work, parallel to the process of "housing filtering."

These issues deserve the most careful investigation. For if job dispersion is depriving poor minorities in the central city of opportunities for improvement, the implications for public policy are clear: to help relieve poverty, we must encourage the dispersion of blacks and other minorities into the suburbs.

Evaluating the Case for Dispersion

To evaluate the dispersion argument we must try to answer two rather complex questions. First, are there enough jobs left in the central cities to employ the remaining resident labor force? Second, how do earnings and occupational status compare as between central cities and suburbs? These questions are difficult to answer for several reasons. First there is the unsatisfactory nature of our statistics. Most of the data we have on employment, type of occupation, and earnings that can be geographically classified refer to the locations where workers live rather than where they work.[39] In strict logic one cannot use such data to compare the characteristics of the suburban and central city "labor markets," since some of the people residing in each place, to whom the data refer, actually work at jobs in the labor market of the other area.

Second, there is the fact that the populations living in the two areas are not identical in their personal characteristics. Blacks living in the suburbs and blacks living in the central city are not random samples of a single black population. Rather they are self-selected groups and may differ significantly in relevant ways. This is, of course, equally true of the white population of the two areas.

How then can we make use of existing data on earnings and occupational status of residents of the suburbs to compare the economic situation there with that in the central city? The answer is that we must assume that the data describe the opportunities open to a worker if he moves to the suburbs and develops the same skills and journey-to-work patterns that present suburbanites have. With this interpretation in mind (and with reservations to be mentioned as we proceed), let us examine the data.

39. The data on job dispersion in Table 3.4 are an exception. They were drawn from the periodic censuses of business, and refer to the actual locations of jobs.

Black Unemployment Rates: Central Cities Versus Suburbs

If it were possible, we would like first to compare the relative "availability" of jobs in the two areas. Since it is difficult to obtain meaningful data on "job openings," the best we can do is to infer the relative availability of jobs from a comparison of unemployment rates: the higher the unemployment rate, the lower is job availability. This is not wholly satisfactory—it requires, for example, that we posit an equal willingness to work in the two areas, as measured by job seekers' "reservation wages" (the lowest wages at which they are willing to accept a job)—but no better alternative is available.

Table 9.5 shows that in 1970 the unemployment rate for all races was slightly higher in the central cities than in the rings of metropolitan areas, which suggests that jobs were less readily available in the core cities. The breakdown by race, however, reveals that the unemployment rate for whites was the same in both areas, while the rate for Negroes was very slightly higher in the suburbs. How then can the overall rate be higher in the central cities? Simply because in both areas the unemployment rate for blacks is almost twice that for whites, and the proportion of blacks is far higher in the central city. If we take the suburban unemployment rate for blacks to represent fairly the job availability that a central city black would face if he moved to the suburbs, we can only conclude that his prospects would be substantially unchanged by the move.

TABLE 9.5

Unemployment Rates by Race and Sex, Inside and Outside
Central Cities of SMSA's, 1970

| | | PERCENTAGE OF LABOR FORCE UNEMPLOYED IN METROPOLITAN AREAS | |
	Total	Central Cities	Outside Central Cities
Total, all races, both sexes [a]	4.5	4.8	4.2
White, both sexes	4.1	4.1	4.1
Male	3.7	4.1	3.5
Female	4.7	4.3	5.0
Negro, both sexes	7.7	7.7	7.8
Male	7.2	7.5	6.1
Female	8.2	7.8	9.9

[a] Includes other nonwhite, in addition to Negro.
Source: U.S. Bureau of the Census, *Current Population Reports*, Series P-23, No. 37, June 24, 1971, Table C and Table 13.

It would be more accurate, however, not to say "his." As the break-down by sex in Table 9.5 reveals, unemployment rates are lower in the suburbs than in the central cities for black men and higher for black women. The same pattern holds for whites by sex.

The data in Table 9.5 confirm the widely observed general rule that no matter what segment of the labor market one looks at, he finds that unemployment rates for blacks are almost twice those for whites. Apparently suburban residence by itself does not overcome the various disadvantages in job retention that burden the black worker. Probably foremost among these disadvantages are discrimination in hiring—the black is often "last hired, first fired"—and lack of suitable training and skill. The force of discrimination is difficult to measure (though we cited some evidence earlier in this chapter); the effects of skill level are more easily shown. Table 9.6 reveals that in central cities in 1970, 61 percent of all resident employed black men and women were in the three occupational categories of operatives, service workers, and nonfarm laborers. Only 32 percent of employed white men and 29 percent of white women were so classified. In every year since 1946, these three categories have shown higher nation-wide rates of unemployment than any other occupational groups. Undoubtedly, the concentration of blacks in these categories contributes importantly to the high rate of black unemployment.

Black Occupational Status and Earnings:
Central Cities Versus Suburbs

For the years 1960 and 1970, Table 9.6 shows both black occupational structure and earnings by occupation and sex in central cities and ring areas of SMSA's. Let us continue to assume that the data for blacks now living in the suburbs fairly represent the prospects that central city blacks with similar skills would face if they moved there. So far as occupational status in 1970 is concerned, the data show that 77 percent of black men living in the suburbs were either blue collar or service workers. Precisely the same proportion obtained among black men in the central cities. Thus, on the basis of current data, there is no reason to believe that moving to the suburbs would improve the black man's chances of shifting into professional, managerial, or white collar occupations (assuming that to be desirable). For black women the situation is slightly less favorable in the suburbs than in the central city. Of those living in the suburbs in 1970, 64 percent were either blue collar or service workers, while the proportion in the central city was 62 percent.

The outcome is quite different, however, if we look at changes in occupational status over time. For both black men and women, the proportion in professional, managerial, and white collar occupations rose

TABLE 9.6

Negro Occupational Status and Earnings by Sex, Inside and Outside Central Cities of SMSA's

	NEGRO MALE				NEGRO FEMALE			
	CENTRAL CITIES		OUTSIDE CENTRAL CITIES		CENTRAL CITIES		OUTSIDE CENTRAL CITIES	
	1970	1960	1970	1960	1970	1960	1970	1960
Occupation of the employed (percentage distribution)								
All occupations	100.0	100.0	100.0	100.0	100.0	100.0	100.0	100.0
Professional, technical, and managerial	11.4	5.8	10.4	3.9	11.9	8.1	13.4	7.0
Clerical and sales	12.3	11.9	13.4	5.0	26.5	13.2	22.6	8.6
Blue collar and service	76.5	82.2	76.5	91.2	61.6	78.9	64.1	84.4
Craftsmen	15.5	11.3	14.1	9.6	0.9	1.0	0.2	0.7
Operatives	31.3	30.9	27.3	25.1	16.0	16.8	15.6	11.7
Service workers	12.0	17.6	13.7	20.3	43.7	60.4	47.3	67.0
Nonfarm laborers	17.5	22.1	18.8	28.5	1.0	0.7	0.2	1.0
Farmers, farm laborers	0.2	0.3	2.6	7.7	—	—	0.8	4.0
	1969	1959	1969	1959	1969	1959	1969	1959
Median earnings of the employed by occupation (in 1969 dollars)								
All occupations	5,828	4,021	5,785	3,529	3,199	1,890	2,943	1,429
Professional, technical, and managerial	6,877	5,219	—	—	6,371	4,083	—	—
Clerical and Sales	6,235	4,900	6,208	—	3,806	3,688	3,675	—
Craftsmen and foremen	6,632	4,800	6,738	—	—	—	—	—
Operatives	5,793	4,414	6,017	3,667	3,331	2,546	3,357	—
Service workers	4,539	3,203	3,875	2,929	2,259	1,345	1,875	1,034
Nonfarm laborers	5,242	3,794	4,728	3,083	—	—	—	—

Source: U.S. Bureau of the Census, *Current Population Reports,* Series P-23, No. 37, June 24, 1971, Table 14 and Table 17.

much more rapidly in the suburbs than in the central cities between 1960 and 1970. It is, of course, possible that this represents nothing more than an increase in the proportion of blacks commuting from suburban homes to high status jobs in the central city. More likely, however, black-held jobs actually located in the suburbs have also been catching up in occupational status with those located in the central city.

Turning to earnings by occupation, we find in Table 9.6 that for black men the median for the aggregate of all occupations in 1969 was slightly higher in central cities than in suburbs. For black women the central city median was substantially higher in 1969. By the criterion of current earnings, then, blacks would seem to gain nothing by moving to the suburbs.[40]

Again, however, the picture alters if we look at changes between 1959 and 1969. Median earnings of both men and women have been rising far faster in the suburbs than in the central cities. The catching up of suburban with central city earnings is the result of two processes. First, as pointed out above, suburban blacks have moved into the higher status occupations relatively faster than central city blacks. Since these occupations enjoy above average earnings, the effect is necessarily a relative rise in median suburban earnings for the aggregate of all jobs. Second, Table 9.6 shows that within occupational categories median black earnings have been rising faster in the suburbs in three out of the four cases for which data are available. Although the data are far from complete, what we do have suggests that black earnings in the suburbs would have improved relative to those in the central city even without relative improvement in occupational status.

Our finding that by the criteria of current unemployment rates, occupational status, and earnings, blacks are as well off in the core city as in the suburbs is consistent with the results obtained by other investigators. Bennett Harrison, for example, has analyzed data covering the 12 largest SMSA's from a Special Survey of Economic Opportunity conducted by the Census Bureau in 1966.[41] He divided the survey responses into three groups according to residential location: central city poverty areas, remainder of the central cities, and suburban rings. He then compared economic performance of nonwhite males in the three areas. Em-

40. Table 3.7 showed median family income for blacks in 1969 to be slightly higher in the suburbs than in central cities, while Table 9.6 shows earnings by occupation to be slightly higher in central cities. The data are consistent, since median incomes of unrelated individuals (i.e., those *not* living in families) are considerably higher in central cities, presumably offsetting the slightly lower earnings of families. See U.S. Bureau of the Census, *Current Population Reports*, P-23, No. 37, June 24, 1971, Table 8

41. Bennett Harrison, "The Intrametropolitan Distribution of Minority Economic Welfare," *Journal of Regional Science*, April 1972, pp. 23–43.

ployment rates, earnings, and occupational status, he found, were lowest in the poverty areas and highest in the remainder of the central city, with the level of performance in the suburban ring standing regularly between these two. He did not compare the suburban ring with the central city as a whole, but the values in his data suggest that in such a comparison, he would have found the current level of well-being about the same in the two locations, just as we have done.

Bernard Frieden's similar conclusions are suggested by the title of his recent study: "Blacks in Suburbia: The Myth of Better Opportunities." After surveying current figures on income, unemployment, and occupational status he wrote that "these data, fragmentary as they are, show little support for the belief that suburban residence is the key to better jobs and higher incomes." [42] Like Harrison, Frieden concentrated on the comparison of central city and suburban job and income data at a moment in time (the late 1960's) and did not report rates of change over recent years. However, the urban system changes profoundly over time (as every chapter of this book has emphasized). One can therefore be easily misled by interarea comparisons that are limited to a single date.

Comparisons Through Time: "The Crossover Pattern"

When twentieth-century socioeconomic data for central cities and suburbs are plotted over time we find repeatedly what might be referred to as "the crossover pattern." At an early date central cities rank above ring areas in rate of population increase, rate of job growth, level of median family income, and so on. As time passes, however, the suburbs typically catch up and, still later, typically surpass the central cities along the same scales of measurement. We referred in Chapter 8 to the fact that prior to 1950 the level of family income was generally higher in central cities than in their suburban rings, but that the suburbs eventually caught up with and now outrank the central cities in that respect. If one had compared central cities and suburbs around 1950 he might have concluded that there was little difference between them in socioeconomic structure because they were then close to the point of "crossover" in terms of many criteria. Neglecting rates of change through time, the analyst would have failed to uncover the fact that this equality was momentary rather than persistent.

It appears that the moment of "crossover" has occurred much more recently for the black population of metropolitan areas than for whites.

42. Bernard J. Frieden, "Blacks in Suburbia: The Myth of Better Opportunities," in L. Wingo, ed., *Minority Perspectives* (Baltimore: Johns Hopkins Press, for Resources for the Future, Inc., 1972), p. 38.

From the data in Table 3.7 it can be inferred that median family income of blacks in the suburbs reached equality with the income of blacks in central cities only in the late 1960's. Thus studies such as Frieden's and Harrison's happened to occur at just the moment when indicators of black economic status in the two areas were close to equality. We have added substantial evidence that in terms of income, occupational status, and occupational earnings, black economic performance has been improving much faster in the suburbs than in the central cities. This suggests that the opportunities for economic improvement open to blacks may, indeed, be better in the suburbs. But we must repeat that data limitations make it difficult to know how much of the observed "improvement" is the result of superior economic opportunity in the suburbs and how much the result of selective black migration to the suburbs or, conceivably, even a rise in the proportion of blacks commuting to jobs in the central city. The question deserves much more study.

It is important to emphasize that the opportunities open to the black population in suburbs versus central cities cannot be judged solely in terms of economic measures such as employment, occupational status, and income. There are many other dimensions along which the welfare of black families might plausibly be expected to differ in central cities as compared with suburbs. Frieden's study examines a great many of these, including school quality, school integration, level of nonschool public services, quality of housing, racial integration of neighborhoods, and prevailing crime rate. We will return to the question of suburban housing for blacks in Chapter 11. Space precludes a detailed review of Frieden's findings concerning the other indicators of welfare. His general conclusion can perhaps best be summarized in his own words: "The suburbs clearly could provide black people with improved access to a series of important resources: to better jobs, schools, housing, and neighborhoods than most blacks have in the central cities. Yet today's black residents of suburbia have not fared much better than those in the central cities, on the average, and the advantages they do have are limited and uneven." [43]

After all these comparisons, where do we come out? Admittedly, it is difficult to establish conclusive proof that blacks have better social and economic opportunities in the suburbs. Yet the existing evidence, seen as another example of the crossover pattern so often observed in comparing central cities and ring areas, does suggest that better opportunity for blacks in the suburbs is not simply a myth. If it is not already a reality it is probably at least on the way to becoming one. It must therefore be given due weight in forming antipoverty policy.

43. *Ibid.*, p. 45.

The Losses Imposed by Segregation

A somewhat different way of analyzing the connection between the ghetto, job decentralization, and minority-group poverty has been developed by John F. Kain. Instead of comparing economic opportunity in central cities and suburbs in an attempt to decide where blacks are most likely to prosper, Kain concentrates on the effects of housing segregation on job opportunities for minorities and on other indicators of minority-group welfare. In a widely discussed empirical study, he tested the following three interrelated hypotheses: that "racial segregation in the housing markets (1) affects the distribution of Negro employment and (2) reduces Negro job opportunities, and that (3) postwar suburbanization of employment has seriously aggravated the problem." [44] Among the important reasons for expecting housing segregation to affect black employment is the fact that segregation limits the individual's freedom to move close to a job location and therefore imposes high travel costs on him that may in fact discourage him from taking otherwise desirable jobs.

To test his three hypotheses, Kain used data for the metropolitan areas of Chicago and Detroit. He started with two sets of facts for each area: a given segregated pattern of black residence and a given spatial distribution of all jobs in the central city and the suburbs. Using statistical techniques, he then examined the effect of the segregated housing pattern on the proportion of blacks in the work force at each job location. Next, he compared the actual level of black employment at each location with an estimate of what its level would be if the black population were distributed evenly over all residential areas instead of being confined to a few ghettos. He found that housing segregation imposed job losses on blacks in both cities. The estimated loss was 22,000 to 24,000 in Chicago and 4,000 to 9,000 in Detroit.

It is but one step from these findings to the argument that the continuing decentralization of jobs within metropolitan areas is likely to reduce black job opportunities still further. Trapped in core city ghettos, blacks will find themselves living at an increasing average distance from the aggregate of job locations. Kain concluded that "the rapid postwar dispersal of employment, accompanied by no reduction and perhaps an increase in housing market segregation, may have placed the Negro job seeker in an even more precarious position." [45]

As Kain has argued elsewhere, the reduction in well-being suffered by blacks as a result of housing segregation goes beyond job losses of the sort estimated above. In addition, those blacks who *do* find employment

44. John F. Kain, "Housing Segregation, Negro Employment, and Metropolitan Decentralization," *Quarterly Journal of Economics*, May 1968, p. 176.
45. *Ibid.*, p. 196.

at outlying job locations are likely to spend more on transportation to work than would be necessary if their housing choices were unrestricted. Finally, the restriction of housing choice imposes a welfare loss on blacks by limiting and distorting their consumption of housing itself.[46] Put very simply, this analysis leads to the conclusion that by limiting freedom of choice segregation cannot help and very probably hurts the segregated minority population. The policy prescription that follows from the analysis is obviously to encourage desegregation, and the appropriate area over which to accomplish desegregation is not just the central city but the entire metropolitan region.

Other Arguments for Dispersion

The case for encouraging voluntary dispersion of minorities gains strength from other considerations as well. In the first place, minorities certainly ought to enjoy equal access to suburban residence as a matter of right. As we will see in Chapter 11, they are presently denied that right by restrictive zoning and other discriminatory practices. Their outward movement would be encouraged by a program that simply guaranteed them the equal access to which they are justly entitled.

Equally important, the national commitment to the goal of an integrated society requires that we take positive action to stem the development of heavily black central cities surrounded by largely all-white suburbs. Table 8.5 showed that the black proportion of central city population rose from 16.3 percent in 1960 to 20.6 percent in 1970, while their proportion of ring area population remained constant at 4.8 percent. Thus at the macrolocational scale, segregation by race has continued to increase. Moreover the rate of natural increase of black populations in central cities is so much higher than that of whites that an enormous rise of black out-migration from the cities would be required during the 1970's just to keep their black/white population ratios constant. That is the compelling reason why dispersion should be thought of not as an alternative to ghetto economic development but as complementary with it. For it is almost inconceivable that dispersion will work fast enough to prevent central city ghettos from growing in size for at least the near future.

The present pattern of macrosegregation by race and income not only defeats the hope of achieving an integrated society, it also undermines the War on Poverty itself. As we will see in Chapter 12, local gov-

46. See J. R. Meyer, J. F. Kain, and M. Wohl, *The Urban Transportation Problem* (Cambridge, Mass.: Harvard University Press, 1965), Ch. 7; and John F. Kain and John M. Quigley, "Housing Market Discrimination, Homeownership and Savings Behavior," *American Economic Review*, June 1972, pp. 263–77.

ernments help to finance a considerable fraction of all public services, including some that are poverty-related. The concentration of poverty within their borders adds to their financial burden while simultaneously weakening the tax base that must bear it. As a result central city residents, including the poor, either receive less in the way of public services or pay higher tax rates to receive the same level than do their counterparts in the suburbs. No one would argue that this outcome is either equitable or consistent with an all-out attack on poverty.

Policies to Encourage Dispersion

A variety of policies have been suggested to encourage the voluntary dispersion of ethnic minorities into the suburbs.[47] Most of these focus on the need to open up the suburbs to low income and lower middle income housing and will be taken up in detail in Chapter 11. Also potentially important are the proposals, outlined in Chapter 12, that call for state assumption of all public education costs and federal assumption of all costs of welfare. These changes in the way we finance public services would help to reduce the opposition of wealthy suburban communities to low income migrants, who, under present fiscal arrangements, are thought to add more to local expenditure needs than they produce in local tax revenues.

In an often quoted passage, the National Advisory Commission on Civil Disorders in 1968 expressed the view that "our nation is moving toward two societies, one black, one white—separate and unequal." Since that date, to be sure, we have managed a modest reduction in the incidence of poverty, including the poverty of minority groups. Unfortunately, however, the geographic projection of the two societies—the separation into poor, heavily black cities and affluent, largely white suburbs—is now more clearly etched than ever before. We cannot fail to recognize the threat that this geosocial pattern poses to the institutions of a democratic society; yet to this moment we have hardly begun to deal with the problem.

---

47. See the articles by Downs and by Kain and Persky cited in note 29, above.

The Problem
of Urban Housing

TEN

Since the Industrial Revolution first began to transform Western life, no aspect of society has aroused the passionate concern of reformers more consistently than the condition, and especially the housing condition, of the urban poor. One has only to walk through a crowded slum district in an American city and look inside a few buildings to understand at once the long history of protest and the unending series of proposals for housing reform—and to be reminded forcefully that despite the protest and despite the reforms, "the housing problem" is still with us. Especially in the older cities of the United States, housing conditions persist that seem to most observers to be wholly unacceptable in the world's most affluent society.

The Housing Act of 1949 contained a famous statement of intent: "the Congress hereby declares that the general welfare and security of the Nation and the health and living standards of its people require . . . the realization as soon as feasible of the goal of a decent home and suitable living environment for every American family . . . ." As housing acts followed one another with bewildering frequency during the 1950's and 1960's, the goal proclaimed in 1949 was sought by means of a continuously changing array of federal programs. Although there was a good deal of improvement in the condition of the nation's housing during those two decades, it was not always clear that public policy had helped very much to achieve it. The frequency with which one widely heralded federal program supplemented or replaced another gave rise finally to the suspicion that it was, not merely the mechanics, but perhaps indeed the very premises of public policy that were mistaken. In the 1970's, the housing problem, and especially the *urban* housing problem, remains high on the nation's agenda of unfinished business.

In order to understand that problem we must first discuss methods of measuring the quality or condition of housing and then sketch a description of the urban housing market that is capable of explaining why it might fail to produce "a decent home and suitable living environment for every American family." Both good and bad housing in the United States are largely the products of our system of free enterprise and competitive markets. It is only against the background of private market action that we can sensibly evaluate public policy toward housing.

MEASURING THE QUALITY OF HOUSING

The word "slum" carries with it the sense of an evil environment. Indeed, for the outside observer there is a kind of visceral reaction to the total environment of the "slum" that seems to render systematic analysis of what he sees unnecessary, perhaps even heartless and undesirable. Yet we cannot have rational discussion or effective public policy unless we can measure the condition of housing on some sort of objective scale. If we define slums as substandard housing, we are obliged to specify the standard. What we really wish to isolate is the quality of service rendered by a given structure. This quality is exceedingly difficult to measure. It certainly cannot be measured along a unidimensional scale. Ideally the dimensions one would like to consider are the following:

1. The physical condition of the structure. Is it sound or unsound— i.e., well maintained or run down?
2. The extent of utilities and equipment. For example, are electricity and complete plumbing provided?
3. The adequacy of the design. For example, does the unit have sufficient light, air, separation of functions?
4. How crowded is the dwelling? How many rooms or how many square feet of floor space does it contain per person?

In each decennial Census of Housing, a series that began in 1940, the Census Bureau has gathered systematic data on the condition of the nation's housing stock. Of the four dimensions of quality listed above, only the third—adequacy of design—has totally eluded the statisticians. To measure physical condition, the Census of 1950 classified units as either "dilapidated" or "not dilapidated," depending on the seriousness and extent of disrepair observed by the enumerator. The Census of 1960 employed a three-way classification: "sound," "deteriorating," and "dilapidated." (Theoretically, since the definition of "dilapidated" was the same in both years, the combined categories of "sound" and "deteriorating" in 1960 should be comparable to the single category of "not dilapidated" in 1950. In practice, however, it is likely that enumerators in 1960, having available the intermediate category of "deteriorating," placed in it some of the housing that would have been classed as "dilapidated" in 1950, when only two categories were used. Thus, comparability of data may have been impaired.) [1] In 1970 the census was conducted by means of mailed questionnaires. Since respondents could not be expected to render consistent judgments about housing condition, the topic was omitted from the questionnaire. In addition, there was considerable doubt about the reliability of the physical condition data in the earlier enumerations.[2]

To measure adequacy of equipment, the census records the presence or absence of a long list of items such as water supply, bathing facilities, toilet facilities, type of heating equipment, and type of cooking fuel. For the principal plumbing facilities a further distinction is made between those shared and those for exclusive use of one dwelling unit. Plumbing facilities have been singled out as the equipment most relevant to an over-all evaluation of housing conditions. By combining information on the extent of plumbing with information on structural condition, U.S. housing agencies arrive at a final set of categories to describe the physical aspect of housing conditions: "standard" housing has been defined as housing that is not dilapidated and that contains all enumerated plumbing facilities; "substandard" housing comprises all units that are either dilapidated *or* lacking one or more of the enumerated plumbing facilities. Since the 1970 Census omitted condition of structure from its questionnaire, the Census Bureau indirectly estimated the number of "dilapidated" units in order to approximate the extent of "standard" and "substandard" housing in all cities and counties. However, the estimates had not yet been published as this book went to press.

To measure crowding, the Census Bureau records the number of persons and the number of rooms in each dwelling unit and then calculates a persons-per-room ratio. Admittedly, this measure leaves out of account differences in the size of rooms among various units at any one date and changes in the average size of rooms over time. However, it does indicate the extent to which a home provides privacy and separation of functions, which a floor-space measure would not do. The persons-per-room ratio can also be faulted for not taking into account "economies of scale" in the use of rooms. For example, one kitchen will suffice for a

1. See the discussion in Martin Anderson, *The Federal Bulldozer* (Cambridge, Mass.: M.I.T. Press, 1964), pp. 214–15.
2. See U.S. Bureau of the Census, *Measuring the Quality of Housing*, Working Paper No. 25, 1967.

six-person family as easily as for a three-person family, so that six people in six rooms are probably less "crowded" than three people in three rooms. But despite these limitations, the persons-per-room ratio is a highly useful index of crowding. A ratio of 1.01 or more persons per room is taken to indicate "overcrowding" according to standards now widely accepted in the United States.

Neighborhood Quality

To this point we have discussed measures of housing quality that are intended to isolate the quality of service rendered in particular structures. A broader definition would attempt to incorporate neighborhood characteristics as well. When people choose housing they take into account, not only the quality of service associated with the particular dwelling unit, but the attractiveness of the neighborhood as a place to live. Desirable neighborhood characteristics include such features as adequate park and recreation facilities, good schools, and, of particular concern at the present, freedom from crime.

Observation of the housing market indicates clearly the importance of neighborhood character. For example, an apartment in a "good" neighborhood will rent for a higher price than a similar unit in a less desirable area, even though both provide internal housing services of equal quality and both are located equally conveniently to the urban center. Households are willing to pay for the neighborhood features that attract them.

Unfortunately, it is no simple matter to incorporate the effects of neighborhood systematically into housing analysis. First of all, neighborhood character is difficult to measure objectively. Second, an attempt to deal with all its dimensions leads the analyst ultimately to consider the entire physical and social environment at the neighborhood level, surely a prohibitively complicated task. Consequently, in the housing analysis of this and the following chapter we will concentrate on the quality characteristics of individual dwelling units rather than neighborhoods. However, the fact that we will frequently refer to neighborhood influences—for example, in connection with housing abandonment, urban renewal, racial segregation, and land-use zoning—should serve to remind the reader of their undoubted importance.

AN "ADAPTIVE" MODEL OF THE HOUSING MARKET

How does the housing market function to produce the mixture of "good" and "bad," or of "standard" and "substandard," or of "crowded" and "uncrowded" housing that is found in every U.S. city?

For the sake of simplicity, the following discussion assumes that the market is entirely a rental one. In fact, only 42 percent of urban housing units are renter occupied. However, focusing on the rental sector is readily justified by the fact that it contains a majority of the overcrowded and substandard urban units. The case is even stronger if we look at central cities of metropolitan areas. Table 10.1 shows that within central cities 52 percent of occupied units are rented and that these units account for 64 percent of the overcrowded central city housing and 79 percent of the units that lack full plumbing. In any case, introducing an ownership sector would add greatly to the complexity of the analysis while not substantially changing its conclusions.

Rapkin, Winnick, and Blank have pointed out that if we use terms from conventional economic theory, the rental housing market in a large city is probably best thought of as an instance of monopolistic competition among a large number of sellers.[3] Competition cannot be described as "pure," since the units supplied are clearly differentiated by size, quality, and location. On the other hand, the very large number of sellers and the small size of the largest in relation to the whole market ensure that effective competition takes place. There is no possibility of monopoly, no collusion among sellers, no tendency for suppliers to become involved in oligopolistic strategies: each building owner behaves as if the market situation were "given" and assumes that his own decisions have no effect upon it. (To be sure, there are some important imperfections in the urban housing market—most notably the prevalence of racial discrimination. We will not neglect these but rather hold them for consideration together with public policy toward housing in the next chapter.)

Because buildings are expensive, durable, and immovable, the housing market differs in important respects from most other consumer goods markets. From the high cost and durability of shelter it follows that in any one year almost the entire supply of housing services is provided by the standing stock. New construction on the average adds only 2 or 3 percent per year to the housing supply of the nation as a whole, and a part of that goes to offset the annual toll of demolitions. If the adjustment of supply to changes in demand could take place only through new construction, the process would be even more cumbersome, slow, and expensive than, in fact, it is. Fortunately, adjustments on the supply side take place not only through new construction but through a series of complex changes by which the quality of existing units, and therefore their rent level, is "adapted" to the pattern of demand expressed in the market for housing services. For example, if a given class of occupants moves out of a neighborhood, the housing they leave behind is usually too

3. Chester Rapkin, Louis Winnick, and David M. Blank, *Housing Market Analysis*, Housing and Home Finance Agency, 1953, p. 22.

244 Urban Economics and Public Policy

TABLE 10.1
Housing Conditions of Renters and Owners in Metropolitan Areas, 1970

	ALL U.S. SMSA'S					
	INSIDE CENTRAL CITIES			OUTSIDE CENTRAL CITIES		
	Total	Renter Occupied	Owner Occupied	Total	Renter Occupied	Owner Occupied
Number of occupied units (thousands)	21,382	11,092	10,290	22,481	6,682	15,799
Distribution by tenure (percentage)	100	51.9	48.1	100	29.7	70.3
Number of occupied units with persons per room = 1.01 or more (thousands)	1,817	1,157	659	1,589	607	982
Percentage with PPR = 1.01 or more	8.5	10.4	6.4	7.1	9.1	6.2
Distribution by tenure (percentage)	100	63.7	36.3	100	38.2	61.8
Number of occupied units lacking complete plumbing (thousands)	684	543	141	704	329	375
Percentage lacking complete plumbing	3.3	4.9	1.4	3.1	4.9	2.4
Distribution by tenure (percentage)	100	79.4	20.6	100	46.7	53.3

Source: U.S. Bureau of the Census, Census of Housing, 1970, U.S. Summary, HC(1)-A1, Table 10 and Table 11.

valuable to be demolished, since it is still capable of rendering service. Hence it will generally be adapted by alteration of its quality to meet the needs of another class. Thus the character of the housing stock in a particular place frequently changes under the influence of market forces in ways that neither city planners nor housing policy administrators can readily control. Probably the greatest weakness in U.S. housing policy has been its failure to acknowledge the power (and therefore to anticipate the consequences) of the adaptive process in the urban housing market. We will therefore return to a detailed examination of that process below.

In analyzing any housing market it is well to keep in mind one seemingly obvious but frequently neglected fact: every family has to live somewhere (though not necessarily in a separate dwelling unit). Hence the function of the market is, broadly speaking, to match up the population of families with the existing stock of housing. Since family income is the principal determinant of housing demand, this function reduces essentially to matching up a distribution of families by amount of income with a distribution of housing units by rent level. The market operates like a game of musical chairs—except that each family ordinarily ends up with a chair. Unless the number of separately residing households or the stock of housing changes, each move that fills one vacancy creates another somewhere else. When the stock increases relative to the number of households, each new unit that attracts a tenant creates a vacancy elsewhere; likewise, each demolition that removes a unit fills up a vacancy in some other part of the stock, unless the number of households is diminishing. Obviously, partial equilibrium analysis restricted to one sector of a city's housing market can be very misleading. It is usually necessary to trace out the consequences of any change for the entire stock within a given market.

The phrase "given market," of course, conceals many ambiguities. The poor family living in a central city slum is not in the market for luxury apartments, though these may stand only a few blocks from where it lives. For the middle and upper classes the choice is certainly wider. Though living in a central city apartment, the well-to-do family probably finds the suburban owner-occupied house a closer substitute for its present home than a slum flat would be. Nevertheless, the central city rental market is best treated as a continuum, for there is a distribution of housing over all rent classes and a distribution of families over all income levels. The market thus provides a series of small steps by which a household can move up or down the scale of housing quality. The possibility of families making these small substitutions binds the entire range of housing into one market, since there are no gaps at which one can draw logical dividing lines.

Varying the Supply of Housing "Quality"

Looked at from the supply side, the urban housing market is bound together by the adaptability of structures. Just as tenants can move from one rent class into the next, so owners can "move" their buildings from one rent class to another by remodeling, dividing, or combining units or by changing the level of outlays for operation and maintenance.[4] It is useful to think of the owner, not just as an "investor" in real estate, but as an entrepreneur who is in the business of operating rental housing. His objective is to maintain and operate his building at the level of quality that will maximize profits. Higher levels of quality of housing service will command higher rents but will also cost more to produce. The owner's task is to find the most profitable combination.

Given the basic structure and layout of a particular building, the quality of housing service produced in it depends on two factors. The first is the annual level of operating outlays incurred by the owner. For example, higher outlays might take the form of increased expenditures for cleaning and painting or for heating fuel, minor repairs, or security against crime. The owner will expand these outlays as long as each dollar of additional expense generates more than a dollar of additional gross income from rents. The most profitable combination occurs at the level of operating expense at which one more dollar of outlay would just return one more dollar of rent. In the conventional terminology of price theory, the owner pushes service output to the point at which marginal revenue equals marginal cost.

The second factor that affects quality in a given structure is the frequency with which deteriorating structural parts or equipment are replaced. In general, major elements of structure or equipment do not suddenly and completely cease to function. Rather they deteriorate gradually, as a plumbing system does, providing less satisfactory service as they grow older. It follows that the shorter the average period over which such elements are replaced, the higher the level of service rendered in the building. But also, the shorter the period of replacement, the higher the annual amount of depreciation that the owner must charge as a cost. Those who wish to enjoy high-quality housing service must be willing to pay a high enough rent premium for new as compared with old equipment to make frequent replacement investment profitable to the owner.

Finally, structures themselves can be altered by investment in re-

4. For further elaboration of this point and for references to earlier literature on the housing market, see James Heilbrun, *Real Estate Taxes and Urban Housing* (New York: Columbia University Press, 1966), Chs. 2, 4. Adaptive models of the housing market have also been formulated by Richard F. Muth in *Cities and Housing* (Chicago: University of Chicago Press, 1969), Ch. 6; and Edgar O. Olsen, "A Competitive Theory of the Housing Market," *American Economic Review*, September 1969, pp. 612–22.

modeling. This is the most obvious way of "moving" a building within the rent distribution to meet changed conditions of demand. Apartments can be divided into smaller units or combined into larger ones, or they can be remodeled to overcome design obsolescence and/or to introduce more up-to-date equipment. The owner will invest in remodeling if the expected return on the required funds exceeds the opportunity cost of his capital.

The Demand for Housing Space and Quality

Rental housing units differ from one another in three important respects: location within the city, size, and quality. In general the rent will be higher the more central the location, the larger the number of rooms, and the higher the quality of the apartment. For a given rental outlay a family can obtain a smaller apartment of higher quality or a larger apartment of lower quality. Each family will presumably choose that combination of space and quality which best suits its needs, income, and tastes.[5]

The two attributes of quality and space that the consumer balances, one against the other, in choosing his dwelling unit are the same attributes that the Bureau of the Census measures under the headings of standard versus substandard (which refers to quality) and overcrowding (which refers to persons per room—i.e., per unit of space). Since quality and space compete for the consumer's housing dollar, it is apparent that given the level of consumer incomes, attempts to raise the quality of housing will, if they require a rise in rents, probably tend to *increase* the degree of overcrowding. Conversely, overcrowding could be reduced by increasing the supply of *low* quality, low price housing. Thus the two major objectives of public policy toward housing—to increase quality and to reduce overcrowding—come into direct conflict with each other, given the constraint of a fixed level of consumer income and rent-paying capacity.

The Effect of Income on the Demand for Housing

The principal factors shaping a family's demand for housing are income and family size. The higher its income, the more it will spend on housing. The response of housing expenditures to change in the level of income is measured by the income elasticity of demand, which is defined as percentage change in expenditure ÷ percentage change in income. In an important theoretical and empirical analysis of urban housing, Muth

5. See Heilbrun, pp. 39–42, and sources cited therein.

found that the income elasticities of demand for housing "tend to cluster around a value just slightly greater than $+1$" in 1950 for a sample of six cities studied individually.[6] Margaret Reid, in another comprehensive analysis, estimated the income elasticity of demand for housing at between $+1.5$ and $+2.0$. In the same study she found that the income elasticity of consumption of rooms per person was only about $+0.5$.[7] This means that although consumption of space rises as family income goes up, the amount spent on increased space can account for only a minor share of the increase in family housing expenditure that occurs as income rises. The major share must therefore be accounted for by a rise in the quality of the space consumed—i.e., by a rise in rent paid per room. In short, these figures imply that the income elasticity of demand for housing *quality* is quite high. As Miss Reid explains it:

> For several decades high quality housing appears to have been an important feature distinguishing the consumption of the rich from that of the poor. Housing improves markedly as one goes up the economic hierarchy of consumers—much more than does food and clothing and probably even more than automobiles . . . with housing as with food, increase in quality rather than sheer quantity accounts for most of the rise in consumption with normal income.[8]

Muth's findings directly confirm the effects of income on housing quality that are only implied in Miss Reid's study. He measured quality by means of the proportion of housing that was "substandard," using the regular census definition of that term. In his sample of six cities he found that the income elasticity of substandard housing averaged about -2.5; in other words, a 1 percent *rise* in the level of income would, on the average, bring about a 2.5 percent *decline* in the proportion of housing that was substandard. For the same cities he found that the income elasticity of overcrowding was also about -2.5.[9] These are very strong relationships. They indicate, for example, that a 20 percent increase in real family income, which might occur over a period of one decade, would cause a 50 percent reduction in the incidence of substandard and overcrowded housing (since $2.5 \times .20 = .50$).

However, the strong relationship between housing quality and income has both encouraging and discouraging implications for the struggle to improve housing conditions in the United States. On the one hand, it means that the secular rise in living standards can be expected to reduce markedly the incidence of substandard housing for the nation as a whole.

6. Muth, p. 199.
7. Margaret G. Reid, *Housing and Income* (Chicago: University of Chicago Press, 1962), pp. 376, 378.
8. *Ibid.*, pp. 377–78.
9. Muth, pp. 199–200.

On the other hand, it also suggests that substandard housing is likely to persist where poverty persists. Therefore, central cities, with their concentrations of low income population, will find it especially difficult to eliminate inadequate housing.

THE HIGH COST OF NEW CONSTRUCTION

For many years one of the major sources of dissatisfaction with the whole enterprise of housing has been the high cost of new construction. Over the years economic progress has greatly reduced the "real cost" of most consumer goods in the United States: historically, per capita income has been rising much faster than the prices of the things people buy, so decade by decade the average family finds its real income, or level of purchasing power, rising. Housing is a notable exception. Through most of this century the cost of new residential construction has been rising much faster than the general price level.

Figure 10.1 illustrates the trend since 1929. From that year through 1972, per capita disposable personal income rose 449 percent. Of course, prices on the average more than doubled over the same period. Real per capita income (i.e., per capita income measured in constant dollars) consequently increased by 122 percent. This last figure means that consumers could, on the average, buy more than twice the quantity of goods and services with their 1972 incomes that they had been able to purchase with their smaller incomes in 1929. Residential construction costs, however, rose 396 percent from 1929 through 1972, more than twice the rate of increase of either consumer prices or wholesale industrial prices. By comparing the 396 percent rise in construction costs with the 449 percent rise in per capita income we can see that the average consumer's ability to pay for new housing has increased very little in more than 40 years. (Admittedly, indexes of construction cost must be used cautiously in analyzing housing problems. First of all, comparisons between widely separated points in time are subject to a degree of error on account of changes in quality and in the mix of physical elements that constitute "housing." Second, the capital cost of housing is only one item among the many that contribute to the annual cost of occupancy—others include maintenance and operating costs, taxes, and insurance.) [10]

Our concern at this point is with the way high construction costs affect the functioning of the housing market: in recent years construction of housing that meets minimum standards in our large cities has been

10. See *A Decent Home*, Report of the President's Committee on Urban Housing, 1969, pp. 118–20.

FIGURE 10.1

Trends in Construction Costs, Other Prices and Per Capita Income, 1929–72

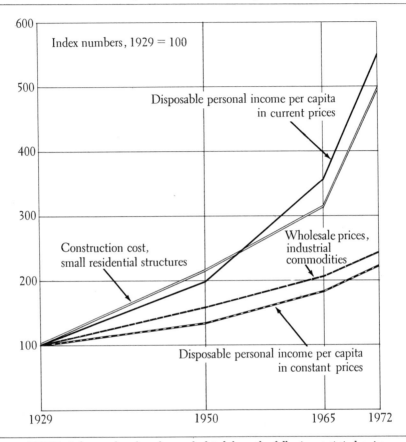

NOTE: Index numbers have been calculated from the following statistical series: U.S. Department of Commerce series on per capita disposable personal income in current prices and in 1958 prices; E. H. Boeckh and Associates, index of construction costs for small residential structures; Bureau of Labor Statistics, index of wholesale prices of all industrial commodities.

so expensive that, roughly speaking, only families in the upper third of the income distribution can afford to live in new dwellings. For example, the President's Committee on Urban Housing estimated that in 1967 a new two-bedroom apartment built without subsidy in Detroit would have had to rent for $2,719 a year (and Detroit had the lowest costs among the large cities).[11]

To live in such an apartment at a rent-income ratio of one-fifth

11. See Table 11.2, p. 287.

(about average for the nation) a family would have needed to earn $13,595 a year. If the family were willing to spend a quarter of its income on rent, the required earnings would have been $10,876. Yet in 1967 only 34.5 percent of all families living in central cities of large metropolitan areas had incomes of $10,000 or more.[12] In the 1970's incomes are somewhat higher, but so are costs. It remains the case that about two-thirds of the families living in large cities are unable to afford new, commercially financed housing. Apart from the possibility of living in new units subsidized in some way by the government, they are consigned to the second-hand market in housing. Of course, this is not necessarily to be deplored. Most people live in second-hand housing—as Grigsby has remarked, even Queen Elizabeth does. The point is, rather, that the inability of most families to afford new housing does clearly shape the process by which new construction is absorbed into the standing stock: new housing, unless subsidized by the government, enters near the upper end of the rent distribution and triggers a series of adjustments by which older housing then shifts down into lower rent classes. This hand-me-down process is known as "filtering." To be sure, some of the low rent, low quality housing still in use was built for the low end of the market to begin with, at a date when minimum standards, and therefore costs, were lower than they are today. A large portion of it, however, reached the low rent category by "filtering down."

THE "FILTERING" PROCESS

Grigsby points out that the term "filtering" seems to cause no misunderstanding when used in casual discussion but that when housing analysts have attempted more precise definitions, they find agreement difficult.[13] This is hardly surprising, since the single term "filtering" must bear the burden of describing a large part of the complex process by which adjustments take place in the match up between the stock of housing units and the tenant population. For our purposes it will suffice to use one of the conventional general definitions and say that filtering takes place when housing once occupied by a higher income group is released by them and becomes available at a lower cost to tenants with lower incomes.

The filtering process gets under way when families in the middle and upper classes move into new housing. The housing thus vacated be-

12. U.S. Bureau of the Census, *Current Population Reports*, P-60, No. 59, April 18, 1969, Table 9.

13. William Grigsby, *Housing Markets and Public Policy* (Philadelphia: University of Pennsylvania Press, 1963), pp. 85–86.

comes available to others, to whom it appears better than the dwellings they had. Let us assume no change in population or in the level of family incomes while this process goes on. In that case, when the well-to-do move out of their old housing, its owners quite certainly will have to reduce rents a bit to attract tenants from the next lower income class. The tenants so attracted will vacate other units whose owners will, in turn, reduce rents to attract a still lower income class. Thus a whole chain of moves will take place, made possible by a series of rent reductions. At the end of the chain the poorest families will, presumably, leave the worst housing for something slightly better, and the worst housing will stand vacant or be demolished.

This is a highly schematic explanation, blessedly simplified by the assumption of static population and income. But let us stick to our simplifications a little longer. Why under these circumstances would the upper income classes wish to move into new housing? Numerous motives exist, provided we do not insist on a completely static world. New neighborhoods become fashionable, old buildings become unfashionable or do not offer the latest equipment and conveniences, new modes of housekeeping lead to changes in interior design, architectural styles change, and so on. These can be regarded as various forms of obsolescence.

It is sometimes suggested that age per se leads to physical deterioration of housing and that the well-to-do move out to avoid this. But housing need not deteriorate with age if it is well maintained. In most cases, therefore, physical deterioration should be regarded, not as an independent causal factor, but as the result of a change in the demand for particular units, which in turn leads to a reduced level of maintenance. As we argued earlier, reducing outlays for maintenance (and for operation, as well) is one of the ways in which owners "move" buildings from one segment of the market to another in response to changes in demand. This view of the matter is supported by the obvious fact that old buildings are often "improved," moved "up" rather than "down," when an old neighborhood becomes suddenly fashionable.

If we introduce the reality of rising living standards, still holding population constant, the filtering process becomes more complicated. If the rich are growing richer, then perhaps they move into new housing because they want something even more opulent than what they had. If the class below them is also growing in wealth perhaps it can move up into the housing vacated by the rich without a reduction in rent. One might then imagine a series of upward moves by all families, while the rents of all occupied housing units remained unchanged. That is too simple, however, since the income classes are not of equal size and cannot fit neatly into the housing vacated by those directly above them. The picture becomes still more complex if we introduce changes in the number, size, and age distribution of households. But there is no need to go further. The details of adjustment will obviously vary with the demands put upon the system. No single description can cover all cases.

Filtering is sometimes defended as the principal way in which we can hope to raise the housing standards of the poor—and often attacked for having failed to do just that. This conflict is correctly resolved by granting that each contention is true in a specifically definable way. In the earlier discussion of the rental housing market it was pointed out that the quality of housing service provided in a given building depends partly on its fixed physical features and equipment and partly on the level of maintenance and operating expenditures applied to them as, so to speak, "variable inputs" by the owner. Filtering *can* raise housing standards insofar as these are concerned with the more or less permanent physical characteristics of buildings; it *cannot* do so insofar as they depend on the owner's inputs of maintenance and operating expense that vary directly with the rent level he is attempting to establish. There are undoubtedly some families now living in standard, filtered-down housing for whom it represents an improvement over what they could have paid for out of the same real income in decades past. The improvement, however, is likely to be, not in the level of maintenance or operating services, but in the physical features of design and equipment: more light and air, more plumbing, fireproof construction, and so on.

On the debit side, it must be admitted that some of the substandard housing now in use has reached its present disreputable state precisely by the process of filtering down. This is hardly surprising, since low income tenants usually require low rent housing, and low rent housing is often substandard. When the supply of low rent units is unsufficient to meet demand, the market is capable of creating more of them either by breaking up larger units or by economizing on maintenance and operating outlays. In the process, additions may be made to the substandard stock. Or, if one thinks in terms of occupancy rather than physical standards, units that filter down may well move into the "overcrowded" category, since lower income tenants economize on rent by using space more intensively. In short, "filtering" is one of the mechanisms by which the adaptive market we have been describing adjusts the services supplied by the housing stock to the demands of the resident population.

Against this background we can now examine recent trends in U.S. housing conditions.

TRENDS IN U.S. HOUSING CONDITIONS

According to all the standard measures, U.S. housing conditions have improved markedly in the last two decades. Table 10.2 shows separately the incidence of overcrowding (more than 1.0 persons per room) and of

TABLE 10.2
Trends in the Condition of Urban and Rural Housing by Race of Occupant, 1950–70

	PERCENTAGE OF ALL OCCUPIED UNITS						PERCENTAGE CHANGE, 1960–70, IN PROPORTION	
	OVERCROWDED (OCCUPIED BY 1.01 OR MORE PERSONS PER ROOM)			SUBSTANDARD (DILAPIDATED OR LACKING COMPLETE PLUMBING FACILITIES)[c]				
	1970	1960	1950	1970	1960	1950	Overcrowded	Substandard
All Races								
Total U.S.	8.2%	11.5%	15.7%	6.0%	16.0%	35.4%	−29%	−62%
Urban	7.6	10.2	13.3	3.1	9.6	21.9	−25	−67
Rural	10.1	15.1	20.6	14.5	32.6	62.4	−33	−56
White [a]								
Total U.S.	6.9	9.7	13.3	4.8	13.0	31.8	−29	−63
Urban	6.3	8.5	—	2.4	7.0	18.2	−26	−66
Rural	8.8	12.9	—	11.4	28.0	59.1	−32	−59
Negro [b]								
Total U.S.	19.9	28.3	32.0	16.9	44.0	73.2	−30	−62
Urban	18.1	24.7	—	8.5	31.8	61.2	−27	−73
Rural	30.1	40.8	—	62.3	85.5	96.3	−26	−27

[a] In 1950 and 1960 this category includes only whites; in 1970 it includes whites and other races, except Negro.

[b] In 1950 and 1960 this category includes all nonwhites; in 1970 it includes only Negroes.

[c] Since data on dilapidation were not available, figures for 1970 refer to plumbing condition only.

Sources: U.S. Bureau of the Census, *Census of Population and Housing,* 1950, 1960, and 1970; and Housing and Home Finance Agency, *Our Nonwhite Population and Its Housing,* July 1963.

substandard housing (units that lack complete plumbing or are dilapidated), as recorded by the census in 1950, 1960, and 1970. Whether one looks at urban or rural areas or at white- or black-occupied units he sees the same general trend—a pronounced decline in both overcrowding and substandard conditions. The only exception to this generalization is found in rural black housing, where the percentage lacking complete plumbing or in dilapidated condition has declined only moderately in 20 years—a tribute, no doubt, to the persistence of the rural out-house.

It comes as no surprise to see in Table 10.2 that the housing condition of blacks is far inferior to that of whites in urban as well as rural areas: the incidence both of overcrowding and of substandard conditions in black-occupied housing averages about three times what it does in units occupied by whites. However, the table also reveals that conditions are improving just as fast in black- as in white-occupied housing. Between 1960 and 1970 the incidence of overcrowding declined among blacks 30 percent and among whites 29 percent, while the incidence of substandard conditions fell 62 percent for blacks as compared with 63 percent for whites. Although housing conditions improved far less, in a relative sense, for rural than for urban blacks, this effect was offset in the black totals by the pronounced decline in the absolute size of the rural black population. Undoubtedly, migration from rural to urban areas accounts for much of the improvement in black housing conditions since 1950, as measured by these Census Bureau categories.

Table 10.3 applies the same definitions of overcrowded and substandard housing to the occupied housing stock of metropolitan and nonmetropolitan areas. By comparing the data for "central cities" in Table 10.3 with the figures for "urban" areas in Table 10.2, we can see whether conditions are better or worse in large cities than in the broader category of urban America that includes small towns. The comparison shows that for the aggregate of all races in 1970 the proportion of housing overcrowded is somewhat higher in central cities than in urban areas generally. However, if we look at the races separately we see that the proportion overcrowded for each race is about the same in central cities as in urban areas. The higher incidence of overcrowding in central cities is clearly associated with the fact that they contain a higher proportion of blacks, and blacks much more frequently than whites live in overcrowded conditions.

The pattern is somewhat different in the case of substandard conditions. In 1970, the incidence of substandard housing for the aggregate of all races was about the same in central cities as in urban areas generally. However, it was markedly lower for blacks and slightly higher for whites in central cities. The very low incidence of substandard housing for blacks in central cities as compared with blacks in any other geographic category

TABLE 10.3

Housing Conditions in Central Cities, Suburbs, and Nonmetropolitan Areas by Race of Occupant, 1960 and 1970

	PERCENTAGE OF ALL OCCUPIED UNITS				PERCENTAGE CHANGE, 1960–70, IN PROPORTION	
	OVERCROWDED (OCCUPIED BY 1.01 OR MORE PERSONS PER ROOM)		SUBSTANDARD (DILAPIDATED OR LACKING COMPLETE PLUMBING FACILITIES)[c]		Over-crowded	Sub-standard
	1970	1960	1970	1960		
All Races						
Metropolitan areas	7.8%	10.4%	3.2%	9.4%	−25%	−66%
Central cities	8.5	10.7	3.2	10.4	−21	−69
Outside central cities	7.1	9.9	3.1	8.3	−29	−62
Nonmetropolitan areas	9.2	13.6	12.2	27.7	−32	−56
White [a]						
Metropolitan areas	6.5	8.7	2.7	7.3	−25	−63
Central cities	6.6	8.4	2.9	7.8	−21	−63
Outside central cities	6.5	9.1	2.5	6.8	−28	−63
Nonmetropolitan areas	7.8	11.5	9.3	22.9	−32	−60
Negro [b]						
Metropolitan areas	17.8	24.7	7.2	28.2	−28	−75
Central cities	17.1	23.5	4.8	24.8	−27	−81
Outside central cities	20.8	29.8	17.2	43.3	−30	−60
Nonmetropolitan areas	26.9	36.0	48.9	77.3	−25	−37

[a] In 1960 this category includes only whites; in 1970 it includes whites and other races, except Negro.
[b] In 1960 this category includes all nonwhites; in 1970 it includes only Negroes.
[c] Since data on dilapidation were not available, figures for 1970 refer to plumbing condition only.
Sources: U.S. Bureau of the Census, *Census of Population and Housing,* 1960 and 1970.

probably reflects two causes. The first is the impact of high central city code standards. Occupancy of housing without full plumbing facilities is now illegal for families in some large cities. The second cause is the filtering process. Many blacks now living in central cities occupy housing recently vacated by whites of a higher income class. Such housing was equipped with full plumbing in order to meet the demands of its higher income occupants, and this physical equipment remains intact as the units filter down to lower income groups. Here is an instance in which filtering does lead to higher housing standards.

The contrast between the things that filtering can and cannot do is illustrated nicely in Table 10.3. Compare the situation of the two races in central cities in 1970. The incidence of housing lacking full plumbing facilities is 4.8 percent for blacks versus 2.9 percent for whites. The absolute difference in this case is small, though on a relative basis, black households suffer substandard conditions 1.7 times as often as white ($4.8 \div 2.9 = 1.66$). On the other hand, the rate of overcrowding for blacks is 17.1 percent versus 6.6 percent for whites. In this case both the relative and the absolute differentials are large. On a relative basis black-occupied housing is overcrowded 2.6 times as frequently as white housing. The relatively low incidence of incomplete plumbing in black central city housing demonstrates that filtering *can* raise housing standards for low income groups insofar as standards are measured in terms of the fixed physical characteristics of structures. On the other hand, in the case of a housing measure such as overcrowding, which is not a structural characteristic, filtering can have little effect in raising standards. Such characteristics tend in the long run to reflect, or adapt to, the income of the occupant. Blacks display a much higher rate of overcrowding than do whites because their incomes are much lower. Improvement is conditional upon rising income.

IS THERE AN URBAN HOUSING CRISIS?

We have seen that census data running from 1950 through 1970 indicate a steady and substantial improvement in housing conditions both for urban areas as a whole and for the central cities of SMSA's. Nevertheless, many economists believe that in our older cities housing conditions have improved little in recent years and may now even be deteriorating. Indeed, the situation is frequently described as nothing less than a crisis.

What can account for the apparent contradiction between what the data show and what experienced observers believe to be the case? The answer has several interrelated elements. First, as average living standards increase year by year, our expectations about the performance of the economy, and therefore our definitions of "adequacy," rise, too. We know this to have been true historically in the case of poverty standards: the definition of a poverty-line income has been raised periodically. Why should it not also be true of nationally defined housing standards? Yet we continue to adhere to a definition of standard housing—"not dilapidated and having complete plumbing"—that was worked out before the 1950 Census. Nothing in this definition measures adequacy of design or of room size. In addition, the term "dilapidated" may fail to comprehend all of those features, such as dirt, disrepair, and malfunction, that together contribute so much to the gut meaning of the word "slum."

Second, though family incomes have been rising in central cities, they have been declining relative to incomes elsewhere and in recent years probably have not kept up with increases in the cost of housing. In 1959 central city median income was 5 percent *above* the median for the nation as a whole. Ten years later the central city figure was 5 percent *below* the national median. (See Table 3.7.) With the rise in real estate taxes, interest rates, and the cost of maintenance and repairs, the total annual cost of providing housing services of standard quality has increased rapidly in recent years. Although changes in such costs over time are difficult to measure with precision, the New York City Rand Institute has estimated that in New York they rose about 6 percent per year between 1945 and 1968.[14] Such a pace is undoubtedly faster than the rate of increase of the rent-paying ability of tenants in the low income sectors of central city housing markets. Frank Kristof has concluded that in cities with large poverty populations "the household budgets of one-quarter to one-third of their households [do] not permit these households to pay the full cost of proper maintenance of older existing housing." [15] Under these circumstances one would expect landlords in low income neighborhoods to reduce the level of maintenance and operating outlays, bringing about a gradual deterioration in the condition of housing. But such deterioration might well occur in ways that available measures of housing conditions do not record.

Indirect evidence for the impact of the relatively unfavorable central city income trend can be seen in Table 10.3. We have already cited Muth's finding that the degree of overcrowding in an urban housing market depends substantially on the income level of occupants. The table shows that for the aggregate of all races the percentage decline in overcrowding from 1960 to 1970 was smaller in central cities than in any of the other

14. Ira S. Lowry, ed., *Confronting the Crisis*, Vol. I of Rental Housing in New York City (New York: New York City Rand Institute, February 1970), Document No. RM-6190–NYC, pp. 6–8.
15. Frank S. Kristof, "Federal Housing Policies: Subsidized Production, Filtration and Objectives: Part II," *Land Economics*, May 1973, p. 171.

geographic areas shown. This is just what we should have expected, since median family income rose by a smaller percentage in central cities during the 1960's than in either the ring areas of SMSA's or U.S. nonmetropolitan areas.

The Problem of Abandonment

The most dramatic evidence cited to demonstrate the existence of an urban housing crisis is the rise, since the mid-1960's, of the phenomenon known as housing "abandonment." In city after city owners of rental housing in low income neighborhoods have simply "walked away" from their properties, usually after allowing them to become uninhabitable by withholding maintenance and operating services and failing to pay taxes and mortgage charges. Abandonment has apparently been encouraged by the growth of crime and vandalism. If an apartment in a building in a high-crime neighborhood falls vacant, it is often immediately vandalized. Damage to the structure and fear of crime cause other tenants to move out. Vacancies increase. Further vandalism follows, soon leaving the building uninhabitable. When finally "abandoned," it frequently becomes a home for criminal intruders and a scene of fires, thus further contaminating the neighborhood for those living in buildings that have not yet reached that extreme state. Clearly, abandonment contributes to, and is itself a function of, neighborhood decline.[16]

Abandonment poses several problems for the housing analyst. First, statistics on the subject must be used cautiously, since it is not always clear what is being measured. Enumerators may find it difficult to distinguish between buildings that have been withdrawn from the market in anticipation of orderly future redevelopment and those from which the owner has definitely "walked away."

Second, the abandonment process itself can be interpreted in diametrically opposite ways. One interpretation would view it as the natural end result of filtering. For example, New York City's population size was approximately unchanged during the 1960's, while a considerable volume of high rent residential construction took place. Under these circumstances, if the filtering process worked in the normal way, one would expect existing units to filter down to tenants with lower rent-paying capacity. At the lower end of the rent scale, when the poorest tenants moved up one notch some units (presumably the worst ones) would be vacated and eventually withdrawn from the market. Thus abandonment

16. For further detail see George Sternlieb, "Abandonment and Rehabilitation: What Is to Be Done?" Papers submitted to the Subcommittee on Housing, Part 1, U.S. Congress, House Committee on Banking and Currency, June 1971, pp. 315–31; and Kristof, pp. 166–69.

could be interpreted as the logical end result of a filtering process that is intrinsically desirable since it brings about a net improvement in housing standards.

A similar interpretation is possible even in the absence of new construction. In many of the cities that have reported high rates of abandonment—St. Louis, Cleveland, and Detroit, for example—population declined substantially during the 1960's. These declines resulted from the exodus of middle and upper income families. What follows might be described as "filtering through population decline." In vacating high rent, inner-city housing, the middle and upper classes would have set in motion a fitering process with precisely the same end result that occurs when population is constant but new construction takes place at the upper end of the rent scale: after a series of moves by tenants, the worst low rent housing would be vacated and withdrawn from the market.

Such an optimistic view, however, overlooks the fact that relatively good housing as well as bad is usually engulfed when abandonment sweeps a neighborhood. For example, of 512 abandoned buildings in Brooklyn demolished by the New York City administration in 1967, 59 percent had been classified as "standard" and only 41 percent as "substandard" in the 1960 Census of Housing. The Rand Institute study of New York City's housing estimated that at least 80 percent of the vast "unrecorded losses" to the housing inventory from 1965 through 1967 were in buildings that had not been classified as dilapidated in a 1965 survey.[17]

The pessimistic interpretation of abandonment stresses the gross inefficiency of a process through which the market loses good housing along with bad, the chaotic nature of the process itself, and the sense it conveys of a complete breakdown of the institutional structure of the housing and property markets in low income neighborhoods. If the pessimists are right and such a breakdown is, indeed, taking place, it is likely to have serious consequences for core city housing for a long time to come.

Causes of Abandonment

Analytically one can separate the causes of abandonment into two classes.[18] The first comprises the "normal" forces of demand and supply. On the demand side, abandonment is encouraged by the low rent-paying

17. The Brooklyn data are reported in Frank S. Kristof, *Urban Housing Needs Through the 1980's: an Analysis and Projection*, Research Report No. 10, The National Commission on Urban Problems, 1968, p. 67; the Rand Institute estimates are from Lowry, p. 6.

18. Philip H. Friedly, "Experimental Approaches to the Amelioration of Housing Abandonment and Neighborhood Decline," *Proceedings* of the American Real Estate and Urban Economics Association, Vol. VI, 1971, p. 154.

capacity of impoverished tenants, and the poorest of all are typically the racial minorities in poverty areas where abandonment has been most frequent. On the supply side, the rapidly rising cost of housing service inputs, described earlier, has made it increasingly difficult to maintain and operate low rent housing at an acceptable quality level.

The second class of causes of abandonment includes those special social and institutional factors that seem to exacerbate the housing problem in low income areas: the high incidence of crime and vandalism, racial tension between landlords and minority-group tenants, unwillingness of financial institutions to make mortgage loans on low income housing, and, finally, the small scale of operation and minimum competence in management of many rental housing owners in poverty areas.

There is ample reason to believe that both sets of factors have been at work and that their interaction makes matters worse. On the one hand, crime, vandalism, and antisocial behavior raise the maintenance costs of building owners, thus reducing the quality of service that they will—or can—offer at any given rent level. On the other hand, the low rent-paying capacity of the poor in the face of rising costs undoubtedly hastened the withdrawal of private financial institutions from their normal role of supporting investment in the maintenance of the low rent housing stock.

However painful and destructive abandonment has been for both tenants and landlords, it has, at least, forced us to clear away some very unhelpful illusions about housing markets and housing policy. As George Sternlieb points out, we have long subscribed to the folklore that slum landlords

> grow very fat, indeed, on the high rents and low input which their tenants and buildings are subjected to . . . a satisfying illusion because it has in turn permitted us the belief that all that is required in low income housing was a repartitioning of an already adequate rent pie. Whether through code enforcement, rent controls, or any of a host of other mechanisms, the problem of good maintenance could be resolved by squeezing some of the excess profits out of the landlord's hands. This process would still leave enough of a residue to maintain his self-interests in the longevity and satisfactory quality of the structure in question. This bit of folklore may have had considerable validity a decade or two ago. It has little relationship to the realities currently.[19]

If it has done nothing else, abandonment has finally dispelled the illusion that slums are highly profitable. We have been forced to recognize that housing for the poor will not be kept up to standard unless the poor can afford to pay the minimum cost of standard housing.

19. Sternlieb, p. 317.

Thus, after four decades in which we attempted to solve the housing problem of the poor by public intervention on the supply side of the market, we are now beginning to understand the fundamental importance of the constraint of low income on the demand side. Much of the recent analysis of urban housing problems emphasizes this new understanding, which is beginning to be reflected in "official" policy pronouncements as well.[20] In the next chapter we will describe the development of urban housing policy in the United States and analyze the many programs that have been either tried or advocated. Before doing so, however, we must examine the rationale for having an urban housing policy at all. We don't have an urban clothing policy. Why should housing, any more than clothing, be an object of special social concern?

THE RATIONALE FOR SUBSIDIZING HOUSING

Urban housing policy comprises a great many actual or proposed forms of public intervention in the markets for land and housing. Some are regulatory in nature, such as antidiscrimination laws and zoning ordinances, and are intended to overcome particular imperfections in the housing and land markets. Most forms of intervention, however, share a different characteristic: they are subsidy programs, such as public housing or below-market-interest-rate loans, whose essential purpose is to increase the supply of housing and/or directly reduce its price to consumers. The funds from which these subsidies are paid have alternative uses in either the public or the private sector. What justifies the particular use to which we put them? Why do we subsidize the output of housing instead of allowing the market to follow its own course in this, as in many other instances?

Over the years, a number of justifications for housing subsidies have been suggested, most of them under one of the following headings:

1. Housing is a "merit want," or "merit good," in the sense first defined by Musgrave.[21] A merit good is something which is better for people than they realize. Consequently, individual consumers, if left to themselves, are likely to consume less of such goods than the amount that would maximize their welfare within the constraints of their income. The concept is easily understood in the reverse case of "demerit goods": we control the use of narcotics on the ground that otherwise many people

---

20. See, for example, the President of the United States, *Third Annual Report on National Housing Goals*, June 29, 1971, pp. 24–25.
21. Richard A. Musgrave, *The Theory of Public Finance* (New York: McGraw-Hill, 1959), Ch. 1.

would use them in ignorance of the harm they cause. In the same fashion, it may be argued that we must subsidize the distribution of, say, education, medical services, or housing because otherwise, largely through ignorance, people would consume less of them than they ought to. Who is to determine the "correct" level of consumption of such merit goods? In a democratic society that is presumably the function of the well-informed, who must then persuade the majority to adopt the appropriate policies.

2. Poverty, or the unequal distribution of income, prevents some families from obtaining housing that meets a socially desirable minimum standard. In order to bring the poor up to the defined minimum standard, the government provides them with more housing than they can or would pay for out of their low incomes. This argument is actually a variant of the first, for it implies that housing is a merit good. If it were not a merit good, it would be unnecessary to provide housing benefits in kind. One could simply grant cash subsidies to the poor—along the lines of the income-maintenance plans discussed in Chapter 9—and rely on them to spend a sufficient portion of the extra cash on housing. Since we do not do that, the argument clearly implies that people do not spend as much of their income on housing as we think they "ought" to—i.e., that housing is a merit good. The only difference between the poverty argument and the merit good argument, then, is that the former suggests, and the latter does not, that above some level of family income we can assume that everyone will voluntarily obtain enough housing.

3. Better housing reduces the cost of providing social services by lowering the incidence of fire, communicable disease, crime, and other social disorders. This is the "external social benefits" argument. If better housing does have these desirable social effects, then individual consumption decisions will result systematically in too little housing being consumed. From the principle of diminishing marginal utility we conclude that the marginal private benefit to the consumer declines as he increases his annual consumption of housing. He reaches his individual optimum by consuming up to the point where the (declining) marginal private benefit he receives from an additional unit of consumption just equals the marginal cost he pays for that unit. But this is short of the socially optimal quantity of consumption because the individual ignores the external marginal social benefits thrown off by his act of consumption. Society would be justified in subsidizing housing so that individual consumption of it is carried to the point where the sum of marginal private benefits plus marginal social benefits equals marginal cost. Since marginal social benefit is positive, this equality will occur at a higher level of housing consumption than the individual would choose to pay for in an unsubsidized market.

4. Housing subsidies are an expedient way of redistributing income to the poor. Thus, one might favor such subsidies while remaining skeptical about the merit good or external benefits arguments. Economists generally have agreed that income redistribution is most efficiently accomplished not by making transfers in kind but by making cash transfers, which leave the recipient free to choose whatever additional goods he most desires. Yet the "realist" who wishes to redistribute income may believe that it is politically easier to legislate adequate transfers in kind than in cash and that this consideration outweighs the contrary argument based on economic efficiency.

Let us examine some of these contentions in greater detail. We have already shown how the merit good argument serves to justify subsidies. Less obvious is the point that it also justifies the use of housing codes intended to keep housing up to a minimum standard of quality. To be sure, housing codes (other than occupancy standards) may be regarded simply as an effort-saving convenience. Instead of letting each tenant see to it that the landlord maintains decent standards in his building, we agree to let an informed specialized government agency do the job for us. A good many regulatory activities of government can be so justified. But there is probably more to it than that. In a competitive setting such as the urban rental-housing market, given normal vacancies, tenants can enforce standards by refusing to live in substandard buildings. Hence our insistence on enacting housing codes strongly implies that some tenants will not insist on high enough standards, either on account of ignorance or because they cannot "afford" standard housing. Given their low incomes, they prefer substandard or overcrowded housing at low prices to standard or less crowded housing at higher prices. In either case, the justification for codes is essentially the merit good argument that at least some consumers fail to realize how important adequate housing is to their own welfare.

Does Housing Confer Indirect Benefits?

What reason can there be for believing that housing is, in fact, better for people than they realize? The answer must lie in the existence of some sort of indirect benefit of which the consumer is not aware, for surely he can judge for himself the direct satisfaction he obtains from housing *qua* housing. The indirect benefits to the consuming family would have to be such things as better physical and mental health, higher educational achievement, and less likelihood of family members turning to narcotics, crime, or juvenile delinquency. These same indirect effects—disease, crime, and delinquency—are an important source of the external costs allegedly thrown off upon society at large by bad housing, and therefore they are also a source of the external social benefits attributable to housing improvement. Thus the merit good argument and the external benefit argument turn out to be rooted in the same phenomenon: indirect effects of housing quality on behavior.

What evidence do we have that such effects actually exist? A virtual utopia of indirect benefits has, of course, been alleged. In the 1930's, when slum clearance and public housing first became objectives of national policy, claims for the beneficent effects of good housing were widely accepted. For example, the Court of Appeals of New York, in an important 1936 decision favorable to public housing, held that:

> The public evils, social and economic, of such [slum] conditions
> are unquestioned and unquestionable. Slum areas are the breeding
> places of disease which take toll not only from denizens but, by
> spread, from the inhabitants of the entire city and state. Juvenile
> delinquency, crime, and immorality are there born, find protection
> and flourish. Enormous economic loss results directly from the
> necessary expenditure of public funds to maintain health . . .
> and to war against crime and immorality.[22]

Such claims now seem astonishingly naive. The logic, or illogic, upon which they were based has been explained lucidly by John P. Dean:

> In city after city . . . slum areas have been shown to be the areas
> of poorest health and greatest personal and social disorder. The
> implication is: "Remove the slums and you remove the social ills!"
> But it would be just as illogical to say that ills of slum areas are
> caused not by substandard housing conditions, but by the absence
> of telephone service, which also correlates with indexes of social
> disorder.[23]

During the 1930's a good deal of "evidence" was amassed to support the extravagant claims of housing reformers. It might easily be shown, for example, that rates of crime, delinquency, illegitimacy, disease, and death were lower in public housing projects than in the surrounding slum areas from which the tenants were selected. At first it was overlooked that the very process of tenant selection accounted for much of the gain. The old, the criminal, the socially disorganized were systematically excluded in favor of stable working-class families with children. In short, public housing tenants were not a random sample of the slum population.

Valid conclusions about the effects of the dwelling environment can

22. Cited in Robert Moore Fisher, *Twenty Years of Public Housing* (New York: Harper & Row, 1959), p. 63.

23. John P. Dean, "The Myths of Housing Reform" (abridged), in Jewel Bellusch and Murray Hausknecht, eds., *Urban Renewal: People, Politics and Planning* (New York: Doubleday, 1967), an Anchor Book, pp. 27–28.

be reached only if the sample of public housing tenants is carefully matched on a variety of socioeconomic characteristics with a selected control group of those remaining in the surrounding slums. A well-known study of the impact of housing on family life conducted in the 1950's employed just that test design.[24] It revealed that public housing is associated with statistically significant improvements in some, but by no means all, of the indexes of health, psychological adjustment, and school performance for which tests were made. The effects of better housing were usually in the expected direction, but the magnitudes of the effects were not very impressive. One would have to attach monetary values to the measured indirect benefits of housing and insert them into a benefit-cost study of a subsidized housing program to determine whether such benefits were sufficient to justify the program's subsidy cost. This task of quantification has defied even the most ingenious investigators. As Rothenberg put it in his very detailed analysis of urban renewal: "The external social costs allegedly generated by the existence of slums probably exist, but it is extremely difficult to find out even roughly how important they are." [25]

The demand for public intervention in the urban housing market has not proven very sensitive to the validity, or lack of it, of arguments concerning the existence of specific, measurable, indirect housing benefits. Beyond the reach of these arguments there remains a widespread conviction that in some fundamental sense housing *does* matter more than other consumer goods. Housing is, after all, the immediate physical environment of one's life. Apparently we do not want people to live—or, worse, to grow up—in a squalid environment. Whether this is because we find physical squalor morally shocking in an affluent society or because we believe such squalor is ultimately a threat to the society itself, is perhaps open to question. What cannot be doubted is that housing has long been, and will probably continue to be, an object of special social concern.

24. Daniel M. Wilner, R. P. Walkley, T. Pinkerton, and M. Tayback, *The Housing Environment and Family Life: A Longitudinal Study of the Effects of Housing on Morbidity and Mental Health* (Baltimore: Johns Hopkins Press, 1962). The volume also contains a useful review of other studies of the effects of housing quality.

25. Jerome Rothenberg, *Economic Evaluation of Urban Renewal* (Washington, D.C.: Brookings Institution, 1967), p. 174. See his Ch. 10 for a review of the conceptual and practical difficulties of measuring the social costs of slum housing.

Urban Housing Policy

ELEVEN

Public concern with urban housing standards has produced, over the years, a considerable range of housing policies and programs. We suggested in Chapter 10 that most of these can be classified as either subsidy programs or regulatory policies. Examining them now in greater detail, we will see that subsidy programs can be further subdivided. The existing major programs—including such a diverse list as public housing, urban renewal, housing rehabilitation, interest-rate subsidies, and rent supplements—form a single class in one important respect. In all of these programs, payment of a subsidy is linked either to the construction of specific new dwelling units or to the rehabilitation of specific buildings. The basic purpose of this kind of "new construction," or "supply side," subsidy is to increase the stock of new or high quality dwelling units as directly as possible, hoping in that way to raise urban housing standards for the whole population. In direct contrast to this is the recently proposed policy of providing cash subsidies in the form of general housing allowances to all low income families. Such a policy would operate directly on the demand side, raising the rent-paying capacity of the poor in the belief that the market would then provide them with an adequate supply of decent, standard, older housing. As the chapter proceeds, we will evaluate these alternative subsidy strategies.

In this chapter we will also discuss regulatory policies that are intended to overcome specific imperfections in the urban housing and land markets. Regulatory policies include the enforcement of housing code standards and antidiscrimination laws and the guidance of land use by means of zoning ordinances. The chapter will conclude with a discussion of proposals to "open up" the suburbs to low income housing—proposals that generally call for combining a variety of the forms of public intervention.[1]

PUBLIC HOUSING

The term "public housing" in the United States refers, not to all forms of government subsidized housing, but only to those units that are owned and operated (or in some cases, leased) by a public housing authority. The federal government had been engaged briefly in building public housing for defense workers in World War I, but its peacetime involvement dates from the Great Depression. Public housing was widely regarded as a radical new departure in the 1930's. It was initiated as an emergency measure to create employment by spending on new construction. In 1933 the Public Works Administration was authorized to include slum-clearance projects and the construction or repair of low cost housing among the works that it undertook, and it was neither required nor expected that such housing projects would be self-liquidating. Two and a half years of legislative battling were required, however, before Senator Wagner's United States Housing Act was passed in 1937, putting the public housing program on a permanent basis. Projects built by the PWA had been federally developed and owned. Under the new law, site selection, ownership, and operation were decentralized to the local level, though under federal guidelines, and have remained so ever since. With the exception of wartime housing, initiation of projects has been restricted to local housing authorities. In a sense, the United States has no "national" public housing policy; it has local public housing programs that are federally subsidized and regulated. The role of the federal authorities is limited to setting standards and making loans, contributions, or grants to the appropriate local body. The choice of whether to build or not remains a local one.

As the program has operated ever since 1937, the federal government, in effect, contributes up to 100 percent of the capital cost of a project as a subsidy to keep rents low. Local governments also contribute substantial subsidies by foregoing ordinary property taxes in favor of much lower payments "in lieu of taxes." Since it is a matter of public policy to restrict

---

1. One omission deserves note. Public policies intended to help reduce housing production costs will not be dealt with. The federal government's experimental cost-reduction program is called "Operation BREAKTHROUGH." For a brief description, see the President of the United States, *Fourth Annual Report on National Housing Goals*, June 29, 1972, pp. 16–17. On the problem of housing production costs see also *A Decent Home*, Report of the President's Committee on Urban Housing, 1969.

these large subsidy benefits to the poor, tenants are not accepted for admission unless their incomes fall below a specified limit. Such limits vary locally. In 1970 the nation-wide median for a four-person family was $4,400, or $430 above the federally defined nonfarm poverty-line income of that year.[2] Consistent with their admissions policy, most local authorities enforce a requirement that tenants vacate when their incomes rise about 25 percent above the maximum level for admission.

Down to the 1960's, public housing rents were expected to cover operating and maintenance costs plus payments in lieu of property taxes made by the local authority to the municipal government. In recent years, however, public as well as private rental housing has faced rapidly rising maintenance and operating costs. In many localities public housing rents had to be raised and/or maintenance outlays cut back sharply. As a result, Congress passed the Brooke Amendment in 1969, authorizing operating subsidies where needed to retain the low rent character of the projects. Appropriations, however, fell short of the amounts required, leaving many local authorities under severe financial pressure.

From 1950 through 1970, as Table 11.1 shows, the inventory of low rent public housing units under management increased from 201,700 to 893,500. Yet at the latter date public housing still accounted for only 1.3 percent of the nation's total housing stock, as recorded in the 1970 Census. The ratio is much higher, however, in many of the larger cities such as New York, Chicago, and Philadelphia.

Political support for public housing probably reached a high point with the passage of the Housing Act of 1949, which authorized construction of 810,000 additional units over a six-year period. During the 1950's, however, congressional appropriations never made possible any such massive program. In the 1960's funds were more plentiful, but by that time the program was running into trouble in the big cities, and available monies were not used to the limit. Local housing authorities were finding it increasingly difficult to obtain politically acceptable project sites. At the same time, earlier enthusiasm by public housing's traditional supporters was giving way to a rising wave of criticism. Only in the early 1970's did the inventory of public housing reach the 1 million unit level that would have been attained much earlier if the six-year program authorized in 1949 had been carried to completion. That comparison provides a dramatic measure of the extent to which public housing lost public support during subsequent years.

2. Henry J. Aaron, *Shelter and Subsidies* (Washington, D.C.: Brookings Institution, 1972), Table B–2, p. 204.

TABLE 11.1

Growth and Composition of the Public Housing Inventory [a]

	PUBLIC HOUSING INVENTORY (THOUSANDS)		*Total U.S. Housing Stock (Thousands)*	*Public Housing as Percentage of Total*
	Under Management	*Under Construction*		
1950	201.7	31.5	45,983	0.4%
1960	478.2	36.4	58,326	0.8
1970	893.5	126.8	68,679	1.3
1971	992.7	117.3	—	—
Composition of public housing inventory, 1971				
Constructed as public housing [b]	868.0	99.5		
Acquired [c]	35.4	5.2		
Leased [d]	89.4	12.6		

[a] As of December 31.

[b] Includes conventionally developed public housing and units built for local housing authorities under "turnkey" contracts.

[c] Existing housing acquired by local housing authorities. "Under construction" indicates units undergoing rehabilitation.

[d] Existing housing leased by local housing authorities.

Sources: *Statistical Abstract of the United States,* 1972, Table 1153; and U.S. Bureau of the Census, *Census of Housing,* 1970, U.S. Summary, HC(1)-A1, p. 6.

How Good (or Bad) Is Public Housing?

Conventional public housing has come in for increasingly severe criticism on a number of grounds. Public housing units typically have been built in large-scale, multibuilding projects, often covering dozens of acres. These vast "developments" have been criticized widely for their impersonality, institutional atmosphere, uninspired architecture, and inhuman scale. Moreover, their interior amenities suffer from the deliberate imposition of a "no frills" policy. Consequently, it has long been argued that public housing projects, though built at great expense, are destined to be the slums of the future. In some respects they have already taken on the characteristics of slum neighborhoods. Certainly, there are frequent complaints of juvenile delinquency and violent crime within projects.

The social design of public housing policy has been criticized as severely as the physical. Income limits imposed on tenants both for admission and for continued occupancy raise seemingly insoluble problems. On the one hand, such limits seem necessary in order to confine the substantial benefits of public housing to those most in need. On the other hand, they produce a public housing population in which the high concentration of poverty and distress may well have destructive effects on individual behavior. Although few families are actually displaced each year because of excessive earnings, the income limitations for continued occupancy do create a disincentive to individual self-improvement.

The classic case of public housing failure, resulting apparently from the overconcentration of poverty in a vast development, is the notorious Pruitt-Igoe project in St. Louis. Completed in the mid-1950's, it consisted of 43 buildings on 57 acres near the city's central business district. By 1970 the project was so ridden by crime and vandalism, and so physically deteriorated as a result of the inability of the St. Louis Housing Authority to keep up with maintenance and repairs, that it was virtually untenantable, and the Authority closed down 26 of its high-rise buildings.[3]

Yet it would be a mistake to take the extreme Pruitt-Igoe case as representative. Because of that fiasco, the vacancy rate in St. Louis public housing in 1967 was a shockingly high 13 percent. But among the 50 largest cities in the United States only 7 others then had public housing vacancy rates above the 5 percent level considered normal in the private rental market. For the 50 cities together, the aggregate public housing vacancy rate was only 2.2 percent. Moreover, the aggregate waiting list for admission numbered 193,072 requests, or 28 times the number of vacancies, an impressive statistic, even allowing for the many persons whose names remained on the list after they were no longer seeking admission.[4] Whatever the critics may say about public housing and however far it may fall short of the expectations with which it was launched in the 1930's, these figures do indicate a considerable degree of tenant satisfaction with the program.

The design of public housing policy has also been criticized for creating inequities among the very people it is intended to help—the low income population itself. Since the stock of public housing is relatively small (see Table 11.1) only a very few of those who meet the income qualifications are actually admitted. Instead of providing uniform benefits to all who qualify, the program provides costly benefits to a few and nothing for the rest. (By way of analogy, imagine that free public elementary education were available only to a small proportion of families and that pupils were selected from long waiting lists.) We cannot be certain what the public housing benefit is "worth" to the family that receives it, but we can try to measure its total cost to the federal and local governments. A study by De Leeuw and Leaman estimates that for two-bedroom

3. *The New York Times,* November 2, 1970, p. 1.
4. *Building the American City,* Report of the National Commission on Urban Problems (The Douglas Commission), 1969, Table 11 and Table 12, p. 131.

units completed in 1971, the total annual subsidy cost—including both cash contributions and the value of foregone taxes—averaged $1,980 per apartment.[5] That is one measure of the difference in treatment accorded to those who are in and those who remain out.

Another criticism leveled at the conventional public housing program is that it fosters racial and economic segregation within neighborhoods of central cities. Nonwhites made up 50 percent of public housing tenantry in 1970, a proportion that was, in fact, far higher than their share of the central city poverty population in the same year.[6] Since projects tend to be large, the high proportion of nonwhite tenants in a project automatically establishes a degree of neighborhood segregation. At the same time, efforts to reduce such segregation by scattering smaller projects through white neighborhoods often arouse intense local opposition from whites, who fear the influx of nonwhite population that they know to be typical in public housing. Realistically, however, it seems doubtful that public housing projects have done much to increase segregation within cities, since most of the black families now living in projects probably would have lived in segregated neighborhoods in any case.

More important is the possibility that public housing helps to maintain segregation at the macrogeographic scale. Because construction depends on local initiative, a good deal of public housing has been built in central cities, very little in the surrounding suburbs. In effect, the public housing program offers a subsidy to blacks on condition that they remain in the central city. As we will see, many current proposals for housing policy reform take it as a principal objective to undo this link between housing subsidies and intrametropolitan segregation.

The Alternative of "Leased" Public Housing

A potentially important change in public housing policy was introduced by the Section 23 leasing program, enacted in 1965. Prior to that date local housing authorities owned and operated their own units, and most were built in large-scale, multibuilding projects, which, as we have already pointed out, were widely criticized for their effects in overconcentrating the poverty population and actually creating segregated neighborhoods. Section 23 permits local housing authorities to lease units in privately owned and operated buildings and sublet them at low rents to the authorities' usual clientele. Thus, public housing beneficiaries can be

5. Frank De Leeuw and Sam H. Leaman, "The Section 23 Leasing Program," in U.S. Congress, Joint Economic Committee, *The Economics of Federal Subsidy Programs*, Part 5, October 9, 1972, Table 2.
6. U.S. Department of Housing and Urban Development, *Hud Statistical Yearbook, 1971*, Table 105, p. 110.

scattered among tenants in conventional buildings and existing neighborhoods instead of being concentrated into socially stigmatized "projects." Congress has sought to encourage use of Section 23 by requiring that 30 percent of assistance funds for future expansion of the public housing stock be contracted for in leased units.

De Leeuw and Leaman estimated that in 1971 the full economic cost of an average two-bedroom leased unit was only $154 per month, as compared with $219 per month for "conventional public housing" built at 1971 construction costs. The "out of pocket" subsidy cost to the federal government is only slightly higher for conventional units; most of the cost difference is accounted for by two "hidden" subsidies to conventional public housing in the form of reduced taxes. First, the typical new conventional unit benefits by an average monthly saving of $21 in foregone local property tax payments. Leased units, on the other hand, pay full property taxes since they are located in ordinary buildings. Second, there is a hidden tax loss to the federal government on conventional units, estimated at $30 per month, resulting from the fact that public housing bonds are tax exempt under the federal income tax.[7]

De Leeuw and Leaman point out that a leasing program, in addition to its primary function of providing decent housing to low income households, can contribute to achieving three other goals. If the units are leased in newly constructed buildings (as some have been), the program may stimulate new construction and help expand the supply of new housing. On the other hand, if units are leased in older buildings and neighborhoods, the program can be used to help arrest housing deterioration, since the rents paid by tenants plus the contributions added by the local housing authority are sufficient to cover standard maintenance and operating costs. Finally, a leasing program can contribute to racial and economic integration by placing tenants in appropriately chosen neighborhoods. These three objectives, however, are competitive within a given budget for the program: the more it emphasizes rentals in new buildings, the less funds will be available to support maintenance of the older housing stock; likewise, the more it stresses rentals in older neighborhoods, the less likely it is to reduce racial and economic segregation.[8]

In the present state of the housing market in the older central cities, the housing supply is shrinking because demand is weak. As the

7. De Leeuw and Leaman, p. 651 and Table 2, p. 655. However, in a paper in the same volume entitled "Federal Housing Subsidy Programs" Henry B. Schechter points out (p. 609) that the higher subsidies in the "conventional" public housing program will lead eventually to debt-free ownership by local authorities of buildings that may have remaining use value and, in any case, of valuable sites. These values will offset some part of the higher subsidies required for "conventional" projects.

8. De Leeuw and Leaman, pp. 656–57.

population in older neighborhoods thins out, relatively good older housing becomes available at moderate cost. Indeed, this may well explain why leased units are currently brought into the program at so much less cost than newly built housing. In such circumstances, a policy that makes effective use of the decent, available, older stock makes more economic sense than one that attempts to stimulate new construction and thereby actually accelerates wasteful abandonment of existing structures. Seen in this light, the leasing program is consistent with a new emphasis on subsidizing the demand for adequate old housing rather than trying under all circumstances to augment the supply of new buildings. If this line of argument is persuasive, the leasing program should be directed away from new construction and toward utilization of the older stock.

URBAN RENEWAL

The Housing Act of 1949, which, as we have seen, authorized a most ambitious public housing program, also gave birth to a new form of government intervention in the housing market that later came to be known as "urban renewal." The unemployment of the 1930's had been succeeded by postwar inflation. Instead of searching for socially acceptable ways to spend money, the government found itself under pressure to cut expenditures in order to check rising prices. Congress sought some means of drawing private investment into the business of improving the nation's housing standards. Urban "renewal," at that time called "redevelopment," was the agreed-upon new program. (The same conservative mood that found this program attractive soon asserted itself in holding the appropriations for the administratively separate public housing program far below the level that the 1949 Act had contemplated.)

Title I of the 1949 Act provided that the federal government would give financial assistance, through local agencies, to make private redevelopment of blighted areas economically feasible. A local redevelopment authority was to select, assemble, and clear a qualified site. It would then resell the site at a loss to a private redeveloper, who presumably could not afford to pay the full cost of acquisition and clearance if he were to earn any profit. The federal government would make its contribution by paying to the local authority a grant equal to two-thirds of the necessary land "write-down," or, in other words, two-thirds of the difference between the sum of site acquisition and clearance cost and the resale price of the land in its new use.

The 1949 Act specified what sorts of site were to be eligible for assistance: a site was required to be predominantly residential either before redevelopment or after, but not necessarily both—rather an odd requirement when measured against the stated intent of the Act—to help the nation realize "the goal of a decent home and suitable living environment for every American family." As Grigsby showed, the flexibility of the housing requirement meant that, in practice, far more sites were residential before than after redevelopment.[9] Moreover, the new housing built on redevelopment and renewal sites has been predominantly for the middle and upper income classes, rather than for the poor. It was widely assumed, however, that although the ill-housed would gain little from redevelopment directly, they would eventually benefit by way of filtering. We return to this troublesome question below.

The Housing Act of 1954 significantly modified the urban redevelopment program. There had been increasing opposition to the "bulldozer method" used in Title I projects. The method took its name from the fact that whole blocks, and often whole neighborhoods, were leveled to provide sites for Title I housing. The earliest opponents were tenants threatened with dislocation, who could not understand why the power of eminent domain should be employed to destroy their neighborhood and their homes in order to build anew for someone else, at private profit. The 1954 Act sought to reduce reliance on the bulldozer by encouraging a combination of selective rehabilitation and conservation, reserving clearance for those structures or blocks that were beyond a reasonable hope of salvation. As a condition of receiving federal aid, localities were required to develop a workable program, coordinating such elements as code enforcement, a master plan, neighborhood planning, relocation procedures, citizen participation, and financial support into a comprehensive whole for the purpose of raising housing and environmental standards. The new emphasis of the program was signaled by changing its name from "urban redevelopment" to "urban renewal."

However, the difference between renewal under the 1954 Act and redevelopment under the Act of 1949 was not sufficient to quiet the opposition, for the logic of the programs remained essentially unchanged. The poor continued to be displaced by application of the majestic powers of the state to make way for the middle class. Criticism mounted.[10] Sociologists and city planners began to realize that many stable and useful social institutions were going down before the unseeing bulldozer. It became apparent that uprooting the poor in order to clear vast sites for

9. William Grigsby, *Housing Markets and Public Policy* (Philadelphia: University of Pennsylvania Press, 1963), p. 324.

10. The intense debate about the virtues and defects of renewal has been conveniently anthologized by James Q. Wilson in *Urban Renewal: The Record and the Controversy* (Cambridge, Mass.: M.I.T. Press, 1966).

renewal was likely to increase the social disorders associated with poverty while achieving, not the elimination of slums, but simply their removal from one neighborhood to another in the wake of the displaced poor.

The use of rehabilitation improved matters very little. Housing rehabilitated to federal standards costs approximately as much to produce as new housing, if full development costs are counted.[11] Low income families were no better able to afford privately rehabilitated housing in renewal areas than private new construction. Nor was the problem of relocation eliminated, since rehabilitation is too time-consuming to permit displaced tenants to camp out in temporary quarters while waiting to return to their original dwelling unit.

Moreover, critics continued to point out that the link between urban renewal and slum clearance had the perverse effect of actually reducing the total housing supply, and especially the supply of low cost housing for the poor. There were two dimensions to this problem. First of all, individual projects took a surprisingly long time to complete. Since tenants were displaced and buildings boarded up or demolished at the beginning of a long process, while new units were ready for occupancy only at the end, there was bound to be an immediate reduction in the housing supply, no matter what long-run plans called for. Second, long-run plans, in fact, often called for constructing fewer units than were demolished. Thus, from its inception the redevelopment-renewal program persistently eliminated more units than it added. Through fiscal year 1968, in 1,495 urban renewal areas, 439,000 dwelling units were demolished and only 124,000 constructed. Additional planned demolition and construction were expected to raise the former figure to 573,000 and the latter to 457,000 when all the enumerated projects were completed, leaving an eventual deficit of 116,000.[12]

In 1969 Congress finally amended the Housing Act to require that each jurisdiction must provide new, standard, low and moderate income housing units equal in number to the total of such units that are demolished in connection with urban renewal. By that time, however, urban renewal had already lost much of its political support. Activity under the program was leveling out and, as long-planned projects came to completion in the 1970's, was expected gradually to decline.

11. For data on rehabilitation costs in New York City, see Ira S. Lowry, "Housing Assistance for Low-Income Urban Families: A Fresh Approach," Papers submitted to the Subcommittee on Housing, Part 2, U.S. Congress, House Committee on Banking and Currency, 1971, pp. 501–02.
12. "Opportunity to Improve Allocation of Program Funds to Meet the National Housing Goals," Report to the Congress by the Comptroller General of the United States, October 2, 1970, p. 18.

MARKET IMPERFECTIONS AND THE
CASE FOR URBAN RENEWAL

Because it was so controversial, the urban renewal program stimulated a good deal of inquiry by economists, political scientists, sociologists,
and city planners. One of the most influential economic analyses was provided by Otto A. Davis and Andrew B. Whinston in 1961.[13] Even though
urban renewal as we have known it is no longer the object of much
enthusiasm, the wave of housing abandonments now sweeping the older
central cities raises once again the question of market-determined land
use versus government intervention and may lead to new proposals for
stimulating redevelopment. The Davis-Whinston analysis remains a very
useful starting point for looking at possible imperfections in the urban
land and housing markets and tracing out their implications for redevelopment policy.

Davis and Whinston explain a number of possible reasons for believing that the urban housing market has not functioned "properly"—in
the sense of providing the optimum amount and quality of housing to
satisfy consumer wants, given the constraints of cost and of limited
incomes. These arguments do not establish the existence of any sort of
"exploitation" of tenants by landlords, but, if valid, they do make a case
for government intervention.

Two kinds of imperfection may be (not necessarily are) present. The
first would result from the strong external effects of one property on the
tenants and owner of another. When a person thinks about renting an
apartment, he takes into account the attractiveness of the neighborhood,
which depends in part on the characteristics of nearby properties. Thus
the rent obtainable by one landlord may be affected by the condition in
which neighboring landlords keep their properties.

We will consider four possible cases that involve this sort of interdependency between two adjacent owners, whom we may call Smith and
Jones.

1. If both owners invest in redeveloping their properties, both can
earn a rate of return that makes the additional investment worthwhile.
Each benefits from the fact that the other has made improvements,
because tenants are willing to pay higher rents for an apartment in an
improved neighborhood than in an unimproved one.

2. Owner Smith can obtain higher rents even if he does *not* undertake redevelopment, provided that his neighbor Jones *does* redevelop.

13. Otto A. Davis and Andrew B. Whinston, "The Economics of Urban
Renewal," in Wilson, pp. 50–67.

Smith's rate of return may even be higher in this case than it would be if he redeveloped too, because he can obtain higher rents without investing any additional capital.

3. If neither of the owners redevelops, both will continue to earn a rate of return lower than they could obtain if both had redeveloped, as in the first case.

4. Finally, if Smith were to redevelop his property while Jones did not, Smith's rate of return might actually drop below what it would be if neither he nor Jones undertook redevelopment, as in the third case.

For the sake of illustration, Davis and Whinston assign hypothetical rates of return to the four cases as follows:

	Rate of Return Earned by:	
Alternative Cases	*Smith*	*Jones*
1. Both invest in redevelopment	7%	7%
2. Jones invests, Smith does not	10	3
3. Neither invests in redevelopment	4	4
4. Smith invests, Jones does not	3	10

It is clear that society benefits most in the first case, where both owners invest in redevelopment. But Davis and Whinston use arguments from game theory (the logic of "the prisoner's dilemma" situation) to show that the actual outcome may well be case 3, where neither property is redeveloped. The argument runs as follows. First examine Smith's situation. When deciding whether to invest in redevelopment he has to consider two possibilities—first, that Jones also redevelops and, second, that Jones does not. When he looks at these two possibilities, he sees that in either case he is best off *not* investing. In the first situation, he can earn 10 percent by not investing (case 2) but only 7 percent by investing (case 1). In the second situation he can earn 4 percent by not investing (case 3) but only 3 percent by investing (case 4). His rational decision is not to invest. Moreover, since Jones as an individual owner is logically in the same position as Smith, each decides not to invest, and no redevelopment occurs, even though such redevelopment would be socially optimal. Here, then, is a case of "market failure" attributable to interdependencies.

Davis and Whinston take as their definition of urban "blight" any case in which the market fails to yield optimum development of the housing stock. They do not equate slums and blight, however, since they recognize that slum neighborhoods may be run down precisely because slum tenants cannot afford anything better. Likewise, "blight" may exist in relatively "nice" neighborhoods, if interdependencies have prevented them from being improved to the optimum extent.

The authors recognize that a suboptimal outcome is due to their assumption of interdependencies that are "sufficiently strong." [14] One can show easily that with interdependencies of a weaker sort, the socially correct outcome will occur. Return to the table and suppose, for example, that we leave cases 1 and 3 as they are but change the outcome of case 2 to Smith earns 6 percent and Jones earns 5 percent; and change case 4 to Smith earns 5 percent and Jones earns 6 percent. We still have interdependency, since one investor's rate of return depends on what the other does. But in this situation it will be rational for Smith individually, and hence for Jones also, to undertake redevelopment.

Interdependencies of the sort described probably exist, but the important question to decide is how strong they may be. The belief that they are strong enough to block redevelopment implies that tenants have substantial demands for housing and neighborhood amenities that go perpetually unfulfilled. The interdependency argument views the tenant as a prisoner of his neighborhood, willing and able to pay for a better environment with higher rent but unable to do so because the system fails to produce the desired amenities. However, if the competitive, adaptive model of the housing market that we described in the previous chapter is accepted as even roughly valid, then the market produces a sufficient variety of housing and neighborhood types and qualities to suit the tastes and rent-paying capacities of a wide variety of consumers. Tenants would consequently be able to select the neighborhood and home in which they live out of a variety of existing neighborhoods and homes because it best suits their needs. We would not then expect tenants in a given neighborhood to nurse latent, unfulfilled demands (which they are able to back with higher rent offers) for something substantially better, if only something better were offered. And if tenants do not have such unfulfilled demands it is unlikely that interdependencies would have the powerful effects on the rate of return hypothesized by Davis and Whinston. The high rates of return from redevelopment hypothesized by Davis and Whinston would occur only if higher income tenants were attracted from other neighborhoods to occupy the redeveloped buildings, but that outcome violates the implicit assumption of their example that it refers to housing for a given population in a given neighborhood.

What little direct evidence we have about tenants in deteriorating neighborhoods supports the notion that they are usually *un*willing to pay for even moderately costly housing improvements. A survey of families in transitional neighborhoods of New York City in 1969 asked respondents whether they were satisfied with specific features of their housing. Those who said "no" were then asked whether they would be willing to pay $30 a month additional rent to correct the unsatisfactory feature. Of tenants

14. *Ibid.*, p. 57, n. 7.

living in units not under rent control, 77 to 78 percent were definitely unwilling to pay the additional rent for those features that would remedy the dissatisfactions they had themselves expressed.[15] While this survey involved too small a sample to be conclusive, its findings are consistent with reports in the daily press of tenants in slum areas who object to proposals to rehabilitate their buildings because they do not wish to pay the higher rent that would be required to finance the job. Given that sort of response, the strong interdependencies hypothesized by Davis and Whinston seem unlikely. The point to be stressed is, not that tenants are unaffected by their neighborhoods, but only that they are not able or willing to pay very much to alter the effects.

The rise of housing abandonment, with its destructive external effects on neighborhood properties, might seem to strengthen the case for the strong interdependencies of the Davis and Whinston example. Can it be that building owners in a neighborhood that is on the verge of slipping into abandonment are caught in the sort of "prisoner's dilemma" situation they described? If all owners could agree *not* to abandon is it possible that none would choose or be forced to? Housing analysts who claim that abandonment is a "contagious, self-fulfilling prophecy" appear to think so.[16] Yet this argument seems to overlook the force of the two most frequently mentioned causes of abandonment, which are inadequate rent-paying capacity and high rates of neighborhood crime and violence. It may well be doubted whether any agreement by owners to stand fast would succeed in neighborhoods where these forces are at their worst.

The Problem of Site Assembly

The second market imperfection cited by Davis and Whinston has to do with "site assembly." They point out that if interdependencies between properties prevent individual owners from undertaking economically desirable redevelopment, then an incentive exists for a single owner to buy out all the others and make improvements over the entire neighborhood himself. By so doing he can realize the high rate of return hypothesized for the case in which all properties are improved. But now the problem of site assembly rises to plague the developer. In the typical American city, property is held in very small parcels. The entrepreneur

15. See Ira S. Lowry, Joseph S. De Salvo, and Barbara M. Woodfill, *The Demand for Shelter*, Vol. II of Rental Housing in New York City (New York: New York City Rand Institute, June 1971), pp. 102–04.

16. See the statements cited by Henry B. Schechter and Marion K. Schlefer in "Housing Needs and National Goals," Papers submitted to the Subcommittee on Housing, Part 1, House Committee on Banking and Currency, 1971, p. 35.

wishing to assemble a large site for redevelopment not only must be will-ing to tie up his capital during the years required to negotiate purchases but must also face the prospect that the last few parcel owners he ap-proaches will be able to demand extraordinarily high sums as the price of not blocking the project.

Moreover, the site assembly problem is not confined to cases involv-ing interdependency effects. Suppose that the optimum redevelopment of a given neighborhood requires that a project be planned on a scale far larger than that of the existing small land parcels. The potential developer is again faced with the need to buy out numerous small holders, one by one, in order to achieve the necessary scale. Real estate developers have long recognized site assembly as a major obstacle, which raises the cost of development and presumably prevents some otherwise desirable proj-ects from going ahead.

The site assembly problem is an important market imperfection with direct implications for public policy. The implication drawn by Davis and Whinston is that when properties in a given neighborhood remain underdeveloped either because of interdependencies that the "atomistic" private market cannot cope with or because the difficulty of site assembly prevents development at an optimal scale, then public intervention is clearly called for. The government is then justified in using its power of eminent domain to assemble a site by purchasing properties at their fair market value. If interdependencies and site assembly problems were the only obstacles to an otherwise profitable renewal, then all obstacles that prevented private development from moving ahead would have been re-moved by the government's action. Consequently, the local renewal authority would be able to resell the consolidated site at cost to a private redeveloper who would then complete the project and earn a satisfactory rate of return without benefit of a land-cost write-down or other special subsidy. Market imperfections thus justify public intervention, but not public subsidy, to make renewal feasible.

Behind this piece of analysis lies the traditional argument that a freely competitive market in land tends, by an orderly process of "succes-sion," to bring about the "highest and best use" of each parcel. The con-cept of highest and best use was introduced in Chapter 6 in explaining how competition between land uses results in an efficient pattern of intra-urban activity location. At that point, however, we did not examine in detail the process of succession by which the highest and best use of a parcel may change over time. If we are to understand fully the general problem of urban change and development (of which "urban renewal" is simply a special case), we must now supply the missing details.

LAND-USE SUCCESSION IN A
COMPETITIVE MARKET

In the course of time both buildings and sites pass through a succession of uses. A building constructed originally as a town house may later be converted to commercial occupancy as the business district of the town expands. Or the reverse process may occur—loft buildings in declining commercial areas may be converted to residential uses. These are successions of use within given structures.

Very frequently evolutionary forces in the development of the city make it profitable to tear down existing buildings and replace them with new ones. In that case, we speak of "land-use succession" rather than succession of uses within given structures. With the rapid growth of cities, two of the most obvious forms of land-use succession have been the conversion of agricultural land to residential uses and the conversion of low density areas of single family homes to higher density apartment house neighborhoods. In either case, according to the traditional view, the evolutionary process of development works to bring about the "highest and best use" of land. If the land market is competitive, we can assume that each new building, at the time it is put up, represents the highest and best use of the plot on which it stands.

Succession via the market process can be explained as follows. First, let us define "highest and best" as that use which can pay the most for a given cleared site. In addition, we may define the following terms:

V_o = the market value of a given site and the building on it, when the building is of the old type, denoted by the subscript o; this value equals the present worth of the expected future returns (gross of depreciation) from the property in the old use.

V_n = the anticipated market value of the same site and the building on it, when the building is of the new type, n; this value equals the present worth of the expected future returns from the property in the new use. V_n includes an allowance for the developer's normal profit.[17]

D_o = the cost of demolishing use o

C_n = the cost of constructing use n, exclusive of the cost of purchasing and clearing the site

17. We have simplified the analysis by omitting from both V_o and V_n the present worth of any future uses that might be expected to succeed them. The omitted item is sometimes called the "reversionary value" of the site. For an analysis of succession that specifically allows for reversionary values, see Wallace F. Smith, *Housing: the*

Let us assume that a building of type *o* actually stands on the given site. At the time it was constructed, *o* was presumably the highest and best use for the site, for the developer who constructed *o* was able to obtain the site by outbidding all other firms for its use. We now wish to see under what conditions the new use, *n*, would replace *o* by means of ordinary market operations.

The cost to a developer of acquiring the given site in order to construct use *n* is V_o, because he has to pay the market price for the old building even though he intends to tear it down. The cost of tearing it down is D_o. Thus, for the new user, we can say that

$$V_o + D_o = \text{cost of acquisition and clearance}$$

On the other hand, the highest price that he can afford to pay for the cleared site and still earn a normal profit by developing use *n* is given by

$$V_n - C_n = \text{maximum value of cleared site to new user}$$

It follows that the new user can profitably undertake development on the site only if

$$V_n - C_n \geqq V_o + D_o$$

which is therefore a necessary condition for the new use to succeed the old through ordinary market processes. As a city evolves, this necessary condition may be fulfilled either because the old use becomes increasingly obsolete, making V_o decline, or because the demand for the new use becomes stronger, making the potential value V_n rise, or by a combination of both changes.

The urban renewal program, by means of its land-cost write-down, speeds up this process of succession. In order to encourage rebuilding, the renewal authority intervenes in situations in which the maximum value of the site to the new user $(V_n - C_n)$ is not yet as large as the cost of acquisition and clearance $(V_o + D_o)$. The government absorbs two-thirds or more of the excess of the latter over the former, thus enabling *n* to succeed *o* at a time when it could not do so by market processes.

To the casual observer this speed-up, which is a principal objective of the renewal program, may seem desirable. To the economist it appears otherwise. If the market functions efficiently, speeding up the process of succession is wasteful, in the sense of unnecessarily destroying economic value. The additional value created by redevelopment of the site from use *o* to use *n* is $V_n - V_o$. But the cost of the resources used up in creat-

Social and Economic Elements (Berkeley and Los Angeles: University of California Press, 1970), pp. 243–50.

ing the additional value is the sum of $D_o + C_n$. Thus redevelopment adds something to society's total economic output only if

$$V_n - V_o > D_o + C_n$$

But by rearranging terms we see that this is equivalent to the market condition for succession:

$$V_n - C_n > V_o + D_o$$

Therefore, if we employ a subsidy to speed up succession, we act irrationally: the costs we incur for redevelopment exceed the additional economic values we create. It is easy to imagine that a person who is concerned about the housing problem might find this conclusion surprising. As he walks through a slum neighborhood he may say to himself: "These buildings are old, run down and depressing. New housing would be a tremendous improvement. There must be something wrong with a system that allows slums such as these to stand decade after decade when we know how to build so much better." He might even add: "Surely these slums do not represent the highest and best use of the land. If we were to start over again on this block we certainly wouldn't put up buildings like these."

The economic analysis of succession can explain these supposed anomalies. Certainly, new housing would be a tremendous improvement. But it is very costly to build. Moreover, before a new building can be economically justified, it must be able to absorb the capital value of the old structure it replaces as its site cost. In other words, succession will not take place until the old property reaches the point where it is worth more as a site than it is as a building. That moment may be indefinitely delayed because old buildings often continue for a long time to have value based on their ability to render services less expensively than new structures. An old building can continue to be operated as long as rent receipts exceed operating costs, maintenance charges, and taxes, whereas a new building will not be started unless prospective rent receipts will, in addition, allow the builder to recoup the cost of construction. Thus old buildings can survive through many decades at a value less than would justify their being constructed anew but greater than would justify their demolition. During such periods they do *not* represent the highest and best use of the land in the sense employed here, since they would not be reconstructed new if the site were cleared for redevelopment. Yet it would be wasteful to tear them down.

Thus our analysis of the economics of succession bears out Davis and Whinston's conclusion that if an otherwise economically desirable redevelopment is blocked only by market imperfections, the government, after intervening to overcome such obstacles, should be able to sell the cleared site to a developer at no loss. Unless additional justification can be found, the policy of subsidizing redevelopment simply to speed up succession is economically irrational.

Cost-Benefit Analysis of Urban Renewal

It is, of course, possible that the additional justification might be found in a complete cost-benefit analysis of an urban renewal project. The market succession calculus that we have described above takes into account only direct, or "on-site," benefits and costs. Perhaps if the indirect, or "off-site," effects were counted as well, the excess of indirect benefits over indirect costs would be sufficient to justify a subsidy. However, as Jerome Rothenberg's careful conceptual analysis of this problem demonstrated, the indirect effects of a large redevelopment project can be expected to ramify in complex ways through the urban housing and real estate markets.[18] Quantification of such effects is extraordinarily difficult and therefore not very persuasive, even when attempted.

For example, one of the most concrete indirect effects of a renewal project is the spillover benefit that might be conferred on neighboring sites. But even if it could be demonstrated that adjacent site values increased as a result of a project, it would remain highly uncertain how much of that increase should be counted as a net gain attributable to renewal, for we recognize that to an undetermined extent subsidized construction may substitute for construction that would have occurred elsewhere in the city without subsidy, and such unsubsidized construction might also have conferred indirect benefits on adjacent sites.

Or consider the important category of indirect benefits that might be associated with urban renewal through a reduction in the quantity of substandard housing. Again, several problems arise in trying to quantify the effect. First, as we have already argued, it is extremely difficult to evaluate the independent effects of better housing, since better housing is usually linked with such tenant characteristics as higher income and more education, the effects of which may well be attributed mistakenly to improved housing conditions. Second, when a renewal project substitutes middle or upper income housing for low rent, substandard housing, it is not clear that the housing condition of the poor has really been improved. Indeed, it may have been worsened by their forcible removal from the housing of their choice, coupled with the destruction of their neighborhood cultural ties.[19]

18. Jerome Rothenberg, *Economic Evaluation of Urban Renewal* (Washington, D.C.: Brookings Institution, 1967).
19. See the papers by Chester Hartman and Herbert J. Cans in Wilson.

Finally, even if a cost-benefit analysis of a project could reasonably demonstrate that its benefits exceeded its costs, there would remain the troublesome question of the distribution of benefits and costs among income classes. There is a strong presumption that many of the benefits go to the middle or upper income families who voluntarily move into the newly built project, while many of the indirect costs are borne by the poor who are forcibly displaced. This has been a principal argument against renewal, and the most potent political opposition to the program has come from *ad hoc* organizations of slum dwellers, whose desire not to be bulldozed out of their homes concretely supports the critics' argument.

SUBSIDIZED PRIVATE HOUSING

As urban renewal declined in favor during the 1960's, Congress enacted a widening array of other subsidy programs that were intended to stimulate new private construction without tying financial aid either to slum clearance or the removal of "blight." For the most part, these programs were designed to reduce rent or ownership costs so that families of moderate or even low income could afford to live in new or rehabilitated standard housing. Because they contained powerful subsidies to private developers, such programs were able to gain important political support from the construction industry. In this instance, unlike the case of public housing during the 1950's, congressional authorization was usually followed by generous appropriations rather than by financial neglect. Some of the programs reached very considerable size by the early 1970's.

Most of the subsidy programs came to be known, for convenience, by the section number of the particular housing act under which they were authorized. The most important for urban areas have been the below-market interest rate program (known as Section 221(d)(3) BMIR), the rental housing assistance program (Section 236), the home-ownership assistance program (Section 235), and the rent supplement program (not usually referred to by number).

Subsidies Under Section 221(d)(3)

Section 221(d)(3), now being replaced by other programs, was added to the Housing Act in 1961. Its purpose was to reduce rental costs by means of an interest rate subsidy given to new units built for middle and lower middle income families. Funds were made available at below-market rates of interest to limited profit corporations as well as to cooperatives and other nonprofit sponsors. The Department of Housing and

TABLE 11.2

Required Rent and Implied Income Level in 1967 for New Apartments Constructed Under Various Federal Housing Programs [a]

	REQUIRED RENT ON TWO-BEDROOM UNIT		REQUIRED ANNUAL INCOME AT RENT-INCOME RATIO OF:	
Program	*Annual*	*Monthly*	*20 Percent*	*25 Percent*
Nonsubsidized housing	$2,719	$227	$13,595	$10,876
Public housing, average	1,161	97	5,805	4,644
Rent supplement, minimum	540	45	2,700	2,160
Section 236, minimum	1,763	147	8,815	7,052
Section 221(d)(3), average	1,993	166	9,965	7,972

[a] Calculations apply to Detroit, where construction costs were somewhat lower than in the very largest cities.
Source: A Decent Home, Report of the President's Committee on Urban Housing, 1969, Table 2–2, p. 63.

Urban Development (HUD), which administered the program, regulated rent levels and established income limits for admission that varied geographically but generally limited entrance to families that were below the local median income level.

From 1965 onward, the subsidy was provided as follows. A 40-year mortgage loan at 3 percent interest was made initially by a bank or other private lender. The mortgage was then immediately sold at par to a government lending institution: until 1968, the Federal National Mortgage Association (FNMA) and since then, the Government National Mortgage Association (GNMA). The benefit to the project equaled the difference between capital costs at 3 percent and those at whatever market rate the borrower would otherwise have had to pay for private funds. The direct subsidy cost to the government was considerably less: the difference between 3 percent and the rate at which the government borrowed to subsidize GNMA.

The estimated effects of various subsidy programs in reducing levels of required rents in 1967 are compared in Table 11.2. In that year a new two-bedroom apartment built under the provisions of 221(d)(3) in Detroit could have rented for $1,993 a year, about $700 less than a comparable unit built without subsidy. However, the average annual direct subsidy cost to the government per unit of housing built under 221(d)(3) was only $112 for units built between 1966 and 1971.[20] This is much less than the amount the tenant was likely to save in rent, as indicated in

20. Schechter, "Federal Housing Subsidy Programs," p. 62.

Table 11.2. The difference reflects the fact that the borrowing rate paid by the government for capital supplied to subsidized housing is much less than the rate ordinary unsubsidized builders would pay to borrow commercially.

After the Section 235 and 236 subsidy provisions were enacted in 1968, the government began to phase out 221(d)(3). A principal factor in the opposition to 221(d)(3) had been that it was a relatively "shallow" subsidy program. As Table 11.2 shows, it was capable of serving the lower middle class but not of pushing rents down far enough to reach the poor. Henry J. Aaron, in his detailed analysis of federal housing subsidies, suggests a number of other arguments that also contributed to its demise.[21] First, subsidies under 221(d)(3) could not be calibrated to the income levels of individual families but were, in effect, passed on as proportional rent reductions to all tenants. Second, given the delays and difficulties involved in building under such a program, its incentives were insufficient to stimulate a great deal of activity. Finally, it had what seemed to federal officials to be an unfortunate time pattern of impact on the federal budget: the full cost of each project appeared as a budget expenditure as soon as GNMA bought the mortgage. Budget makers much preferred a system—similar to the arrangement for financing public housing—in which subsidies could be paid out over the life of a project instead of being charged as a lump sum at the beginning.

Rent Supplements: A "Deeper" Subsidy

The first attempt to remedy the defects of the below-market interest rate program was the "rent supplement" plan authorized by the Housing and Urban Development Act of 1965.[22] The initial proposal to Congress called for a plan to assist families whose incomes were too high to qualify them for public housing but too low for them to afford units built under Section 221(d)(3). On behalf of such families the government would make subsidy payments to a qualifying nonprofit or limited-dividend developer of a new building. These payments would cover the difference between fair market rent and 20 percent of family income. Thus, for the first time, the amount of a government housing subsidy would be geared directly to the beneficiary's income level. The higher the family's income, the less subsidy it would receive in a given housing unit. If income rose high enough, the subsidy would automatically end, but the tenant would not

21. *Shelter and Subsidies*, pp. 132–33. Aaron's book compares the benefits, by income class of beneficiary, of various direct federal subsidy programs and also of the important indirect subsidies to housing owners that come through provisions of the federal income tax.

22. *Ibid.*, p. 133.

have to move. It was hoped that in this way new housing could be developed that would contain both very low income families and families that had achieved success and were "on the way up." In short, the plan was expected to provide socioeconomic integration.

The program that Congress finally enacted was a good deal less sweeping. Tenants were required to contribute 25 percent rather than 20 percent of income toward rent. Eligibility was limited to those with incomes below rather than above the public housing admission level and who were *also* elderly, handicapped, displaced by government induced demolition, or previous occupants of substandard housing. In case these restrictions did not sufficiently limit the program's scope, Congress concluded the matter by appropriating minimal funds for its support.

Insofar as funds have been made available, however, rent supplement benefits do reach far down into the income distribution. Aaron reports that in 1969 the median income of families in the program was only $2,089, and that their median monthly rent was $127, of which the government paid $81 and the tenant only $46.[23]

Among the most actively used provisions of the rent supplement program is one that permits payments on behalf of tenants admitted to projects that are also subsidized under other sections of the law. Thus a double subsidy, or "piggy-back" arrangement, is authorized under which it becomes possible to provide a limited number of families with a very deep subsidy indeed.

Subsidies Under Sections 235 and 236

In 1968 Congress enacted Sections 235 and 236 of the housing law, a pair of subsidy plans by which 221(d)(3) was eventually replaced. Each employs a subsidy formula that is similar in some respects to the provisions of the rent supplement plan and was designed to meet the objections that had been raised to 221(d)(3). Under the rental assistance provisions of Section 236, HUD contracts with a qualifying sponsor (who will develop and operate the project) to pay a monthly rent subsidy geared to the level of each eligible tenant's income. In general, eligibility is restricted to tenants whose income does not exceed the admission limit for public housing by more than 35 percent. The amount of subsidy is determined in the following rather complicated way. The sponsor obtains a mortgage loan at the going market interest rate. The tenant must pay at least 25 percent of his income in rent. The government then pays a subsidy on behalf of each tenant equal either to the difference between (1) "market" rents based on the mortgage costs actually incurred and

23. *Ibid.,* p. 135.

the rent that would be required if mortgage interest were only 1 percent, or (2) "market" rents and 25 percent of the tenant's income, whichever is less.

Under this plan, not only may each tenant be subsidized to a different extent, but the subsidy each tenant receives will decline gradually as his income rises (all other things remaining the same). As intended, the plan does provide a "deeper" subsidy than was achieved under 221(d)(3). (See Table 11.2.) The median income level of tenants in Section 236 units is therefore somewhat lower than under 221(d)(3).[24] However, the subsidy is not deep enough to allow very low income families to participate unless they are willing to spend far more than the required minimum 25 percent of their income on rent.

The average subsidy payment per unit was in the neighborhood of $1,000 a year in the early years of the Section 236 program.[25] That is six or eight times as high as payments per unit under 221(d)(3). In part this reflects the "deeper" subsidy per unit: down to the equivalent of a 1 percent rather than a 3 percent interest rate on the mortgage. But also, in part, the greater budgetary outlay results from the fact that Section 236 projects are built with mortgage funds obtained at the private market rate of interest, which is much higher than the rate paid by the U.S. Treasury for funds used to build under Section 221(d)(3). It should be noted, however, that the difference between these two borrowing rates does not represent any difference in "real" social costs. The fact that the Treasury can borrow at a lower interest rate than a private developer does not reduce the real cost of a housing unit, which is measured by the quantity of labor, land, and capital used to produce it. Because of the formula employed in the Section 236 program, the annual subsidy cost will, of course, vary over time, depending upon trends in tenant income and in the cost of housing operation.

The homeownership assistance program, enacted as Section 235, is similar in structure to the rental plan under 236. Families whose incomes fall within the qualifying limits receive subsidies to help them meet the monthly carrying cost of a commercially financed mortgage on either a new or existing single-family home. The beneficiary must spend at least 20 percent of family income on monthly mortgage payments. The government pays a subsidy equal to the lesser of (1) the difference between the beneficiary's monthly payments and the actual monthly cost, including property taxes and insurance, or (2) the difference between the cost that would obtain with a 1 percent mortgage and the actual monthly

24. *Ibid.*, Table 8–1 and p. 137.
25. *Ibid.*, p. 166.

cost, *not* including property taxes and insurance. Although renters under Section 236 are required to pay 25 percent of income toward housing, owners under Section 235 pay only 20 percent because they must, in addition, bear the maintenance and operating costs that are included in rent.

Figures assembled by Aaron suggest that the median family income of owners in Section 235 housing is slightly higher than that of renters under Section 236. This difference, however, is more than offset by the larger average size of families in the ownership program. Annual budgetary cost per unit is about the same as under Section 236.

Unlike the rent supplement program, Sections 235 and 236 were supported by generous federal funding and soon produced a large volume of subsidized construction. They became, in fact, the leading subsidy programs employed by the federal government in its effort to achieve the National Housing Goals, beginning in 1969.

The National Housing Goals

In 1968, the same year that it added Sections 235 and 236 to the housing statutes, Congress passed a Housing and Urban Development Act that included a timetable for achieving "National Housing Goals." The purpose of adopting specific goals was to redeem the unfulfilled promise of "a decent home and suitable living environment for every American family" that had been set forth in the Housing Act of 1949.

For the ten-year period from 1969 through 1978, Congress set a goal of constructing or rehabilitating 26 million housing units, including 6 million subsidized units for low and moderate income families. As goal details were eventually worked out, the latter figure was to consist of 5 million new and 1 million rehabilitated units. The remaining 20 million units were to be unsubsidized private construction, including 16 million conventional units and 4 million mobile homes.

The 26 million total figure was based on the assumption that

> the nation's housing problems could be substantially solved in a single decade by producing enough unsubsidized and subsidized housing units to offset expected new family formations, replace substandard housing and losses from the housing stock, increase the vacancy rate and provide income assistance in the form of housing subsidies for families who could not afford the cost of standard housing . . . .[26]

26. The President of the United States, *Fourth Annual Report on National Housing Goals*, June 29, 1972, p. 27. See Chart 9, p. 26, of the report for the estimate of "needs" on which the 26 million goal figure was based.

We had, in other words, adopted a "new construction strategy" for solving our housing problem.

The announced goal for new construction (excluding mobile homes) came to an average of 2.1 million units per year over a ten-year period—an ambitious undertaking when compared with the annual average of about 1.45 million units actually achieved from 1959 through 1968. However, the housing industry, backed by federal credit and subsidies, was able first to meet and then, in the early 1970's, to surpass the annual production goals set by the President. The major categories under which housing was produced are shown in Table 11.3. Subsidized production more than tripled during the first four years of the ten-year goal period, and the Section 235 and 236 programs became predominant.

Subsidies under Sections 235 and 236 are deep enough to reach what might be called the "upper low income population" but not the poorest of the poor. The great bulk of *un*subsidized new housing goes, of course, to middle and upper income families. Clearly, then, the new construction strategy embodied in the national housing goals implies a reliance on filtering to improve housing conditions for those at the bottom

TABLE 11.3

Housing Production Toward the National Housing Goals
(Fiscal Years, Thousands of Units Produced)

	1969	1970	1971	Est'd 1972	Est'd 1973
Total production of new units	1,969	1,762	2,233	2,750	—
Unsubsidized production, total	1,806	1,466	1,794	2,330	—
Construction	1,437	1,063	1,359	1,780	—
Mobile homes	369	403	435	550	—
Subsidized production, total	163	296	439	420	496
1- to 4-family homes	32	108	207	212	249
Section 235	8	70	136	137	157
Other	24	38	71	75	92
Multiple dwellings	132	189	232	209	247
Public housing	64	83	92	57	62
Conventional	36	29	25	19	15
Turnkey and leased	28	55	68	38	47
Section 236	1	49	100	134	158
Rent supplement	16	22	15	10	18
Section 221(d)(3)	39	24	11	4	1
Other	12	11	14	4	8

Source: The President of the United States, *Fourth Annual Report on National Housing Goals*, June 29, 1972, Table 1, p. 9, and Table B–2, pp. 44–45.

of the income distribution.[27] We must therefore examine carefully the connection between subsidies, filtering, and housing standards.

HOUSING SUBSIDIES AND THE FILTERING PROCESS

In the preceding chapter we described the filtering process as one in which housing originally built to rent at a higher price to a higher income class gradually "filters down" to a lower rent level and a poorer class of tenants. It has often been argued that subsidies to stimulate the construction of moderate (or even upper) income housing are justified because they encourage this filtering process, which eventually raises housing standards for lower income groups as well as for those better off families who initially move into the subsidized housing. How credible is this argument?

Undoubtedly housing built with the benefit of subsidy can rent for less than unsubsidized new construction of similar quality. As long as there is some price elasticity to housing demand, subsidies are therefore likely to increase the volume of new construction. Consequently, they are also likely to increase the number of already built housing units that filter down to lower rent levels. However, there may well be substantial substitution between housing built with subsidies and new units that would have been put up commercially without such aid. A degree of substitution is certainly to be expected if the subsidized housing is built to rent above the minimum at which new commercially developed construction is feasible.

Given the high cost of new construction, that outcome is unlikely under programs such as 221(d)(3), 235, or 236, in which income limits for eligibility are below the median value for local family income. It may well have occurred, however, under urban renewal, since many of the units built on renewal sites have been "semi-luxury" housing.[28] The point is that one cannot take it for granted that all subsidy programs make a one-for-one contribution to increasing the volume of new construction and, therefore, to accelerating the filtering process.

One of the justifications frequently offered for building relatively high rent housing on urban renewal sites has been that it would help to

27. For a systematic analysis of alternative strategies see Anthony Downs, "Housing the Urban Poor: The Economics of Various Strategies," Ch. 6 in his collected papers entitled *Urban Problems and Prospects* (Chicago: Markham Publishing, 1970).

28. See Martin Anderson, *The Federal Bulldozer* (Cambridge, Mass.: M.I.T. Press, 1964), Figure 4-1, p. 58.

keep the middle class from fleeing to the suburbs and so contribute to the maintenance of an economically and socially balanced central city. It should be noted, however, that in many cities this argument is now incompatible with the claim that urban renewal also encourages filtering. Take the case of an older central city where, in the absence of urban renewal, the number of middle class families in the central city would either be stable or declining. Under these circumstances, if the middle class families who move into renewal projects had emigrated to the suburbs instead, their former middle class housing would nevertheless have been vacated. Consequently, the same housing units would have "filtered down" with or without renewal. To the extent that a subsidy program "holds" the middle class in the central city, it makes no net contribution to the filtering process. One cannot have it both ways.

Granted that subsidies for middle income or lower middle income housing will, under the right conditions, accelerate the filtering process, the question remains: how much is that likely to improve the housing condition of the poor? The answer has already been suggested by the analysis of filtering in the preceding chapter. Insofar as permanent structural characteristics of buildings are concerned—for example, room dimensions, plumbing and heating installations, access to light and air—filtered-down housing can raise standards at the lower end of the rent distribution. The situation is quite different for other aspects of housing service, such as expenditures on cleaning, repairing, maintaining, and operating a building. In providing "variable" services of that sort, building owners will adapt to the rent-paying capacity of their tenants. When housing filters down to a lower income class, owners are almost certain to reduce these outlays, thus deliberately moving the building down to a lower quality level. Indeed, structural characteristics, too, may be altered in the process of adaptation: for example, large rooms or large apartments can be subdivided by remodeling. The end result is that good housing may gradually be converted to bad in the process of filtering.

Casual observation suggests that much. Some systematic evidence is provided by Muth's study of housing on Chicago's South Side. Muth employed multiple regression analysis to examine the degree of association between a large number of variables and the incidence of substandard housing in a sample of census tracts. He found that with the level of 1960 income and other variables "controlled for," there remained a significant inverse relationship between the proportion of housing classified as substandard in a tract in 1960 and the median income level in that tract in 1950. This is consistent with the hypothesis that housing conditions in 1960 were adapting gradually to income levels that had been established ten years earlier. Muth concluded that "this indicates that if anything, dwelling unit condition adjusts over time to changes in the income level of its inhabitants rather than the reverse." [29]

A final criticism of the filtering process as a way of raising the housing standards of the poor concerns its connection with housing abandonment. The outcome of the filtering process as seen at the low rent end of the market used to be described as the "withdrawal" of the least desirable buildings from the stock of available housing. But in many cities where there is now a large poverty population, the normal process of "withdrawal" has become the chaotic sequence of "abandonment," with all the deprivation of housing services and all the social turmoil that the word implies. In such urban housing markets we must acknowledge that a policy of encouraging filtering is also a policy of encouraging abandonment and is likely to increase the housing ills of the poor in the short run, whatever it may do to relieve them over a longer period.

NEW DIRECTIONS FOR HOUSING POLICY?

We have seen that government housing policy during the early 1970's produced a record quantity of new, federally assisted, low and moderate income dwelling units. Yet, as early as 1971, housing programs were again in trouble with their critics, and in 1973 the federal government decreed a freeze on further commitments and moved to reexamine the whole array of housing subsidy programs. The immediate cause of the freeze may have been a desire to "regain control" over federal spending by reining in programs such as 235 and 236 in which modest initial-year outlays led automatically to substantial, though somewhat uncertain, long-run spending commitments. In addition, there were intimations of waste, inefficiency, and scandal. Many of the new homes sold to low income families under Section 235 were badly constructed; many of the old ones were drastically unsound and/or greatly overpriced.[30] Section 236 was criticized as providing overly generous benefits to investors.[31] (Ironically, the objections to Section 236 were reminiscent of those that had been raised against Section 608, the federal government's principal rental

29. Richard F. Muth, *Cities and Housing* (Chicago: University of Chicago Press, 1969), p. 265.
30. See *Interim Report on HUD Investigation of Low and Moderate-Income Housing Programs*, U.S. Congress, Hearing before the House Committee on Banking and Currency, March 31, 1971.
31. James E. Wallace, "Federal Income Tax Incentives in Low and Moderate Income Rental Housing," in U.S. Congress, Joint Economic Committee, *The Economics of Federal Subsidy Programs*, Part 5, pp. 676–705.

housing program of the early postwar years.[32] We seem to have difficulty formulating schemes that can stimulate a large flow of new, moderately priced urban rental housing without at the same time creating substantial windfalls for some investors.)

No doubt, however, the impulse to economize and to avert scandal was reinforced by widely expressed doubts about the fundamental direction taken by urban housing policy in the United States. Housing analysts both inside and outside the government began to question the wisdom of the new construction strategy on which that policy rested.

If we look at the history of urban housing policy from the early postwar years down to the present, we can discern two major periods, defined by the policy-dictated links connecting slum clearance, subsidized new construction, and the provision of benefits to tenants. The first period began with the birth of urban renewal (then called "redevelopment") in 1949. Urban renewal and the older, low rent public housing program became the principal elements in urban housing policy. These programs shared several characteristics: both provided subsidies that were linked to new construction; both linked new construction in some degree to slum clearance; in both cases the subsidies went initially to the supplier of new housing, whether private or public, rather than to the demander, or occupant.

The second period in housing policy began in the 1960's. The growing unpopularity of urban renewal, and to a lesser extent of public housing, was based partly on their link with a slum clearance and the resulting destruction of low income housing and neighborhoods. The new programs of the 1960's—221(d)(3), 235, 236, and rent supplements—severed the connection between subsidies and slum clearance. They did not, however, remove the link with new construction; they merely changed its form. In linking benefits for specific income classes to occupancy of specific newly constructed dwelling units, they strongly resemble the conventional public housing program: however much they differ in other respects, both are part of a new construction strategy.

Recent criticism of U.S. housing policy concentrates on precisely that point. Many analysts now argue that we should cut the tie between subsidies and the supply of newly constructed units and instead pay "demand-side" subsidies to the poor, to be spent, with only a few restrictions, on old, new, or middle-aged housing at their choice. Of all the policies so far discussed, this is the one most clearly consistent with the adaptive model of the housing market described in Chapter 10. It rests on the assumption that if we use subsidies to bring the demand for hous-

32. *Ibid.*, p. 692, n. 15. For a description of the 608 "scandal," see Charles Abrams, *The City Is the Frontier* (New York: Harper & Row, 1965), pp. 87–90.

ing up to an adequate level, the market process, largely by its own motion, will supply an adequate flow of standard quality housing services.

HOUSING ALLOWANCES:
A "DEMAND-SIDE" SUBSIDY

A number of proposals for subsidizing the housing demand of the poor have been made since the late 1960's. While these housing allowance plans differ from one another in important details, they share an underlying logic that we can conveniently examine in the version developed by Lowry.[33] As Lowry points out, subsidies for housing demand, rather than for the supply of new construction, look particularly attractive in the market context of the 1970's. The census reveals that 45 percent of all central cities of metropolitan areas lost population between 1960 and 1970. Of the 21 cities that had populations greater than 500,000 in 1960, 15 suffered population decline during the ensuing decade. There is every reason to expect continuing population loss in the older central cities. Consequently, the existing housing stock, plus the new construction that would take place without subsidy, should make up an ample supply of shelter in such cities during the 1970's. The widespread incidence of abandonment provides direct evidence that there has, in fact, been an excess supply of housing in many cities.

The problem is one, not of insufficient quantity, but of inadequate quality. To a considerable extent (as we have already argued), the inadequate quality supplied by owners of rental housing is their way of adapting to the low rent-paying capacity of tenants, given the fact of rapidly increasing maintenance and operating costs.

In such circumstances does it make sense to attack the housing problem by means of subsidies to accelerate the pace of costly new construction? Advocates of housing allowances think not. Instead, they propose giving subsidies to low income tenants that will enable them to pay the rents needed to cover adequate maintenance and operation of the existing, usable, older housing stock.

Lowry describes his housing allowance proposal as follows:

> In each community a housing assistance agency would determine the rents needed to support full costs of ownership . . . for well-maintained older housing units, a standard amount varying with size of unit. Low-income families would apply to the agency for

33. Ira S. Lowry, "Housing Assistance for Low-Income Urban Families: A Fresh Approach," Papers submitted to the Subcommittee on Housing, Part 2, U.S. Congress, House Committee on Banking and Currency, June 1971, pp. 489–524.

assistance, providing a Federal income tax return or other evidence of income. Applying a formula or schedule that takes into account income and size of family (and possibly other factors), the agency would determine how much the applicant could afford to contribute toward the cost of his housing. The applicant would be issued a rent certificate whose face value was equal to the difference between that amount and the standard full cost of a housing unit whose size was appropriate for the applicant's family. The certificate would consist of twelve dated coupons, covering a calendar year of rent assistance, each bearing the name of the recipient and the number of family members.

With the additional purchasing power provided by these coupons, the applicant would then seek private rental housing whose location and physical features were congenial to his needs and preferences and whose rent was within his now-augmented budget. Negotiations with the landlord over rent and conditions of occupancy would be solely the responsibility of the applicant; he could and should request evidence that the building was free of violations of the City's housing code. Once accepted as a tenant, he would present his assistance coupon in partial payment of the contracted rent, supplying the balance from his own pocket. Because each dollar of rent above the face value of the coupon would come out of the tenant's pocket he would have a clear incentive to choose housing within his means and to pay no more than the going market price for the housing he chooses.[34]

Lowry suggests a sophisticated formula for calculating individual benefits that would take into account, not only disposable family income and the minimum standard rent for an apartment of appropriate size, but also the minimum requirements for nonhousing consumption. Less complex proposals usually provide that benefits equal minimum standard rent for a unit of appropriate size, minus some constant fraction (generally 25 percent) of family income. In that formulation it is easily seen that as a household's income rises, the benefit payment diminishes, finally disappearing when the family can pay for standard housing by spending 25 percent of its income. Although the discussion here and below is in terms of rent, housing allowances could be extended also to low income homeowners under appropriately adjusted formulas.

Housing Allowances and Code Enforcement

It is worth examining briefly the interconnection between housing allowances and code enforcement. Most cities have housing codes that require dwelling units to be supplied with specific facilities such as plumb-

---

34. *Ibid.*, p. 505.

ing, heating, and ventilation and to be kept in a state of cleanliness and good repair.[35] In rental buildings it is the responsibility of the landlord to see that essential services are maintained. Periodically it occurs to housing reformers that a "code enforcement drive," with real muscle behind it, could force owners of deteriorated slum housing to bring it up to par and keep it there. Such drives are not necessarily useless, but their frequent repetition suggests, at least, that they do not achieve long-lasting improvement. This failure is probably explained by the inability or unwillingness of tenants in slum housing to pay rents that would cover the cost of operating a violation-free building. For if tenants were willing and able to pay such costs there would seem to be no reason why the landlord would not wish to satisfy them by providing the necessary services. On the other hand, if tenants were not willing and able to pay, landlords would seem likely to resist incurring the extra cost of providing such services.[36]

If this explanation seems unduly simpleminded, consider the case of a well-run, middle class apartment house. No one supposes that the owner of such a building keeps it clean and in good repair only because of the threat of housing code penalties. Rather he does so because his tenants want, and are prepared to pay for, a well-run building. Ideally, by providing low income tenants with enough rent-paying capacity to support well-maintained housing, an adequate rent certificate program would make code enforcement as routine and secondary a matter for low income housing as it is today for middle income structures. However, there would probably be a long transitional period following the introduction of housing allowances during which code enforcement would be essential to achieve rapid improvement of the housing stock and to establish a new level of expectations among both tenants and landlords. Hence the emphasis on code enforcement in every housing allowance proposal.

Lowry's plan includes a provision, with teeth in it, for ensuring the maintenance of decent housing standards: rent certificates would be cashed by the housing agency only for owners of buildings that were free of all housing code violations. Thus the power of the tenant to insist on adequate maintenance (which he can now afford to pay for) as a condition of continued occupancy would be supported by the power of the housing agency to make the entire building ineligible for rent certificate payments. Landlords catering to a low income clientele would find this a strong incentive to keep their buildings up to full code standards, while

35. For a detailed description of housing codes in the United States, see *Building the American City*, 1969, Part III, Ch. 4, "Housing Codes."

36. For a more extended argument of this point, see James Heilbrun, *Real Estate Taxes and Urban Housing* (New York: Columbia University Press, 1966), pp. 10–23.

the public would be assured that rent subsidies were not being paid for substandard housing.

The Issue of Equity

It is generally agreed that a housing allowance plan would be far more equitable than our present new construction strategy. Under present programs, a relatively small number of families receive very large benefits per household, while the majority of low income families, equally qualified according to eligibility standards, receive nothing. By contrast, a housing allowance plan would provide less ample benefits per family but would reach all eligible households rather than a somewhat arbitrarily selected minority. The typical benefit formula under a rent certificate plan provides that assistance payments are gradually reduced to zero as family income rises. Together with universal coverage for low income families, this feature ensures the equitable result that no one receiving assistance is thereby made better off than someone else who is not. Such an outcome is *not* assured under the patchwork arrangement of present housing subsidy programs.

The "disappearing benefit" formula also solves a problem that has greatly troubled administrators of local public housing projects: what to do when a family's income rises too high. To expel such families is not only harsh but prevents the project from gaining a balanced tenantry. To allow them to stay means conferring large benefits on middle class households while numerous poor families remain on the waiting list. Under a housing allowance formula, this dilemma cannot arise. A family can "work its way off assistance" without having to give up its home. To be sure, this is also a feature of the current 235, 236, and rent supplement formulas.

A Cost Comparison: Housing Allowances Versus New Construction

A housing allowance plan would be far less costly than a new construction strategy per dwelling unit brought up to standard. Lowry estimated that in New York City in 1969 the rent needed to cover the full cost of a well-maintained four-room apartment in an older building ranged from $100 to $150 per month. The equivalent full cost for either new public housing or new Section 236 units was approximately twice as high.[37] Consequently, the subsidy needed to enable a family of a given income class to occupy well-maintained older housing would be far lower than the subsidy needed to put the same family into a newly constructed unit.

37. Lowry, "Housing Assistance for Low-Income Urban Families," pp. 500–01.

Precise comparisons are difficult to carry out. However, for all families not on welfare but eligible for the proposed rent assistance program, Lowry estimated that in 1969 the average rent certificate payment would have been $642 per year.[38]

The above calculations are for New York City only. Nation-wide average costs have been estimated for other rent assistance schemes not greatly different in approach from Lowry's. For example, Aaron analyzed the cost of a plan under which each family would pay 25 percent of adjusted income in rent and receive a subsidy equal to the difference between that amount and the shelter cost reported by the Bureau of Labor Statistics for a low income family living in decent housing. The average annual benefit payment per household in 1967 would have been $397.[39]

This figure, as well as Lowry's, is far below the subsidy cost of either new public housing or housing built under Section 236. De Leeuw and Leaman estimated the full annual subsidy cost for a two-bedroom unit of conventional public housing completed in 1971 at $1,980. Of that amount, $1,368 was the direct federal cost, $360 was the federal revenue loss through tax-exempt financing, and $252 the local government cost equal to foregone property tax receipts less housing authority payments in lieu of taxes.[40] Neither of the last two costs occurs under a rent certificate plan, since private structures ordinarily are not financed by tax-exempt borrowing and pay full real estate taxes. But even the direct (or out-of-pocket) federal costs per unit would be far less under a rent certificate plan than for public housing.

Section 236 units are less heavily subsidized than public housing. We have cited an average federal cost of about $1,000 per unit in the early years of the program. However, Section 236 housing does not reach as far down in the income distribution as either public housing or the typical housing allowance plan. For the sake of cost comparison one should therefore look at the unit subsidy cost when the present rent supplement benefits for low income families are "piggy-backed" with benefits under Section 236. In that case one would add an estimated $600 to the cost of the 236 program, bringing the current total subsidy per unit almost to the level of public housing.

Although unit costs would be relatively low under a housing allowance program, the wide coverage of such a plan would make it quite costly in the aggregate. Whether it would turn out ultimately to be more expensive than the combined policies that now make up our new con-

38. *Ibid.*, p. 509 (corrected from $615).
39. Aaron, Table 10–3, p. 170.
40. De Leeuw and Leaman, Table 2, p. 655.

struction strategy depends partly on how far the latter are carried. The national housing goal calls for subsidies to 5 million new units and 1 million rehabilitated units. If this program were carried through, the yearly federal subsidy, at an average of $800 to $1,000 per unit, might easily reach $5 to $6 billion.[41] (It should be emphasized that all these unit cost predictions are risky, since the size of future payments per family will depend on trends in both tenant income and housing costs.) By way of comparison, the housing allowance scheme analyzed by Aaron would have cost an estimated $4.9 to $6.2 billion in 1967. While these figures are not for the same dates, they do suggest that annual budgetary costs might ultimately reach the same order of magnitude under the two approaches. However, the housing allowance plan would reach that level at once and would therefore cost far more than the new construction strategy during the years while the latter was building toward the limits set by the national housing goals.

To put these cost figures in perspective, we should keep in mind that a much larger housing subsidy is already provided by the Treasury to the American homeowner in the form of specially favorable tax treatment. As we pointed out in Chapter 3, the U.S. income tax discriminates in favor of homeowners as compared with investors in other assets because it allows them to deduct real estate taxes and the interest cost of home ownership from their taxable income without also requiring that they report as income the imputed annual rental value of their home. On the basis of a sample of 90,000 federal tax returns, Aaron estimates that this favorable treatment reduced homeowners' income tax payments by $7 billion in 1966. Sixty-four percent of the saving accrued to households with incomes above $10,000 a year.[42] The concentration of benefits among the middle and upper classes occurs partly because home ownership increases with income, partly because any saving through deductibility is worth more to those in a high tax bracket than to those farther down in the scale.

Favorable tax treatment of homeowners is defended—when it is discussed at all—as a means of "encouraging home ownership." But that is just a pleasant way of pronouncing the word "subsidy," and it is perfectly reasonable to insist that other housing subsidies not be rejected out of hand, on account of their cost, while this most costly one is retained unnoticed.

In evaluating alternative housing programs, we must look at probable

41. Charles L. Schultze, *et al.*, *Setting National Priorities: The 1972 Budget* (Washington, D.C.: Brookings Institution, 1971), p. 290.
42. Aaron, Table 10–1, p. 162.

effectiveness as well as probable cost. It can be argued that a considerable part of the outlay on a new construction strategy will ultimately run to waste so far as raising housing standards is concerned. Because low income tenants cannot afford to pay its "upkeep," much of the housing that filters down as a result of subsidized new construction is likely to deteriorate into later model slums. Our costly efforts would then be futile, much like those of a man who tries to fill up his swimming pool without first mending the leaks in the bottom. Housing allowances are aimed precisely at those leaks. They are designed to prevent filtered-down housing from sinking below acceptable standards.

Housing Allowances and Income Maintenance

It probably will not have escaped notice that a housing allowance plan under which benefits decline as income rises resembles structurally an income-maintenance scheme (such as the one outlined in Chapter 9) that incorporates the same feature. The impacts of the two plans on housing expenditures, however, would certainly differ. Income-maintenance schemes leave beneficiaries free to spend as they choose, while housing allowance plans are designed specifically to stimulate outlays on shelter. Even a fairly generous income-maintenance plan would be unlikely to increase housing consumption as much as a housing allowance program would. For example, if standard urban housing for a family of four costs $125 a month (or $1,500 a year), then the income-maintenance plan illustrated in Table 9.4 would still leave families with earned incomes of less than $4,500 unable to afford standard housing unless they spent more than 25 percent of their income on rent. Many of them would be unwilling to do that. On the other hand, a housing allowance program would give low income households the means to pay for standard housing and would relieve some of the pressure on their budget in doing so, but it would by no means ensure that they could afford a decent minimum of other goods.

In principle there is no reason why both programs could not be employed simultaneously. The combined cost would be high, but it would be much less than the sum of the separate costs, since payments under either heading would go far toward meeting obligations under the other. A combined program would have the advantage of adding to the basic income maintenance allowance a regionally differentiated housing component that would compensate for some of the interarea differences in living costs in the United States.[43]

43. *Ibid.*, p. 173.

Will Supply Respond to Increased Demand?

Those who are skeptical about housing allowances raise one very serious issue. They argue that such a program is likely to drive rents up by increasing demand without augmenting supply:

> Proponents of tying housing subsidies to the construction of new units offer a major counterargument against proposals for housing allowances. They point out that a combination of zoning laws, racial discrimination, and similar restrictions would make it impossible for many recipients of housing allowances to find decent older housing. As a consequence, the allowances would simply drive up rents in low-income areas.[44]

Such arguments, however, seem to confuse three possible effects of housing allowances. The first effect is an *intended* increase in rent payments for given dwelling units. As Lowry's approach makes clear, housing allowances are intended to provide low income tenants with the rent-paying capacity to support improved quality of service in the buildings where they already live. If landlords *do* supply improved service—and the adaptive model of the housing market suggests that they will—rents would certainly be expected to rise. Consistent with this argument, it is not implied by advocates of housing allowances that tenants would have to move to achieve improved quality, though they might do so, and a credible threat of moving would certainly be useful.

The second possible effect is the *unintended* one that rents might rise *without* an improvement in quality—an effect that might be called "pure rent inflation." [45] This is certainly a conceivable result of a housing allowance program. It seems unlikely to occur, however, in cities that are now undergoing population decline and that therefore may be presumed to have surplus housing stock now en route to abandonment. In any event, the coupling of rent assistance with code enforcement should provide landlords with the necessary incentive to bring their properties up to acceptable standards once tenants are able to pay the cost of doing so.

A third possible effect is a combination of the first two: rents rise in order to cover the cost of improved quality, but they rise more than that, indicating a degree of pure rent inflation. Such an outcome would add to the cost of a housing allowance program for two reasons. First, assistance payments per family would be greater. Second, with higher rents, more families would become eligible for assistance. This possibility accounts for the range of program cost estimates given by Aaron and cited above.

44. Schultze, *et al.*, p. 295.

45. For an attempt to measure the response of rent to differences in tenant income see Frank De Leeuw and Nkanta F. Ekanem, "The Supply of Rental Housing," *American Economic Review*, December 1971, pp. 806–17.

Residual doubts about the extent to which pure rent inflation might occur can be resolved only by trial runs of a housing allowance system under various actual market conditions. The Department of Housing and Urban Development began to conduct such experiments in 1971.

Consumer Choice Versus Planning

The choice between housing allowances and subsidized new construction is also to some degree a choice between the strengths and weaknesses of the free market and those of urban planning. Some new construction-oriented programs, such as public housing and urban renewal, give local planning authorities the opportunity to choose project sites that support their long-run plans for change and development. On the debit side, all new construction subsidies tie government obligations to particular buildings in particular locations. A wrong decision can lead to disastrous loss to the government, as in the case of Pruitt-Igoe. We do not know how many other such errors the government may now be committing itself to through long-run subsidy contracts on particular buildings.

Unlike new construction subsidies, housing allowances are not something that local authorities can use to reshape or direct the pattern of urban development. That is their debit side. On the credit side, because housing allowances are geographically mobile, they cannot become permanently locked-in to the wrong neighborhood or the wrong city, as new construction subsidies may. Instead, they move automatically to wherever people wish, and are able, to spend them. Although this mobility deprives local authorities of some leverage in planning, it also reduces the risk of serious public investment errors.

More important, housing allowances have the virtue of greatly increasing the freedom of choice for beneficiaries. If the program were set up nation-wide, low income families could obtain equivalent benefits anywhere. Within a given city they would be free to choose any building and neighborhood they could afford, instead of being constrained to live in designated subsidized projects. As between city and city, or city and suburb, they would be free to move, without losing benefits, to any place offering moderate-priced accommodation. Consequently, although housing allowances would not help local authorities to accomplish the traditional jobs of urban physical planning, they might contribute to achieving one thing that has eluded planning itself: a reduction in the degree of racial segregation within cities and between cities and suburbs.

SEGREGATION AND DISCRIMINATION
IN HOUSING

Housing segregation is certainly a major social problem in the United States. Within large cities the increase in black population has not been accompanied by an increase in racial integration. Old black neighborhoods expand outward, new enclaves of black settlement grow until they, too, are large, all-black communities, but few neighborhoods achieve and retain racial balance. As we pointed out in Chapter 9, segregation imposes losses on blacks both because it reduces their employment opportunities and because it limits and distorts their housing choices. In addition, it surely makes school integration difficult, if not impossible, to achieve.

Segregation by race obviously exists in U.S. cities. Is that fact sufficient to prove the existence of racial discrimination in housing markets? Or might the observed degree of racial segregation be explained entirely by economic factors, such as the location of low skill jobs and of old, inexpensive housing, which would cause low income blacks to concentrate in particular neighborhoods? The answer is that economic forces alone cannot explain what we see. Anthony Pascal tested the hypothesis that economic factors could account for racial segregation by estimating multiple regression equations to predict black residential location in Chicago and Detroit. He found that economic variables could "explain" only one-third to one-half of the observed degree of segregation.[46]

But perhaps blacks are so highly segregated because they choose voluntarily to live in predominantly black neighborhoods? After all, other urban ethnic minorities have tended to cluster out of preference for their own culture and kinfolk. Pascal tested this possibility, too. Using data for Chicago, he compared the observed degree of segregation for Italian-Americans—who are reputed to have a strong tendency toward self-segregation—with that of middle to upper income nonwhites. The segregation index for nonwhites was more than five times that for Italian-Americans. Such a difference could hardly be attributed to voluntary self-segregation alone.[47] In any case, the stated preference of most blacks in Pascal's study was for integrated housing. If anyone doubted the existence of racial discrimination in housing markets, studies such as Pascal's offer sufficient evidence that it exists.

Such studies also indicate, however, that economic factors *do* account for a portion of observed segregation by race. Consequently, hous-

46. Anthony H. Pascal, "The Analysis of Residential Segregation," in John P. Crecine, ed., *Financing the Metropolis* (Beverly Hills, California: Sage Publications, 1970), p. 407. Also see John F. Kain, ed., *Race and Poverty, The Economics of Discrimination* (Englewood Cliffs, N.J.: Prentice-Hall, 1969), editor's introduction, pp. 21–27.

47. Pascal, pp. 409–10.

ing allowances would probably help significantly to diminish segregation. By giving low income families the purchasing power with which to compete for lower middle income housing, they would facilitate movement out of racial ghettos for those who wished to move out. Housing allowances will not end discriminatory practices; that can be accomplished, if at all, only by educational campaigns and by legal prohibitions and remedies. What housing allowances can do is to weaken the support that income inequality has hitherto lent to discriminatory practices in reinforcing racial segregation. We treat antidiscrimination and antisegregation policies in greater detail in the next section of this chapter, which deals with proposals to "open up" the suburbs to low and moderate income families and to racial minorities.

"OPENING UP" THE SUBURBS

A recurrent topic in any book that deals with urban economic problems in the twentieth century is the ongoing process of job and population dispersion within metropolitan areas. We have emphasized the fact that population dispersion has been highly selective rather than uniform by income and race. That fact helps to shape almost every policy issue raised in this book. In Chapter 8 we showed that poverty is increasingly concentrated in the central cities and that racial segregation as between central cities and suburbs is increasing rather than diminishing. We argued in Chapter 9 that job decentralization puts the central city poor at an increasing disadvantage in their struggle to improve their condition. In Chapter 10 we showed that the concentration of the poor in the central city has led to a virtual breakdown of private housing institutions in many neighborhoods. We will argue in the chapter following this one that the unequal distribution of the poverty population between central cities and suburbs raises serious issues of both equity and efficiency in metropolitan public finance.

Indeed, at this moment in the history of U.S. metropolitan development, the increasing disparity in racial composition and income level between central cities and suburbs is at once probably the most difficult, pervasive, and alarming of "urban problems." Proposals that the suburbs be somehow "opened up" to low income and lower middle income families have therefore received increasing attention since the late 1960's. Because these proposals raise questions of housing policy first and foremost, it is appropriate to discuss them in this chapter. Because they relate housing issues to many others in urban economic policy, it is appropriate that they should make up the chapter's concluding section.

In earlier portions of the book we described the complex of forces that account for the present pattern of settlement of rich and poor in metropolitan areas. To recapitulate briefly, the poor are attracted to the center for several reasons. First, it has by far the largest concentration of old and therefore cheap housing, which is all that the poor can afford unless they are subsidized. Second, the central city still offers easy access to the largest single concentration of employment. On the other hand, as their incomes rise, the middle and upper classes find it increasingly desirable to pay the price of higher transportation costs in order to buy spacious housing in the suburbs. These "natural" economic forces, acting alone, would probably have sufficed to produce a pattern of richer suburbs and poorer central cities in the course of metropolitan growth. But they have not been acting alone. Rather they have been reinforced by public policy and by class and race prejudice. At the level of national policy, the provisions of the federal income tax favor home ownership over home rental. Since the incentive to ownership becomes more powerful the higher the individual's tax bracket, the middle and upper classes far more than the poor are induced to move into home-ownership territory, and home ownership is far more prevalent in the suburbs than in central cities. Equally important are the exclusionary zoning policies that suburban communities themselves can use to let the well-to-do in while barring the poor and the lower middle class. While there seem to be several motives behind exclusionary local policies, race and class prejudice are probably important among them.

Exclusionary Zoning

The poor and the lower middle class can be kept out of a suburban community by a few simple provisions in the local zoning ordinance. For example, a community can zone itself for single family housing only. Thus all multiple dwellings, including such relatively inexpensive forms of construction as garden apartments, are effectively banned. If that is not thought to be a sufficient barrier, the zoning ordinance can also require a large building lot for any new home—say, two acres or more—instead of the quarter of an acre lots on which so much suburban housing has been built in the past. With land costs rising rapidly in the suburbs, a large lot requirement adds substantially to the cost of a home. In addition, builders are reluctant to put inexpensive homes on large lots. Thus zoning provisions can be used to raise the minimum cost of a new home high enough to exclude newcomers whose incomes are less than solidly middle class.[48]

48. See *Building the American City*, Part III, Ch. 1, "Land-use Controls: Zoning and Subdivision Regulations"; and Linda Davidoff, Paul Davidoff, and Neil N. Gold, "The Suburbs Have to Open Their Gates," *The New York Times Magazine*, November 7, 1971.

Comprehensive zoning in the United States is usually dated from the adoption of a zoning resolution by New York City in 1916. As originally conceived, zoning was to be a form of land-use control that would keep incompatible uses from impinging on one another or prevent overintensive development of one site from imposing burdens on its neighbors. Incompatible uses could be kept apart by zoning certain areas for residential development to the exclusion of all industry and others for residential, commercial and light industrial uses, while confining truly "noxious" activities, such as glue factories or stockyards, to peripheral locations. In the same zoning ordinance, individual improvements could be prevented from blocking the light and air of their neighbors or imposing other burdens on them by regulating the height and bulk of buildings or requiring open space along lot boundaries.

The noxious odors that a stockyard sends into the neighborhood or the deep shadows that a huge building casts upon adjacent properties are both examples of land-use "externalities." As we pointed out in Chapter 6, these arise when one person's actions impose costs on other people that the injured parties can neither avoid nor readily collect compensation for. This kind of imperfection in the land market does, or could, occur frequently when people are living at typical urban densities and, when it occurs, will prevent the market from yielding optimal results. Consequently, most land economists and urban planners accept zoning as a legitimate way of regulating the land market by reducing the destructive effects of externalities.

Exclusionary zoning in the suburbs is a different matter, however. Its intent is not to correct market failure but to impose unnecessary restrictions on consumer choice, thus actually restraining free market activity. There would be no objection to a plan under which a town reserved some areas exclusively for single-family homes, while allowing multiple dwellings in others, since zoning can be defended as a way of preserving certain neighborhood amenities. But when we find that a town has been enacting acreage requirements and building codes far more restrictive than those that prevailed during most of its own period of development, we can hardly doubt that the intent is exclusionary.

Under the regime of local autonomy regarding land-use decisions that prevails in the United States, even public housing cannot breach the exclusionary walls of the suburbs. Although the federal government subsidizes low income public housing, it is planned and built by local authorities. If a town does not want any, it simply does not participate in the federal program. Nor can the housing authority of one town undertake to build or operate units in another. Thus we have in the United States neither federal nor metropolitan agencies empowered to determine the location of subsidized housing.

Motives for Exclusionary Practices

There are at least three important motives for exclusionary practices in the suburbs. The first is a financial motive. Under our multilevel system, local governments are financially responsible for an important share of public services. Despite state and federal aid, a heavy local tax burden remains. As we will demonstrate in Chapter 12, the citizens of any municipality stand to gain financially by excluding those in-migrants who are likely to contribute less to local tax and grant-in-aid revenue than they will add to local service costs. The property tax is the most important source of local revenue. Suburban voters therefore have a strong financial motive for trying to ensure that low or even middle income housing is not built in their town, because it will not "pay its way" in terms of taxes. The same financial motive that induces suburbs to keep low or moderately low income families out encourages them to bring clean, tax-paying industry in. An approach that combines both elements has been dubbed "fiscal zoning." It is a deliberate "beggar-my-neighbor" policy. The town that successfully practices it gets the industry while some other municipality is forced to bear the cost of public services for the factory's workers.[49]

A second motive for exclusionary practices is a desire to preserve neighborhood amenities. If a family moved into a suburb because they liked its "rural" character, they will probably want to keep it that way by prohibiting apartment house construction and perhaps even by slowing down further intrusion of single-family homes. The unexpressed impulse is "now that we're in, let's slam the door to keep others from following."

Finally, there is the motive of opposition to racial and/or socio-economic integration. The distinction between feelings about race and about class is potentially significant since, if class prejudice plays an important part, we should expect opposition to integration to diminish as racial minorities converge toward the majority in socioeconomic characteristics.[50] Because race and class feelings are not freely expressed, it is difficult to know how much of the opposition to integration should be attributed to these antagonisms and how much to other motives. In recent years the situation has been further complicated by the growth of crime and delinquency as a major personal and social concern. Consider the case of the extraordinary local opposition that developed in 1972 to siting low income public housing in the middle class Forest Hills neighborhood of New York City. The housing project would not have affected neighborhood tax or expenditure levels, since these are established on a city-

49. See Julius Margolis, "On Municipal Land Policy for Fiscal Gains," *National Tax Journal*, September 1956, pp. 247–57.
50. Pascal, pp. 410–12.

wide basis. Hence, there was no financial motive for opposition. It might have affected the neighborhood's physical character in some degree, but certainly not enough to account for the ensuing uproar. Quite clearly, residents were expressing opposition to the entry of low income families who they knew would be heavily black and Puerto Rican and who they feared would bring an increase in crime and juvenile delinquency to what had been a relatively "safe" neighborhood.

What Would Be Gained by Opening Up the Suburbs?

A program that succeeded in opening up the suburbs to low and moderate income families might be expected to produce a variety of benefits. First of all, by encouraging the movement of blacks into the suburbs, it would obviously help to slow the trend toward macrosegregation in metropolitan areas: increasingly black central cities surrounded by still largely white suburbs. If *de facto* integration is ever to be achieved in U.S. society, it is essential that the suburbs accept a substantially greater proportion of the metropolitan black population.

Second, it would promote freedom of choice in housing location for groups whose choices are now heavily restricted by exclusionary practices. Such freedom from imposed restrictions is a matter of right that also has practical economic consequences. The growth of suburban job opportunities was discussed in Chapter 9. It was argued that restraints on freedom of choice in housing systematically limit the access which minorities, now concentrated in the central cities, have to these attractive opportunities and also impose losses on them by limiting and distorting their consumption of housing itself. Those who do work in the new suburban plants and offices are likely to find themselves bearing unnecessarily heavy travel costs, since they cannot live near their jobs. Davidoff cites the case of the suburban town of Mahwah, N.J., about 25 miles northwest of the center of New York City. Mahwah's biggest tax resource is a recently built automobile assembly plant. The town makes a practice of excluding housing even for moderate income families. Consequently only 88 of the factory's far from impoverished 4,200 workers actually live in Mahwah. Some commute from as far away as Newark and New York City.[51]

Finally, removing housing restrictions in the wealthier suburbs would help to even up tax costs and service levels among different local governments. The well-to-do would no longer be able to use self-segregation as a means of escaping responsibility for sharing the cost of local public services provided to those with lower incomes. (It is a curious fact that one of the important consequences of the twentieth-century revolution in transport

51. Davidoff, Davidoff, and Gold, p. 46.

technology has been to facilitate this self-segregation.) Low and moderate income families moving into wealthy communities would benefit either by receiving a higher level of service or paying lower tax rates than before.

Policies to Encourage Racial and Economic Integration

Policies to encourage racial and economic integration within metropolitan areas can be divided, for purposes of analysis, into two groups: "permissive" policies and "active" policies. Permissive policies would remove the barriers of exclusionary zoning and discriminatory practice but would not bring housing costs down by means of subsidies. Active policies, on the other hand, would provide subsidies to bring suburban housing costs within the reach of low income groups.

We take up permissive policies first. Among those already in force is the Civil Rights Act of 1968, which prohibits racial discrimination in the sale or rental of housing. Numerous state laws do likewise. It is not easy to know how effective these statutes have been. Kain points out that antidiscrimination laws and the public attitude that lie behind them "have caused opponents of open housing to resort to more subtle and secretive methods." Unfortunately, evidence concerning such methods is likely to be anecdotal, difficult to evaluate, and hence, in social scientific terms, inconclusive.[52]

Whether or not the "retail" sort of discrimination that may occur in individual housing transactions can be curbed, it is certainly possible to do something about the exclusionary zoning regulations that now lend the color of legality to discrimination when it is practiced at "wholesale." Local zoning ordinances are written under authority of state law. Consequently, the states have the power to abolish them or to require that they conform to nonexclusionary standards or even to a state-wide plan. If local political interests are strong enough to block such reform in state legislatures, a more fruitful approach may be to attack exclusionary zoning through the courts. "Class" actions can be brought in state court on behalf of low income or minority groups. As a result of such a suit, a New Jersey court in October 1971 set aside the entire zoning ordinance of Madison Township. The court found that the ordinance dictated such high housing costs that it would automatically exclude 90 percent of the area's population from moving into the town and held that it therefore failed to meet the test of advancing the general welfare.[53] Indeed, successful suits may eventually force state legislatures to enact basic zoning reform.

52. Kain, editor's introduction, pp. 24–26.
53. *The New York Times*, October 30, 1971.

Because residents of the suburbs are genuinely concerned about the extra tax burden they would take on if they allowed an influx of low income households, appropriate public finance reforms would undoubtedly help to weaken support for exclusionary policies. For example, if local school outlays were to be fixed at a state-wide uniform level per pupil and financed entirely by a state property tax, and if all local welfare costs were to be absorbed by either the state or the federal government, then the financial motive for opposing low income in-migration would all but disappear. More generally, any form of grant or revenue sharing, or any reassignment of functions that shifts the responsibility for financing services to a higher level of government, would help to weaken the financial motive for exclusionary policies. Much has already occurred along these lines. With the states now under pressure to assume the full costs of education, and Washington looking periodically into welfare reform, there is reason to expect more action as time goes by. (We will discuss these problems of public finance at greater length in Chapter 12.)

The policies considered to this point are permissive only. They would help to eliminate practices that now inhibit the free play of market forces in suburban housing, but they would do nothing to help the poor pay market costs. Since the new private housing that might be constructed when the barriers fell would remain beyond the reach of low income families, permissive policies would at most open the suburbs to the lower middle class. The poor would be encouraged to move there only if they received support from active subsidy policies.

A nation-wide housing allowance scheme is an active policy that could help to reduce intrametropolitan racial and economic segregation. If allowances were usable over an entire metropolitan housing market, such a plan might help some of the urban poor move out into the nearer suburbs, where relatively inexpensive older housing is available. However, it would certainly not move them into new, single-family suburban homes, since the subsidy payment would be geared to the cost of standard older housing, not new construction.

Any really effective policy to move low income households into the suburbs would probably have to include subsidies directed specifically toward those areas. One approach would be to establish metropolitan area housing authorities with the power to build or lease subsidized, low rent public housing anywhere within the region. The authority could make plans on the basis of regional rather than purely local criteria and, if necessary, carry them out by overriding exclusionary local zoning ordinances. However, political resistance by the suburbs currently makes the creation of metropolitan housing agencies with coercive powers look highly unlikely. As a result of such resistance, New York's Urban Development Corporation, which takes the entire state as its field of operation, was deprived, in 1973, of its former power to construct housing without conforming to local restrictions.

It may be that cooperative regional efforts under the aegis of metropolitan planning agencies can proceed without the need to invoke extraordinary powers. The virtue of cooperation is that if every suburban jurisdiction were willing to accept a fair share of low income housing, none would be asked to absorb very much. Such an arrangement would relieve the fear that "once we let down the barriers, a flood will follow." The voluntary approach has been successfully launched in the Dayton, Ohio, metropolitan region, where more than two dozen municipalities agreed on a plan that assigned each of them a share of expected, federally subsidized housing.[54] This sort of arrangement is not likely to sweep the country, however, unless municipalities are given some incentive to cooperate. The federal government could exert pressure by withholding various categories of grant funds from recalcitrant municipalities or by rewarding with special generosity those that cooperate. A logical extension of this policy would be a grant program specifically designed to help defray the cost of municipal services in towns that accept subsidized low income housing under a regional plan. Morton Schussheim suggests funneling such aid through regional agencies that have full authority to override local zoning, acquire land and build low income housing, but there would seem to be no reason why it could not also be used in support of essentially voluntary regional efforts.[55]

The Consequences of Alternative Policies

Present housing and land-use policies, far from helping to promote racial and economic integration of city and suburb, have probably had just the opposite effect. Broadly speaking, the new construction strategy we have been pursuing to meet the nation's housing needs produces subsidized new construction in the cities and unsubsidized middle and upper class housing in the ring areas. Subsidized low income housing built in the cities tends to anchor the poor there. At the same time, our new construction strategy as a whole reinforces this effect, for it produces a substantial amount of filtering, and it is the older housing at the center that filters down to the lowest rent level. As Downs argues, the macrolocational outcome of a strategy based on new construction plus filtering is that the poor remain concentrated in the central city while the well-to-

54. *The New York Times*, December 21, 1970.
55. Morton J. Schussheim, "National Goals and Local Practices: Joining Ends and Means in Housing," Papers submitted to the Subcommittee on Housing, Part 1, U.S. Congress, House Committee on Banking and Currency, June 1971, pp. 157–58.

do settle in the outlying growth areas.[56] It goes without saying that these broad tendencies are further reinforced by the exclusionary land-use policies permitted under our system of local planning autonomy.

What would happen if we now put an end to exclusionary practices by adopting policies that permit but do not subsidize low and moderate income housing in the suburbs? The result would probably be an increase in the quantity of new moderate income housing built in the ring area and a more even distribution of such housing among localities of varying income levels. We have already cited the gains in the form of increased housing, job, and locality choice; reduced transportation costs; and improved public services that would accrue to those who could afford the new housing. In a society dedicated to freedom of individual choice and equality of opportunity, such gains are ample justification for the necessary policy changes.

Ironically, however, policies that help only the middle or lower middle class to move to the suburbs may have the effect of aggravating social and economic conditions in the central city for those who remain behind. Consider, for example, the simple arithmetic of income levels. Suppose that a suburb that had used exclusionary zoning to keep out families with incomes below $18,000 a year now lowers the bars so that new housing becomes available to families with incomes as low as $13,000 a year. If the median family income in the central city is only $10,000 or $11,000 it is probable that the new out-migrants will have income levels below the median in the suburb to which they move but above the median in the city from which they came. In that case, their migration would lower the medians at both places and could well increase rather than narrow the difference between them. A reduction in the level of median family income in central cities would, in turn, exacerbate some of the most serious problems that they now face, including the inadequacy of the local tax base and the deterioration of neighborhoods that is associated with housing abandonment. In short, opening up the suburbs only by means of permissive policies would help a substantial number of middle and lower middle class families—but very possibly at the expense of weakening the capacity of the core city for helping the poor who remained behind. Active policies to help move the poor out of the central cities are therefore important for two reasons. First, they are the only way of ensuring that low income families can take advantage of the opening up of the suburbs, when that occurs. Second, they will help prevent further relative deterioration of the social and economic condition of the remaining central city population.

It is always true, of course, that increased aid to localities or the

56. Downs, p. 172.

assumption of fiscal responsibility for local services by higher levels of government could be used, to whatever extent the public is willing, to offset the undesirable consequences of central city poverty. But as we will argue in Chapter 12, other ends might be sacrificed in that process. Americans place a high value on local government autonomy. Depending on their form, policies intended to bring about financial equality between richer and poorer communities may reduce the real independence of local governments. To the extent that the demands for financial equality and for political autonomy are in conflict, a policy that would help to redistribute population so as to make local income levels more nearly equal becomes that much more attractive. This argument for an active rather than only a permissive policy of opening up the suburbs is ultimately a political one, but it may well be the most important of all. Unfortunately, the outlook is not encouraging. Permissive policies will probably continue to gain momentum, but there is currently no sign that active policies will do likewise.

Organizing and Financing
the Metropolitan Public Sector

TWELVE

In the catalog of urban and metropolitan problems, government finance and organization occupy a special place. Unless the metropolitan public sector is efficiently organized and adequately financed we cannot expect local government to contribute optimally to the solution of any of the other urban problems, be they in housing, education, poverty, pollution, transportation, or land use. Consequently, our anxieties about the state of metropolitan public finance have grown in step with our commitment to solve other urban problems. Yet when we begin looking into the matter we realize that, ironically, the same forces of change and growth that have generated those other problems have also rendered our traditional local financial institutions increasingly inappropriate for the tasks we now urgently wish them to accomplish. Thus every systematic discussion of metropolitan public finance ends inevitably with proposals for substantial reform.

THE MULTI-LEVEL PUBLIC SECTOR

The structure of the public sector in the United States can best be described by a two-dimensional diagram, such as Figure 12.1. Along the vertical scale we mark off the three levels of government: federal, state, and local. It is conventional to treat local government

317

FIGURE 12.1

Structure of Government in the United States: A Two-dimensional View

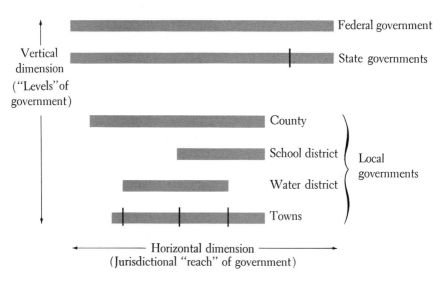

as though it were a single level. In fact, the local sector in most places consists of many overlapping layers: cities, counties, school districts, water districts, and so forth. An attempt is made to show these schematically in the diagram. The degree of complexity at the local level is suggested by a few statistics: there were no less than 81,248 local governmental units in the United States in 1967, and only 18,048 of these were "municipalities." The 227 SMSA's then recognized by the census alone contained 20,703 governmental units.[1]

The horizontal dimension of the diagram measures schematically the jurisdictional reach of the units of government in each of the layers. The pattern is clear enough at the federal and state levels. At the local level it becomes complex and unsystematic because the jurisdictions of the units vary in size both within layers and between them. A county may be larger or smaller than a city. A school district may take in one or more towns as well as unincorporated rural areas. A special district may overlap cities, counties, or towns. A single citizen may thus live under a bewildering array of local governments stacked one above the other.

The Dimensions of the Metropolitan Fiscal Problem

The horizontal and vertical dimensions of Figure 12.1 can usefully be thought of as the two dimensions of the metropolitan fiscal problem. The functions of government and the power to raise revenue by various means are distributed along the vertical scale among the federal, state, and local governments. The vertical problem in metropolitan public finance, sometimes called the problem of "fiscal imbalance," arises from the mismatch between the assignment of functions and the distribution of revenue-raising powers among the three levels.

We will show below that as a result of this mismatch, local governments in recent years have been put under intense and destructive fiscal pressure. What they face has, in fact, often been described as a "fiscal crisis."

Population, together with its needs, income, and resources, is distributed horizontally across the map of states and localities. The horizontal problem in metropolitan public finance also results in part from a mismatch: the needs of the population for public service and the income and resources out of which the revenue to pay for those services can be raised are not similarly distributed across governmental units at the local level. Serious inequities among individuals and between social classes arise from this geographic mismatch. But the horizontal problem has another aspect, too: the haphazard jurisdictional arrangement of governments within and across the local level prevents the local public sector from providing services at an optimum, or perhaps even acceptable, level of efficiency.

We will begin by analyzing the vertical dimension of the metropolitan fiscal problem, then take up its horizontal aspects, and conclude by examining some of the fundamental reforms that have been proposed to ameliorate both. First, however, a brief discussion of the economic functions of local government.

THE ECONOMIC FUNCTIONS OF LOCAL GOVERNMENT

Apart from regulatory action, government brings its influence to bear on the economy through the operation of its budget, which affects economic activity by means of both taxes and expenditures. In his highly influential treatise on public finance Musgrave usefully divides the budgetary objectives of government in a market economy into three classes.[2] The

2. R. A. Musgrave, *The Theory of Public Finance* (New York: McGraw-Hill, 1959), Ch. 1. The normative approach to problems of public finance adopted in this chapter is based largely on the work of Musgrave as applied to metropolitan areas by Brazer, Break, Netzer, and Tiebout (see subsequent references to these writers).

first of these he calls "allocation," the second "distribution," and the third "stabilization." The task of allocation consists of providing those goods and services that, for a variety of reasons, the private sector cannot provide at all or cannot provide at prices and in quantities that are optimal. The task of distribution might better be labeled *re*distribution, since it consists of transferring income among individuals to correct the pattern of private market rewards in order to arrive at an ethically more desirable distribution of well-being. Last, the stabilization task involves using the fiscal powers of government to smooth out fluctuations in the level of aggregate economic activity.

In a unitary political system the three budgetary functions would be performed and, ideally, coordinated by a single government. Under the multi-level system of federal, state, and local governments that we in the United States enjoy—or should one say, tolerate?—matters become much more complicated. Lack of coordination among governments, overlapping of jurisdictions, the mismatch between a government's objectives and its resources all contribute—not haphazardly, but systematically—to preventing the public economy as a whole from functioning efficiently. To say this is not to argue that we should abandon multi-level government, which has indispensable virtues as well as characteristic defects, but rather to explain why the search for more effective forms of federalism is now so intense.

Under a multi-level system, state and local governments perform few stabilization functions. Quite rightly, they leave stabilization largely in the hands of the federal government. In this they really have no choice. The economies of states and localities are so wide open to the influence of the national economy, through trade, that it would be hopeless for them to attempt local stabilization by means of fiscal policy, even if they were permitted by their own constitutions to do so. As economic base analysis assumes, the level of local activity is influenced significantly by the strength of outside demand for local products. Any stimulus or any restraint that local authorities might contrive to counteract outside forces would soon dissipate its effects in the larger national economy.

Providing Local Public Goods and Services

Allocation activities are the dominant concern of local government. Local citizens want and are willing to pay for public goods and services such as parks, sanitation services, and police protection. One of the principal objectives of the local public sector is to provide such services, in accordance with citizen preferences, just as the private sector provides bread and shoes and washing machines in accordance with consumer preferences.

Since the early 1950's economists have devoted much thought to the problems of satisfying the demand for publicly provided goods and services and have found that many difficulties stand in the way of an optimal solution.[3] The private sector makes use of prices to achieve an allocation of output that accords with consumer preferences. The public sector could certainly make use of prices in the form of user charges more often than it has done to produce services in the quantities that its citizens want. But in most cases, public-service pricing is either technically impossible or inefficient because it is too costly. How could the city charge a fee for police protection, public health services, or city planning? For the most part one must hope that a democratic voting procedure somehow succeeds in registering citizen preferences for public services in the same way the market does for private ones.[4]

Redistributing Income from Rich to Poor

In Musgrave's ideal scheme the tasks of allocation and distribution are logically separated, even though both may be performed by the same government. Under the heading of allocation, the government provides public goods and services to the extent that citizens want them and are willing to pay for them with taxes. If a redistribution of income is desired the most efficient way to carry it out is by making transfers in cash, rather than in services, from the rich to the poor. So clear a distinction between allocation and distribution is not, however, maintained in practice by any of the three levels of government in the United States. True, under the heading of welfare, about 12 percent of which is paid for out of local taxes, municipal governments do make cash transfers to the poor. But they also adopt policies in which allocation and redistribution objectives are more or less deliberately joined. One might mention, for example, policies to encourage the wider distribution of services, such as medical and hospital care or education, that the majority of citizens regard as particularly meritorious, by providing them at less than full cost or perhaps entirely free. The redistributive effect of such policies can be explained most clearly in the case of education: in a given community, benefits are received by rich and poor families in equal amounts per child, but the rich pay far higher school taxes than the poor. Even where the redistribution objective is not consciously acknowledged, however, the effect is the same. Local governments provide the poor with more service benefits than they pay for in taxes and the rich with less. The local budget consequently redistributes real income from the rich to the poor.

3. See, for example, *ibid.*, Ch. 4.
4. See Roland McKean, "The Unseen Hand in Government," *American Economic Review*, June 1965, pp. 496–505.

The extent of this redistribution cannot be observed directly. It can be approximated, however, by estimating separately the incidence of local tax payments and the incidence of local expenditure benefits by income class and then comparing the two estimates. Using data for 1957, Netzer compared the incidence of the property tax with the distribution by income class of the local expenditure benefits it finances. He found that on the average, families with incomes below $7,000 received more in benefits than they paid for in taxes, while those with incomes above that level paid more in taxes than they received in benefits.[5]

Economists often assert that the function of redistributing income, like that of stabilization, should be left entirely to the federal government. They argue that the capacity of the lesser jurisdictions to redistribute income among their citizens is limited severely by the mobility of both taxpayers and expenditure beneficiaries. A city that taxes the rich to provide benefits for the poor to a greater extent than other cities do will tend to attract the poor and repel the rich. This response may well make redistribution at the local level a self-defeating process. Nevertheless, as we have seen, local communities *do* engage in a degree of income distribution. Partly they can get away with it because not all resources are highly mobile. Partly they do not get away with it because mobile resources *do* sometimes move when local fiscal pressure becomes sufficiently heavy. As we will see below, the self-defeating nature of locally financed income redistribution is among the strongest arguments for reexamining the assignment of fiscal responsibilities within our multi-level system of government.

THE PROBLEM OF VERTICAL FISCAL IMBALANCE

We have noted already that the vertical aspect of the metropolitan fiscal problem is the result of a mismatch between functions and revenue-raising powers at the local level. To understand the nature of this mismatch we must look at both the expenditure and the tax revenue sides of the budget.

Rapidly Rising Expenditures

Local government expenditures have been rising very rapidly since the end of World War II. As Table 12.1 indicates, this is true of purely "allocative" functions such as police, fire, and sanitation services; of func-

---

5. Dick Netzer, *Economics of the Property Tax* (Washington, D.C.: Brookings Institution, 1966), pp. 59–62.

TABLE 12.1
Direct General Expenditure of Local Governments Compared with Gross National Product
(Fiscal Years)

	1949–50	1959–60	1970–71	COMPOUND ANNUAL RATE OF GROWTH (percentage)	
		(millions of dollars)		1950–60	1960–71
Gross national product [a]	$284,400	$503,700	$1,046,800	5.9%	6.9%
Total direct general expenditure [b]	14,763	34,090	94,196	9.0	9.7
Education	5,819	15,323	43,613	9.9	10.0
Public welfare	1,374	2,183	7,708	4.5	12.2
Health and hospitals	801	1,898	5,806	9.0	10.7
Highways	1,745	3,358	5,792	6.8	5.0
Police	691	1,612	4,430	8.8	9.6
Fire	488	995	2,303	7.9	7.9
Sanitation and sewerage	834	1,727	4,087	7.9	8.2
Parks and recreation	304	770	2,109	9.9	8.6
Housing and urban renewal	452	850	2,522	6.5	10.4
All other	2,246	5,374	15,826	9.1	10.3

[a] Calendar years 1950, 1960, 1971.
[b] Includes expenditures financed by intergovernmental aid; excludes expenditures of utilities, liquor stores, and insurance trust funds.
Sources: U.S. Bureau of the Census, *Census of Governments,* 1962, and *Governmental Finances* in 1970–71.

tions that combine allocative and redistributive intent, such as health, housing, and education; and of purely redistributive functions, such as welfare. Between 1960 and 1971 the rates of growth of expenditures on major functions varied from a high of 12.2 percent per year for public welfare to a low of 5.0 percent per year for highways. The combined total for all functions has regularly grown faster than the gross national product. Table 12.1 shows that between 1960 and 1971 local government outlays financed from all sources increased at a compound rate of 9.7 percent per year, while the gross national product rose at a yearly average rate of 6.9 percent. During the preceding decade expenditures had increased at a rate of 9.0 percent per year, while GNP rose 5.9 percent annually.

It will be helpful to have a formal measure for the relationship between changes in local government expenditures and changes in GNP. Let us define the GNP elasticity of local spending, E_{LS}, as follows:

$$E_{LS} = \frac{\text{percentage change in local government expenditure}}{\text{percentage change in GNP}}$$

The value of E_{LS} will be greater than one at any time when local government expenditures are increasing at a faster rate than GNP. From the data in Table 12.1 we can calculate that E_{LS} had a value of 1.40 between 1960 and 1971 and of 1.53 in the preceding decade.

The reasons for local expenditure growth are many and complex. For analytical purposes public expenditures may be regarded as the product of two factors: the number of units of service provided and the average cost of providing a single unit. Increases in both factors have contributed to the growth of total local expenditure. Consider first the growth in quantity of services provided.

Urbanization and the Demand for Public Service

In a highly urbanized society it becomes necessary for government to provide some services such as sewage disposal, water supply, and recreation facilities that in a rural or village society the individual often provides for himself. In addition urban society, because of its physical density and high level of socioeconomic interdependence, intensifies the need for such functions as police and fire protection, public health services, and public transportation. It is convenient to think of individual citizens as having demands for public service just as they have demands for such private goods as bread and shoes. Using the ordinary terminology of economic analysis we can then say that we would expect the per capita demand for units of local government service to increase rapidly simply as a result of the urbanization process itself.

Yet it seems likely that, quite apart from urbanization, rising living standards also have contributed to the relative growth in demand for public services. When living standards were low, as in the nineteenth century, people spent most of their incomes meeting the intense daily need for ordinary private goods such as food, clothing, and shelter. They held government spending to a bare minimum. As living standards rose, however, they chose to spend an increasing proportion of their income on the whole range of local government services, many of which were complementary to private spending. The increase can be viewed as a demand partly for a greater quantity of existing services, partly for better quality, and partly for the introduction of entirely new government functions. (In formal terms this amounts to arguing that the income elasticity of demand for government services—defined as the percentage change in demand for government services divided by the percentage change in income—has probably been greater than one.)

Rising Costs per Unit of Service

An increase in the per capita quantity of public services supplied undoubtedly accounts for much of the relative growth in local public expenditures during the twentieth century. However, in recent years the rising average cost of supplying each unit of service has also been a significant factor. Unit costs have been rising in the local public sector because public employees' wages and fringe benefits have gone up rapidly in recent years while output per employee has apparently risen little, if at all. The trend of wages is shown in Table 12.2, which compares monthly earnings in the local public sector with monthly earnings in manufacturing industries, from 1966 through 1971. Whether one looks at all cities, at cities with a population of 50,000 or more, or at the four largest cities— New York, Chicago, Los Angeles and Philadelphia—the percentage increase in monthly earnings is greater for municipal employees than for the national average of private sector manufacturing workers. If fringe benefits were included, in order to measure total compensation, the margin in favor of public employees would probably be still wider.

Although wages are rising faster in the public sector, output per employee is evidently increasing more rapidly in private industry. The result is that unit labor costs (which equal wages per man-hour divided by output per man-hour) have probably gone up much faster in the public than in the private sector. The relative rise in the unit labor cost of public services would then help to explain why local public expenditures have increased so much faster than the aggregate of public and private expenditures, as measured by GNP.

Admittedly, broad statements about cost per unit of output in the local public sector are difficult to substantiate because in many cases we

TABLE 12.2

Comparison of Monthly Earnings in Municipal Employment and in Manufacturing

	1966	1971	Percentage Increase, 1966–71
Average monthly earnings in common municipal functions [a]			
All cities	$505	$ 733	45.1%
Cities of 50,000 or more	557	811	45.6
New York City	674	999	48.2
Chicago	627	986	57.2
Los Angeles	736	1,009	37.0
Philadelphia	542	899	65.8
Average monthly earnings in U.S. manufacturing [b]	554	720	29.9

[a] Average for October of each year.
[b] Average of 12 months.
Sources: U.S. Bureau of the Census, *City Employment, 1966* and *1971,* Tables 2, 3, 4; U.S. Department of Commerce, *Survey of Current Business,* National Income Issue, July 1968 and July 1972, Table 6–5.

lack the measures of physical output needed to carry out precise unit cost calculations. Nevertheless, most analysts would agree with the conclusion reached by Bradford, Malt, and Oates, after a careful study of the available data, that "rising unit costs have been a major . . . source of recent increases in local public budgets." [6]

Local government activity is much more labor-intensive than is the output of the federal and state governments. Consequently, localities feel much more budgetary pressure when civil service wages rise than do the higher levels of government. Wage pressure in recent years has been greatly increased by the advent of municipal civil service unions. Wage demands by these unions are difficult to resist for two reasons. First, the unions typically control output of public services for which there are no ready substitutes and which cannot be stockpiled by consumers in anticipation of strikes. Second, they represent sizable blocs of local voters whom mayors are not eager to antagonize by taking a hard line against wage increases. Table 12.2 suggests that municipal civil service unions have helped public employees in large cities to obtain wage *increases*

6. D. F. Bradford, R. A. Malt, and W. E. Oates, "The Rising Cost of Local Public Services: Some Evidence and Reflections," *National Tax Journal,* June 1969, p. 201.

(though not necessarily wage *rates*) far in excess of those in private manufacturing.

Yet it is important to remember that the cost pressure on local governments is the result, not just of wage increases, but of wage increases combined with productivity lag. If municipal wages do no more than keep up with wages in private firms while output per man-hour fails to increase as fast in municipal employment, then unit costs will continue to rise faster in the public than in the private sector.[7] In effect, local expenditure will have to rise relative to GNP simply to maintain a given level of public service.

Unfortunately, there is no easy solution to this problem. On the one hand, municipal civil service unions are unlikely to become less militant. On the other hand, the very nature of public services such as education, the police, or hospitals and health makes it difficult to economize on the use of labor. Realistically, therefore, we must expect unit costs of local public services to continue to increase. And when increasing unit costs are combined with a continued rise in the quantity of service demanded, it seems clear that expenditure for services of the type now provided by local governments will continue to increase faster than GNP. (Whether some of those services will eventually be assigned to a higher level of government is another matter and will be discussed below.)

LOCAL GOVERNMENT REVENUE

Budgets involve income as well as outgo. Local government receipts, apart from borrowings, consist of local taxes, user charges, income from utilities and other enterprises, and aid from the state and federal governments. The yield from each of these sources is shown for selected years in Table 12.3.

If local governments are under financial pressure, it must result from some sort of mismatch between receipts and expenditures. The nature of the mismatch can best be understood if we ignore other sources and assume for the moment that local communities must raise all revenue from local taxes.

At this point some additional definitions will be helpful. Each local tax has its own tax base: the financial aggregate to which the tax rate is applied. In the case of the property tax, the base is the assessed value of taxable local property. For a retail sales tax, the base is the annual value of taxable retail sales. The yield of any tax is the product of the base times the rate.

7. See William J. Baumol, "Macroeconomics of Unbalanced Growth: the Anatomy of Urban Crisis," *American Economic Review*, June 1967, pp. 415–26.

TABLE 12.3
Local Government Revenues
(Fiscal Years)

	(millions of dollars)			COMPOUND ANNUAL RATE OF GROWTH (percentage)		DISTRIBUTION BY SOURCE, 1970–71 (percentage)	
	1949–50	1959–60	1970–71	1950–60	1960–71	Total General Revenue	Tax Revenue
Total general revenue [a]	$14,014	$33,026	$91,964	8.9%	9.7%	100.0%	—
Tax revenue	7,984	18,081	43,434	8.5	8.3	47.2	100.0%
Property tax	7,042	15,798	36,726	8.4	8.0	39.9	84.5
Sales and gross receipts taxes	484	1,339	3,662	10.7	9.6	4.0	8.4
Income tax	64	254	1,747	14.8	15.6	1.9	4.0
Licenses and other taxes	394	692	1,289	5.8	5.8	1.4	3.0
Charges and miscellaneous general revenue	1,602	4,831	14,058	11.7	10.2	15.3	—
Intergovernmental revenue	4,428	10,114	34,473	8.6	11.8	37.5	—
From federal government	211	592	3,391	10.8	17.2	3.7	—
From state governments	4,217	9,522	31,081	8.5	11.3	33.8	—

[a] Excludes revenues from utilities, liquor stores, and insurance trust funds.
Sources: U.S. Bureau of the Census, *Census of Governments*, 1962, and *Governmental Finances in 1970–71*.

Just as we defined the GNP elasticity of local expenditures, so we can define a GNP elasticity for each local tax. This measure, E_{LT}, indicates the relationship between changes in the revenue from a tax and changes in GNP, on the assumption that tax *rates* and the definition of the base are held constant. Thus,

$$E_{LT} = \frac{\text{percentage change in local tax revenue}}{\text{percentage change in GNP}}$$

The reason revenue from a particular tax changes when GNP changes, even though tax rates and definitions are held constant, is that economic growth usually causes growth in the tax base. Thus E_{LT} can be thought of as a measure of tax base elasticity as well as a measure of revenue elasticity with rates held constant.

We can now see that if the value of E_{LT} for the aggregate of taxes were equal to the value of E_{LS} for the aggregate of expenditures, and if all expenditures were paid for out of tax revenues to start with, then local governments could finance the growth of expenditures as GNP increased year by year with no increase in tax rates. This happy circumstance would prevail because the growth of GNP would induce just enough expansion of the local tax base to provide the revenues needed to pay for growing expenditures. In fact, however, the value of E_{LT} in the years since World War II has been far below the value of E_{LS}, and this contributes to the persistent financial pressure under which local governments have been operating.

It should be pointed out that the GNP elasticity of expenditure may depend in part on the GNP elasticity of the tax base. When the latter is smaller than the former, it probably exerts a restraining influence: expenditures will increase less rapidly when the increase requires a higher tax rate.

The value of E_{LS}, the GNP elasticity of local government expenditures, can be calculated directly from readily observable data on total local expenditures and GNP. We have already seen that it has been about 1.4 in recent years. Tax elasticity is more difficult to calculate since the object is to measure changes in the size of the tax base, with definitions and rates held constant, rather than changes in observable tax revenue. As Table 12.3 shows, the property tax accounts for about 85 percent of local tax revenue. Estimates of its GNP elasticity for the United States as a whole vary from a low of 0.8 to a high of 1.3, but the majority of such estimates place its value in the range between 0.8 and 1.0. Sales and gross receipts taxes rank second in importance, producing 8 percent of local tax revenue. On a nation-wide basis the general sales tax is estimated to have an elasticity of between 1.0 and 1.27, with the majority of estimates falling at precisely 1.0. Except for the income tax, which accounts for only 4 percent of local tax revenue, the other sources of general revenue (other than intergovernmental aid), such as taxes on particular commodities and miscellaneous fees and charges, probably have elasticities well below unity.[8] When these parts are added together it appears that E_{LT} for the aggregate of local taxes and charges is at most about 1.0 and perhaps somewhat less.

With an expenditure elasticity of about 1.4 and a tax elasticity of 1.0 or less it is clear that local governments would find themselves under constant pressure to raise tax rates or adopt new taxes if they had to finance the growth in expenditure entirely from local revenue sources. Fortunately, a substantial part of the gap between rapidly growing outlays and slowly growing tax bases has been covered by grants from the federal and state governments. As Table 12.3 shows, intergovernmental grants have been one of the fastest growing categories of local revenue. By 1971 they supplied 37 percent of local receipts as compared with only 32 percent in 1950.

Since the growth of intergovernmental grants does not close the gap entirely, tax rates at the local level have been increasing steadily. With thousands of overlapping local governments collecting many different taxes, it is impossible to calculate a meaningful average local tax rate with which to measure this trend. The best that can be done is to approximate the trend from indirect measurements. Let us assume that E_{LT} has had a value of 1.0—a generous estimate—during the last two decades. In that case, if tax rates had remained constant from 1950 to 1971 and no new taxes had been added by local governments, the percentage change in tax revenues would have equaled the percentage change in GNP. The latter increased by 268 percent. If local tax revenues had increased by the same percentage they would have amounted to $29.4 billion in 1971. In fact they rose to $43.4 billion. This implies rate increases (plus new taxes adopted) of 48 percent (since $43.4 \div 29.4 = 1.48$). If we assume that E_{LT} had a value of only 0.9 instead of 1.0, then the figures imply a tax rate increase of 60 percent instead of 48 percent.

Revenue Growth at Higher Levels of Government

We described earlier the vertical problem in metropolitan finance as resulting from the mismatch between the assignment of functions and the distribution of revenue-raising powers among the three levels of government. The fact that the higher levels of government have been able to finance a sharp increase in grants to the local sector is evidence of this mismatch. Historically, the situation of the federal government has been just the reverse of that of the localities. Because Washington relies so heavily on a progressive income tax for revenue, the GNP elasticity of the

8. These estimates were compiled from a variety of sources by the Advisory Commission on Intergovernmental Relations. See Commission Report No. M–74, *State-Local Finances: Significant Features and Suggested Legislation, 1972 Edition,* Table 134, p. 301.

federal tax base as a whole is very high. As living standards rise with the growth of the economy, families move into higher tax brackets and pay a larger percentage of their incomes in tax. Consequently, federal income tax receipts increase much more rapidly than family incomes do as the economy grows, and a 1 percent rise in GNP leads to much more than a 1 percent rise in total federal revenues. Until recently, except during periods of hot war, federal revenues at given tax rates consistently grew faster than federal expenditures on existing programs. A growth-induced surplus, or "fiscal dividend," was therefore available, which could be disposed of either by cutting tax rates or developing new programs. Consequently the federal government was able to take care of its own needs, increase its grants to state and local governments, and at the same time gradually *reduce* federal income and excise tax rates. Since the mid-1960's, however, federal spending for domestic purposes has grown much more rapidly than before. With normal expansion of currently existing programs, it appears likely that federal expenditures in the near future will rise at least as fast as federal revenues can be expected to grow with a given tax structure. The fiscal dividend out of which new programs or tax cuts could be financed has at least temporarily disappeared.[9]

As far as the balance between needs and resources is concerned, state governments are somewhat better off than the localities but not so well off as the federal government. States can and do make use of income taxes at mildly progressive rates, while local governments rarely do. This makes for a somewhat greater tax elasticity for state governments. Nevertheless, the states have had to increase their tax rates markedly in order to finance their rapidly growing expenditures. These expenditures, of course, include sharply increased state aid to localities.

The vertical problem then comes down to this: at the federal level, the supply of revenue grows fast enough to finance a substantial increase in expenditures, including aid to lower levels of government, without increased tax rates. At the state and local levels, expenditures tend to grow faster than the supply of revenue at constant tax rates plus aid from the federal government. Consequently, tax rates must be increased regularly and new taxes adopted in order to avoid deficits.

Why Not Let Local Tax Rates Rise?

The steady, seemingly inexorable increase in tax rates probably explains why we so frequently hear the term "fiscal crisis" applied to the current budgetary problems of local government. However, we have been living through a period in which local expenditures increased at an un-

9. See Charles L. Schultze, *et al., Setting National Priorities: The 1973 Budget* (Washington, D.C.: Brookings Institution, 1972), Chs. 12, 13.

precedented rate without causing more than a few public authorities to miss payment of their bills. Why should this successful expansion of programs be described as a "crisis"? The answer is quite simple. Historical experience teaches us that a "fiscal crisis" exists whenever, in the space of a few years, a government finds it necessary repeatedly either to raise its tax rates or to institute new levies. Such has been the unhappy fate of local governments in recent years. The federal government, too, has greatly increased its expenditures, but it has thus far done so to the accompaniment of falling tax rates. Consequently, one does not hear the federal budget situation described as a "crisis."

Yet we must ask ourselves why we should be especially concerned about the local "fiscal crisis." Is it just a matter of psychology, a sort of "tax illusion" under which people feel the pain of rising rates on a fixed base more intensely than the pain of stable rates on a growing base, even though the latter combination may increase the dollar amount of their tax payments more rapidly than the former? The answer is "no"; we are concerned not about the psychology of taxpayers but about the real consequences of the fiscal pressure on local government. Three of these are of major importance.

The burden of property taxes. First, there is the special problem of the property tax, a levy that accounts for 85 percent of local tax revenue. Other taxes are possible at the local level, and some might be preferable to the present form of the property tax. Unless these are adopted and used aggressively, however, higher local tax rates will continue to mean higher property taxes, and the property tax has many drawbacks. Undoubtedly its worst feature is the burden it puts upon housing.[10] A 3 percent tax on the market value of housing is approximately a 25 percent tax on housing rent before tax. In large cities the rate is frequently even higher. In view of our general dissatisfaction with housing standards and our national commitment to improve them, a consumption tax of 20 percent to 30 percent on housing services is, to say the least, paradoxical.

It is true that housing services receive some offsetting tax advantages as compared with other forms of consumption because they are exempt from retail sales taxes and are treated favorably under the personal income tax. Since sales taxes average only about 5 percent, the offsetting advantage in that case is a relatively small one. Favorable treatment of owner-occupied housing under the income tax, however, is a more important matter. As we explained in Chapter 3, this tax benefit has two parts. On the one hand, owner-occupants are not taxed on the imputed net annual rental value of their home. On the other hand, they are allowed to deduct

---

10. For an analysis of the impact of the property tax on urban housing and of the effects of possible property tax reforms, see James Heilbrun, *The Real Estate Tax and Urban Housing* (New York: Columbia University Press, 1966).

from taxable income the interest and property tax costs of owning the home, even though these are really costs of generating the imputed rental income on which they are *not* being taxed. The tax saving to the owner-occupant is greater the higher his tax bracket.

The combination of heavy property taxes on all housing plus off-setting benefits to owner-occupants thus results in two biases: it favors high income versus low income owners, and it favors owners as a whole versus renters. For wealthy owners the combination may well encourage housing consumption. For low income renters, who make up a large proportion of the ill-housed, it certainly has the very undesirable opposite effect.[11]

The problem of maintaining progressivity. A second issue that arises in connection with vertical fiscal imbalance is the preservation of progressivity for the tax system as a whole. A tax system is called progressive if it takes an increasing proportion of income from an individual as his income increases. It is called regressive if the proportion paid in taxes drops as income increases. The American tax system as a whole is only mildly progressive. The federal sector is moderately progressive due to the influence of the personal and corporate income taxes. The state and local systems taken together are mildly regressive, however, since they rely heavily on sales, excise, and property taxes. Incidence estimates for both sectors and for the system as a whole as of 1961 are presented in Table 12.4. If we examine the row showing total for all taxes, we see that from the lowest income class up to the $10,000 level there is virtually no progression. The regressive impact of state and local taxes almost wholly offsets the progressive effect of the federal structure over that range.

The reader should be warned that the numbers in Table 12.4 are, indeed, "estimates." The incidence of taxes on various income classes cannot be observed and measured. It can only be estimated on the basis of numerous assumptions about economic behavior, some of which are arbitrary and controversial. However, if the estimates in Table 12.4 are even approximately correct, it is clear that the long-run effect of a tendency to hold federal income tax rates constant, or even to reduce them, while raising state and local sales, excise, and property tax rates will be to render the system as a whole less and less progressive. Given our national commitment to reduce poverty, this, too, would be a paradox.

The problem of "tax competition." The third problem arising from the vertical mismatch between expenditure responsibilities and tax resources concerns what is called "tax competition" among local governments. Business firms frequently enjoy a degree of freedom in the choice

11. See Dick Netzer, "Housing Taxation and Housing Policy," in Adela A. Nevitt, ed., *The Economic Problems of Housing* (New York: St. Martin's Press, 1967), pp. 132–34.

TABLE 12.4
Taxes As a Percentage of Total Income: Estimates for 1961 for All Families, by Income Class [a]

| | INCOME CLASS | | | | | | | | | |
	Under $2,000	$2,000 to 2,999	$3,000 to 3,999	$4,000 to 4,999	$5,000 to 5,999	$6,000 to 7,499	$7,500 to 9,999	$10,000 to 14,999	$15,000 and Over	Total
Federal taxes, total	12.8%	14.1%	17.4%	17.8%	18.4%	18.4%	19.1%	21.8%	35.7%	20.2%
Individual income tax	2.0	3.4	4.9	7.0	7.5	8.4	9.6	10.9	17.6	9.0
Other federal taxes	10.8	10.7	12.5	10.8	10.9	10.0	9.5	10.9	18.1	11.2
State and local taxes, total	14.4	12.2	12.0	11.3	11.0	10.3	9.7	9.1	8.4	10.3
Property taxes	6.7	5.1	4.7	4.2	4.0	3.8	3.5	3.1	2.4	3.8
Sales and excise taxes [b]	5.7	5.3	5.3	4.9	4.9	4.5	4.2	3.8	2.5	4.3
Other state and local taxes	2.0	1.8	2.0	2.2	2.1	2.0	2.0	2.2	2.8	2.2
Total, all taxes,	27.3	26.3	29.4	29.1	29.4	28.6	28.7	30.9	44.1	30.5

[a] See original source for definitions and for assumptions on which these incidence estimates are based.
[b] Also includes some other minor taxes.
Source: *Tax Burdens and Benefits of Government Expenditures by Income Class, 1961 and 1965* (New York: Tax Foundation, Inc., 1967), Table 3, p. 14.

of location—not that any place is as good as any other, but there may be many almost as good as the best. Consequently, local governments fear that if they impose on business tax burdens much above those prevailing in other places, they will find firms moving away and the tax base shrinking. Even businesses that serve a local market may be able to move within the metropolitan area to reduce tax costs. As we will see below, families, especially the well-to-do, also may move in response to tax differentials. Therefore, introducing a local income tax in order to avoid raising property taxes or other levies that affect business may not eliminate the revenue-base erosion that results from taxpayer mobility.

It is probable, although it cannot be proven, that the fears associated with tax competition have, as Netzer puts it, "restrained the increase in local taxes and thus have had feedback effects on the output of public services." [12] These fears are related inversely to the size of the taxing jurisdiction. The federal government can ignore the remote possibility that higher taxes will drive resources out of the country. States are sensitive to the potential mobility of taxpayers but have less to fear than localities. Businesses serving local markets and wealthy taxpayers commuting to local jobs are less likely to be able to move across state lines than across municipal boundaries in response to tax differentials. Thus, because of tax competition, the vertical mismatch between tax resources and expenditure needs may lead to a smaller provision of public services than would occur if more of the required revenue were to be raised by higher levels of government.

It should by now be clear that a general solution to the vertical problem in metropolitan public finance must involve either shifting the responsibility for some major functions upward to higher levels of government, or increasing the downward flow of grant funds to local governments, or some combination of these policies. We will return to a discussion of these alternatives after examining the horizontal dimension of the metropolitan fiscal problem.

THE PROBLEM OF GEOGRAPHIC DISPARITIES BETWEEN NEEDS AND RESOURCES

The horizonal problem has two quite distinct aspects. The first is the geographic disparity between needs and resources across the map of local areas. The second is the haphazard jurisdictional arrangement of local governments. We will take them up in that order.

12. Dick Netzer, "Federal, State and Local Finance in a Metropolitan Context," in Harvey S. Perloff and Lowdon Wingo, Jr., eds., *Issues in Urban Economics* (Baltimore: Johns Hopkins Press, 1968), p. 444. Concerning the effects of tax differentials on business location, see Netzer's extensive citations on the same page.

Because local government plays such an important role in American life, geographic inequality in the distribution of local needs and resources is a serious issue. Rich towns can provide a higher level of service than poor ones. It may not matter *who* you are, but it does matter *where* you are. From the point of view of the individuals and social classes involved this appears to be an inequity, a denial of social justice. From the point of view of society it is more than that: the maldistribution of local resources impedes progress toward achieving major social goals such as better education, improved health, and reduced poverty.

Within metropolitan areas the distribution of resources and population between central cities and suburban rings has been shifting rapidly. As we pointed out in Chapter 8, the influx of the poor to the central cities, combined with the outward migration of middle and upper income families to the suburbs, has reversed the earlier pattern in which median family income was higher in central cities than in the ring. Today income levels are distinctly higher in the suburbs, and the gap is widening steadily. (See Table 8.4.) At the same time, under the influence of forces described in earlier chapters, business as well as personal wealth has been dispersing to the suburbs.

The casual observer may suppose that despite the dispersal of industry and middle and upper income population to the suburbs, the typical central city, with its towering CBD and dense development, must have a stronger property tax base than the suburbs. In fact, such is not the case. Netzer compared per capita property tax values in outlying portions of SMSA's and in central cities for 32 large SMSA's in the period from 1957 through 1961. According to his estimates, values were higher in the ring areas in 18 out of 32 cases, equal in 2 cases, and lower in only 12. In the Northeast and North Central regions, where the older and larger central cities are concentrated, per capita suburban values were higher in 12 out of 15 cases. Ten of the 12 cases in which central cities had higher per capita values were in the newer metropolitan areas of the South and West, where, as Netzer puts it, "Much of the area beyond the frequently extensive central city boundaries is still largely rural," a factor that would make for lower outlying-area property values.[13] Given the continuous dispersion of industry, trade, and high income residence from central city to ring in recent decades, one would expect to find the ratio of per capita central city to suburban property tax values steadily declining. Although historical data on the subject are only fragmentary, Netzer shows that they confirm this expectation.[14]

Thus, whether we look at income or at property values, we see the

13. Netzer, *Economics of the Property Tax*, pp. 117–19.
14. *Ibid.*, pp. 119–20.

same picture: the per capita level is now lower in the central cities than in the ring areas of SMSA's, and the margin in favor of the ring grows steadily larger. In short, there is a widening tax-base differential in favor of the suburbs. This contrasts strongly with the situation 40 or 50 years ago. Then as now the data suggest that residential property value per capita was higher in the suburbs than in the central cities. But this disparity was offset by the overwhelming central city concentration of commercial and industrial property. Although the core cities then contained large populations of the immigrant poor, they were also centers of wealth that could be taxed for the support of local services. In recent decades, however, the evolving pattern of metropolitan settlement has inexorably turned the tables against them: the central cities house an increasing proportion of the nation's poor whom they must service out of taxes on a decreasing proportion of the nation's wealth.

The national commitment to eradicate poverty and reduce inequality depends heavily on programs for better education, improved health, and more effective social services. Local governments bear heavy responsibilities for these programs. Unfortunately, the tendency toward segregation of the national population by income classes at the local level automatically creates an inverse relationship between local expenditure needs and local financial resources. The poor are increasingly concentrated in the central cities, which, partly for that very reason and partly because of the dispersion of business activity, are increasingly at a disadvantage in financing the services that the poor require and that national policy commits us to provide for them. To finance an equal level of services from a smaller per capita tax base, poorer communities, if they received no compensating outside aid, would obviously have to tax themselves at a higher rate than their more well-to-do neighbors. The difficulty of doing so would tend to reduce their output of local public services below the level that would obtain if they had an ampler tax base. That the opposite situation obtains in the more well-to-do localities in no way compensates for this, since the issue is precisely one of maldistribution of needs and resources between communities.

Differences in "Tax Effort"

Localities do, of course, receive aid from higher levels of government in financing local services. However, as between central cities and suburbs or between richer and poorer communities outside central cities the pattern of distribution of such aid has not been such as to eliminate interlocal differences in needs and resources. Comparative studies suggest the following general pattern: among local jurisdictions outside central cities, expenditures per capita tend to be higher where property value per capita is higher; at the same time, property tax rates tend to be lower when property value per capita is higher. In effect, richer communities provide themselves with a higher level of service than do poor localities and succeed in doing so at lower rates of taxation.[15]

The central city versus suburb comparison is somewhat different. Central cities tend to spend more per capita than do suburbs in the same metropolitan areas.[16] However, their income and property value per capita tend to be lower. Central cities must tax themselves at a higher rate than do the suburbs in order to provide the going level of service. Netzer's comparison of estimated property values and property tax rates in 32 SMSA's cited above showed that property tax rates were higher in central cities in 24 cases, lower in 6 cases, and approximately equal to suburban levels in 2.

Additional evidence on this point that covers all local taxes rather than just the property levy comes from a study that compared local "tax effort" in the central cities and suburbs of the 22 largest SMSA's in 1962. "Tax effort" was defined as per capita local tax revenue divided by per capita local income. In 21 of the 22 cases, central city tax effort was greater than suburban tax effort. The mean rate of tax on per capita income was 7.6 percent in central cities as compared with 5.7 percent in suburbs.[17]

In all such comparisons one must allow for the possibility of "tax exporting" by local jurisdictions. This may occur, for example, when a tax is levied on local business property. If the taxed firm sells some of its output outside the local community it may, in effect, "export" some of the tax burden in the form of higher prices. Or, if the tax reduces profits and the firm is owned by nonresidents, some of the burden may be exported through lower dividends to outsiders. Netzer points out that the export percentage tends to be higher for central cities than for suburbs because a higher proportion of central city taxable property is commercial. In general, however, this difference in the capacity to export taxes is not large enough to eliminate the difference between local tax burdens in central cities and suburbs.[18]

---

15. *Ibid.*, pp. 124–27.

16. See, for example, Harvey E. Brazer, "Some Fiscal Implications of Metropolitanism," in B. Chinitz, ed., *City and Suburb* (Englewood Cliffs, N.J.: Prentice-Hall, 1964), p. 138.

17. Woo Sik Kee, "City-Suburban Differentials in Local Government Fiscal Effort," *National Tax Journal*, June 1968, pp. 183–89.

18. Dick Netzer, "Impact of the Property Tax: Its Economic Implications for Urban Problems," in Wm. E. Mitchell and Ingo Walter, eds., *State and Local Finance* (New York: Ronald Press, 1970), pp. 166–68.

The Effects of Redistributive Local Budgets

Up to this point the discussion of geographic disparities has concentrated on differences in the average level of taxes or the average level of expenditures between central cities and their suburbs. Average tax levels and average benefit levels within localities do not tell the whole story, however. We have already shown that local budgets tend to redistribute income from rich to poor by giving the poor more benefits than they pay for and the rich less.

We now wish to examine the process of income redistribution in greater detail and to show, in particular, how differences between communities in the average level of income interact with redistributive policies within localities both to create horizontal inequities—that is, violations of the ethical rule requiring equal treatment of equals—and to speed up the counterproductive process of tax base erosion.

Following the argument of James M. Buchanan, let us define fiscal pressure on the taxpayer as the difference between the sum he pays in taxes and the value of the benefits he receives.[19] Buchanan labels this difference the "fiscal residuum" of the individual. It is defined as positive if his tax payments exceed his benefits, negative if benefits exceed taxes, and zero if they are equal.

Table 12.5 presents a hypothetical comparison of the fiscal residuals received by taxpayers in two towns that differ in average level of income. Each town has three citizens. Wealthy taxpayers, each of whom owns residential property worth $50,000, are denoted W1, W2, W3. Poor taxpayers, whose residential property is worth only $5,000, are denoted P1, P2, P3. The wealthy town consists of two wealthy taxpayers and one poor one; the poor town reverses these proportions. Each town raises all its revenue by a 2 percent tax on residential property.

In each of the hypothetical towns benefits are distributed on an equal per capita basis (probably close to the actual circumstances for locally financed services in American cities). Since tax payments are proportional to wealth, while expenditure distribution is regressive to wealth, the rich in both towns pay more in taxes than they receive in benefits, while the poor receive more benefits than they pay for in taxes. Thus both towns redistribute income from rich to poor. The right-hand column labeled "fiscal residual or net gain" shows the extent of the redistribution. It indicates that both rich and poor are better off in the wealthy town. Each individual pays the same amount of tax no matter where he lives, but the benefit level is higher in the rich town because the tax base there

19. James M. Buchanan, "Federalism and Fiscal Equity," in R. A. Musgrave and C. S. Shoup, eds., American Economic Association, *Readings in the Economics of Taxation* (Homewood, Ill.: Richard D. Irwin, 1959), p. 99.

TABLE 12.5

Taxes and Expenditure Benefits As a Function of Local Per Capita Wealth: A Hypothetical Example

	Value of Residential Property	Tax Payments at 2% of Prop- erty Value	Benefits Received	Fiscal Residual or Net Gain
Wealthy Town				
Citizen W1	$ 50,000	$1,000	$ 700	−$300
W2	50,000	1,000	700	−300
P1	5,000	100	700	+600
Total	$105,000	$2,100	$2,100	0
Poor Town				
Citizen P2	$ 5,000	$ 100	$ 400	+$300
P3	5,000	100	400	+300
W3	50,000	1,000	400	−600
Total	$60,000	$1,200	$1,200	0

is larger. In the wealthy town the poor man enjoys a net gain of $600 via the public budget. If he lived in the poor town he would gain only $300. In the wealthy town the rich men lose $300 on account of budgetary transactions. Their counterpart in the poor town loses $600.

Thus, differences in the fiscal resources of local communities, when coupled with redistributive tax-expenditure systems, create inequities: people of like income or wealth status are treated differently by the local government depending on whether they happen to live in a rich or a poor community. This is the equity problem in local public finance.

These differences in treatment in turn lead to the problem of tax base erosion. Both rich and poor could improve their situation by moving from poorer to richer communities. The rich are able to do so at their own option. The poor can do so also, if the move involves migrating from the relatively low income areas of Appalachia, Puerto Rico, and the rural South to the relatively more affluent northern or western central cities. But within a given metropolitan area the situation is different. The rich are able to improve their fiscal lot by moving from the central city to the suburbs, where the average income level is still higher. But the poor are effectively prevented from following them, not just by racial discrimination and large-lot zoning, but by the absence in the suburbs of a plentiful supply of the old, low rent housing on which they typically rely and by the high transportation costs required for suburban living. Selective migration consequently speeds the erosion of the central city tax base. Of course, this argument is not meant to suggest that the outward migration of the middle and upper classes is explained solely or even principally by calculations of tax-expenditure gain. But since we have sufficiently emphasized in earlier chapters the many other forces that are also at work, their repetition is not required here.

Thus far we have examined only the effects of differences in community income level. What happens if we also introduce differences in "redistributiveness"—that is, in the rate at which communities attempt to redistribute income via the local budget? It turns out that differences in redistributiveness affect the relative attractiveness of communities to rich and poor quite apart from differences in average community income level.

Obviously as between two localities where average income is the same, the poor will be better off in the one in which the budget is more redistributive and the rich in the one where it is less so. Differences in "redistributiveness" between any two towns, however, can offset the effects of differences in average income level in generating fiscal gains for either the rich or the poor family, but not for both, and in so doing will necessarily have the opposite effect on the choice presented to the other income class. Thus the low income family will prefer the rich community unless the poor town offsets its disadvantage in wealth level by redistributing income more strenuously than does the rich; but in that case the poor town becomes even more repellent to the well-to-do. The latter will prefer the poor town if it is sufficiently less redistributive than the rich one; but in that event the poor town becomes even more repellent to families of low income.

Within our large metropolitan areas, the first case seems currently more relevant than the second. The war on poverty, coupled with the nation-wide effort to overcome the accumulated harm of centuries of discrimination, puts the older central cities, with their concentrations of the impoverished and of ethnic minorities, under great pressure to direct more and more public resources to the benefit of the lowest income classes. Thus they face a painful dilemma: if they spend more on the poor, they increase the fiscal pressure that encourages the rich to move out, thus eroding the tax base and undermining future prospects for those who remain; if they attempt to defend the tax base by choosing policies that are less redistributive, they fail in their obligation to press the war against poverty and inequality.

These difficulties are compounded by the considerable mobility of business firms within metropolitan areas. Businesses are not likely to perceive much direct benefit to themselves from that part of the local budget that finances services to individuals. Thus if central cities in their effort to increase service levels for the poor raise tax rates on business much above those in the surrounding suburbs, they simply hasten the dispersion of industry that is already under way for other reasons, thereby further encouraging tax base erosion.

Do the Suburbs "Exploit" the Central City?

The fiscal-spatial relationship between central cities and suburbs has often been discussed in terms of "exploitation." As Julius Margolis has put it:

> The central cities argue that the suburbanite crowds their streets, demands police and fire protection while he shops and works, and then retreats outside the municipal boundaries into his valuable residential property, which the central cities believe should be taxed to pay for these public services. The suburban governments argue that they must educate the boom baby crop of the commuter; they must protect his family and his property, but the lucrative tax base which should support these services—the factories and office buildings—is located in the central city.[20]

We have already noted that local public expenditures per capita are generally higher in central cities than in the surrounding ring areas. The initial evidence for "exploitation" was uncovered by Amos H. Hawley, who found a significant positive correlation between the proportion of ring population to central city population in metropolitan areas and the associated level of per capita central city expenditures.[21] This finding is consistent with the hypothesis that the daily "contact population" that enters from the suburbs caused an increase in the cost of "running" the central city.

Higher central city expenditures, however, do not suffice to support a finding of exploitation, since the daily contact population may add enough to central city taxable sales, income, and property to equal or even outweigh the extra service costs its presence imposes. This issue could be resolved only by attempting to apportion central city costs and revenues between the central city and the contact populations, an almost impossible task given the collective nature of so much public service consumption.

The case for exploitation rests much more firmly on other grounds. In Chapter 11 we described the exclusionary housing and land-use policies by which the suburbs have tried to prevent lower middle class and lower class families from moving in. This deliberate self-segregation by the sub-

20. Julius Margolis, "Metropolitan Finance Problems: Territories, Functions, and Growth," in Universities-National Bureau Committee for Economic Research, *Public Finances: Needs, Sources, and Utilization* (Princeton, N.J.: Princeton University Press, 1961), p. 256.

21. Amos H. Hawley, "Metropolitan Government and Municipal Government Expenditures in Central Cities," in Paul K. Hatt and Albert J. Reiss, Jr., eds., *Cities and Society*, rev. ed. (New York: The Free Press, 1957), pp. 773–82.

urban middle and upper classes reduces their own burdens at the expense of those remaining in the core cities. In that sense there is surely "exploitation."

Yet the word "exploitation" is itself inadequate. It has an almost exclusively ethical connotation, as of taking more or giving less than one ought to do. In fact, there is much more at stake than who pays the bills: the disparity between needs and tax-paying capacity at the local level is not only inequitable; it also reduces the commitment of resources we make toward meeting the national problems of inequality and poverty.

What can be done to overcome these disparities within metropolitan areas? Possible solutions to the major problems of metropolitan public finance will be taken up at length below. In addition, the reader should recall that in Chapter 11 we analyzed a variety of policies designed to open up the suburbs to poor and lower middle income families. One purpose of these policies is to give racial minorities the opportunity to exercise wider choice of residential location within metropolitan areas. There are sufficient arguments in favor of this as a matter of right, but, in addition, a relatively uniform geographic distribution of the poor (if one may speak in such crude terms) would also make it possible to use the entire metropolitan tax base in financing local services for that part of the population that does not "pay its own way." However, even the most active policies to open up the suburbs could hardly work fast enough to count as a solution to present metropolitan fiscal inequities.

To be sure, evolutionary forces, such as the aging of housing in the older suburbs, are already helping to bring about some movement of poor and lower middle income minority families into the suburbs and will continue to do so. But the dispersion of poverty that takes place as a result of natural evolutionary forces may well have its own unfortunate fiscal results. If low income families concentrate in a relatively small number of older suburban towns, those areas are likely to face the same sort of fiscal squeeze now endured by the central cities. The natural processes of metropolitan development are not likely to eliminate intra-metropolitan fiscal disparities in the foreseeable future.

THE PROBLEM OF ACHIEVING A RATIONAL ARRANGEMENT OF FUNCTIONS AND BOUNDARIES

We come now to the second aspect of the horizontal problem in metropolitan public finance: the haphazard, irrational arrangement of functions and boundaries at the local level. The extent to which present arrangements interfere with efficient public sector operation can best be understood if we review the various goals of local government and see what criteria for drawing boundaries and assigning functions must be met in order to achieve each of them. The goal of providing adequate services for those citizens too poor to pay their own way has already been discussed in detail. Four other objectives remain to be examined. It will become clear that in the assignment of functions and the drawing of boundaries there may be inescapable conflicts between the patterns that would maximize the fulfillment of each of the objectives taken separately. Any comprehensive "solution" is therefore likely to be a compromise involving only partial achievement of many desirable ends.

Providing the Optimum Level and Combination of Public Services

Producing the optimum level and combination of public services is the task of "allocation," described at the beginning of the chapter. For most public services there is not (nor could there be) a market through which individual demand would be more or less automatically registered and satisfied, as happens in the private sector. A political voting process must therefore be relied on to shape the provision of public goods and services in accordance with citizen preferences.

The "Tiebout Solution." It is tempting to argue that satisfaction of voters' preferences for public goods proceeds best when political jurisdictions are small and their populations are homogeneous in taste. As jurisdictions grow smaller, sensitivity of government to individual preferences is likely to increase because government and citizen are "closer." The possibility of homogeneity of tastes also increases as area size decreases, and the more homogeneous the desires of the population the more likely it is that the citizen who fits the local norm will find all his wants nicely fulfilled. In fact, as the late Charles M. Tiebout argued, if there are enough minor jurisdictions within a metropolitan area and if individuals are not denied the choice of locality through discrimination, zoning, or lack of income, one might expect people with similar preferences to flock together in order to create communities congenial to their particular set of tastes.[22] Clearly the "Tiebout solution" to the problem of preference satisfaction could only work if governmental units within metropolitan areas remained small and very numerous.

Economists have by now offered a variety of criticisms of the Tiebout solution. One of these goes directly to the question of preference satisfaction. From the high degree of daily mobility in the metropolitan way of life—the fact that many people work, live, and shop in three or more different jurisdictions—it follows that metropolitan residents regularly

22. Charles M. Tiebout, "A Pure Theory of Local Expenditures," in Mitchell and Walter, pp. 21–29.

consume public services in several places, while expressing their preferences through voting in only one. In these circumstances it is not clear that small homogeneous communities maximize the possibility of preference satisfaction for their resident citizens.

One might go further, however, and question just how much importance we should concede to the objective of satisfying local differences in the "taste" for public services. If we are moving toward acceptance of the idea that citizens are entitled as a matter of right to substantial equality in the level of public services no matter where they live, then we have already begun to chip away at differential preference satisfaction as a criterion. A community containing many retired couples may prefer to spend very little on schools, but if the state sets a standard, then the community cannot be allowed to express its preferences by violating the standard.

The wide variation in both the aggregate level and functional pattern of local expenditure is explained by a number of factors besides differences in local "tastes"—for example, by differences in per capita income, state and federal aid, and geographic and demographic characteristics. An upper middle class family may move from the central city to the suburbs because it finds public services there more suited to its "wants." But one suspects that a good deal of the improvement consists in being able to receive back as service benefit most of what it pays out to the local tax collector instead of seeing a substantial part of its tax payments go to provide services for the poorer families that do not "pay their way" in the tax-expenditure calculus, and who are found mostly in the central city. This is not an improvement that we can properly label as "better preference satisfaction," except to the extent that many people have a preference for not paying other men's bills.

Other things being equal, a maximum opportunity for satisfying individually different preferences for public services is, of course, desirable. But other things are not unaffected, if we maintain small jurisdictions for that purpose. For small jurisdictions within metropolitan areas certainly hamper effective area-wide planning, create demonstrable fiscal inequities, and may possibly prevent the realization of economies of scale in local government.

The problem of externalities. The process of satisfying local demand for public goods and services is seriously impeded by the existence of benefit and cost externalities, or spillovers. These occur when a service produced by one town for itself also yields benefits for or imposes costs on neighboring towns whose interests have not been taken systematically into account. Metropolitan areas are, by definition, densely settled, and the localities within them are systematically interdependent. In such a setting externalities are probably more the rule than the exception.

FIGURE 12.2

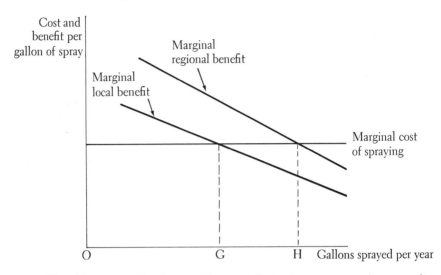

Consider a very simple case. Suppose that a town engages in mosquito abatement by means of chemical spraying within its own boundaries. The rational course of action for the single town would be to expand the program to the point where the marginal cost to the town of additional spraying just equals the marginal benefit to the town of the resulting additional abatement. The situation is depicted in Figure 12.2. The horizontal scale measures gallons of spray applied per year. The vertical scale shows marginal cost and marginal benefit (in dollars) for each additional gallon used. We assume that the cost of buying and spraying the chemical is constant per gallon. Hence the marginal cost curve is a horizontal straight line. The marginal benefit from incremental gallons of spray, however, declines over the relevant range because there are diminishing returns in mosquito abatement as more gallons are used. From the town's point of view optimum program size is OG gallons per year. To the left of G marginal town benefit exceeds marginal town cost: it pays to continue expanding the program. To the right of G marginal town benefit is less than marginal town cost: the program has been overexpanded. The optimum from the town's point of view is therefore at the point where the two curves intersect and marginal town benefit and cost are just equal.

If we consider the welfare of society, however, rather than of the single town, the optimum-size program is larger. Mosquito abatement in one town confers external benefits on neighboring localities. Regional benefit equals the sum of town benefit plus benefit external to the town. Therefore the curve showing marginal regional benefit must lie above and to the right of the town benefit curve. From the point of view of society as a whole it would be desirable for the town to expand the program to point *H*, where marginal cost just equals marginal regional benefit. This case illustrates the general rule that when externalities exist ordinary decision-making processes usually lead to socially suboptimal outcomes.[23]

Benefit or cost spillovers probably exist for many urban public services. The subject of externalities has received a good deal of attention in recent years and will not be treated in detail here.[24] Suffice it to say that local education is now thought to produce nation-wide external benefits, local pollution control clearly yields external benefits over a wide region, and even the activity of the local police force in suppressing crime probably confers benefits far outside the local jurisdiction.

There are two responses to the problem of externalities in the public sector, either of which would help to overcome distortions due to geographic spillovers and bring us closer to the optimum level of output for a given service. (1) Enlarge the jurisdiction providing the service until it takes in most of the area over which significant cost or benefit spillovers occur. In this way externalities are "internalized," and the interests of the jurisdiction become identical with those of society. Therefore the enlarged jurisdiction could be expected to make socially optimal output decisions. (2) In the case of external benefits, arrange for a higher level of government to subsidize the local agency providing the service by means of open-ended, matching, functional grants.[25] In the case illustrated in Figure 12.2 it would be necessary to contrive a subsidy that would increase program size from *OG* to *OH*.

Supplying Public Services at Minimum Unit Cost

Whatever services are to be supplied to satisfy citizens' preferences ought to be produced at the lowest possible unit cost. It is therefore important to discover how unit cost varies with the size of the jurisdiction

23. Under-supply when external benefits exist, as in the text example, was once thought to be the general case. More recently it has been shown that with reciprocal externalities among suppliers, over-supply is also a possible outcome. See J. M. Buchanan and M. Z. Kafoglis, "A Note on Public Goods Supply," *American Economic Review*, June 1963, pp. 403–14; and Alan Williams, "The Optimal Provision of Public Goods in a System of Local Government," *Journal of Political Economy*, February 1966, pp. 18–33.

24. See, for example, the discussion in Werner Z. Hirsch, *The Economics of State and Local Government* (New York: McGraw-Hill, 1970), *passim.* and the sources cited therein.

25. The case for such "optimizing grants" has been set forth lucidly by George F. Break in *Intergovernmental Fiscal Relations in the United States* (Washington, D.C.: Brookings Institution, 1967), Ch. 3.

in the output of particular local services. Although it is difficult to measure the output of a public-service-producing agency, economists have published some useful studies of unit costs in recent years, and the question continues to receive a good deal of attention.[26] If the technical conditions of production are such that a range of decreasing unit costs is followed by a range of increasing unit costs as the size of the jurisdiction increases, then the average cost curve is U-shaped, and unit cost is lowest for a jurisdiction whose size corresponds to the bottom of the U. Thus, if the average unit cost curve for a particular public service is U-shaped, the minimum unit cost criterion can indicate the best jurisdictional size for that service. Of course, if average unit cost curves are approximately horizontal, indicating that unit costs do not vary with the scale of output, then this criterion becomes irrelevant.

The situation is made more complicated if we allow for the fact that "producing unit" need not be synonymous with "jurisdiction." It is sometimes possible for smaller jurisdictions to purchase services from larger ones or from large private contractors. In that way governmental units can remain small without sacrificing the possible advantages of economies of scale in the production of local services. This sort of arrangement, sometimes called the Lakewood Plan, has been used successfully in Southern California.[27]

It is important to note that the minimum unit cost criterion can indicate when jurisdictions are too large to be efficient as well as when they are too small. Further study of public service costs may reveal, for example, that very large cities are now encountering *dis*economies of scale in public output, and that unit costs could be reduced by the decentralization of production, at least for some public services. This is only speculation, however, and the recent strong interest in the decentralization of urban services takes its impetus less from considerations of economic cost than from a desire to increase democratic participation and to make government more accessible to the governed. These political objectives are the next category to be discussed.

Political Participation and Accessibility

Political as well as economic objectives must, of course, be taken into account in discussing the arrangement of metropolitan functions and boundaries. It is in the American tradition to favor small local governments on the ground that they encourage voter participation, are accessible to

26. See Hirsch, Chs. 7, 8.
27. See Robert Warren, "A Municipal Services Market Model of Metropolitan Organization," *Journal of the American Institute of Planners,* August 1964, pp. 193–204.

the citizen in the conduct of his daily business, and are sensitive to local needs. The influence of this very old tradition has been reinforced since the early 1960's by new demands within the larger cities for neighborhood government, community control, and administrative decentralization. Philosophic support for these demands has come from a new generation of radical critics who, almost without exception, seek to reduce central authority and return power to "the people" or "the community." [28]

No doubt there is an element of romanticism in all this, but no one who has lived in a large city is likely to dismiss the charge of excessive centralization or unresponsive bureaucracy as unfounded. Cautious as well as incautious observers these days are seeking ways to improve local government by redistributing functions and powers. As George F. Break has written:

> Among the major challenges to the U.S. federal system in the next few years, it now seems clear, will be the formation of more rational and effective systems of local government. While the solution of some of the most important urban problems requires integrated, areawide policy action, groups with special tastes and needs for public services are primarily concerned with local autonomy. What seems to be needed is some magic blend of centralizing and decentralizing changes that will create simultaneously both larger and smaller units of local government than any that now exist.[29]

It should be borne in mind, however, that public services differ greatly in the extent to which they involve politically sensitive issues. Voters by and large are not much interested in having access to the officials who operate the Fire Department, inspect meat markets, or distribute the water supply. On the other hand, they are most certainly concerned about access to the School Board and the Police Department. The criterion of political accessibility does not apply with equal force to all services.

Planning and Coordination

The metropolitan area is in its very nature an interconnected, organic whole. Consequently, many of its governmental functions ought to be planned on an area-wide scale. Transportation, recreation, and environmental protection are only the most obvious of these. A more ambitious reckoning would certainly include area-wide planning of land-use densities and housing policy.

---

28. See, for example, Milton Kotler, *Neighborhood Government* (Indianapolis: Bobbs-Merrill, 1969).

29. George F. Break, "Changing Roles of Different Levels of Government," in Universities-National Bureau Committee for Economic Research, *The Analysis of Public Output* (New York: Columbia University Press, 1970), p. 182.

The typically fragmented pattern of metropolitan jurisdictions makes such planning very difficult. Local units, sanctioned by the strong tradition favoring the right to local self-government, can often prevent effective action being taken on a metropolitan-wide scale. Nevertheless, area-wide planning *is* on the increase. Partly this results from a growing recognition that in the long run planning and coordination can be in everyone's interest; partly it results from pressure applied by the federal government. Since the mid-1960's many federal grant programs have carried the stipulation that recipient local projects must be part of a comprehensive regional plan, and special grants have been made available to help finance new metropolitan planning agencies.

Meanwhile, within the larger cities, the new drive for neighborhood autonomy and decentralization has further complicated the process of planning and coordination. This movement had its origins in neighborhood opposition to the incursions of highway and urban renewal schemes. Its success in halting many of these projects has made both planners and politicians highly sensitive to the need for reconciling conflicting interests as part of the planning process. Of course, there is no technically "correct" way of doing that, if it can be done at all. This nicely illustrates the conflict between the various objectives of local government: if we increase the number of minor jurisdictions in order to maximize the formal representation of neighborhood interests we run the risk of seriously impeding large-scale urban planning.

A SUMMARY OF THE MAJOR FISCAL PROBLEMS

Very briefly, the three major problems of metropolitan public finance are:

1. The vertical mismatch between the assignment of functions and the distribution of revenue-raising powers among the three levels of government.
2. The geographic disparities between needs and resources of local jurisdictions.
3. The haphazard, irrational arrangement of functions and boundaries of local governmental units.

In recent years, numerous major reforms have been proposed, and one has been enacted, to meet these problems. Some of these reforms promise to mitigate several problems at once. Thus, while we have several stones to kill each bird, we also have some that will probably bring down more than one bird at a time. In short, the solutions are interrelated and must be discussed as nearly as possible simultaneously. Let us begin with reforms intended to relieve the vertical problem.

RELIEVING THE VERTICAL PROBLEM

As we have shown already, the mismatch between functions and revenue-raising powers has had several unfortunate consequences. Over a period of more than two decades, state and local tax rates have risen rapidly, while federal tax rates were periodically reduced. This has made the aggregate U.S. tax system more regressive, may have slowed the expansion of local public services to an undesirable extent, and has certainly increased the property tax burden, which, in turn, reduces housing consumption and restrains the improvement of housing standards.

Several solutions to the vertical problem were discussed intensively from the mid-1960's on, and one proposal, general revenue-sharing, was finally adopted in 1972. Since this single act is unlikely to make more than a moderate dent in the problem, other proposals remain very much alive and worthy of careful comparison with it.

Reforms intended to mitigate the problem of vertical mismatch fall into two groups. Those in the first are strictly financial. They would increase greatly the flow of funds from the federal government to states and localities as a way of relieving financial pressure on the lower levels of government. But they would do this without much altering the mix of functions for which each level traditionally accepts significant financial responsibility. Included in this group are three major proposals: (1) general revenue-sharing, which has already been enacted; (2) an increase in conditional grants; and (3) a revision of the Internal Revenue Code to allow a federal tax credit for income taxes paid to state and local governments.

Revenue-Sharing

Revenue-sharing is a system of relatively unrestricted federal grants to the state and local governments. The idea was first developed by Walter W. Heller and Joseph A. Pechman in the mid-1960's as a way of using expected surplus federal tax revenues to relieve financial pressure on state and local units.[30] When the war in Vietnam eliminated the expected federal surplus, the proposal was temporarily shelved. It was revived later in a somewhat different form by President Nixon, who renamed it "General Revenue-Sharing" (to distinguish it from his plan for "Special Revenue-Sharing," which we will discuss in connection with conditional grant programs).

The essence of general revenue-sharing is that it employs the federal tax base, with its high GNP elasticity, to supply funds that will relieve the pressure on the much more slowly growing state and local tax bases.

30. For a thorough statement of the case for revenue-sharing, see Walter W. Heller, *New Dimensions of Political Economy* (New York: W. W. Norton, by arrangement with the Harvard University Press, 1967), Ch. 3.

The State and Local Fiscal Assistance Act, adopted in the fall of 1972, authorizes $30.2 billion of federal funds for general revenue-sharing to be paid out in a series of installments covering the five years beginning January 1, 1972. Thus the Act provides an average of just over $6 billion per year in grant money to the states and localities. To put this sum in perspective, we must look at it as an increment to the total of $26.1 billion in federal grants received by state and local governments in fiscal year 1970–71. Clearly the program provides a substantial increase in the level of federal assistance. Just as clearly, the sums involved are not large enough to be thought of as "solving" the problem of vertical fiscal unbalance. That is why other programs to cope with the vertical problem will continue to find strong support.

Funds allotted to general revenue-sharing are granted to the states, and through them to all "general purpose" local governments. School districts and other special districts are thus not eligible for any part of the funds. The calculation of allotments has been summarized as follows:

> General Revenue Sharing funds are distributed among States on the basis of one of two formulas. The "three-factor" formula distributes the funds on the basis of population, tax effort, and per capita income. The "five-factor" formula includes two additional factors, urbanized population and State income tax collections. Each State amount is determined by the formula that maximizes its share. If the total of the shares is greater than the available authorization, all shares are reduced proportionally.
>
> Within the State one-third of all funds go to the State government, two-thirds to local governments. Distribution among local governments is based on the three-factor formula.[31]

It is an important feature of revenue-sharing that it redistributes income from rich states to poor. In part this results from the fact that allotments are weighted inversely to per capita state income. But some redistribution would occur even if each state's share were strictly in proportion to population, with no special adjustment for income levels. Poor states contribute a much smaller amount per capita to federal tax revenues than do rich ones. Since they contribute less per capita, but would receive back equal per capita benefits, they would clearly make net gains from equal per capita revenue-sharing as compared, let us say, with the alternative of having the federal government turn back a certain percentage of its income tax revenue to the state of origin.

31. Executive Office of the President, Office of Management and Budget, *The United States Budget in Brief, Fiscal Year 1974*, p. 55. A detailed explanation of general revenue-sharing formulas and procedures can be found in U.S. Department of the Treasury, Office of Revenue Sharing, *What General Revenue Sharing Is All About*, undated.

As originally conceived by Heller and Pechman, revenue-sharing allotments were to have "no strings attached," a system of completely "unconditional" grants. Advocates of revenue-sharing believed that federal aid to states and localities had relied excessively on "conditional" (also known as "categorical") grants. These were thought to involve too much red tape, to provide too little incentive for creative innovation in program design by the lower levels of government, and, through their matching provisions, undesirably to distort local choice among objectives. As finally passed by the Congress, however, general revenue-sharing did attach a few "strings." States may use the funds for any legal purpose except to match federal grants under other aid programs. Localities may use the funds only for "priority" expenditures as defined in the statute. These include (1) ordinary and necessary capital outlays and (2) maintenance and operating expenditures for public safety, environmental protection, public transportation, health, recreation, libraries, social services for the poor or the aged, and financial administration—a list long enough to be relatively unconfining. In addition, the fungibility of funds makes it impossible in the long run to say which dollar went where. If revenue-sharing funds are applied, let us say, to public safety, then funds that otherwise would have gone for that purpose can be used for another not eligible for revenue-sharing support.

Some opponents of revenue-sharing contend that states and localities will be more apt to waste such funds than monies raised through their own tax effort. Although there may be a problem here, this way of putting it is mistaken. Since each state's and locality's allotment under revenue-sharing is fixed by a legislated formula, the grant it receives is truly a "lump-sum" payment. Economists are in rare agreement in stating that lump-sum payments do not distort behavior at the margin. If a locality receiving revenue-sharing funds spends money wastefully, the dollars it wastes are the marginal dollars it raised through taxation, which it need not have raised had it been less wasteful, not the dollars it receives willy-nilly from the federal government. Perhaps an analogy will make the point more clearly. If a policeman aged 50 retires from the force on a fixed pension and supplements that by working at another job, we do not suppose that he spends his money less responsibly on account of the pension than he would if he earned all of it by working.

It can be argued, however, that intergovernmental aid does lead to a certain weakening of moral fiber at the lower levels of government. The more such aid becomes an accepted fact of life, the more local public officials seem tempted to blame all their troubles on its inadequacy. Blaming Washington or the state capital for insufficient aid becomes the all-purpose response to criticism. It is unclear how much real effect this rhetoric has. Unfortunately, if voters find it persuasive, they may fail to hold local officials responsible for keeping their own house in order. And since local government is now a large-scale enterprise by any economic standard, keeping it in order is an economically important task.

Conditional Grants

The second major proposal for enlarging the flow of funds from the federal to the state and local governments is simply to increase conditional grants more rapidly than heretofore. Advocates of this position argue that the federal government has both a duty and a right to set national standards for the use of funds it supplies. They incline to the view that the federal government has promoted socially useful innovation more often than the state and local governments and contend that it is demonstrably less subject to either outright corruption or manipulation by special interests. Consequently they believe that a considerable degree of federal oversight of grant programs is desirable.

A frequent criticism of conditional, or categorical, grants has been that the number of separate grant programs, each with its own narrowly defined objectives and specific matching requirements, has multiplied out of all reason. This criticism can be met rather easily, however, by adopting a consolidated grant framework along the lines proposed by President Nixon. Within major functional areas, such as urban community development, education, manpower training, and law enforcement and criminal justice, his "Special Revenue-Sharing Program" would provide that grant programs be combined, matching provisions dropped, requirements simplified, and objectives broadened.[32] The federal government would thus retain the power of directing its funds toward nationally defined and ordered objectives while leaving more responsibility in the detailed choice of means to state and local officials.

Tax Credits for State and Local Income Taxes

The third financial proposal for relieving vertical fiscal imbalance calls for amending the federal income tax law to give taxpayers a credit against federal tax liability for some portion of the income taxes they pay to state and local governments. At present, taxpayers may count state and local income taxes paid among their itemized deductions. Such taxes may therefore be deducted fully from adjusted gross income in arriving at taxable income. This deduction allows the taxpayer to save an amount equal to the product of his state and local income tax payment times the highest federal tax bracket rate that he pays. For example, if he is in

32. See excerpts from the President's 1974 Budget Message in *The United States Budget in Brief, Fiscal Year 1974*, pp. 14–15.

the 20 percent bracket and deducts $100 in state income tax, he saves .20 × $100 = $20.00

Instead of a deduction from income, a tax credit, in effect, allows a deduction from tax liability. One widely discussed plan would allow a credit of 40 percent.[33] In that case the taxpayer cited above would be allowed to deduct from his federal tax liability 40 percent of his state and local income tax payments. He would save .40 × $100 = $40.00 as compared with $20.00 under present law. A taxpayer in the 40 percent rate bracket would neither gain nor lose by this change. Those below that level would benefit. Taxpayers in brackets above the 40 percent level would be allowed to continue using the itemized deduction instead of the tax credit and hence would be unaffected.

The purpose of the tax credit would be to encourage states and localities to use the income tax much more heavily than they have done in the past. The virtues of this tax are, of course, that it does not distort relative prices, that it can readily be made progressive, and that it has a GNP elasticity greater than one—characteristics not shared by the excise, sales, and property taxes that currently supply the bulk of state and local tax revenue. The tax credit would encourage heavier state and local use of the income tax by reducing its burden on the taxpayer: he could automatically recoup 40 percent of his state and local payments in the form of reduced federal liability. In effect, the federal government would be offering to match state and local income tax revenues without limit on a 40–60 basis. States not now using the tax would be encouraged to do so, and others would be inclined to use it more heavily.

As compared with revenue-sharing or conditional grants the tax credit proposal has a number of drawbacks. First, it is not redistributive among states: poor states, lacking the resources to support adequate public services, will be no better off than before. Second, the initial benefit goes to taxpayers. There may well be a lag before states or localities respond to the credit stimulus by raising rates. Indeed, some state constitutions currently prohibit the use of an income tax. Third, the proposal does little to overcome the expenditure-inhibiting effect of tax competition at the state and local level.

Reorganizational Proposals

We come now to the second group of proposals for relieving the problem of fiscal imbalance. These are essentially reorganizational rather than financial. Instead of relieving budgetary pressure at the lower levels

33. Advisory Commission on Intergovernmental Relations, *Federal-State Coordination of Personal Income Taxes*, Washington, D.C., October 1965, pp. 14–19.

by providing federal funds for all or a broad range of state and local services, these proposals would give relief by shifting to a higher level of government the major responsibility for a few. They would therefore radically change the mix of functions for which each level accepts important financial responsibility.

The case for radically altering financial responsibilities is based on a reassessment of the strengths and weaknesses of each level of government. As Richard Ruggles points out, "The federal government should be the instrument for developing national policy." [34] It is also an efficient instrument for collecting taxes and disbursing funds. It is not well suited, however, to administering the details of complex public service programs at the point of delivery. If the public decides that as a matter of national policy every citizen is entitled to a first-rate education, good health care, and relief from poverty, then, according to this line of argument, it is the duty of the federal government to guarantee that this takes place by providing sufficient funds so that, despite geographic differences in wealth, every locality will be well served at equitable tax rates. In the language of economic theory, such services as health and education have nation-wide externalities. Therefore decisions about the proper level of "output" must be reached nationally and made effective everywhere.

The strength of state and local government lies in the production, coordination, and delivery of public services at the regional and local levels. Therefore these governments should be entrusted with the administration even of those programs for which the federal government sets minimum standards and provides basic funds. If state and local governments wished to exceed the national standards they could do so by adding revenue from their own sources. For services not charged with a national interest, such as police and fire protection, sanitation, and correctional institutions, state and local governments should have both financial and administrative responsibility. With some or most of the burden for "national" services lifted from their shoulders, they would have no difficulty financing the rest of their needs.

A variety of proposals has been based on this sort of logic. The least sweeping and most likely to be adopted calls for the federal takeover of all welfare costs up to some acceptable national standard. Considerably more ambitious is the recommendation by the Advisory Commission on Intergovernmental Relations that the federal government assume all welfare costs and the state governments, thereby relieved of a heavy burden, in turn relieve localities of the major responsibility for the cost

34. Richard Ruggles, "The Federal Government and Federalism," in Harvey S. Perloff and Richard P. Nathan, eds., *Revenue Sharing and the City* (Baltimore: Johns Hopkins Press, 1968), p. 70.

of elementary and secondary education.[35] Most far-reaching of all is the suggestion by Ruggles that the federal government take over the costs, not only of welfare, but also of providing a minimum standard level of education and health care.[36]

SOLUTIONS TO THE PROBLEM OF GEOGRAPHIC DISPARITIES

The proposals discussed up to this point were presented as solutions to the problem of fiscal imbalance between the levels of government. They would also, in varying degrees, help to relieve the second fiscal problem of metropolitan areas—the geographic disparities between needs and resources among local jurisdictions. We have already explained the consequences of these disparities in detail. To summarize briefly: tax rates are generally higher and service levels lower in poorer communities. Central cities are generally poorer than their suburban rings and are losing ground steadily. High taxes encourage well-to-do families and mobile business firms to leave the central city, with the result that geographic disparities in wealth within metropolitan areas tend to be self-reinforcing. The poor are effectively barred from the wealthier suburbs and must therefore endure rising tax rates and deficient services in the central city.

The effect that geographic disparities in needs and resources have on local tax and service levels could be completely eliminated only in one way: by abolishing state and local taxes entirely and financing all local services out of federal funds, appropriately distributed to local authorities. Of course, no one advocates such a sweeping revolution in the American political system. A close approach to eliminating the effects of geographic disparities could be achieved, however, by less drastic means: federal and state grant programs could be made strongly inverse to the local income level and strongly dependent on the local need for service. Wealthy communities might still wish to provide themselves with a higher level of service than poor communities, but if grant levels were generous enough, remaining differences in tax rates and service levels would not be highly significant. However, neither revenue-sharing nor the conditional grant programs now in existence or suggested thus far are sufficiently redistributive or large enough in scope to make more than a modest start toward eliminating geographic fiscal disparities. Finally, the impact of geographic disparities could be reduced greatly by federal assumption of

35. Advisory Commission on Intergovernmental Relations, *Urban America and the Federal System*, Washington, D.C., October 1969, pp. 22–27.
36. Ruggles, pp. 62–68.

fiscal responsibility for welfare, education, and health outlays along the lines suggested by Ruggles.

Equalization at the State Level

It now seems almost certain that significant moves toward equalization will come first at the state level. In the case of *Serrano v. Priest*, the California Supreme Court in August 1971 held that to finance education by a local property tax violated the "equal protection" clauses of both the federal and the California constitutions. The court based this finding on the fact that local property-tax financing of education leads inevitably to great disparities among districts in the level of spending on education. (Subsequently, the case was returned to the trial court for further proceedings.) Similar suits have now been brought by aggrieved families in federal or state courts in a majority of states. The first federal case to reach the United States Supreme Court came from the state of Texas. In March 1973 that tribunal overturned the lower court decision in the case of *Rodriguez v. San Antonio School District* and held that the Texas school finance system, though based on the local property tax and fraught with inequalities, was not in violation of the federal Constitution.

The Texas decision, however, will certainly not halt the drive for equalization at the state level. Suits brought under state law have already been successful and cannot be appealed to the federal courts. For example, the New Jersey Supreme Court in April 1973 held that the state's system of educational finance failed to fulfill a mandate for equal educational opportunity in the state constitution. Furthermore, many states were already studying the possibility of full state assumption of all educational costs, or of other reforms to bring about greater educational equality, even before the recent flood of suits began. Under the pressure of court action, all will now be pushed in that direction.

It seems unlikely, moreover, that the drive for equality should stop with educational services. For if citizens have a right to equal provision of education within the state, why not also to equality in the provision of other essential public services? If this view represents the temper of the times, we should soon expect far-reaching changes in state-local fiscal relations, as the states move toward genuine equalization of the whole spectrum of local services.

Equalization Within Metropolitan Areas

Within metropolitan areas themselves geographic disparities in the capacity to support public services could be reduced or even entirely overcome by setting up some form of metropolitan-wide local government.

The degree to which such a government would overcome the effects of geographic fiscal disparities would obviously depend on the weight of the services for which fiscal responsibility was surrendered to it versus the weight of those (if any) for which such responsibility was retained by the smaller units. In recent years supporters of metropolitan unification have not been inclined to advocate setting up monolithic metropolitan regional governments. Instead, they have tended to favor less centralized forms such as metropolitan "federation." This is a two-tiered system in which some functions are assigned to the metropolitan government to be conducted uniformly throughout the region, while others are left to be performed within the discretion of the constituent local governments.

The best-known example of federation is the Municipality of Metropolitan Toronto. It was established in 1954 as a federation comprising the central city of Toronto and 12 suburbs. A reorganization in 1967 consolidated the 12 suburban municipalities into 5 Boroughs and increased the powers and responsibilities of the Metropolitan Government. The success of Metropolitan Toronto has undoubtedly stimulated interest in federation in the United States.

Under certain circumstances county governments in the United States appear to offer an alternative way of achieving two-tiered metropolitan government. In many cases an entire metropolitan area lies within a single county. It is then possible to use the existing county government as the metropolitan unit to which localities surrender selected functions.[37]

RATIONALIZING THE ARRANGEMENT OF LOCAL FUNCTIONS AND BOUNDARIES

The power to overcome geographic fiscal disparities is not the principal argument in favor of either federation or other two-tiered systems of metropolitan government. Rather, these sophisticated proposals are usually offered as the ideal solution to the third problem of metropolitan organization and finance—the haphazard and irrational arrangement of functions and boundaries at the local level.

Analysis of the problem of boundaries led to the conclusion that for each public service they should ideally be drawn so as to: (1) eliminate significant externalities; (2) minimize the unit cost of production; (3) provide political accessibility for services where that is important; (4) facili-

37. For a description of the Toronto experience as well as other versions of the "two-level" approach, see John C. Bollens and Henry J. Schmandt, *The Metropolis* (New York: Harper & Row, 1965), Ch. 15. An extended discussion of alternative plans for reforming the presently haphazard arrangement of local governments in the United States can also be found in the Advisory Commission on Intergovernmental Relations' report, *Urban America and the Federal System*, Ch. 4.

tate area-wide planning and coordination. Even for a single service these criteria may well conflict. For example, political accessibility is important in the case of public housing, indicating the desirability of small jurisdictions. Yet housing policies ought to be planned on a regional basis, which indicates the need for a single metropolitan jurisdiction. For each service, therefore, even in an ideal system, it might be necessary to compromise among objectives in drawing boundaries. A second round of compromise is necessary in combining many functions under the jurisdiction of one or a few local governments. The alternative of setting up a separate "government" for each function in order to enjoy the optimum size jurisdiction for each one is obviously absurd, since it would make planning and coordination of services at the local level virtually impossible and, by dividing power among a multitude of elected officials, would seriously weaken political accountability.

It is precisely these considerations that make federation or other two-tiered systems so attractive as a way of organizing the whole metropolitan public sector. Under a two-tiered system, functions with important externalities or economies of scale or requirements for area-wide planning would be assigned to the "central government" of the federation. Functions that lacked those characteristics, or in which political access was an over-riding consideration, would be left in the hands of the traditional, smaller local units. To the extent that fiscal equalization was also a goal of the federation, those services left for purposes of administration in the hands of the local governments could be financed in whole or in part by uniform federation-wide taxes. Unfortunately, however logical and attractive this scheme may appear to civic reformers and to students of economics and public administration, it has not yet impressed American voters sufficiently to be adopted in more than a few places.[38] Except for those instances in which the courts have been able to intervene on constitutional grounds, changes in the structure and performance of American local government occur more readily through gradual adaptation to new conditions than through sweeping reform. A less polite way of putting it would be that we are strongly committed to a policy of "muddling through."

Policies for "Muddling Through"

Response to the problem of governmental fragmentation in metropolitan areas has taken three forms in recent years: the creation of metropolitan-wide special districts for selected functions, the formation of

38. See Bollens and Schmandt, Ch. 16, for a discussion of "the politics of reform."

regional planning and coordinating councils of local governments, and the increasing reliance on the states as effective regional authorities. Let us consider these responses in order.

Most special district governments are set up to perform a single function such as water supply, transportation, fire protection, sewerage, or housing and urban renewal. A few are empowered to perform multiple functions. To finance themselves special districts are given the power to levy taxes and/or charge fees, receive grants, and incur debt. The 228 SMSA's defined as of 1967 contained no less than 7,049 such units, which averages out to 32 per SMSA and provides ample evidence that most special districts are not metropolitan area-wide jurisdictions. However, the Advisory Commission on Intergovernmental Relations did find that 527 of the units existing in 1967 were "multi-county districts that deal with 'large-area' functions such as air pollution, airports, and mass transportation." [39] A well-known example is the Port of New York Authority, which owns and operates bridges, tunnels, bus terminals, part of the rail transit system, and numerous port facilities as well as the major airports in the bi-state (New York-New Jersey) port region.

Along such lines, special districts can and do perform functions across entire metropolitan regions that at the level of general purpose local government are almost hopelessly fragmented. But the horizontal coordination and planning that the special district may (but does not always) achieve for a single function is bought at the price of making coordination between functions more difficult than ever in the vertical direction, of fragmenting responsibility and accountability, and of weakening citizen influence in decision-making. Special districts continue to proliferate, but they are a far from satisfactory response to the problem of metropolitan jurisdictional fragmentation.

The need for area-wide planning and policy coordination among local governments within metropolitan areas has fostered the growth of various kinds of regional planning agencies in recent years. The federal government actively encouraged this trend, first, by making many of its grants conditional upon review of programs by an area-wide body with planning responsibilities and, second, by offering grants to defray the cost of planning itself. The Advisory Commission on Intergovernmental Relations found that by late 1968, 208 of the nation's SMSA's were served by some variety of area-wide planning agency, though these agencies did not always have jurisdiction over an entire SMSA.[40] While such intergovernmental planning and coordination are better than nothing at all and may, indeed, be the most we can hope for at the present time, no one would

39. *Urban America and the Federal System*, p. 77.
40. *Ibid.*, p. 62.

suggest that they are an adequate substitute for more thoroughgoing structural reform of metropolitan government.

The vacuum left by the inability of metropolitan areas to cope with their own problems has to some extent been filled by state governmental action. As Netzer points out, "state governments under our constitutional system have very broad powers . . . . The states are the best regional governments we have, and they may be the best we are likely to get." [41] Since the 1960's state governments have played an increasingly active role in developing transportation, housing, open space, and other programs that require large-scale planning for metropolitan regions within their boundaries. There is good reason to believe this role will continue to grow. We have seen, in addition, that the states are being compelled, by the pressure of demand for equality, to take over a much greater share in the financing of local education. In the long run we can look forward to still further involvement of state governments in matters once regarded as strictly local in character.

PROSPECTS FOR REFORM

Of the three great problems of finance and organization discussed in this chapter, we can say that there is real hope of mitigating two within this decade. Before the end of the 1970's we will probably see further substantial change in the manner in which local public services are financed. In all likelihood the federal government will take additional steps to mitigate vertical fiscal imbalance, either through more generous revenue-sharing, through tax credits, or by assuming greater responsibility for some functions now paid for in large measure by state and local governments. Simultaneously the courts, moving with the opinion of the times, have agreed to extend the ancient American claim to equality by putting irresistible pressure on the states to overcome geographic disparities among needs and resources within their own boundaries. It is only the third problem of governmental fragmentation at the local level that seems likely to resist resolution.

Finally, it needs no remarkable insight to add that the progress we make toward solving the financial difficulties of localities may well be bought at the price of further eroding their political autonomy. There will be alarms and debates, as indeed there should be, for the dilemma we face is an aspect of the great problem of all highly technological societies, the conflict between diversity and uniformity that is implicit in our national motto: *e pluribus unum.*

41. Dick Netzer, *Economics and Urban Problems* (New York: Basic Books, 1970), p. 180.

Postscript: Problems
of Decline and Growth

THIRTEEN

Writing in the early 1960's, Scott Greer found that two visions of the future metropolis shaped the analysis of those concerned with solving the "metropolitan problem." On the one hand there were the "ideologists of return," who believed that the old central city could and must be preserved and revitalized as the natural center of a newly reorganized metropolitan area. At the other extreme were the "utopians of dispersion," who argued that the technology of transportation and communications now made it possible to dispense with large cities entirely and resettle mankind into clusters of smaller, balanced, integrated communities, without sacrificing the material advantages of modern specialization. Greer did not expect either of these visions to be realized, and so far time has confirmed that judgment.[1]

Metropolitan areas have continued to grow in a pattern that is satisfactory to neither sort of visionary. Under the impact of changing technology and rising income, they are still rapidly decentralizing. Growth in the ring areas, however, has taken place, not in the form of discrete and identifiable communities, but rather as an almost continuous and undifferentiated carpet of settlement. As for the central cities, though they are far from withering away, the evidence of a declining number of jobs and shrinking population, presented in earlier chapters, certainly indicates that their position as the focus around which the metropolitan area is spatially organized

1. Scott Greer, *The Emerging City* (New York: The Free Press, 1962), pp. 178–80.

continues to grow weaker. Many of the older cities have been losing population since the 1950's. No one now talks seriously of "return."

PROBLEMS OF DECLINE AND GROWTH

Apart from the issues of segregation and unequal income that now loom so large, the major problems of both cities and suburbs arise from the simple facts of population and employment growth in the ring and their simultaneous decline at the center. The United States has always been a growth-oriented society, in which problems were not so much solved as outgrown. When the central cities were expanding, they could often pay the cost of adjusting to the dictates of technological and other economic change by borrowing, so to speak, against the present value of expected future growth. If the old infrastructure of streets, water supply, schools, housing was becoming obsolete, it could readily be replaced by the new facilities that would, in any case, be needed to meet the requirements of rapidly rising demand. Old errors could be buried under new construction. Someone was always willing to pay for a second chance.

Today most of the older central cities are losing jobs and population. Expected future growth no longer attracts private and public capital resources out of which to pay for the replacement of obsolete structures and unsatisfactory neighborhoods. One might think that as its population declined a city's need for capital outlays would drop substantially, because additional capacity in schools, hospitals, and other expensive facilities would not be required. Budgetary relief from that source is minimized, however, by the facts of neighborhood change and the intra-urban redistribution of population. The old facilities, even if not obsolete, are often located in the wrong place to serve current demands.

In general, adjustment to change becomes more difficult when change is accompanied by decline. For example, widespread housing abandonment would seem to provide an opportunity for the creation of attractive parks and open spaces in old, formerly crowded slum areas. But the cities do not seem to know how to go about planning such change or how to pay for it even if they did. Instead of orderly, purposeful reduction in density, we get empty lots filled with garbage and neighborhoods that look like the aftermath of a firebombing. Coping with decline in all its implications is not easy. As yet, the cities have scarcely begun to face the problem.

The issues are quite different in the suburbs, for it is growth rather than decline that causes their major problems. Unlike the older cities, the suburbs are now in a position to reap the benefits of growth as a convenient source of capital and energy with which to modernize and adjust their infrastructure. But, ironically, this same growth threatens the very basis of suburban life, for it strikes at the amenities that are their fundamental attraction. If density in the cities was sometimes excessive, it was nevertheless the source of their advantages. In the suburbs it is quite otherwise. There, increasing density gradually obliterates the very features people came in search of: the easy access to open space, the uncongested facilities, the dream of escaping from communal pressures and hard social choices into the quiet, family-centered life of the single-family house and the back yard. Just as cities have to learn how to take advantage of their own population decline, so the suburbs must learn how to cope with continued growth. As we have seen, many of them would like to close their gates and divert the crowds elsewhere. But no matter how successful some towns may be in that effort, there is no possibility that such measures will halt the growth of suburban population as a whole.

Is There a Natural Limit to Metropolitan Size?

Will the process of agglomeration into metropolitan areas go on indefinitely? Economists have long wondered if there is an ultimate limit to economies of scale obtainable within the firm. One may ask analogously whether there is a point beyond which the disadvantages of further agglomeration begin to outweigh the gains. It is easy to point out some of the diseconomies, such as traffic congestion, smog, and lack of access to open space, that accrue as metropolitan regions increase in size and density. Yet such areas continue to grow and to attract industry and population that are free to choose other locations if they wish. It remains unclear, then, whether, in a nation that relies largely on market forces to determine the location of industry and population, there will be any natural limit to the size of metropolitan areas. Some city planners and a perhaps smaller number of economists would assert that as a matter of public policy we ought to *impose* limits on their size. That, to paraphrase Scott Greer, is a subject worthy of discussion—but not in these pages.

Between 1960 and 1970 metropolitan areas as a whole gained 23.5 percent in population. Only 2 of the 56 areas whose population exceeded 500,000 in 1960 failed to grow during the following decade, and these 2 —the Pittsburgh and Jersey City SMSA's—each lost only .2 percent of their residents. These figures suggest that metropolitan areas have not yet reached a natural limit to their size, if indeed such a limit exists.

Central cities, of course, present a very different picture. We have pointed out that 15 of the 21 that had a population above 500,000 in 1960 actually lost residents in the next ten years. Were these losses related to the development of diseconomies of agglomeration? If so, we would expect the largest cities to display the largest declines. Loss of population was heaviest in the older cities of the North and East. Examining the 12 largest in this group, we find that population in the top 3 (New York, Chicago, and Philadelphia) declined only .9 percent from 1960 to 1970, while in the next 9 it fell by 9.1 percent.[2] These figures do not support the more colorful recent fantasies about the largest cities strangling themselves to death in the congestion generated by their own uncontrolled growth. They show, rather, that it is the older cities of middle rank that have suffered the heaviest loss of function in recent decades, while the largest cities have fared much better.

Because simple extrapolation from the economic past is almost always wrong, we cannot be certain precisely what combinations of metropolitan growth and decline the future will bring. One can safely predict only that as the years pass the pattern of settlement will continue to shift. Changes in technology, the growth of population, the rise in income, continually alter the economic environment, urging men and organizations to move once again in search of the ideal location, which, in a world of flux, they can never attain for long. Moving over the land, however, men cannot take their buildings with them but must leave them behind as monuments to another time and another pattern. It is the mobility of men and the mutability of their functions together with the immobility of cities and the permanence of structures that gives urban problems their unique and historic character.

2. In order of size in 1970 the next 9 were Detroit, Baltimore, Washington, Cleveland, Milwaukee, Boston, St. Louis, Pittsburgh, and Buffalo.

Index

New York City, 33, 65, 69, 309, 366
  hinterland, 88–89; table, 90
  housing:
    low rent, 269
    operating costs, 258
    rehabilitation costs, 276
    subsidy costs, 300–301
    transitional neighborhoods, 279–280
  income differentials, table, 187
  mass transit orientation, 133
  municipal wages, table, 326
  nonbasic-to-basic ratio, table, 153
  population change, table, 38
    density and, 35, 36
New York City Rand Institute, 258, 260
New York Court of Appeals, housing decision, 265
New York State Urban Development Corporation, 313
Nixon, Richard M., 353, 354
Nonmetropolitan areas:
  family incomes in, 53; table, 54
  growth of population, 30; tables, 27, 31
  migration by race, 49–51, 56; tables, 50, 52
  poverty in, 179, 182; tables, 180, 181
Nourse, Hugh O., 2, 76, 91, 118, 149

Oakland, William H., 227
Oates, W. E., 326
Obsolescence, housing, 252. *See also* Succession
Occupational earnings of blacks, by area, 233–234; table, 232
  231–234; table, 232
Occupational status of blacks, by area,
Office of Economic Opportunity, 194, 199
  and minority-owned business, 224
Old age assistance, 211; table, 210
Olsen, Edgar F., 246
Operation Mainstream, 200; table, 199
Opportunity cost, 4, 109, 247
Organizing the metropolitan public sector. *See* Local government functions and boundaries
Otis, Elisha Graves, 32
Output effect, of transport cost reduction, 96–98
Overcrowding (housing), 241–243, 247, 248, 253–255; tables, 244, 254, 256
Overflow effect, 34–36, 128

Park, Robert E., 89, 126
Parks and recreation, 242, 349, 353; table, 323

Partial equilibrium method, location theory, 71–72
Pascal, Anthony H., 204, 306
Pechman, Joseph A., 351, 353
Perishability-fragility gaining or losing processes, 60; table, 72
Perloff, Harvey S., 335
Persky, Joseph J., 185, 188, 191, 222, 238
Person-per-room ratio (housing), 241. *See also* Overcrowding
Pfouts, R. W., 139, 153, 174
Philadelphia, 21, 225–226, 269, 366
  income differentials, table, 187
  input-output study of, 156
  municipal wages, table, 326
  nonbasic-to-basic ratio, table, 153
  population change, table, 38
    density and, 35
Philbrick, Allen L., 82
Pinkerton, T., 266
Pirenne, Henri, 9, 10
Pittsburgh, 83, 365, 366
  locational advantages of, 64, 68
Planning:
  and housing policy, 305
  and metropolitan regional problems, 349–350, 360–362
Plumbing, and housing conditions, 241, 246, 255, 257; tables, 244, 254, 256
Police services, 349, 353; table, 323
Pollution:
  and automobiles, 134
  local policy toward, 173–174
Population. *See* Central cities; Cities; Density; Metropolitan areas; Rural areas; Suburban rings
Population change, effect on:
  land use patterns, 125, 128, 132–133
  market area size, 80, 94, 99
  urban hierarchy, 94, 99, 100–102
Port of New York Authority, 361
Ports, and location of activity, 11, 65–66, 83
Poverty. *See* Income, level of
Power orientation, 69; table, 72
Preference satisfaction, in public sector, 320–321, 344–345
Prescott, James P., 166
President's Committee on Urban Housing, 249, 250
Prest, A. R., 135, 202
Production-cost orientation, 67, 68–70, 83; table, 72
Profit-maximization, and location decisions, 58, 131
Property tax:
  elasticity of, 327, 329